monsoonbooks

RAFFLES AND THE BRITISH INVASION OF JAVA

Tim Hannigan is an author and journalist specialising in Indonesia and the Indian Subcontinent. *Raffles and the British Invasion of Java*, his second book, won the 2012 John Brooks Award, UK, for historical nonfiction. His other works include *Murder in the Hindu Kush* (The History Press, 2011) and *A Brief History of Indonesia* (Tuttle, 2015). For more information about the author, visit: *www.timhannigan.com.*

Praise for *Raffles and the British Invasion of Java*

'... lively, original and daring ... It's seldom that history makes such wonderful reading ...' *Bali Advertiser*, Indonesia

'... fascinating stuff ... what kept me reading was the lyrical force and energy of Tim's writing ...' *Expat Living*, Singapore

'... a vivid portrait... a gripping narrative...' *The Straits Times*, Singapore

'An excellent, authoritative account of the brief period of British rule, and the role of Raffles in the early 19th century ...' *Lonely Planet Indonesia*

'... spellbinding ... packed with a wealth of background ...' *Jakarta Expat*, Indonesia

'A controversial reassessment of the mythical Raffles that seeks to question most of our comfortable assumptions about the "founder of Singapore"' Nigel Barley, author of *In the Footsteps of Stamford Raffles*

'... necessary reading in the troubled times we live in ..." Farish A. Noor, *New Straits Times*, Malaysia

'Hannigan's clear enthusiasm for his subject matter is infectious. His relish for the project of history itself ... is equally as captivating' *Hello Bali!*, Indonesia

'... sheds new light on the man, his exalted place in history, and the dark side of British colonialism ... in a vivid, cinematic writing style ...' Tom Benner, *The Straits Times*, Singapore

the 2013 John Brooks Award, UK. His other works include *Murder in the Dark* (The History Press, 2011) and *A Brief History of Indonesia* ... For more information about the author, please visit ...

Raffles
and the British
Invasion of Java

Tim Hannigan

monsoon

monsoonbooks

First published in 2012
by Monsoon Books Ltd
No1 Duke of Windsor Suite, Burrough Court,
Burrough on the Hill, Leics. LE14 2QS, UK
www.monsoonbooks.co.uk

This updated 4th edition published in 2019.

ISBN (paperback): 978-981-4358-85-9
ISBN (ebook): 978-981-4358-86-6

Cover design by Cover Kitchen.

Frontcover portrait of Raffles ("Engraved by Thompson, from a
Miniature in posession of Mr. Raffles"). Frontcover sketch of a view of
Gunung Salak, near Buitenzorg. Backcover sketch of a fight between a
tiger and buffalo from JJX Pfyffer zu Neueck, *Skizzen von der Insel Java
und derselben Verschiedenen Bewöhnern* (Schaffhausen, 1829).

A Cataloguing-in-Publication data record is available from the National
Library, Singapore.

Printed and bound in Great Britain by Clays Ltd, Elcograf S.p.A.
21 20 19   4 5 6

Contents

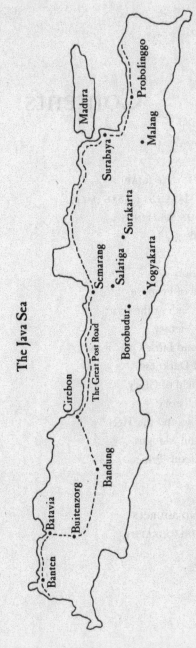

JAVA 1811-1816

The Java Sea

The Southern Ocean

Madura

Probolinggo

Malang

Surabaya

Surakarta

Salatiga

Semarang

Yogyakarta

Borobudur

The Great Post Road

Cirebon

Bandung

Batavia

Buitenzorg

Banten

CENTRAL JAVA 1811-1816

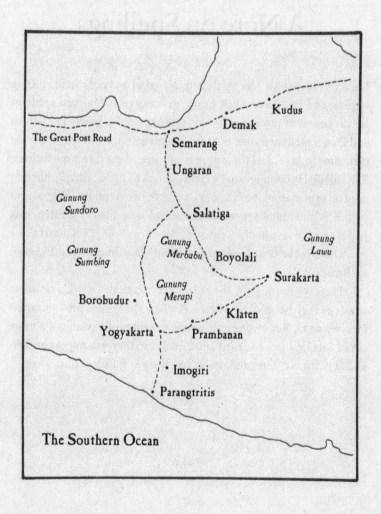

Kudus

Demak

The Great Post Road

Semarang

Ungaran

Gunung Sundoro

Salatiga

Gunung Merbabu

Boyolali

Gunung Lawu

Gunung Sumbing

Gunung Merapi

Surakarta

Borobudur ·

Klaten

Yogyakarta

Prambanan

· Imogiri

Parangtritis

The Southern Ocean

A Note on Spellings

Modern Indonesian uses a delightfully logical and consistent spelling system, and so I have stuck firmly to Modern Indonesian spellings for the names of places and people throughout this book. The British and Dutch used their own systems of representing local words during their time in Java, and these appear in some of the direct quotations. The colonial version is usually close enough to the modern spelling to need no explanation, but there are a couple of exceptions: Yogyakarta (which is colloquially pronounced – and occasionally written – as Jogjakarta), was usually written by the British as 'Djocjocarta', or just 'Djocjo'; the British outpost of Bengkulu in Sumatra was known as 'Bencoolen'.

There is something of an academic convention of writing Javanese words as they 'should' be with an A where the typical pronunciation involves an O. But no one ever spoke or wrote colloquially of a town called Sala or a prince called Dipanegara, so they will appear as Solo and Diponegoro here, and others like them will follow suit.

Glossary

Alun-Alun the great grassy square at the centre of a traditional Javanese city

Babad a Javanese chronicle, usually written in verse in formal language

Bibi an Indian term of address for a woman; in the 18th and early 19th century it was often used by the British in Asia as the term for the native concubine of a European man; the Dutch used the term *nyai* to the same effect in Indonesia

Candi a Javanese Hindu or Buddhist temple

Dalang the puppet-master in the *wayang kulit*, and in metaphorical terms anyone who orchestrates events from the background

Djinn an invisible, and often malevolent, spirit. The term is of Arabic origin, and djinns are mentioned in the Koran as beings resembling humans, but made of fire. In many countries, including Indonesia where it is usually spelt *jin*, the term is used as a more generic catch-all for all sorts of ghoulies, ghosties and things which go bump in the night

Dukun a shaman, witchdoctor or spiritual healer

Dwarapala the monstrous guardian statues that flank entranceways of Javanese temples and palaces as a deterrent to evil spirits

Gamelan Javanese orchestra featuring gongs and xylophones

Haji a Muslim who has completed the Haj pilgrimage to Mecca

Jago a fighting cock, or the head of a rebel band or criminal gang

Jawi the modified Arabic script traditionally used for writing Malay before the 20th century

Joglo a Javanese tiered pyramid roof, traditionally reserved for the homes of royal or noble families, or those of the descendants of the founders of a village

Kampung a settlement or group of houses; in rural terms a hamlet; in an urban setting a quarter

Kawi classical literary Javanese, a language with its own Sanskrit-derived script used for many of the chronicles and epics of old Java

Kebaya a lightweight Indonesian woman's blouse, traditionally made of silk or cotton

Klenteng a Chinese temple

Kraton a Javanese palace or royal residence

Kris a ceremonial dagger and essential part of the outfit of a formally attired Javanese man, often an heirloom object, and frequently believed to have magical powers

Kromo High Javanese, the respectful form of the language used for addressing those of superior rank

Memsahib a hybrid Anglo-Indian term for a white woman. *Sahib*, pronounced 'saab', is a respectful Indian term for a man in a position of authority; it was given racial connotations when the British misappropriated it and applied it to themselves. They ditched the correct feminine equivalent – *sahiba* – and came up with memsahib for their wives

Ngoko Low Javanese, used between equals, or to inferiors

Pasisir literally 'the Littoral'; usually used for the northern coastal regions of Java, and in Javanese terms implying an area outside the cultural and historic heartlands – if not beyond the pale, then somewhere very close to it

Patih the prime minister of a Javanese court

Pendopo a traditional Javanese pavilion, usually topped with a *joglo* roof

Perahu an Indonesian open boat

Peranakan literally 'descendent', usually used for people of mixed

Chinese and Malay or Javanese origins

Pusaka sacred Javanese royal regalia and heirloom items

Ratu Adil 'The Righteous Prince', a messianic figure in Javanese folklore, first mentioned in the 12th-century Joyoboyo Prophecies, set to save the island in times of trouble

Sayyid an Arabic title for a man claiming descent from the Prophet Mohammed

Sajen offerings of flowers, petals and other small items, left at tombs, temples and other places associated with spiritual power

Sepoy an Indian soldier in the army of the British East India Company

Stupa a Buddhist monument

Susuhunan the royal title taken by the kings of Mataram, and retained by the rulers of Surakarta, sometimes abbreviated to *sunan*.

Tapa Javanese ascetic exercises and meditation, practiced in search of mystical power and enlightenment and ranging from *tapa ngalong* – hanging upside-down from a tree – to *tapa metak* – eating nothing but rice for long periods.

Wali Songo The semi-mythical 'Nine Saints', said to have converted Java to Islam

Wayang Kulit the Javanese shadow-puppet theatre

Introduction

The Past Perfect

'It would have been better if we had been colonised by the British, not the Dutch.'

I remember very clearly the first time I heard that strange and discomfiting sentiment voiced by an Indonesian. I was sitting at the head of an air-conditioned classroom beneath a whiteboard scrawled with tortuous explanations of the past perfect continuous tense; a callow young English teacher in an oversized shirt and a terrible tie, not long arrived in the seething Javanese city of Surabaya.

This was my favourite class. The other groups I taught were reticent undergraduates or obese infants who fiddled sulkily with their mobile phones throughout their twice-weekly hour of extracurricular English. But this class was different. There were eight of them, senior high school students whose conversational tastes ranged well beyond shopping malls and celebrity gossip. They were clever, boisterous and funny, and they had a talent for leading me down tangents away from tenses. That was what had happened now: we were talking about Indonesian history and politics.

All of them were from the privileged elite of Indonesia's second largest city, young men and women bound for Singaporean healthcare and American educations. But they partook with gusto in the peculiar Indonesian pastime of doing down their country in extravagantly hyperbolic terms, bemoaning its corruption and chaos.

I tried to remonstrate with them, to point out calmly that despite its manifold problems Indonesia had actually done remarkably well during its improbable half-century existence. For a start it had managed the formidable task of not disintegrating; it had achieved impressive economic development, attained near-total literacy, undergone a successful transition to democracy, and seemed to be forging a strong course in a new century.

But I couldn't convince them. They were wealthy enough to have travelled; they had seen how the other half lived.

'Look at Singapore and Malaysia,' they said. 'Look at how much richer and more modern they are!'

I pointed out the unfair advantages of their pint-sized neighbours. Indonesia has 17,000 islands, several hundred languages and an infinity of divergent histories. Malaysia has a population of less than 30 million; Singapore is the size of the Isle of Wight.

But they would not have it, and what was more, they had a neat historical explanation for the fact that life was better on the other side of the Straits of Melaka: 'It would have been better if we had been colonised by the British, not the Dutch.'

It was enough to stop an earnest young Englishman in his tracks. It certainly stopped me in mine and they roared ahead with tales of the gold-paved streets of former British territories. Look at Singapore's skyscrapers! Look at Malaysia's motorways! Look at Hong Kong's hotels and shopping centres! These were places they had visited on holiday; they knew. Look at India …

'India?' I muttered dreamily, still off-kilter, and started to protest. But they ignored me; they knew their current affairs and India was a rising superpower. Bangladesh, Pakistan and vast swathes of Africa were blithely dismissed as irrelevant aberrations; for them the evidence was irrefutable: the centuries of Dutch rule were to blame for all Indonesia's problems – if only the British had conquered these islands instead then all would be prosperity and progress.

It was not a sentiment I had expected to hear from the bright young things of a rising postcolonial nation – a retrospection and regret, not that their country had been colonised at all, but that it had been colonised by the *wrong people* ...

By the time I had recovered my repose we were out of time. Class was over and the past perfect continuous tense would have to wait until next week. The students wandered out into the corridor nudging each other triumphantly – they had put paid to my carefully crafted lesson plan yet again, and in the next room a horde of obese eight-year-olds with mobile phones were waiting.

* * *

I first came to Indonesia to travel and to learn the language – the national lingua franca which will get you by from the tip of Sumatra to the marches of Papua New Guinea – and then, a little while later, to live and to work as an English teacher in Java. From my base in Surabaya – a warm, earthy Javanese city of potholed roads, slithering canals and spicy sauces – I travelled whenever and wherever I could. I climbed volcanoes in Bali and Lombok, walked through green uplands in Sulawesi, endured terrible bus rides in Sumatra and chewed betel nut with ancestor worshippers in the scattered outposts of Nusa Tenggara. But above all, I explored the heartlands and the hinterlands of Java itself, the lodestone of the archipelago, heading out of Surabaya on weekends and holidays on my battered little Honda motorcycle. I saw the countless classical Hindu and Buddhist temples that still stud the countryside, nailing the green carpet of Java onto its historical floorboards, and I spotted the little piles of leaves and curls of burnt-out incense in the inner recesses, suggesting that centuries after the island turned to Islam, someone was still venerating these places. I shivered in morning mists amongst pineapple fields and casuarinas, and stopped my bike on the elbows of mountain roads to wonder how this empty green space could be the most densely populated island on earth. I wrestled too with the big cities, and saw the blunt ugliness of modern Indonesian suburbia, tempered only by good food on roaring roadsides.

And as I travelled on the ground I journeyed into the past too, hungrily consuming every book I could find about Java and the island state beyond it. I read of the heady years of new nationhood in the middle years of the 20th century, and of the upheavals that had gone before; I read of the 19th-century colonial heyday and of the days of spice and piracy when Europeans had first plied the waters of the archipelago. And I read of the glittering realms of Old Java, the dynasties that had left the island speckled with temples, palaces and legends: Sanjaya, Singosari, Majapahit and Mataram.

But even long after I had become hopelessly hooked on this green and sprawling land's limitless supply of stories and strangeness, and had moved on from English teaching to the tenuous trade of freelance travel writer, the history of Java seemed irredeemably distant. The past, they say, is a foreign country. I had already dabbled in the historical episodes of 19th-century India, and there I had found a mass of manuscripts written in my own first language, by men from my own country – Britain. Characters, incidents and episodes had come cascading clearly down the decades from the flimsy ink-splattered sheets and colonial gazetteers. But in Indonesia those same sources would be written in Dutch and classical Javanese; even Standard Indonesian was of little use. I was left to make do with the overviews and the academic texts, and they made for a poor substitute – an almanac of dates and names, a declination of dynasties and a rote-learnt recitation of colonial contexts. It was hard to populate this second-hand past with palpable figures. Dutch governors-general were distinguished only by their dates of retirement and their administrative reforms; Javanese princes were little more than an unpronounceable name and a year of ascendancy. Whole dynasties were diminished to a paragraph, and battles were fought out over a single sentence. In my mind entire generations of colonial Dutchmen amounted only to an amorphous image of red skin, white trousers and coal-black tops and tails.

I had long since grown used to hearing that unsettling comment I had first encountered in that air-conditioned classroom: 'It would have been better if we had been colonised by the British, not the

Dutch'. I had heard it from market traders and businessmen, mystics and punk rockers. And though I always tried to proffer a polite counterargument, at times I was almost inclined to agree with them, if only because a British-dominated colonial Indonesia would have left me with much easier access to the past.

But the slabs of standard Indonesian history did offer one small, glittering jewel that instantly fired my imagination. At first glance it seemed only to be a glitch, a curious anomaly in the list of grandly named Dutch governors-general. In the first decade of the 19th century, the colonial possessions of the Netherlands in Southeast Asia were ruled by a man with the mellifluous name of Daendels. He was succeeded early in 1811 by the spiky-sounding Jan Willem Janssens, and in 1816 the post was taken by the initial-laden Baron G.A.G. Ph. Van der Capellen. But between Janssens and Van der Capellen there was a gap. For five years there was no governor-general; instead there was something called a lieutenant-governor, a man with a name that was unmistakably English, and not just English, but also vaguely familiar – Thomas Stamford Raffles.

Java and the core of colonial Indonesia, it turned out, *had* been ruled by Britain, albeit for just five years.

* * *

I set about trying to find out more about the episode known today as the British Interregnum, but the details were elusive. Major histories gave the topic a few paragraphs at most: it was little more than an obscure footnote, and the most far-flung sideshow of the Napoleonic Wars. If I wanted more, I realised, I would have to dig deeper. I started tentatively, with a couple of modern reprints of early English accounts of Java. I read them during a bout of travelling in the tiny, stepping-stone islands of Indonesia's far southeast where Asia runs out towards Oceania. On the top decks of rusting ferries, rolling under blank skies, I snatched excitedly at 200-year-old descriptions of places I knew well, and underlined accounts of military manoeuvres.

While seasick pigs grunted unhappily in the hold and old women dozed on dirty blue mattresses, I envisaged columns of red-coated Indians and Englishmen marching along the Javanese roads that I had previously peopled only with those hazy black-coated Dutchmen. When the journey was over, and bookshops and internet connections were back within reach, I tracked down more reading material.

The British occupation of Java had been dealt with for a general audience in one context and in one context only – in the middle chapters of the myriad biographies of Sir Thomas Stamford Raffles. I had, like many people, been half-aware of Raffles for years, had stumbled over his sainted name every time I passed through Singapore, and held somewhere in the back of my imagination a loose vision of jungles, exotic flowers, temples, scholarship, decency and heroism. But already, after what I had learnt about the British occupation of Java on those long-haul ferry rides, I wasn't entirely sure that this was the whole story. I needed more to go on.

I ordered eye-wateringly expensive and aggravatingly obscure accounts from the small body of academic work that deals with Java under Raffles; I scoured the scholarly journals, and then, finally, I went back to the source. Over a long, hot summer back in the United Kingdom I slept on friends' sofas in London and spent eye-straining days in the bowels of the British Library. The archive material dating from the British occupation of Java was a mere drop in the eternal ocean of the old India Office Records, but Raffles' own personal correspondence alone – bound and bundled in burgundy boxes – amounted to hundreds of thousands of words. There were five years' worth of weekly newspapers on microfilm, countless reports from provincial administrators marooned in remote Javanese hill towns where the arrival of a British tourist would still raise eyebrows even today, replies and responses from Calcutta and Batavia, maps, measurements, account books, secret missives, journals, and much else besides.

Out of it all a picture slowly emerged – of both the period, and the people involved. The strange half-decade during which Java and its outlying satellites had belonged to Britain, not to Holland, had been *far* more than an irrelevant interlude, far more than a mere change of the name above the door. For a start, the conquest itself had been all high military drama amidst muddy ditches, and more bloody battles had followed. Raffles had tried to institute radical administrative reforms – and had failed badly in the attempt. He had ordered the creepers stripped from the flanks of epic temples, and, in jealous contest with a gaggle of other scholar-administrators who produced a shelf-full of competing compendiums, he had laid the foundations for modern Southeast Asian Studies.

But the period had been characterised by controversy and bitterness as much as by study and scholarship. The whole occupation itself was a rogue operation, a wilful overstepping of the Supreme Government-defined mark. Disgrace and scandal came sniffing around Raffles' Buitenzorg back door; military men fell out with civilians, civilians fell out with other civilians, and everyone reported tetchily back to headmaster in Calcutta. There was tragedy and death, hatred and hypocrisy, drama and drunkenness, and some very dark doings indeed. And as for Raffles himself, it didn't take long leafing through those sheets of creamy white paper in the Reading Room of the British Library for the liberal vision bestriding the burgeoning skyline of modern Singapore to melt into something else entirely, something rather less savoury. In Java, I soon discovered, Raffles made for a *very* strange sort of hero.

And then I stumbled upon another source, one which the Raffles-worshippers had always ignored: the other side of the story. An account existed of the years when Raffles ran Java, laid out in the allusive stanzas of high Javanese, written by a local aristocrat. It revealed in stark relief what I had already begun to suspect – that the strange half-decade of British rule had been an episode of sustained and epoch-changing trauma for a centuries-old society.

And suddenly, with a return to Indonesia and a desk in a rented room in Yogyakarta at which to write beckoning, the real significance of the story came into focus. The Anglo-Dutch rivalry, the reforms and surveys, and the schoolyard feuds of the colonial administrators were all well and good. But the grand set-piece of the British Interregnum had been an event of such earth-shattering impact that I simply could not understand why everyone in Indonesia, not to mention Britain, seemed to have forgotten it. Just one year into his rule in Java Raffles had ordered something which no Dutch governor-general in the preceding two centuries had ever dared or dreamed to do. In an effort to impress the people of Java with the might of British power, Raffles had attacked, wrecked, cowed, and humiliated the most powerful native court in Java, Yogyakarta, the glittering receptacle for all the inherited magic and mythology of an ancient order. It was an event that would set the tone for a century.

The beating heart of the story of the British invasion of Java, I now felt, was a clash of civilisations, between a new and energetic European colonialism and the grand old courts, between a class of men for whom profit was the order of the day, and a world where power descended from long-dead dynasties and where sultans consorted with the mythical Queen of the Southern Ocean. It had been threatening for centuries, but it came to a head in the brief window between 1811 and 1816 with Raffles leading the charge for the European side.

All too often Indonesians today express that strange and disquieting regret that their country was not colonised by Britain. But it *was* colonised by Britain, and though the experience was by no means a happy one, the forgotten episodes of the period were of enormous consequence. Exactly two hundred years later, I knew for certain that it was a story well worth telling.

The Land of Promise

The little boat ground onto a suppurating shoreline scattered with dead fish and a man leapt out with a shriek of delight. He was dressed as a pantomime pirate. He skipped over the lengths of waterlogged driftwood and tiptoed around the banks of rotting seaweed. The tassel on the top of his red fancy-dress fez swung in wild circles as he went. At the head of the sticky beach a dreary expanse of mud, marsh and morass opened, shimmering in the yellow heat of a dry season afternoon. It was hardly a promising spectacle, but the man was exhilarated none the less. He took a deep breath of the fetid air, waved his antiquated pistol at the bleached tropical sky, and brandished his Sinbad-style cutlass at a gaggle of scrawny hens that had been picking through the flotsam and jetsam. They clucked irately. The man drew another deep breath and sighed with delight. Java! Java! The Land of Promise lay before him!

It was 4 August 1811. A short way from the landing spot was the ramshackle fishing village of Cilincing, a cluster of stilt huts at the mouth of a muddy river on the north coast of the great green island of Java. Eight miles west through the marshes and fishponds stood the grand old colonial capital, Batavia, Queen of the East. This pestilent Javanese littoral, with its trade, immigration and malaria, had been a possession of Holland for the best part of two centuries, but the pantomime pirate was no Dutchman. His name was John Leyden. He was a Scottish scholar, a posing polymath and a poet of the very worst kind, and with his spectacularly self-indulgent leap from the bows of the landing craft, he had just made himself the first foot soldier of the British invasion of Java.

Behind him the broad bight of Batavia Bay was bristling with tall ships. Eighty-one frigates, sloops and cruisers rode at anchor on the slick white surface. Union Jacks and the red and white ensigns of the British East India Company fluttered at their topmasts.

Back down at the water's edge the other occupants of the first landing craft were scrambling ashore with a little more decorum than John Leyden. They were all professional soldiers, their grey breeches already smeared with mud, their red jackets already sodden with sweat. They watched the be-tasselled Leyden striking his pose on the skyline with expressions of distaste. But what could they do? He was a man of letters and a part of the inner circle, one of the clique of sainted civilians gathered around the person of a certain fey young man with a lazy eye and a seedy wife who had the ear of the Governor-General, and who was, right at this very moment, breathlessly watching the unfolding scene from the deck of a ship moored just offshore. If the proud arrival of mighty Britannia on the shores of the island of Java and the opening of a brave new chapter in the history of European imperialism was to be heralded by a versifying orientalist dressed as a pirate and met by a flock of angry chickens, then so be it.

The soldiers came stomping up the beach, boot leather squeaking, gun metal clinking, brass buckles jangling. At their head was a tough forty-five-year-old colonel with the improbable name of Rollo Gillespie. He was a small Irishman with foxy features, furious sideburns and dark receding hair that rose in wayward tufts above a broad brow. Despite being blighted with a moniker more appropriate for a music hall entertainer – and despite being decidedly short of stature – he was a ruthless, determined and talented commander, a hero no less, and a man with a testy temper to boot. He had killed more men and bedded more women than he could ever count, and had fought furious battles all over the globe.

Gillespie brushed past Leyden and looked back to the north. Offshore, things were not going entirely to plan. The commanders of the fleet had chosen this spot for their invasion carefully, for reconnaissance had revealed that the Dutch usually left it unguarded. They had decided on a precise and orderly schedule of landing: each longboat was supposed to crunch onto the beach at its allotted moment, artillery pieces coming ashore at the same time as their gunners, horses prancing through the shallows in time for their officers to leap into the saddles. However, they hadn't counted on the vagaries of nature. A warm, damp land breeze was blowing offshore from the line of distant volcanoes, carrying with it all the strange and unsettling scent of the island beyond, and the tide run was flooding out of the Cilincing estuary and racing for the open sea. It was as if Java itself was trying to deflect the invaders.

The rowboats backed and spun in the current. Oars crashed together; there were collisions, terrified horses whinnied and frantic oarsmen bawled at one another. Here and there a redcoat slipped and plunged into the murky waters of the bay as he struggled down a rope ladder to disembark from the frigates. It was impossible to maintain order; an exasperated command was given to land freely, and the overloaded boats began to pull for the shore willy-nilly. It was fortunate that the only defence of Cilincing had been that offered by the chickens – and Leyden had already vanquished them.

Gillespie was followed up the beach by the overall commander-in-chief of the entire operation, Sir Samuel Auchmuty. There was nothing they could do about the shambolic order of landing, and so, as the British Army came ashore in Java piecemeal, they hurried on across the marshy flatlands between lines of drooping palms, thundered across a low wooden bridge over the river, took possession of Cilincing village and raised the first British flag over Javanese soil. There was not a Dutch soldier in sight, and the road to Batavia lay open before them.

Back in the bay, on the high rear deck of a dapper little frigate with the rather inappropriate name of *Modeste*, a clutch of overheated civilians had watched the sabre-wielding party-pirate's hostile encounter with the chickens, and the subsequent chaos of the landing with breathless delight. Foremost amongst them was the dandyish sixty-year-old Governor-General of the British East India Company's Asian possessions, Gilbert Elliot, the first Lord Minto.

Standing beside him was a man precisely half his age, who had laboured for the past year under the rather wordy title of Agent to the Governor-General with the Malay States, but who was destined for much greater things. As the coppery sun slipped down over the dark line of the coast and the loaded longboats continued to make their lumbering progress onto the Cilincing beach Minto's young companion was filled with a sense of perfect delight. It was, he later wrote, one of 'the times in which I am as happy as I think it possible for a man to be ... one of these life inspiring moments'.

Modesty had never been one of his most notable characteristics, and he had a decided tendency to overstate the importance of his own role in great events. But as a humming tropical dusk fell over the long low coastline and the green, mountainous hinterland to the south, Thomas Stamford Raffles did indeed have good reason to be excited. The improbable event that he and the pantomime pirate had dreamed of for much of the past year had actually come to pass: Britain was invading the old Dutch colony of Java, a land loaded with all the unsettling strangeness that Asia had to offer for romantic young Europeans. And what was more, Raffles, who had been little more than a clerk twelve months earlier, was assured of the key post in the new administration.

If, as he stood on the deck of the *Modeste* that sticky August evening, Raffles could have known all that the coming five years would bring – the violence and the sickness, the scandal and the failure, the uprisings and bitter arguments, the economic catastrophes, the ruined reputations and the endless round of personal tragedies – perhaps he might have smiled a little less broadly. But he would not have changed course. Raffles, a nobody risen from nowhere, was a man of insatiable and aggressive ambition, and Java would be the making, or the breaking, of him.

* * *

Swimming on its side under the equator, beneath Borneo, southeast of Sumatra and punching well above its weight, Java has long been the jewel in the Southeast Asian crown. A rough, horizontal oblong, it is only 600 miles in length, and barely a hundred miles across at its widest point, but it has nurtured mighty civilisations. Variously influenced by Chinese trade and Indian religion in the first millennium, and then by Islam and European colonialism in the second, it has been home to emperors and sultans, and has given rise to some of the greatest artistic and architectural traditions on earth.

And yet, for most of modern history, Java and the shattered island arc of the Indonesian archipelago have lain just beyond the horizon of the western, English-speaking imagination. There are some half-familiar superlatives: the world's largest archipelago state, and its most populous Muslim-majority nation, covering a distance, top-to-toe, equal to that between Dublin and Baghdad. More than half of that mighty populace, and most of the Muslims, are crammed into Java, the lodestar of the archipelago, an island the size of England with 138 million inhabitants. In that context a vision of Jakarta – the modern capital, squatting atop the bones of Dutch Batavia – as a howling Third World megalopolis and a dark maelstrom of hungry humanity makes perfect sense. But how does that fit with those other images of an island-long chain of jungle-clad volcanoes, of concertinaed rice terraces, and the most productive agricultural land on earth?

And the same confusion surrounds the peoples and the cultures of Java: there are the tumbling scales of *gamelan* music, the late-night flicker of a *wayang kulit* shadow puppet, a recollection of refinement, classical dance and sumptuous batiks beneath a lavender haze of humidity. There are crumbling temples and stone gods in the forest and slender girls in tight sarongs and lacy *kebayas*. Quite how all that interlocks with newsreel footage of skinny youths throwing stones, bombs in international hotels and angry Islamist radicals with smooth cheeks and sparse beards is impossible to say. The place-names are left as an evocative confusion: Jakarta, an image of concrete and greenery; Surabaya, a place at the end of the world to which rakish sailors run off; and Java itself, a whiff of sweet black coffee, earthquakes and petrol bombs.

It all amounts to a place beyond the pale.

At the turn of the 19th-century Java was all the more baffling a prospect for Europeans. If we had been able to take wing on the hot tropical air in those years, and to follow the wheeling cattle egrets upwards on the eddying thermals, we would have seen the island laid out below us like a long green lozenge.

At each of its furthest extremities are shallow droplets of dense jungle – Ujung Kulon in the west, Alas Purwo in the east – places of ghosts and tigers. At the northwest tip of the island stands Banten, the little sultanate that once housed the rival trading houses of the spice race. Fifty miles to the east are the mildewed mansions and pestilent canals of Batavia, the colonial capital – and beyond it that little fishing village at Cilincing. All along the meandering northern coast, runs a slab of level, fertile country, alternately narrowing and broadening as the highlands push forward and ease back. Here solid ground gives way uncertainly to the shallow waters of the Java Sea – long stretches of cloying mud open at low tide, and tangled ranks of mangroves mask whatever foreshore exists. This is a private sea, walled off by great hulks of land from the storms of the Southern Ocean. The waters are calm and benign – hidden sandbanks notwithstanding. There is much shipping here, and wherever a river the colour of milky coffee pushes through the drowning fields and slippery mudflats there is a port. Some are nothing more than a cluster of stilt huts and a muddle of moored outrigger canoes, but others are grand international entrepôts.

Heading east from Banten and Batavia we can pick out the mildewed red rooftops and the cluttered laneways of Cirebon with its royal courts, the point where Java-proper starts,[1] of Tegal, and

---

1 Not everyone in Java is Javanese. The most westerly third of the island is the realm of the Sundanese, ethnically and linguistically a world apart from their eastern counterparts.

of Pekalongan with its batik workshops. Beyond that we see the old-established colonial town of Semarang. Crowding its river there are boats of all countries – Gujarati dhows find moorings alongside Chinese junks; amongst the Dutch trading ships there are a handful of permit-paying merchantmen from other European nations, and a few worn-out Portuguese hulks from the forgotten outposts of Timor and Flores. On either side are tied dozens of white, high-prowed *padewakang* schooners, Bugis boats from Sulawesi which ply between the islands and out as far as the lost northern reaches of Australia. Sweeping low over the steaming alleyways we can catch the rising babble of strange languages: Javanese in soft and harsh versions from the locals of varying classes; pared-down Malay tossed back and forth between the immigrants; the chatter of Balinese and other unidentifiable tongues belonging to lost eastern islands from the load-carrying slaves, and other, more outlandish languages too – bubbling Bengali or Gujarati; chirruping Chinese dialects, sand-scoured Arabic rasps, Dutch demands and a few snatches of pidgin Portuguese.

Heading on eastwards along the coast we skim the housetops of Kudus, Demak and Jepara, the anteroom of Islam in Java. Onwards, beyond a stretch of wilder coast, a southern turn takes us past the one-time Muslim powerhouse of Gresik, and neighbouring Surabaya, another polyglot port with a colonial quarter, Chinese *klenteng* temples full of Confucian and Buddhist altars under clouds of incense smoke, teakwood mosques where old men of Arab extraction teach the Koran to small boys in white skullcaps, and crowded Malay *kampungs* with fighting cocks under wicker baskets. Madura Island rides offshore and ships shelter in the channel; a few more minor harbours – Pasuruan, Probolinggo, and Situbondo – swelter on the yellow flatlands and then Java is cut abruptly short before Bali.

This strip of northern shore is known as the *Pasisir*, 'the Littoral' – the place where the sea and all its influence leaches into Java, making it by turns more Dutch, more Muslim, more Chinese, more Malay, rougher, tougher, cruder, and less refined. But rising right behind the Pasisir in great purple cones, some of them still trailing smoke from their hollow summits, are the volcanoes, walling off this heterogeneous antechamber from the Javanese heartlands.

The mountains run the length of the island, rearing below us from a blanket of creamy cloud. They begin in a knot of green ridges south of Banten and Batavia, thicken to the east, pushing their outliers right down to the uneasy southern shore, rise higher still behind Semarang and then tail out towards the end of the island in a series of punchy up-thrusts. Up amongst those mountains there are sacred springs where, when the moon is full, the invisible gateway to long-fallen realms opens. There are the tombs of Muslim saints who are also Chinese holy men. There are hermits practicing mystical mortification of the flesh in hidden caves, and secret places to meditate in search of the great energy that runs through all of Java. And in the deepest forest on the steepest slopes there are the camps of robber bands and rebel princes, men with tousled, shoulder-length hair and the gifts of second sight.

South of these great green fire-mountains is a coastline very different from the soft shores of the Pasisir. Here Java has teeth – sharp black outcrops of basalt – and they bite into an angry sea. There are few harbours along this coast with its buttressing green headlands, its pockets of dark jungle and its wave-lashed beaches. There is only a scattering of fishing hamlets where a few sun-scarred men protected by powerful amulets dare to work in the realm of the Queen of the Southern Ocean.

Between these two coasts, and amongst these monumental uplands, are the basins of the great rivers: the well-watered cradles in which kingdoms have grown, teetered, toppled, and grown again. There is the Brantas Delta behind Surabaya that once nurtured the Hindu Majapahit Empire, the narrower saddle between the Tengger and Arjuno-Welirang massifs that harboured the Singosari Dynasty. And then there is the power-charged triangle of rich green land in the very middle of Java, running south from the sharp summit of the Merapi volcano, threaded by the pale, winding bands of the

Bengawan Solo, the Progo, and the Bogowonto Rivers. This country above all others has spawned kingdom after kingdom. The people who built the great Hindu and Buddhist temples that we can pick out here and there between the treetops ruled from here; the mighty Sultanate of Mataram came to prominence from this quarter even as the Dutch were rising in the 17th century, and even now it is still home to a pair of magnificent rival kingdoms – Yogyakarta and Surakarta.

* * *

The first European travellers came to this long green island following the sweet, musky scent of spice. In past centuries the Indonesian archipelago was the condiment store of the world. Pepper grew in great strings like green necklaces in the hills of West Java, and there were other, still more exotic aromas emanating from the spreading starburst of islands beyond: cloves burst from the branches in the orchards of Ambon and Ternate, and nutmeg, the base-note of a thousand Christmases, was found only in the Bandas, an archipelago of miniscule landfalls like a cluster of old acne scars on the smooth face of a tropical sea. Maluku – the scattered confetti of watery landfalls including Banda and Ambon which fills the gap between the vast, turkey-shaped mass of Papua and the dancing spider of Sulawesi – found a place in fable as the Spice Islands, and its fragrant harvests launched a thousand ships. Java became the final way-station on this maritime spice route.

Traditionally the flow of spices into Europe had been controlled by the Arab traders who crossed the Indian Ocean in fast-sailing dhows, and the Venetian middlemen who channelled their wares to cold northern kitchens and apothecaries at astronomical prices. But at the end of the 15th century the Portuguese, sailing in castellated carracks with long banners streaming from the topmasts, rounded the southern tip of Africa, headed east, and managed to tap directly into the source. For a century these Iberian pioneers had the trade to themselves. They ousted the Arabs, built forts among the nutmeg groves, signed treaties with island kings, threw their own spicing of vocabulary into the stew of the Malay lingua franca – the words for butter, windows, tables, flags, churches and Sunday – and launched a thin, cracked halo of Catholicism through the eastern archipelago. But with each darkening generation, as the communion wine soured and the mildew sprouted on the white walls of the churches, they drifted further from home. When the competition turned up in the early years of the 17th century, they were in no position to fight back.[2]

Though English ships did ply the Indonesian seas, and did drop anchor off the coasts of Java, in these early decades – and though their crews did indeed take part in all the violence, treachery and debauchery of the period known to the Dutch as the *Wilde Vaart*, the 'Wild Voyages' – it was Holland that ultimately came to dominate the trade. Their first fleet to reach the Spice Islands had returned a 400 per cent profit, and in 1602 a consortium of Dutch trading houses set up a conglomerated spice company on a truly global scale. They gave their new monopoly the exhaustingly spiky name of *Vereenigde Oost-Indische Compangnie*, the United East India Company, known forevermore in the interests of brevity as the VOC, the corporation that became an empire. Before long they had ousted the last of their European rivals from the tropical seas of the archipelago, and had established the city on the north coast of Java that would become a grand colonial capital in the coming centuries – Batavia, Queen of the East.

Batavia was founded in 1619 after an absurd three-way battle between the Dutch, British and Javanese. There had long been a small port called Sunda Kelapa – named for the local abundance of

2 The Portuguese were the first in and the last out. Though theirs was nothing more than a vestigial empire even by the 17th century, they lingered on years after the Dutch and English had faded from the Asian scene. Goa, that long-declined seat of conquest and Catholicism, remained Portuguese territory until the Republic of India invaded in 1961 (as did the tiny enclaves of Daman and Diu); East Timor mouldered under the disinterested auspices of Lisbon until 1975, and Macau only went back to China ten days short of the end of the 20th century.

coconuts – at the mouth of the Ciliwung River, but a century earlier it had been hyperbolically renamed Jayakarta, 'Glorious Victory', and turned into a vassal of the Sultan of Banten.

Rival British and Dutch fleets got tangled up in a dispute between Banten and the recalcitrant vassal prince of Jayakarta, and then turned on each other. A small force of Dutch shopkeepers and feverish sailors ended up besieged in a little fort beside the river, while their governor-general, Jan Pieterszoon Coen, fled to the Spice Islands in search of reinforcements. When he returned three months later, all fired up for a great battle, he found that both the British and the Javanese had lost interest and vanished, and that his countrymen inside the fort had spent most of the siege getting drunk, praying fervently to a Calvinist Christ, and dying of malaria. The highlight of the episode had come on 12 March 1619, when some unnamed Dutch soldier, inspired either by religious mania, inebriation or malarial delirium, came up with the idea of renaming their miserable outpost after a much-mythologised Germanic tribe who had stomped around the marshy flatlands of the Rhine Delta two thousand years earlier – the Batavi. The old Dutch headquarters in the East Indies had been far away at Ambon in the Spice Islands; Coen had long planned to shift operations south to Java, and now he had both a convenient location, and a suitably patriotic name for his capital.

As the spice trade gradually went to seed in the later 17th century, the focus of the VOC's empire shifted from the Spice Islands and consolidated in Java, where there were other export commodities to be found. The Dutch built barn-like churches beneath the volcanoes, and upland mansions with heavy shutters on the green hillsides. And they became ever more entangled in the convoluted politics of the native courts. Batavia, meanwhile, grew as a grand and dignified city. By 1670 it was home to around 130,000 people. It had a grid of canals lined with broad-canopied tamarind trees and flanked by heavyset buildings with whitewashed walls, shuttered windows and hipped, red-tiled roofs. At the head of the town stood a stocky, four-cornered fort with cannon-lined ramparts; behind it was the canal-cut walled city, and beyond that the outlying garrisons gave way to the coconut groves and the rice fields. Batavia's climate was atrociously morbid; the whole place teemed with malaria and dengue (a new arrival from Europe was said to have no more than a fifty-fifty chance of surviving his first year), and the city was occupied largely by slaves, immigrant Chinese, and the kind of Dutchmen one early governor-general described as 'the scum of the earth'. For all the downsides, however, Batavia was probably the most sophisticated European settlement east of Suez.

But for the other nascent colonial nations of Europe, not least Britain, none of this was of any interest whatsoever. The English East India Company was becoming increasingly entrenched in India; the days when nutmeg cost more than gold had been forgotten, and Indonesia and Java had fallen off the map, vanishing into a historical obscurity from which they would never return – except during that strange five years between 1811 and 1816.

* * *

The events that led – by many tortuous byways and detours – to John Leyden's fancy-dress pratfalls on the Cilincing beach in 1811, had taken place a decade-and-a-half earlier, and many thousands of miles to the west.

In the chilly tail-end of December 1794, a world away from the Javanese tropics, the rampaging Corsican general Napoleon Bonaparte sent his French Republican forces across the frosty flatlands of northwest Europe and into Holland. The fifth Prince William of Orange fled across the choppy English Channel in a small boat, begged the protection of the British, and was installed in what critics regarded as indolent luxury in the genteel London suburb of Kew. He quickly began sending begging letters to the governors of his colonies, ordering them to surrender their territories to the King of England. The Netherlands had been by no means stable in the previous decades, and support for the House of Orange was by no means universal, so it was not entirely surprising that few of the far-flung Dutch governors, sweating behind the shutters of mildewed mansions on Indian Ocean islets, immediately ran a Union Jack up the flagpole. They waited to see which way the wind was blowing, and as far as the British Government was concerned the sum total of Dutch overseas possessions – a scattering of remote landfalls in sultry seas, a few forgotten ports on muddy shores, and of course, the strange green island of Java – became enemy territory.

Of course, Java was beyond the pale, and there were much more pressing concerns in Europe itself. But over the coming years a few tentative forays were made into Dutch waters. In 1797, outposts in Malaya and Maluku were seized by British fleets, and that same year the prime minister, William Pitt the Younger, stressed to the governor-general in India the need for tackling Java itself. Almost nothing was known about the place beyond the facts that it was green, fertile, Muslim, and apparently woefully mismanaged by the Dutch. But still, Pitt felt that Java had potential, and would make a useful staging post on trade routes into the South China Sea and beyond.

In the event, however, more pressing distractions in India itself saw the Prime Minister's plea politely ignored, if not entirely forgotten, until 1810 when back in Europe Napoleon set about consolidating his empire. He annexed Holland and placed his brother Louis on the throne; the country was no longer simply a conquered French vassal: it was actually a part of France. There could be no more procrastination. The Secret Committee of Britain's East India Company – still running India on quasi-commercial lines on behalf of the crown at the time – gave urgent orders for the Dutch to be ousted from Java. The following year that huge fleet of eighty-one frigates, sloops and cruisers sailed for Java.

Four decades earlier, in 1770, the celebrated Captain James Cook had come limping through the archipelago aboard the *Endeavour* at the end of his first successful round-the-world voyage. He had crossed the Pacific, mapped New Zealand, and made first contact with the East Coast of Australia. Cook and his crew had experienced every hostile climate from the dreary doldrums to the storms of Cape Horn; they had dodged crocodiles and poison arrows, and had coped with scurvy and shipboard dysentery. But they decided that Batavia, with its mosquito-ridden drains and cloying humidity, was the unhealthiest place they had ever seen. Indeed, Cook declared that the Batavian climate 'was a sufficient defence or preservative against any hostile attempts, as the troops of no nation would be able to withstand, nor would any people in their senses, without absolute necessity, venture to encounter this pestilential atmosphere.'

But now, whether in their right minds or not, whether compelled by necessity or some darker driving force, an army of Englishmen and Indians were on their way down the Straits of Melaka with every intention of making this pestilential place their own. And for the man who would have the key role in the adventure, whether it proved to be a triumph or a catastrophe, any ominous warnings about the effects of the Javanese climate would have been blithely dismissed. Thomas Stamford Raffles was on the brink of the future he felt he deserved. He had come a very long way in a very short space of time.

The First Sigh of the East

The island of Penang rose out of a milky sea in the lavender light of a tropical dawn. A misted bank of hills stood above a ledge of foreshore and beyond it the dark forests of the Malay Peninsula rolled away under the swelling saffron stain of the coming sun. The ship was scarcely moving over the cloudy, shoal-stirred water. The sails hung limp and heavy in the moist air, shifting and settling uneasily from time to time on the whispers of a warm land breeze which carried with it a strange, unworldly scent: a hint of heat, leaf mould and unknown blossoms, of dry, scratchy coconut husks and fresh-cut teakwood, a whiff of sweat and steam and Chinese laundries, of fish cooked in hot oil, and an odour of tar, spice, old rope and cluttered drains.

The passengers stood on deck, not yet sweating, but skin still clammy from sleeping in cramped cabins in the hot darkness. They looked out at the slowly rising island, taking in that strange smell as they did so. Even for those long familiar with Asia it was a powerful moment of arrival, but for the first-timers it was utterly intoxicating. Joseph Conrad would write of his own experience of this 'first sigh of the East' eight decades later. It was, he declared, 'impalpable and enslaving, like a charm, like a whispered promise of mysterious delight'.

For one of the passengers standing on the deck of the ship that September morning in 1805, six years before the British fleet moored off Cilincing, the promise carried in that first scent of the land must have been particularly tantalising. He was a twenty-four-year-old clerk, newly married and newly promoted; a small man, with

39

hunched shoulders and limp brown hair that flopped down from his brow in a damp and unkempt fringe. One of his eyes pulled slightly askew of true and he had a nervous tendency to shift and fidget. Thomas Stamford Raffles had arrived in the East.

* * *

Raffles is one of the strangest, most conflicted and conflicting members of the vast and motley crew of thieves, heroes, geniuses and charlatans who make up the *dramatis personae* of the British Empire. He has also, despite having been something of a disgrace by the end of his own career, ended up with a posthumous reputation rendered from pure Teflon. Though here and there an angrily patriotic Dutch historian, or a drearily earnest post-colonial scholar has tried – in the obscurest annals of academia – to portray him as the devil incarnate in a frock coat, in popular consciousness he has become precisely what he never was in life: a hero. A new adoring biographer has emerged in every generation since his death, each polishing and plagiarising the work of his predecessor in a ceaseless relay of beatification, until the Raffles reputation, inextricably braided into the shimmering status of modern Singapore, has assumed an unassailable air. A Good Man in the East, they say; a sensitive scholar and an administrative genius, and the Last Colonialist It's OK to Like. While Mintos, Mayos and Victorias have been righteously obliterated from the roadmaps of India, Raffles remains like a rash all over Singapore, his name immortalised in schools, hotels and hospitals.

Though Raffles' own most notable characteristic was furiously energetic ambition, even he, as the ship called the *Warley* swung into the Georgetown dockside in Penang, could not have imagined such an outcome. But still, at the age of just twenty-four, he had already done rather well for himself.

Raffles was born on 6 July 1781 aboard a slave ship called the *Ann*, lumbering north from Port Morant, a sweltering harbour town of rum and bananas on the southeast coast of Jamaica. His father was the captain of the ship, which belonged to Hibberts and Co., a firm of Glasgow slave brokers. Raffles was the first of six children. One of his younger siblings, a boy, died in infancy; those who survived were all girls, and he grew up an only son. Raffles himself was responsible for writing the first draft of the myth that his future biographers would so eagerly embellish, and in later years he liked to proclaim a past of penury, most notably claiming that his family had been unable to afford candles during his childhood. It certainly seems that Captain Raffles made no great fortune from the slave trade, and left no great inheritance when he died in the last years of the century. But at worst the life that he provided for his wife and his children was that of the frustrated lower middle class, rather than the hand-to-mouth grind of true poverty. Raffles grew up in a 'genteel substantial dwelling house' in Islington, and was schooled at 'a respectable academy at Hammersmith'.

When he was fourteen a shadowy maternal uncle pulled some strings, called in some favours, and got him a job as a junior clerk in the offices of the British East India Company. The position brought his formal schooling to a terminal halt, but for a middle-class youth in the late 18th century an entry into the world of work at fourteen was nothing unusual, and a post in the ranks of the East India Company, no matter how lowly, was a point of departure with serious potential. For Raffles it would be the first way-station on a long and mercurial journey eastwards to Java and Singapore.

East India House, the headquarters of the East India Company, stood amongst a jumble of chimneypots on Leadenhall Street in the City of London. It outstripped its space amongst the inky offices of long-forgotten little trading companies like a cuckoo chick in a wren's nest, a forest of Doric columns soaring from the pavements towards an apex crowned by a statue of Britannia in all her haughty glory. The Company, formed in 1600 with spice in mind, had grown exponentially – and earned a little more respectability – since the early days of pillage and piracy. Like the Dutch VOC, its advance into territorial acquisition had been, if not entirely accidental, then by no means part of the original plan. But by the end of the 18th century the Company had turned into a quasi-empire, and the Leadenhall Street headquarters had become home to a sprawling pseudo-civil service and an army of underpaid clerks.

Raffles spent a decade at his desk in Leadenhall Street, coming of age in the department of the Company's secretary, William Ramsay. At night he schooled himself in all he had failed to learn in his two-year academic career, and by day he pored over account books and reports, round shoulders hunched over the ink-splattered table-top as he totted up totals of incomes and outgoings for obscure posts in Indian backwaters he had never seen and could never imagine. These inky years, on £70 per annum, were Raffles' apprenticeship.

As a clerk and a junior administrator he was certainly energetic. He could produce vast quantities of paperwork in an improbably short period of time, and when he had been given a task by a superior he would go to it with admirable determination. Raffles' eager diligence did not always endear him to his co-workers, if the reminiscences of another young company servant who accompanied his father on a visit to East India House in 1803 are anything to go by. While the father went in to a meeting with the Company directors behind an oak-panelled door, the son 'was left in a room occupied by two clerks':

One of these was standing in front of a fire, when the other came and, with a kick, sent him away. The one who was removed from the fire in so undignified a manner was Mr Raffles who became the celebrated Sir Stamford Raffles.

There would be plenty of others who would seek to land a firm kick upon his person in the years to come.

Doubtless Raffles' employers were pleased with his hard work, but still, his rise from obscurity in East India House was sudden, unexpected, and has never been satisfactorily explained. In 1805 he was plucked from the ranks on a salary that had increased by a factor of *two thousand per cent*, and shipped off for an administrative post in Southeast Asia. He had been gazetted as assistant secretary to the newly appointed Governor of Penang, a freshly upgraded British outpost drifting off the Malay coast near the head of the Straits of Melaka.

There are two stories, neither entirely convincing, to explain how Raffles came by this remarkable and exotic promotion. The first – that told by the Rafflesophiles – has it that the East India Company Secretary, William Ramsay, was so impressed by the young man's earnest pen-pushing abilities that he felt compelled to exert his influence and offer him an almighty leg-up. The other version, whispered maliciously by the Rafflesophobes, is positively scurrilous. Just six days after the official notice of Raffles' new appointment came through, a low-key but distinctly unusual wedding took place in the parish church of St George in the scholarly London district of Bloomsbury between a twenty-four-year-old clerk with suddenly improved prospects, and a thirty-four-year-old widow with a murky past. The two events, the gossips hissed, were by no means unconnected.

Olivia Mariamne Raffles (*ex* Fancourt, *née* Devenish) was an enigma wrapped in a mystery swaddled in a scandal. Her origins were shady, her character dubious, and the responses she elicited from the men who met her were utterly contradictory. She prompted poets to verse and cynics to sneers; some grown men tumbled headlong into the pools of her 'flashing black eyes'; others sniggered and muttered of mutton dressed as lamb. Raffles' second wife – who was also his first biographer – sought to expurgate her predecessor entirely from the pages of history, and despite the aggrieved protestations of the man himself he was never entirely able to shake off the rumours that his first union, sealed in the Bloomsbury church that March morning, had been not just a marriage of convenience, but one of outright connivance. The eager-to-please clerk from the Secretary's office, the gossip-mongers said, had sacrificed himself at the marital altar to rid his boss of an embarrassment, and shamelessly to advance his own career. Olivia, they claimed, was the mistress of William Ramsay, and he was desperate to offload her, either because of her advancing years and diminishing charms, or because she had simply become too much of a handful. It was not a very nice thing to suggest, but some years later the claim even made it as far as the pages of the *Biographical Dictionary of the Living Authors of Great Britain and Ireland*, which stated that 'Mr Raffles went out to India in an inferior capacity, through the interest of Mr Ramsay, Secretary to the Company, and in consequence of his marrying a lady connected with that gentleman'.

Whatever the truth of the matter, the first Mrs Raffles was certainly a little odd. She was born, most probably in India, in 1771, and seems to have sprung from a subset of a clan of Irish gentry, though family legend would have it that those flashing black eyes were the product of an exotic descent. Olivia's mother, rumour had it, was a Circassian.[3]

Whatever the genetic origins of her looks, by the age of twenty-two she had already put them to effective use and as a consequence her reputation was already marked by an indelibly scandalous stain. On a ship called the *Rose*, sailing from England to Madras, the young Olivia had flashed her black eyes at the captain, a much older married man named Dempster, and trusting to old clichés about the passing of nocturnal ships the pair embarked on a torrid affair. Nine months later a little girl called Harriet was born in an outraged Madras. Dempster demonstrated an admirable sense of duty: he took the child

---

3 The Circassians are a magnificently ambiguous people, straddling the imaginative gap between Orient and Occident. Their homeland lies in the Caucasus, and for those peering fascinated from points west they have always managed to have one milky-skinned foot in the courts of old Europe, and the other in the harem. Like their Caucasian kin, the Armenians, they were everybody's Other, with low-key diaspora communities scattered from Calcutta to Cairo. Their women were said to be very beautiful indeed, and they have popped up – skin whiter than white, eyes blacker than black – in the seraglio of the mind's eye of orientalist poets and painters since time immemorial. In later ages their image was used to sell beauty products

on, raised her, and eventually made her his heir. Olivia, however, seems to have had nothing to do with her illegitimate daughter after the birth, and showing a remarkable resilience to scandal she had found a willing suitor with honourable intentions within the year.

She married her first husband – an assistant surgeon in Madras by the name of Jacob Fancourt – while her second husband was still a scrawny thirteen-year-old, reciting his times-tables in that 'respectable academy at Hammersmith'. The physician was apparently not equipped to heal himself however, for he died of fever in the Punjab in 1800, and the next time the widowed Olivia emerges from the ether it is as she presents herself at East India House in 1804, demanding a pension on the strength of her deceased husband's service (she got one – one shilling and eight pence a day). She may have first encountered the barely post-pubescent Raffles at this point, but it is hard to imagine that they had much in common.

Raffles displayed a typically British reticence about his relationships with women in his otherwise expansive and emotional writings, and between that and the obliterating editorial efforts of his second wife it is rather hard to gain a firm impression of Olivia. But she did sign up as a committed – and occasionally unhinged – player in Team Raffles as her husband's star rose, and whatever its original motivations their marriage does seem to have become a close, if somewhat strange, one.

And in any case, the half-young-half-not-so-young couple had plenty of time to get to know each other. In April 1805 Mr and Mrs Raffles set sail from London for the five-month voyage to Penang. A turbulent decade would pass before the younger spouse saw his homeland again; his wife would never return to Europe.

* * *

Penang, a crushed cube of land some fifteen miles long, lies across a murky channel from the dark green foreshore of the Malay state of

Kedah. In the early years of the 19th century it was the preeminent port of the Straits of Melaka, and an unlikely British toehold in Southeast Asia. It had been leased in 1786 from the Sultan of Kedah on behalf of the East India Company by a gallivanting sea captain from Sussex by the name of Francis Light, and a little European township called Georgetown had been laid out amongst the palms at the head of the island. The outpost grew quickly under Light's command as a 'port of refreshment for the King's, the Company's and the Country Ships', and it soon drew trade away from Dutch harbours further down the Straits and out in the islands beyond. It was also chosen as the spot at which to develop new shipyards replacing scarce English oak with abundant Asian teak, and in 1805 the East India Company's government decided to upgrade Penang from a mere outpost to a presidency, a territory under the rule of a governor on par with Madras, Bombay and Calcutta. Raffles – now on £1500 a year – was the most junior member of the new administration.

For the old-established administrators of Penang, the arrival of the new presidency government, shipped in wholesale from overseas, was akin to a very large elephant suddenly boarding a very small boat. The place had long been used to toddling along at its own pace, and more than a few sunburnt noses were put badly out of joint as a consequence. But the new arrivals – and the new money – did bring a certain buzz to the little island. There were banquets, buggy rides and drinks parties. A newspaper was founded which filled its columns with adverts for ladies' dresses and six-month-old news from Europe. There were occasional shooting parties in pursuit of green pigeons; of an evening the ladies would sing cheery airs to the off-key tinkle of damp-ravaged pianos, and alcohol was consumed in oceanic quantities. Even before the 1805 upgrade Penang seems to have laboured under the effects of mass alcoholism. In one eighteen-month stretch of bacchanalia in the 1790s the island's Government House alone had managed to put away 1,020 bottles of claret, 588 of beer, 300 of port, a relatively modest 30 of cherry brandy (for the ladies, perhaps?) and a head-splitting

1,404 bottles of Madeira.

Meanwhile, beyond the confines of the drink-addled European society, Georgetown grew as a polyglot port of many races. There were Chinese shopkeepers, Indian labourers, Malay sailors, and all manner of hawkers, hookers, cooks and criminals.

For the young and ambitious Raffles, in the thick of all this, Penang was a place of possibilities. He spent five years there, living in a little bungalow on the forested slopes behind Georgetown, and rapidly expanding the remit of his job description to take on every vacant role as fever, incompetence and corruption felled his fellows. Though he had landed in what was indeed 'an inferior capacity', before long he was a veritable paragon of multitasking. He assumed the role of acting First Secretary when the official occupant of that post fell out with the Governor and was shipped off on an extended leave of absence; he became the Agent for the Navy, the licenser of the press, and even took over the role of official Malay translator to the Government.

According to the hero-worshippers, Raffles, with his love of self-improvement and formidable intellect, was already fluent in Malay by the time he disembarked from the *Warley* at Georgetown in 1805. He had spent the five-month voyage from England earnestly poring over the primers and conversing with the Asian crewmen.

Malay, as far as foreigners were concerned, was the 'Hindustani of the East'. An Austronesian language loaded with Sanskrit and Arabic ballast – as well as with a subtle spicing of Chinese, Persian and Portuguese – it most likely emerged from the basin of the Palembang River in the steamy south of Sumatra sometime in the 7th century. It had become the first language of those regions, and of the Malayan mainland. But Malay was a much longer tongue than that alone, and it licked the shores of every landmass in Southeast Asia. It was the linguistic starch that bound the polyglot Pasisir ports of Java; a little pidgin Malay would get you by on docksides everywhere from Bangkok to Dili, and a Malay missive mailed to any corner of the sprawling Indonesian archipelago stood a good chance of being understood.[4] And all this utility was coupled to a relative ease of acquisition.

For this reason the oft-repeated claim that Raffles' facility with Malay made him somehow unusual needs to be taken with a certain pinch of salt: most old Southeast Asia hands could speak the language quite well; many of them could speak it much better than Raffles. In the Dutch territories there were some who spoke it by preference, especially amongst the locally-born Dutchwomen and the Indo-Europeans. Also, the claim that Raffles knew the language perfectly is not entirely sound. He certainly seems to have made energetic attempts to improve his fluency from the outset, but he could never make much shift with the written language. He always relied on translators to pen his letters to native courts,[5] and indeed, even after he had been in the region for several years he often had verbal translators on hand for his meetings with kings and courtiers. And

---

4 Today Malay remains by far the most widely spoken language in Southeast Asia. As well as the national language of Malaysia and Brunei, it is also one of the official tongues of multilingual Singapore, and is spoken in dialect form by the Muslims of southern Thailand. There are also pockets of Malay dialect spoken in Burma and amongst Southeast Asian-descended communities in Sri Lanka and on Australia's Christmas Island; a few words are still remembered by older members of South Africa's Cape Malay community, descended from exiles of the colonial era. By far the biggest body of Malay-speakers, however, is in Indonesia. The national Indonesian language, spoken from the tip of Sumatra to the marches of Papua New Guinea, is simply a rebranded form of Malay, chosen as a unifying vehicle of nationalism by 20th-century independence activists. As *Bahasa Indonesia* it is spoken by at least 200 million people, and though the versions used in Indonesia and Malaysia reflect the divergent histories of the two nations – with Javanese and Dutch vocabulary added to one, and English loanwords to the other – they remain mutually comprehensible.

5 Malay (in both Malaysian and Indonesian forms) is written today in the Roman alphabet. Until the early 20th century, however, it was usually penned using a modified Arabic script called *Jawi*, and students of the language who wanted to read the sagas and write to the kings would need to knuckle down, go right to left, and learn their *alif-ba-ta* ...

judging from the way Raffles transliterated Malay vocabulary in his own writings, he never learnt to detect the subtle but crucial terminal consonant of many words: when he listened and when he spoke, it seems, Raffles could not differentiate between a house-brick – *bata* – and the people of the North Sumatran hinterlands, the Batak. And in any case, at the time he stepped down from the decks of the *Warley* it is *highly* unlikely that Raffles could manage more than a few halting, ill-pronounced sentences, and as official 'translator' his role would have been mainly one of supervision.

But still, at a very tender age, Thomas Stamford Raffles had arrived in the corner of the globe that he was to make his own. He had a wife who, in his own words, 'would soothe the adverse blasts of misfortune and gladden the sunshine of prosperity', he had a rudimentary facility with the local language, and all manner of prospects as a growing fish in the poky pond of Penang.

The image of Raffles during these early years is that of a man of prodigious energy – perhaps a little too much for some tastes. Rival writers have given varying versions of Raffles' status in Penang society over the years. Some have made him the object of ostracism, an outcast beset by scurrilous rumours about his marriage. Others leap to his defence and crowingly quote contemporary sources that make him the very life and soul of the Penang party. At a glance the two visions seem contradictory, but in fact they probably both represent the truth.

For old-established stick-in-the-muds who had been in Penang since the days of Francis Light, Raffles – with his rapid rise, his swottish tendency to leap into any vacant position, and his infuriating ability to do most jobs well – likely became the lightening rod, the figurehead for all they resented. Rumours about the reasons for his preferment had almost certainly been shipped out in private letters from Leadenhall Street and propagated in dockside taverns, and the fossil of Olivia's earlier scandal had doubtless been prised from the memory of rum-sodden country-boat captains sailing in from Madras (rumours and circumstantial evidence also strongly suggest that

Olivia was a little too fond of a drink herself – not that that would have counted against her in Penang). On the other hand, there seems no reason to doubt the writings of an acolyte who stated that Raffles was 'of a cheerful lively disposition and very fond of Society', or those of the visitor who stated that he was 'the life and soul of what little society (European) there was gathered up and down among the cocoa-nut trees'.

And herein lies the crux of Raffles' character, and the reason why some were utterly beguiled by his company while others couldn't stand the sight of him. If you were part of Raffle's circle of friends and collaborators, if you were invited to his 'gay gatherings', shared his world view and committed yourself to the clique, then he was an utterly charming man, full of intelligence, kindness and bright ideas. If, on the other hand, you were not invited, or had no inclination to attend, then he was an absurd and obnoxious egomaniac, prancing preposterously atop a mountain of self-interest. Depending on the point of departure, both impressions were probably valid. The sheer volume of people who intensely disliked Raffles cannot simply be dismissed as the result of wrongheaded bitterness, but neither can the legions who fell at his feet be simply scoffed at as dupes and ingénues.

One man who was very much invited to the Raffles party, and was certainly no ingénue, had arrived in Penang just a month after the instalment of the new presidency government. Eccentric, academic, poet and pirate, he was to prove a radical inspiration to the young administrator, a vessel for his further advancement, and the sharp and shining third corner of a bizarre consensual love triangle.

* * *

John Caspar Leyden landed in Penang on 22 October 1805 in a parlous state of health. If Raffles' own journey from the decks of a slave ship to a promising post in Southeast Asia had been an unlikely one, then Leyden's trajectory had been positively fantastic. He was born in 1775 in the village of Denholm on the banks of the

Teviot River in the low hills of the Scottish Borders. His father was a shepherd.

The peasants of 18th-century Teviotdale were apparently an unusually literary lot: little Leyden was taught to read by his grandmother, and feasted his youthful imagination on copies of the works of Homer, the *Arabian Nights*, and *Paradise Lost*, all borrowed from neighbours' cottages. At the age of nine he entered the village school, and six years later he set out on foot to take up a place at Edinburgh University. Though his classmates laughed at his 'homespun coat' and 'homely speech', Leyden excelled in the study of Hebrew, Arabic and theology, and by the age of nineteen he had 'confounded the doctors of Edinburgh by the portentous mass of his acquisitions in almost every department of learning'. Quite what the earthy folks of Denholm made of him when he came home for the holidays, Hebrew Bible under his arm and a sheaf of Arabic poetry poking out of his satchel, is hard to imagine, but they were perhaps pleased to hear that the little prodigy was leaning towards the priesthood. After draining the academic wells of Edinburgh he shifted to St Andrews where he earned his license to preach. But by this stage he had changed his plans and embarked on training as a physician, gaining his medical doctorate in double-quick time. All this marks Leyden out as some kind of genius, but what makes his character so striking is that he was no staid and bookish bore; by his late teens the boy who had started out minding the flocks on heather-clad hillsides had decided to strike the pose of a sophisticated dandy. He had also discovered the joys of poetry.

Leyden's verse is monumentally awful – all leafy bowers and fiery breasts – but it was the kind of stuff that went down well at the turn of the 19th century, and he soon fell in with Walter Scott, and collaborated with him on collections of wildly romantic 'border minstrelsy'. He could quite easily have made a career for himself as a poet, or a priest, or simply as a country doctor. But this was not enough for the budding polymath. His linguistic studies had already fired an interest in the more exotic quarters of the globe, and his decidedly free translations of Persian and Arabic poetry had made him a forerunner of the orientalist literary tradition of Edward FitzGerald and Richard Burton. He had already completed a work on the exploration of Africa without ever having been there; now he was determined to visit weird and wonderful places for himself.

In early 1803 he was offered a medical post in Madras. The prospect of all the glorious literary and scientific treasures of the Subcontinent left Leyden in a spin, and he was all set for an immediate departure. At the last minute, however, he was felled by 'a severe attack of cramp in his stomach', and he missed the boat. This turned out to be a piece of great good fortune, for his intended vessel, the *Hindustan*, only got as far as Margate before going down in a storm. Leyden eventually got underway a couple of months later, and in August 1803 he arrived in Madras where he was placed in charge of the General Hospital.

The recollections of those he treated suggest that, whatever his poetic and linguistic talents, Leyden was not much of a medic, and like Olivia Raffles' unfortunate first husband he showed that unnerving tendency of British doctors in India to chronic ill health. He had not been in Madras long before he began to embark on a series of excursions into the interior in search of a climactic cure. Reading Leyden's own accounts of these journeys it is instantly apparent that he was a British traveller of the light-footed and self-effacing kind – a Robert Byron rather than a Wilfred Thesiger – and that he was by no means shy of spinning a yarn. There were encounters with brigands and 'monstrous tigers', purple poetry at breakfast, and plenty of slightly ridiculous derring-do. There was also serious botany, ethnography and linguistics. However, there was no respite from the stomach cramps, and in September 1805, in search of some serious relief, he set sail from the steamy Keralan port of Kollam, bound for Penang, which in its early years had obtained an entirely undeserved reputation as a sanatorium.

He was the only European on board the leaky little ship, owned by a Parsee, mastered by an Arab and crewed by a gaggle of Maldivians 'prodigiously addicted to sorcery'. With a certain satisfaction Leyden noted in his journal that 'I very much question, if ever Sinbad the Sailor sailed with a more curious set'.

It was a decidedly eventful voyage. There were furious storms; the boat turned out to be little better than a seaborne sieve, and there were endless rounds of Arabic chanting, and tortuous theological debates when Leyden suggested reviving some fatigued crewmen with a tot of gin (they ultimately decided that it was permissible to drink the *haram* liquor, as they were taking it as medicine rather than for pleasure). The most dramatic moment came when they encountered a prowling French frigate, which swung at them 'like a leopard at a fawn', prompting the Maldivians to embark on a bout of particularly frantic Koranic chanting. Convinced that 'everybody had been going stark staring mad' Leyden made his own preparations for battle by addressing a poem to his Malay dagger[6] and by plotting to ambush any perfidious Frenchmen who came aboard. Fortunately the wind blew them clear, and a few days later they limped into the Straits of Melaka with the ship by now full of 'The tainted odour of spoiled rice, and rotten salt-fish' and infested with 'myriads of cock-roaches and ants'.

Leyden was delighted to come ashore, but less than pleased with the lodgings in which he found himself – 'a kind of naval tavern where all around me is ringing with the vociferation of tarpaulins, the

---

6 Leyden later wrote the poem down as the *Address to My Malay Krees* [kris], *While Pursued by a French Privateer off Sumatra*:

Yet still my trusty Krees prove true,
If e'er thou serv'dst at need the brave,
And thou shalt wear a crimson hue,
Or I shall win a watery grave...

And so on for six purple verses. Between Leyden declaring rhymes to a piece of antiquated weaponry at one end of the deck, and the Maldivian blethering in Arabic at the other, the French lookouts must have been tumbling from the topmasts in fits of hysterics ...

hoarse bawling of sea oaths and the rattling of the dicebox'. It was no place for an invalid, especially after such a trying voyage, and Leyden was thrown into a state of despair. But then there descended a pair of angels – one with drooping shoulders and a wonky eye, the other markedly more mature than her companion. The poet was spirited away to an airy bungalow where everyone promptly fell madly in love with each other.

* * *

Raffles seems to have met Leyden entirely by chance, but it was an encounter of mighty consequence. As the poet gradually recovered his health under the Raffles' roof, fiery intellects and flashing dark eyes met. As a self-schooled drop-out Raffles could quite easily have resented the houseguest's plethora of degrees, but instead he was utterly beguiled by Leyden's learning. He doted on him; he sat at his feet and heard tales of eastern philosophy and of Asian literary traditions every bit as convoluted and complex as the Greek. Very quickly Raffles – with his as yet imperfect knowledge of the Malay language and his casual interest in local history – was all set on becoming a great orientalist scholar. He even sent a request back home to England for a Hebrew dictionary.

Leyden meanwhile, found himself utterly undone by the Circassian eyes and tender nursing skills of Olivia, and was soon sitting up in bed to pen soaring paeans to her beauty – 'The saffron-tinted flower of love, Its tulip-buds adorn the hair, Of none more lov'd amid the fair'! Raffles was apparently delighted that his wife – who another, less enamoured visitor of the period described as 'a rather elderly lady, dressed rather fantastically' – should receive such attentions from such a man. The household was all awash with effusive adoration.

It was almost certainly sometime during the joyous months of Leyden's convalesce that Raffles first took serious notice of the name of a long, lozenge-shaped island, a thousand miles to the south.

The Southeast Asian sideshow of the Napoleonic Wars was well underway by the time Raffles reached Penang. Melaka, further down the Straits, had been captured by a British fleet a decade earlier, and other lightweight warships sailed out from Penang from time to time to hassle the more remote of the Dutch outposts in Indonesia. There must also have been idle talk of an oft-discussed, long-delayed project actually to seize the jewel in the VOC's crown, Java itself. But it was in conversation with John Leyden that Raffles first came to think of Java as 'the Land of Promise', the place where all his own dreams of glory might eventually be realised.

The poet was the very epitome of the 19th-century orientalist, with his misappropriation of Asian literature, his inclination to equate the past glories of the East with those of the Classical world, and his love of the arcane and obscure – all coupled to a tendency to view the current inhabitants of the Orient as superstitious fools and benighted cowards. Java was the great lodestone of high culture in Muslim Southeast Asia; flowery fantasies of the Mataram and Majapahit empires would certainly have been raised in the little Penang bungalow as Raffles hung wide-eyed on every word and Olivia applied cold compresses to the fevered genius' forehead, and the idea that these two men, these kindred spirits of high brow and low birth, might one day lord it together over that fabled island would have been quite in keeping with the tone of the discourse. It was certainly an idea that they would become increasingly attached to over the next half-decade, and in their own self-penned legends the fact that a British invasion of Java had been on the cards, and had indeed even been abortively attempted, long before either of them ever arrived in Asia would be conveniently forgotten.

But that all lay some way ahead across a torrent of effusive correspondence. By January 1806, Leyden had recovered sufficiently to return to his Indian duties, and as soon as Penang was out of sight he began penning love letters, declaring Olivia 'a living saint' capable of the 'sublimest miracles', and putting the finishing touches to his *Dirge of the Departed Year*, unashamedly dedicated to Olivia. To quote all seventeen syrupy stanzas would be too much for anyone; the final four are enough to convey his feelings, not just for the lady, but also for her husband:

> But chief that in this eastern isle,
> Girt by the green and glistering wave,
> Olivia's kind endearing smile
> Seem'd to recall me from the grave.

> When, far beyond Malaya's sea,
> I trace dark Soonda's forests drear,
> Olivia! I shall think of thee; –
> And bless thy steps, departed year!

> Each morn or evening spent with thee
> Fancy shall mid the wilds restore
> In all their charms, and they shall be
> Sweet days that shall return no more.

> Still may'st thou live in bliss secure,
> Beneath *that friend's* protecting care,
> And may his cherish'd life endure
> Long, long, thy holy love to share.

Whatever charms Olivia possessed, they certainly seem to have worked on Leyden.

Plenty of Leyden's other letters to the lady – and to Raffles himself – have survived, but only one of her own replies remains. It is, in fact, one of only two written traces of the first Mrs Raffles that we have, and it doesn't offer the most favourable of impressions. Written from Penang in 1808 in a hand that wavers like dune grass in the wind, she begins by declaring to Leyden that 'I feel an affection for you such as I feel for my only and beloved Brother,' before descending to pouting protestations that he seems to have forgotten her. She then goes on, referring to herself in the second person and using certifiably hysterical language (she had been at the brandy perhaps), to relate her husband's troubles with some members of the old Penang establishment. Raffles had apparently fallen out with John Dickens, the Penang judge and magistrate whose appointment dated back to 1801:

His old <u>enemy</u> Mr Dickens is going back to Calcutta with his heart full of rancour and his mouth full of scurrility against him – for what Olivia? [Be]cause he [Raffles] has proved himself <u>almost</u> as learned in the law as himself, 'Great Judge and M.', because he has saved the Government, bad as it is, from his insolent and unmerited attacks – [be]cause he has proved himself above him in all things and has persevered in politeness to him... he [Dickens] is really the most <u>impudent, ignorant, affected</u>, envious ungrateful old <u>Jay</u> I ever heard of ...

If this kind of thing was the norm it is, once again, not difficult to understand why there were people who took against the Raffles couple. Indeed, from the rest of Olivia's letter it seems that there were plenty of other 'little paltry wretches' in Penang who had issues with her husband, though 'They may bark as a dog does at the Moon with as much effect'.

The merry gatherings at the Raffles bungalow in Georgetown were, of course, a mere dress rehearsal for still gayer get-togethers at a much grander upland retreat on a much larger island, and the yapping of the paltry wretches of Penang were but an overture for the barking of much bigger dogs in years to come. Leyden ought to have been right alongside Raffles and Olivia for all of it, but it was not to be. Amidst the deluge of the *Dirge of the Departed Year* there was a passage of prophesy:

Fore-doom'd to seek an early tomb,
For whom the pallid grave-flowers blow,

I hasten on my destin'd doom,
And sternly mock at joy or woe.

He would get to see Java, but not very much of it.

* * *

The island of Raffles' and Leyden's dreams had not been faring well in recent years.

The Dutch had spread their net beyond Java and the Spice Islands, to take in footholds on jungle foreshores across the archipelago. But the cost of maintaining an ever-expanding network of residencies and military outposts was enormous, and as the outgoings had spiralled over the course of the 18th century, the returns had dwindled. The Council of the Indies – the cluster of administrators who sat in session with the Governor-General twice a week in Batavia – would justify military entanglements in the internal affairs of native courts by way of the advantageous treaties that were usually signed as a result. But treaties couldn't be wrapped, weighed, bundled up and traded for hard silver in the docks, and the sheer bloated scale of the VOC's empire had turned the one-time golden goose of the Dutch East Indies into a dead economic duck, floating around the Southern Ocean belly-up with its feet in the air. Many stations, out amongst the islands, had turned into weeping economic ulcers. Expenditure was often well over double the returns; in the case the Bandas, the one-time honey-pot of the spice trade where a small box of nutmeg once rendered an entire round-the-world voyage a success, running costs topped incomes by a factor of fifteen!

It was not only bad luck and mismanagement that had precipitated the slump; it was also corruption. From its earliest days the VOC in Indonesia had attracted the very worst kind of people. For most Europeans, Java and the rest of the Indies were rough, remote, and spectacularly unhealthy. With a handful of exceptions amongst dedicated soldiers and born administrators the only people who would actually *want* to go there were those with the worst possible motives, namely greed, desperation and the fact that they couldn't cut it back at home. VOC out-stations often ended up in the charge of men deemed totally unemployable in Holland. Company staffers were not paid particularly well, and they sometimes had to meet the full running costs of their postings out of their own pockets. With shutters peeling, white walls flaking, and death by teatime a permanent possibility, it was little wonder that so many succumbed to graft on a grand scale. The perpetual pilfering did nothing for the financial health of the company.

Even the Queen of the East was beginning to look like a ropey old charwoman. The population had dwindled; many corners of the city had been abandoned and the buildings were beginning to crumble. The four-cornered fort at the river mouth was falling to pieces; counting-houses that had chimed with the clink of accumulating coin a century earlier were now the abode of cobwebs and ghosts, and the canals were choked with all manner of unspeakable filth. Sewage, household waste, and general junk were routinely tossed into the oozing black water, and 'every now and then a dead hog, or a dead horse, is stranded upon the shallow parts, and it being the business of no particular person to remove the nuisance, it is negligently left to time and accident'.

The coastline on either side of the river mouth, meanwhile, was 'a dismal succession of stinking mud-banks, filthy bogs, and stagnant pools', noted one appalled visitor; 'along this shore the sea throws up all manner of slime, mollusca, dead fish, mud, and weeds, which putrefying with utmost rapidity by the extreme degree of heat, load and infect the air with their offensive miasmata.' This insalubrious shoreline, together with the carcass-filled canals, the low-lying marshes inland, and the general state of decay combined 'in a greater or lesser degree, their baneful influence to render Batavia one of the most unwholesome spots on the face of the globe.'

The mortality from tropical diseases was horrific. Everyone was in a state of permanent ill-health with a 'wan, weak, and languid' appearance, and the sheer regularity of deaths engendered a bleak sort of cynicism amongst the survivors. Those Europeans who could afford to had abandoned the original walled city and moved out into the countryside where the atmosphere was claimed to be a little better, but no matter where you housed yourself, the fever would still come calling with alarming regularity. A pall of constant gloom hung over Batavia, and according to one visitor the entire European society was in the grip of 'discontent and dejection':

The only resource for those who are in this state of listlessness, approaching to torpidity, is, to seek relief in society, and to endeavour to kill the heavy hours in the most frivolous manner: smoking tobacco, uninteresting and useless conversation, drinking and card-playing, form the sum of their amusements; and having, in this manner, spent the day and part of the night, they rise the next morning, utterly at a loss how to pass the many tedious hours of the day they enter upon; and devoid of all inclination for reading, either for amusement or instruction, they are compelled to go the same dull round, and are only solicitous to make choice of such ways of killing time, as least interfere with their beloved state of motionless repose.

It was a damning indictment of an entire colonial project in a state of terminal decline.

When Napoleon invaded Holland in 1794, one of the first things his new republican administrators had done was to take a close and critical look at the VOC's accounts: a 200-year-old trading corporation that had been racking up enormous debts by way of cooked books and short-term loans to pay the dividends demanded by its shareholders was exactly the kind of decadent aristocrat that the guillotine was designed for. The appalled auditors discovered that the company was a credit-crunching 85 million guilders – equivalent to something like half a billion pounds sterling today – in the red. The Seventeen Gentlemen, the board who had presided over this ruin, had been kicked out of their chambers, and four years later, on the very first day of the very first year of a brand new century – a century that would be the heady golden age of European colonialism – the VOC was officially disbanded and its assets transferred to the Napoleonic-Dutch state. The East Indies were nationalised, though they were in such a mess that even an army of squeaky-clean civil servants with administrative superpowers would have been hard-pressed to set them straight.

* * *

In Britain's own much more modest Southeast Asian empire, meanwhile, a young clerk with significant – if not quite super – powers knew nothing of Dutch woes below the equator; he was continuing to build his own career, to correspond with John Leyden, and to dream of a shining future. At times the stress and the heat took their toll. Bouts of fever began to drag Raffles down, and with them came a creeping depression – a black dog that would emerge from the shadows from time to time throughout his career. But the man who would provide Raffles with every opportunity he had ever dreamed of – and who would license events that would change the course of history in Java – had already arrived at his post. There was not long to wait.

Gilbert Elliot, the First Earl of Minto, had arrived in Calcutta in 1807 as the most powerful Briton in Asia, the East India Company's governor-general. A middle-aged Scotsman with a busy but exemplary career behind him, he had thinning white hair, a smile of permanent amusement, and a touchingly sincere long-distance relationship with his wife (who had remained at home in Scotland). He had been chosen by the Board of Directors as a safe pair of hands to put right the carnage wrought by his nightmarish predecessor, Richard Colley, the Marquis Wellesley, an arrogant hothead who had stacked the Company's debts to an eye-watering £31.5 million (well over £1 billion in today's money). One of Minto's earliest initiatives on arrival in India was to encourage the learning of local languages amongst British administrators. This, inevitably, brought him into contact with a fellow Scot, by then installed in Calcutta as Professor of Hindustani. The link was forged – Raffles to Leyden, Leyden to Minto – and Java, the exotic Land of Promise, began slowly to rise from the far horizon as something more than wild fantasy.

In the monsoon months of 1810 Thomas Stamford Raffles visited the hub of Britain's nascent empire in Asia for the first time. A rickety country ship had carried him to Calcutta, and once he disembarked on the banks of the Hooghly, he enjoyed a joyous reunion with John Leyden, got to read a paper he had written on the Malays to the Bengal Asiatic Society, and was soon spinning through the rarefied upper atmosphere of colonial India. There had been an uptick in the volume of talk about the Dutch territories that year, and a British fleet had recently captured the one-time Spice Islands, Maluku.

As one of the most promising young civil servants in Penang, and as a man with a personal recommendation from Leyden, it was unsurprising that Raffles was granted an audience with the Governor-General. There had actually been some suggestion that Minto might appoint him governor of Maluku. Raffles soon learned that this was not to be, but he and Leyden had wilder dreams anyway, and he was quite unconcerned:

I met with the kindest reception from Lord Minto. I found that, though the appointment to the Moluccas had not actually taken place, it was promised to another. I, in consequence, relinquished all idea of it, and at once drew his Lordship's attention to Java, by observing that there were other islands worthy of his Lordship's consideration besides the Moluccas: Java, for instance. On the mention of Java, his Lordship cast a look of such scrutiny, anticipation, and kindness upon me, as I shall never forget. 'Yes,' said he, 'Java is an interesting Island; I shall be happy to receive any information you can give me concerning it.'

This passage, written much later, is Raffles at his mythomaniac worst. His apologists have engaged in semantic spin-doctoring over the years to claim that he really meant something quite different by his version of the genesis of the Java project, but the inference is as obvious as it is absurd: he, Raffles, a talented but relatively lowly secretary from the most obscure of the Company's four presidencies, had been entirely responsible for planting the idea of invading Java in the mind of the Governor-General. Aside from everything else the claim is insulting to Lord Minto.

The idea of invading Java had been batted around by Old India Hands since Thomas Raffles was in short trousers, and an abortive attack on Batavia had actually been launched back in 1800 when he was still filling in the account books in Leadenhall Street. Even while he was actually in India in 1810, offering his suggestions and plotting with Leyden, Lord Minto received a detailed memo from the Company's Secret Committee. Napoleon had now completed the total annexation of Holland, it told him, and he was to 'proceed to the conquest of Java at the earliest possible opportunity'. Any scrutinising anticipatory glance Minto cast at Raffles on the mention of the island was not that of a man hearing a novel idea for the very first time, but that of well-informed politician recognising a sparky young talent who might have a key role in a project whispers of which had long been heard on the monsoon wind.

But whoever really came up with the idea, Raffles now found himself in possession of an exciting new job: it was time to say goodbye to Penang, and to move one step further south towards the Land of Promise. No naval assault on Java could be contemplated until the sodden months of the southern monsoon had passed, but in the meantime Raffles would be employed as a forerunner of the invasion, an intelligence-gatherer sent to scout out the ground. He was appointed 'Agent of the Governor-General with the Malay States', armed with a great sheaf of 'gorgeous letter paper' for writing missives to the sultans and rajas of Indonesia, and provided with all manner of rich silks, satins, guns and gifts to offer them as bribes. A neat little cruiser called the *Ariel* was placed at his disposal, and he sailed for Melaka to set himself up as the erstwhile promoter of a grand military adventure.

'From this moment on', he wrote, 'all my views, all my plans, and all my mind were devoted to create an interest regarding Java as should lead to its annexation to our Eastern Empire'.

* * *

Melaka, a steamy port 250 miles south of Penang, was the perfect listening post for a man looking to gather news of happenings out amongst the islands. It stands on the eastern shores of the narrowest section of the straits that bear its name; the forests of the Malay hinterland sprawl behind it, and on the far side of the milky channel Sumatra and the sea lock hands in a mesh of mangrove-girt islands and pirate hideaways. Fleets from the east had been calling there for centuries.

If you had visited Melaka sometime in the final months of 1810 you would probably have found Raffles earnestly quizzing some white-turbaned sailor from Sulawesi or some batik-clad emissary from Sumatra. Native scribes in slate-blue jackets would have been scribbling away in *Jawi*, writing replies to far-off rajas, while waiting patiently in a hallway would have been some villager from the forests behind the town who, having heard that the white man paid good money for the odds and ends of the natural world, had brought in a basketful of fungi and scorpions to sell him. Olivia, in some dim corner of the house, would have been tirelessly quizzing the servants in her quest to improve her language skills – 'How do you say this? What's that in Malay?' – and startled visitors might even have spotted an orang-utan wearing trousers, waddling from room to gloomy room (it had been a gift from the Raja of Sambas in southern Borneo).

There was much to do, and much to investigate, for news had leached out of Java in recent years that a certain vigour had returned to the Dutch administration. Most of that vigour seemed to be emanating from one man, Napoleon's personal appointee as Governor-General: Marshal Herman Willem Daendels.

Daendels was a dark-haired, square-headed man with big ideas and a bad temper. He had arrived in Batavia at the very height of the wet season in January 1808, and had, the reports would have it, already demolished the old fort at the head of the city and replaced it with a modern bastion called Meester Cornelis, some eight miles inland. He had also laid out the foundations of a grand new colonial city between Cornelis and Old Batavia at 'an airy site, the land of which is dry and the vicinage little marshy'. It had been dubbed 'Weltevreeden', or 'Well Contented', for it was as close to that as you could get in the vicinity of Batavia. More important, however, Daendels had also ordered the biggest construction project Java had seen since the temple-building heyday of the 8th century. He had, on Napoleon's direct orders, forced an 888-mile highway the entire length of the island, connecting Batavia with all the other colonial ports of the Pasisir. It was called *de Grote Postweg*, the 'Great Post Road', though its *raison d'être* was always the military rather than the mail. He had also, if the reports were to be believed, done a great deal to antagonise both the Dutch old guard and the native Javanese aristocrats who were their partners-in-crime, with his newfangled republican ideals.

To the north, in Melaka, Raffles scraped together all there was to be known about these goings on – and about much else besides. The reports he wrote ran to hundreds of thousands of words. Every scrap of information about Dutch territories, about Daendels' road and fort-building projects, about agricultural and administrative systems in the Javanese hinterlands, about the archaic stratifications of the native courts, about trade winds and sailing routes, about the role of the Chinese immigrants in Indonesia, and about the strength and composition of the Dutch armies was gathered in and written out on sheets of heavy, cream-coloured paper, always signed off in a series of bombastic up-and-down arcs: 'Thomas Raffles'. In India, meanwhile, Dutch prisoners were being interrogated and more questions about

Java framed for Raffles to answer: 'Can the natives be employed in carriage; are cattle easily procurable & where; where is forage procurable?'

And as well as intelligence-gathering work, the propaganda campaign had begun. Hoary old tales about VOC perfidy in the days of the spice trade were dusted off and polished up. Word of slavery and torture in Batavia was spread, and Daendels, 'the Thundering Marshal', was made out to be a monster. Lord Minto declared of him that 'none of the worst of the Roman pro-consuls ever vexed and scourged the provinces, too distant for control, with more extortion and cruelty than this villain.' These were stories that would continue to drift around the English-speaking ether for ever more and that still echo faintly in the modern discourse about Dutch colonialism in Asia.

By far the most important part of his work in Melaka, Raffles felt, was to start a correspondence with the native courts of Indonesia. They would, he was sure, be natural allies against the demonic Dutchmen. He sent letters, written by local scribes in florid Malay, to the petty fiefdoms of southern Borneo, to Madura, and to Palembang, across the Straits of Melaka. The Dutch had always left the great green hulk of Sumatra well alone, but they had a small outpost in Palembang in the south of the island. Raffles wanted to encourage the Sultan there to oust the isolated clutch of fever-stricken Europeans and throw his lot in with the British. In the event nothing happened in Palembang until long after Java had fallen to the British, but Raffles would have cause to remember the letters he had penned to its ruler from Melaka with discomfort in the years to come: he had, his Dutch critics would argue, instigated a massacre. We will hear more of this grubby and gruesome episode later.

Beyond the royal correspondence, Raffles had other serious concerns to wrestle with, foremost amongst them the question of what would become of Java after a successful invasion. The problem lay in the instructions issued to Lord Minto by the East India Company in Leadenhall Street. He was indeed to attack Java as soon as possible, but having toppled its Dutch-Napoleonic government and destroyed their fortifications, the British were to 'hand the island over to the Javanese'. The Directors' reasoning was purely financial – after the wild and unrestrained expansions of Wellesley in India the last thing they wanted was another huge tranche of territory of questionable economic value added to their domains.

But the idea of leaving Java to the natives horrified Raffles. He had envisaged a new 'Eastern Empire' for Britain with himself and Leyden gallivanting through its palm groves as lords of all they surveyed. A sharp, short attack and a sudden retreat to Penang was *not* part of his plan. Fortunately, Lord Minto was also horrified. In early 1811, with preparations for a great naval assault on the Dutch territories already under way in India, he wrote to Raffles in Melaka:

I must tell you in confidence, that I have received the sanction of the Government at Home for this Expedition, but that the views of the Directors do not go beyond the expulsion of the Dutch power, the destruction of their fortifications, the distribution of their arms and stores to the natives and the evacuation of the Island by our own troops. I conclude, therefore, that the disruptive and calamitous consequence to so ancient and populous a European Colony, the property and lives of which must fall as sacrifice to the vindictive sway of the Malay Chiefs ... have not been fully contemplated; and I have already stated my reasons for considering the modification of all their orders ...

He had simply decided to ignore the wishes of the Directors altogether. He had concern for the fates of Dutch and Chinese civilians as moral justification, and more important, a hit-and-run was simply not the British way of doing things. Raffles was delighted.

* * *

At the end of April 1811 the first British troop ships appeared in the Melaka Roadstead. Looking out at their forested masts and their fluttering pennants – the starburst of the Union Jack and the crimson of the East India Company flag – Raffles must have felt a terrible pride. All those meetings and mutterings in Calcutta the previous year, all the long months of report-writing while Olivia practiced her Malay and the orang-utan tripped over its trousers, had paid off. The invasion was actually going to happen, and better yet – both Minto and Leyden would be there to see it.

Lord Minto had astonished the other members of the East India Company Council in Calcutta with his decision to join the expedition – 'They threw up their hands in horror at the Governor-General demeaning himself over a paltry place like Java' – but the project had caught his imagination. Leyden, meanwhile, had been appointed as a sort of translator, advisor and general expert on matters Oriental, and had tagged along with every expectation of a senior place alongside Raffles in the future administration of the island. Military matters had been placed in the hands of the impeccable New York-born veteran Sir Samuel Auchmuty, with Colonel Rollo Gillespie as the commander of the first division.

Some 12,000 soldiers, English and Indian, had embarked from Madras in mid-April. The entire expedition very nearly came to grief immediately when a violent tropical storm came howling out of the Bay of Bengal and drove several of the troop carriers straight back onto the Indian beaches. Most of the ships, however, were already well offshore, and besides the loss of forty horses which panicked and suffocated in the hold of one vessel as it pitched over the rollers, there was no further damage done, and soon the Straits of Melaka were thick with ships, and the open land around the port was speckled with tents.

One wide-eyed local wrote of his astonishment at the wild assortment of Indians in the Company's army, and marvelled at their weird ways:

[A]mongst them were various races of Hindus and Musselmen

and I saw others who ate like dogs, to wit, they licked their food with their tongues; while there were others, who, on being seen eating, would throw the food away, would chase you, as if they would kill you, they were so angry ... and there were others, who tied three strands of thread around their belly before they ate, nor did they stop eating until that thread had broken; there were others who took white and red earth and smeared it on their breasts, with three stripes on their arms and brow: then they bowed themselves in front, then to the right and to the left, then to the back, then off they ran into the sea ... others there were who could not taste fish and flesh or things of blood, but only vegetables ...

And all these men were heading for Java.

Throughout May more and more ships arrived, and more and more red-coated soldiers disembarked. The young officers organised horse races, Raffles conjured up a Melaka Asiatic Society and convened a meeting, and Leyden dashed off inland on a mini-expedition and found the natives to be a 'clean, healthy, stout looking race'. There was a moment of high drama when a store-ship loaded with gunpowder caught fire and had to be cut loose and shoved off into the channel where it exploded spectacularly, but the whole business had the air of a grand picnic.

The first ships sailed from Melaka on 11 June 1811. Raffles and Minto were comfortably installed in the *Modeste* under the command of the Governor-General's son, George Elliot; Leyden was soon rifling the dressing-up box on an accompanying brig, and before long they were all slipping past the low and muddy islet that would one day be Singapore, and out into wide, warm waters of the Java Sea. The journey took six weeks – good going for a massive flotilla of laden troopships sailing against the wind. Along the way there were near misses with hidden reefs and moments of panic in sudden storms, while on calmer days the passengers of the *Modeste* were entertained with games of charades (a talent for which Lord Minto had discovered on the journey out from India) and the antics of a troop of strapping young sailors dressed as 'young, accomplished and generally sentimental ladies of quality' (the soldiers aboard the other ships must have peered through their spyglasses in utter horror).

And then, at the very start of August, a long line of dark land rose from the southern horizon, with a great stacked buffer of pearly cloud riding above a ridge of spiny green mountains. On that sticky afternoon of 4 August the invasion began, Leyden leapt ashore dressed as a pirate, and Raffles – the boy born on a slave ship thirty years earlier – looked out for the first time at the shores of the island that had consumed all his energy and all his imagination for more that twelve months. It would continue to do so for the coming five years, but it would also kill his closest friends, and bring him to the brink of disgrace.

As for the native inhabitants of the island, the people of the villages and the palaces beyond the volcanoes, they had no way of knowing just what kind of storm was bearing down on them.

Glorious Victory

The road was strewn with coffee beans. They crunched under the feet of the little party of British riflemen as they moved into Old Batavia. Above them a pale sun pulsed in the blank white sky and a hot breeze shifted through the branches of the trees that lined the street. Here and there a frightened woman's face showed for a moment in an upper floor window as the soldiers approached, before disappearing behind the snap of slamming shutters. The two captains at the head of this little advance – ordered to feel their way carefully into the town – moved slowly, peering right and left, approaching each new corner delicately. The heat was intense. Every so often a Dutch scout mounted on a pint-sized pony would clatter from some side alley ahead of them and, catching sight of the redcoats, would wheel about and thunder away towards the southern suburbs before the first English rifle could be raised. The Dutch military had, it seemed, abandoned Old Batavia to its fate – and that fate was to be looted by the locals.

The Javanese, Sundanese and Malays who lived around the town had clearly decided that the coming battle was no concern of theirs, but they had been shrewd enough to conclude that Dutch days were numbered. As soon as they realised that all of the soldiers and most of the European civilians had fled the old town they had headed for the government warehouses (which had been left conveniently unlocked), flung the stockpiled coffee into the streets, and made off with the more valuable goods. As the Englishmen advanced they passed groups of shirtless men in rolled sarongs padding swiftly for the countryside with looted bundles balanced on their heads. The eyes of the men of both parties would have met briefly and suspiciously as they passed, but they were engaged on different businesses and they hurried quickly on in opposite directions.

These uneasy, wordless encounters between looters and redcoats were not much of a first contact for the British and Javanese nations, but they still amounted to more than what had gone between the invaders and their erstwhile enemies. Four days had passed since John Leyden had pranced ashore at Cilincing, but the British had still seen little more of the Dutch-Napoleonic forces than those fleeting glimpses of panicky scouts, hightailing it for the hills.

* * *

It had taken almost twenty-four hours to complete the disembarkation of 12,000 troops from the ships off Cilincing. The British forces were almost evenly split between European and Indian regiments. It had been assumed that the Indians would cope with the Javanese climate more successfully than their European compatriots, but it quickly became apparent that no one was immune to the marshy miasma and scorching sun. There had been no hostilities, but the 'putrid air' had already slayed its first swathe of foot soldiers by the end of the first day, and it would claim its first high-profile victim long before the conquest was complete.

Over the next two days the British army had edged its way along the coast towards Batavia. They saw nothing of the enemy, but the ground was so 'intricate' – so intersected with canals and drains, so patched with flooded paddy fields and stitched with banks of trees – that the advance was painfully slow. As the sun set on 7 August the red roofs of Old Batavia finally came into view. No cannonade and no grapeshot whistled out from the walls, but as the last of the daylight faded along the coast towards Banten the soldiers could see the shifting, wavering orange glow of flames: the Dutch were burning the bridges and the looters were already at work in the town. That night the entire British advance crossed the Ancol River in single file over a hastily convened bridge of boats, and in the milky grey light of the dawn they were in the outer suburbs of the city. As the exhausted Englishmen and sweat-soaked Indian sepoys settled down to a meagre breakfast amongst the palm trees, Sir Samuel Auchmuty, Colonel Rollo Gillespie, and the rest of the commanders tried to decide what to do next.

The disparate Dutch suburbs that would one day melt into the cauldron of modern Jakarta were laid out in a long north-south line along the meandering course of the Ciliwung, known to foreigners as the Great River. At its head lay the original settlement of Batavia; three miles south, through rice fields, palm groves, native *kampungs* and sprawling Chinese cemeteries, was the more salubrious and well-contented new settlement and garrison of Weltevreeden. Another three miles towards the mountains, beyond a stretch of forest, fields and gullies, was the modern fort at Meester Cornelis, and then a long thirty-mile uphill run led to Buitenzorg, a mountain retreat and a staging post on the Great Post Road.

The British had expected first to engage the Dutch at Batavia itself, and then, with the enemy bogged down amongst the filthy canals and crumbling warehouses there, to pull the rump of the army back east to Cilincing and to march cross-country, straight for Cornelis. The Dutch, they assumed, would retreat stage by stage – Batavia to Weltevreeden, Weltevreeden to Cornelis, Cornelis to Buitenzorg – with a series of decisive battles fought at each stop. But it now seemed as though the Dutch had declined the offer of a first engagement, and had already retreated to Weltevreeden, or perhaps even as far as Cornelis. It was impossible to be certain, however: perhaps it was trap; perhaps they were waiting just to the south for the British to swarm into the city where they could be pinned down.

While they were worrying over the troubling possibility of ambush a visitor arrived at the camp – it was the woe-begotten Dutch mayor of the old town, a Mr Hillebrink, all set to throw himself on the mercy of the newcomers. The British had always been hoped that the Dutch civilians residing in Java would show little loyalty to the new Napoleonic administration, and according to the nervous, perspiring mayor, most of the 'respectable inhabitants' had been ordered out of their houses for fear that they would assist the invaders, and compelled to join a pre-emptive retreat to the south. Old Batavia had been all but abandoned, he said, and those who remained were desperate for British protection. It was gratifying news, but the officers still feared a trick and a trap. And so, with the heat rising, the bridges smouldering, and the sun blazing, that little advance party under the command of Captains Watts and Thorn was sent into the city to wade through the scattered coffee beans and find out what was really going on.

What was going on, they soon discovered, was very little besides the looting. They headed for the cobbled, tree-studded square at the heart of the city and took possession of the townhouse – the sturdy, clock-towered original seat of government in Batavia. The looters, meanwhile, on seeing these strangely clad and decidedly sweaty white men and their uncouth-looking Indian companions – all bearing arms – had decided that they had already reaped enough of a windfall and headed for home.

Not a shot had been fired but Batavia, it seemed, had fallen. Word was sent back to the eastern suburbs and the main body of the advance – some 800 men with Gillespie in charge – headed for the townhouse; a Union Jack was run up a seafront flagpole, and when the watchers still squinting at the skyline from the decks of the fleet offshore spotted it fluttering in the evening breeze they went wild and fired off a royal salute with all their cannon. Back on the steps of the townhouse the assorted Dutch and Chinese who had nervously gathered to get a look at the newcomers flinched at the sound of the firing in the bay, but they were reassured that all was well and that they were now under British protection. The troops were told to find quarters for the night in the warehouses around the square and issued with strict orders not to accept any of the offers of liquor and rice wine from the remaining residents. This boozy hospitality was in fact a cunning piece of Dutch sabotage: they had ordered that large quantities of alcohol should be placed in easy reach in the old city. The ruddy-cheeked Hollanders had apparently assumed that British soldiers were men after their own hearts and that the invaders would descend into an arak-induced stupor on their first night in Batavia and thus make the easiest of targets. It was not to be, however, for the orders to stay sober were honoured.

At sunset the first direct communications between the British and the Dutch Governor-General were opened. To the relief of the invaders the man who had looked likely to be truly formidable adversary in Java – the thundering Marshal Daendels – had been recalled to Europe just three months earlier. His replacement – the feisty, French-speaking Dutch nobleman Jan Willem Janssens – was still a foe of considerable stature, however. He was an experienced soldier and politician, a headstrong commander, and a firm adherent to Napoleon's cause. But the British now took the chance of inviting him to give up without a fight. A Dutch-speaking English officer called William Robison – who would have a troubled and troubling role to play in the years of the coming occupation – was sent off alone towards Cornelis carrying a flag of truce and a summons to Janssens demanding his outright and immediate surrender.

While they waited for Captain Robison to return with Janssens' reply, Gillespie and the other commanders invited the perspiring Mayor Hillebrink and a clutch of stray Napoleonic officers who had been loitering around the square to dinner in the hastily requisitioned dining room of the townhouse. This was the early 19th century, and that was how war between civilised Europeans was conducted, but the British officers did not fail to notice that the mayor seemed to be 'particularly alarmed the whole time of supper' and that the Frenchmen were behaving in a 'suspicious and extraordinary manner'. Rumours had been doing the rounds all evening that the Dutch were planning to descend on Old Batavia from Weltevreeden during the hours of darkness, and it seemed as though the uncomfortable dinner guests might have some inkling of what was going on.

At ten o'clock a breathless Captain Robison returned from his excursion through the lines. The Dutch sentries had blindfolded him and led him past Weltevreeden all the way to Cornelis where he had delivered his message to Janssens. The Dutchman's response to the demand for capitulation was not favourable: he had declared that he was a general of the Napoleonic Republic, and that as such he was duty bound to fight to the last. Janssens was a proud and haughty man who wrote his letters to the enemy in florid French, beyond a histrionic English address – 'My Lord!' His signature was spectacular: some twenty vicious up-and-down lashes of the pen that sent wild sprays of ink all over the paper. As the Java campaign continued this final flourish became more and more furious until the point where it took up half a page, but his first verbal communication, offered to Robison on the night of 8 August, was little more than a blunt 'no'. Janssens had already presided over one defeat by the British: in 1806 he had been governor of the South African Cape Colony when it fell at the Battle of Blaauwberg. According to legend Napoleon had issued him an ominous warning before sending him to Java to organise its defence: 'Know, sir, that a French General is not offered a second chance'. He had reasons beyond mere pride not to capitulate.

After receiving this negative response, Robison was blindfolded once more and led back north through the lines towards Old Batavia. But though his eyes were shut, his ears were open, and when he reached the townhouse he reported to Gillespie that he had heard the unmistakable sounds of an army on the move, of the creaking wheels of gun carriages and the bustle of boots and hooves. What was more, it sounded very much as if they were heading for Batavia. Gillespie called the men back from their quarters, checked for signs of insobriety, and ordered them to line up with guns loaded under the trees of the square. Scarcely had they fallen in when the sound of firing erupted from the southern gate of the city. On hearing it the duplicitous dinner guests – Mayor Hillebrink and the French officers – leapt up from the commander's table and bolted for the door, but they were grabbed by the guards and placed under a firm and unhappy arrest.

Outside in the darkness a huge column of Dutch and French soldiers had attacked the outlying British sentry posts and the night was soon crackling with gunfire. They had obviously expected the British to be drunk, and they obviously knew nothing about Colonel Rollo Gillespie. He lived for exactly this kind of desperate situation – a small British force (most of the troops were still back on the coast towards Cilincing) vastly outnumbered and all but surrounded. He came thundering out of the townhouse, sabre clattering at his side, boots cracking at the cobbles, conjured up a fast-moving column, and bore west out of the city to loop around and surprise the attackers with a furious assault on their flank. 'This movement had the desired effect', wrote one observer who was straining his ear to the night sky from inside the city walls; 'The firing soon afterwards ceased, and the enemy were no more heard or seen during the remainder of the night.' What exactly had happened was not recorded, but Gillespie, blazing unexpectedly out of the Javanese night with his sabre swinging, had somehow managed to send several thousand Dutch soldiers and French officers scurrying back up the road to Weltevreeden without a single British trooper killed. For anyone who knew the little colonel's history, it was a far from surprising outcome.

* * *

Hugh Robert Rollo Gillespie was a very small man who had crammed a very great deal of overcompensation into his turbulent forty-five years. His life was littered with medals, corpses and broken noses, and his character seems to have comprised three parts James Bond, two parts Indiana Jones, and a tempering one-part hint of Harry Flashman. He was a swashbuckler of the highest order and the shortest stature, and if it wasn't for the portraits in oils, the contemporary reports and the original letters you'd have to suspect that someone had made him up.

Gillespie was born at Comber in County Down on 21 January 1766 into the same kind of low-level Irish aristocracy that later threw up Olivia Raffles. His grandfather was a Jacobite rebel who had fled Scotland at the turn of the 18th century, and since then the family had proved moderately prosperous on their Comber estates. Mr and Mrs Gillespie seem to have been very indulgent of little Rollo (and he was very little indeed: comments about his height pepper contemporary accounts). He was shipped across the water at a tender age to enjoy an expensive private education at Norland House School in Kensington, and so as to be close at hand for holidays and weekends his parents rented a house in the decidedly genteel West Country town of Bath. Honey-coloured sandstone, Roman spas, and the company of the frivolous and indolently rich hardly constitute the ideal environment in which to raise a youth destined for gory glory on the battlefields, and indeed Old Man Gillespie seems to have been appalled at the idea of his diminutive son – then endowed with flowing locks and rather delicate features – facing any kind of physical danger. He rather hoped that he would go to Cambridge and become a lawyer. However, being spoilt rotten from an early age did nothing for young Rollo's academic inclinations. In a last gasp attempt to salvage his education his parents turned him over to the tuition of a Reverend Tookey in Newmarket, but to no avail: Cambridge was not for Gillespie, and before his 18th birthday he returned to Bath and declared that he was going to join the army.

In the 1780s the British Army was decidedly in the doldrums. The American War of Independence was over, Napoleon was still a student at Brienne, and for the first time in decades the chances of a soldier actually being killed during service seemed to have receded. Gillespie's father gave his grudging consent and purchased him a commission in April 1783. He embarked immediately on the decidedly undisciplined life of a young commissioned officer in a time of peace. If he wanted action, he would have to seek it away from the battlefield, and once his regiment was transferred to Ireland his adventures began.

Riding out near barracks in County Tyrone one summer morning in 1786, the twenty-year-old Rollo crossed paths with a charming young lady by the name of Annabell Taylor. It was love at first sight (perhaps it was fortunate that Gillespie was on horseback at the time – their eyes had met before she had chance to realise how short he was), and after a few moony months the pair eloped, dashed to Dublin, and married in secret. From now on in would be drama and daring the whole way. Gillespie had bagged himself a bride; now it was time to slay his first enemy. Sometime in early 1787, after returning to his regiment at their new posting in Kildare with Annabell in tow (the young couple had spent the winter in 'mirth and festivity') a 'violent altercation there took place in the apartments of Mr. Gillespie'. The fight was between a brother officer called Mackenzie and the hoodlum son of a local squire named William Barrington. Quite what they had fallen out about is unclear, but these were still the days of duelling, and after the first fisticuffs, a meeting with pistols amidst the Irish mists of the Barrington estate was fixed for the following morning. Gillespie was to act as second for his insulted comrade.

After a good deal of huffing, puffing and cockerel-like strutting at dawn the next day the two young men fired their pistols. Both missed. In such circumstances it was usually agreed that mutual honour had been salvaged, and indeed after this abject failure of marksmanship a gentlemanly handshake seems to have been suggested. What happened next is unclear. According to the aggrieved Barringtons – who were known locally as the 'Mad Barringtons' – it was the short-statured second who threw a tantrum at the prospect of a bloodless end to the affair. Gillespie's defenders meanwhile had it that it was the squire's son who took such a belligerent line and began to heap 'opprobrious epithets' on him. The pistols came out again – at point blank range this time. Gillespie suffered a slight scratch (he was a small target, after all); Mad William Barrington ended up with a bullet through his heart.

The business of duelling was something of a legal grey area at the time; the circumstances of this particular fire-fight were far from regular (a duellist didn't expect to be shot by his opponent's second, after all), and the Barringtons went even madder than usual at the loss of their scion. A warrant was issued; a reward was raised for Gillespie's arrest, and his young wife descended into a state of nervous collapse at the news. For the first time – but not the last – Rollo Gillespie went on the run. Over the coming months he flitted in disguise between Dublin, Scotland, and his family's Irish seat (where all concerned decided to keep the fact that his son was wanted for murder from the ailing Gillespie Snr.) before finally turning himself in and appearing before the court. The judge decided without hesitation that the foul-mouthed Barrington had brought his bloody fate entirely on himself. Gillespie was acquitted.

Urged on by his overwrought wife – who had found the whole business a terrible trauma – and with tender concern for the nerves of his aged father, Gillespie now toyed with the idea of leaving the army and setting himself up as a country gentleman on his family's money. But the adrenalin-rich months on the run had obviously rather appealed to him, and when his father died in 1791 he disregarded Annabell's fevered beseeching and embarked as a lieutenant for the West Indies, where the bullets had recently started to fly.

On arrival in Jamaica Gillespie was given a bed in which a man had died of yellow fever the previous evening, and after a night between the infected sheets he went down with the illness himself. After two grim months sweating on the edge of consciousness he recovered, hauled himself upright and threw himself into the chaotic fray of the Caribbean. The French Revolution had spilled over into the tropics; slave uprisings had turned into civil wars, and Saint-Domingue – later to become the partitioned island of Haiti and the Dominican Republic – was in a state of bloody rebellion. It was the perfect place for a piratical young swashbuckler. Over the coming decade Gillespie racked up a catalogue of eye-popping adventures. He swam ashore at Port-au-Prince with a sword between his teeth and a summons in his pocket, saved himself from being executed by the French Jacobin commander Léger-Félicité Sonthonax by proffering a Mason's Handshake, was wounded any number of times, and earned a reputation for bravery that strayed well beyond the point of recklessness. On his way east for a visit home in 1794 he was shipwrecked in the English Channel and lost all his baggage, and during a stopover in Cork while heading back in the opposite direction the following year he ended up on the run from the police once more.

Gillespie had gone ashore from the troopship one evening for a night at the theatre. Never less than a patriot, he took extreme umbrage when the man in the seat beside him refused to stand or to remove his hat during the national anthem. Clearly unaware just what kind of person the indignant little soldier was, the offender remained stubbornly seated and hatted in the face of Gillespie's increasingly furious demands. Rousing himself to an indignant rage Gillespie knocked the offending hat to the ground, and moments later fists were flying and chairs tumbling – presumably with God Save the King still playing decorously in the background. The hat-wearer had 'the bridge of his nose demolished in the fray', and when his fiancé subsequently saw the state of his face and heard how he had failed to defend himself against the wild haymakers of the pint-sized patriot, she cancelled the engagement. A broken heart and a broken nose are guaranteed to incite bitterness: he pressed charges for assault. Another warrant was issued for Gillespie's arrest, and the young hero was on the run once more. This time he escaped altogether – by slipping past the guards at the dock and getting aboard his departing ship disguised as a woman with a borrowed baby under his arm (his height surely aided the ruse).

Back in the Caribbean there were more violent shenanigans. One night in Saint-Domingue, Gillespie woke to the sound of fighting on the ground floor of his quarters. He clattered downstairs, sword in hand, and discovered that eight assassins had broken into the house, murdered his servant, and were on the point of swarming up to the first floor to slay him in his sleep. Eight murderous villains against one small, bleary-eyed soldier was a far from equal match, but neither yellow fever, Mad William Barrington, nor the hat-wearer of Cork had managed to vanquish Rollo Gillespie, and when a startled patrol arrived at the house a few minutes later they found him standing in his gore-splattered nightshirt, bleeding profusely from a bullet wound at his temple, but with the mangled corpses of six of his would-be murderers strewn around him – the two survivors having fled for their lives. This spectacular event did a great deal for Gillespie's already heroic reputation. When he met George III several years later the king reputedly asked: 'What, can it be possible that this little man is the person who performed so great an exploit in Saint-Domingue?'

Once he had recovered from this latest set of wounds he found himself in charge of his own regiment in Jamaica. He soon proved that as well as dab hand in close combat, he was a very capable commander of men and manager of barracks. His 20th Light Dragoons were renowned as not only one of the most professional, but also one of the healthiest and happiest regiments in the entire West Indies. Gillespie ensured extra rations, sanitary conditions and – by the generally gruesome standards of the day – decent medical care for his men. This is all very much worth bearing in mind in light of the furious disputes that would later arise in Java, and the ill-tempered issues that Raffles would take with Gillespie's ideas about how to run a colony and an army.

By now a new century had begun, Gillespie was well into his thirties, and had been promoted to the rank of lieutenant-colonel. The long golden locks had thinned, darkened, and been cropped to a suitably soldierly length, and the once girlish features had taken on a foxy sharpness. His had not been the most likely trajectory for a short, spoilt, lazy brat from the ranks of the landed gentry. Elopement and duelling may have fallen under the category of youthful hell-raising, but they marked him out for the life of a London libertine, not that of the military hero he had quickly become. He might be inclined to beat to a pulp someone who refused to remove his hat, but the respect and admiration of both his juniors and seniors and the accolades he won as a commander in the Caribbean suggest that the undeniably short fuse was attached to a cannon that was anything but loose. Gillespie's own letters were always plain and unadorned, with scant hyperbole or hauteur and more praise for his compatriots than himself; there is no hint of the affectation and self-indulgence that his early upbringing could well have engendered. He certainly did plenty to glorify himself, but by way of deeds rather than words. In short, Lieutenant-Colonel Rollo Gillespie was everything that Thomas Stamford Raffles was not. It is hard to think of two men less suited to being left together in charge of a new and complicated colony.

But before all that Gillespie had to make the same eastward journey from the Caribbean to Java that had formed the thread of Raffles' own early life story. He did so by way of England and India, and with his forties fast approaching he showed no sign of slowing down. In autumn 1802 he returned to Europe, doubtless to the delight of his wife and aging mother. This English interlude was not without its drama: Gillespie ended up facing a court martial after allegations of corruption in Jamaica. So well run and well off had his regiment been, the gossips had it, that its financing must have been irregular. The case was a lengthy one, but it was ultimately dismissed out of hand. Far from lining his pockets, Gillespie was by now mired in the kind of debt that fast-living officers of empire so often accrued.

With these debts in mind and in the hope of finding the kind of fortune that a career in the East could often provide, he exchanged regiments for a command in the 19th Light Dragoons, then garrisoned in the dusty little Indian township of Arcot, west of Madras on the road to Bangalore. Poor Annabell – who must at times have bitterly regretted ever taking that fateful morning ride all those years ago in Tyrone – was left behind again in 1805 as her husband set out on the far from well-trodden overland route to India (although she outlived him, she disappears entirely from the records of his life at this point; Gillespie earned a certain reputation as a Lothario in India, and it is possible that he never actually saw his wife again).

Quite why Gillespie decided to go by land rather than booking the more conventional passage to India aboard a ship is unclear. He was several centuries too late for the Silk Road, and at least 160 years too early for the Hippie Trail, but the journey inevitably threw up more high drama. In Eastern Europe he prefigured the spy games of the Cold War by being pursued by French agents. Sometimes he fell back on the disguise techniques he had learnt in his days as a wanted murderer to escape them. He had his guns stolen by a passing Russian general in Poland, had a brush with pirates on the Black Sea, and won a swordfight with a Frenchman in Constantinople.

The Gaul had reacted spectacularly badly when Gillespie refused an invitation to dinner, and declared that 'he should be glad to kill an Englishman'. He could not, of course, have chosen a worse person for an attempt to satiate such an ambition. As Gillespie later told it, he replied coolly that, 'As it is your wish to kill an Englishman, I am come to give you that satisfaction, by trying your skill upon me'. Out came the swords, and within a few seconds the Frenchman was 'wounded and disarmed' and in possession of a valuable lesson: 'to avoid treating with contempt persons of an unassuming appearance'. Next up came an encounter with a party of Arab bandits in the Syrian desert, and a plot to murder Gillespie for his baggage – a plot which he averted by curing the head bandit's stomachache. Then there was time for a little sightseeing in the bazaars of Baghdad, before he finally clambered aboard a dhow for the quick hop across the Arabian Sea to Bombay followed by a brisk trot across the Deccan to take up his new post. It was 1806, and Gillespie would hardly have time to unpack before embarking on a legend-making escapade that would surpass even his eight-to-one assassin-slaying in Saint-Domingue.

On the morning of 10 July 1806, Rollo Gillespie was out early on his horse, trotting through the haze and raucous birdsong of a South Indian dawn. Perhaps he was hoping to repeat his Tyrone triumph by encountering some delectable regimental wife or daughter out for her own morning ride (Gillespie, it was said in India, was by no means averse to such liaisons). He had an invitation to breakfast later in the morning from an old comrade from Caribbean days – Colonel Fancourt, then in charge of the stocky, crenulated fortress at Vellore, sixteen miles west of Arcot – but for now he was enjoying the transient cool of first light, before the white bullet-hole of the sun soared into the hollow sky. The tranquillity did not last long, however, for at 7 a.m. Gillespie encountered not a fragrant damsel, but a bruised, bloodied and terrified soldier on a hyperventilating horse bearing a mortifying message: breakfast was cancelled, Fancourt was dead, and the sepoys of Vellore had mutinied.

The Vellore Mutiny of 1806 was the first major rebellion by Indian soldiers against their colonial officers. It predated the great 1857 uprising by half a century, and mysterious events in Central Java at the tail end of the British occupation – of which more later – by a decade. The mutiny caught the British very much by surprise, and they later did their best to explain away the episode as the result of either a 'Muhammedan Plot', the meddling of the mischievous sons of the recently deposed Tipu Sultan, or better yet the wicked work of 'some Frenchmen dressed as Fakeers'. In truth, as in 1857, the trouble came about when the spark of cultural insensitivity was added to the powder-dry kindling of general discontent.

The previous year a set of new dress regulations had been issued to the sepoys of the Madras Presidency Army. The more exotic of their accoutrements were forbidden – Hindu caste marks were to be wiped from foreheads during parades; extravagant moustaches and beards must be trimmed, and most unsettling of all, a new tight little turban that looked very much like an English top hat was to be worn at all times. Clean-shaven faces and English hats were closely associated in the eyes of the sepoys with Christianity, and what with the interdiction against brightly barred brows, a dark rumour was soon circulating over chai and chapattis at tiffin time that the British were plotting forcibly to convert the entire army to their own religion. There was low-level unrest throughout the spring of 1806. Here and there sepoys refused to wear the new turbans or to submit to the razor. They were brutally punished for their disobedience – two men in Madras were subjected to a horrific 900 lashes each. Reports of disquiet over the dress code from all over South India were forwarded to the commander-in-chief, but he dismissed them as nothing more than a little local difficulty, best ignored.

In Vellore itself – a small and isolated garrison – rumours of rebellion first reached the ears of the English officers on 17 June when a sepoy named Mustapha Beg reported that a mutiny was being planned. Beg was tossed in jail for gossiping. The next day his story was repeated by a certain Mrs Burke, but Mrs Burke was an army widow who had chosen to remain in the cantonment after her husband's demise. She had therefore earned an unfortunate reputation as a woman of questionable morals, and her story was dismissed as the scandalous tittle-tattle of a harlot. Regimental heads were thrust firmly into the sand until two in the morning on 10 July when the garrison rose as one, slaughtered some 200 English officers and their families, and raised the banner of Tipu Sultan over the gate of Vellore Fort. By the time Gillespie's morning ride was so rudely interrupted only a last desperate handful of Englishmen – NCOs and surgeons for the most part – were barricaded in a corner bastion and fighting for their lives.

Gillespie quickly spurred his horse to a gallop, roused his entire garrison, and with an advance party of twenty hard-riding heroes he thundered off in the direction of Vellore. At 8.30 the desperate defenders spotted a whirlwind column of dust pirouetting down the Arcot road. According to later legend one of them breathlessly declared that 'If Colonel Gillespie be alive, that is he, and God Almighty has sent him from the West Indies to save our lives in the East'.

Gillespie was hauled up into the redoubt at the end of a rope made of soldiers' sashes. He led an instant bayonet charge along the ramparts, had the main gate of the fort blown open in time for the arrival of the main body of the 19th Light Dragoons, and by 10 o'clock the British flag was flying once more over Vellore. Gillespie's men, meanwhile, had discovered mutilated English corpses in the garrison hospital and had gone on a reciprocal rampage, slaughtering every Indian they could find. At one point Gillespie himself had 100 of them lined up against a wall and annihilated with canister shot. This kind of thing, however, was exactly what was expected of 19th-century heroes of the British Empire, and Gillespie was hailed as a saviour of saintly status. Any wider uprising fizzled out before it began, and the more offensive aspects of the new dress codes were discreetly dropped. The wider lesson – that there was only so much abuse and exploitation that sepoys would stand from their European masters – was not learned, however, as 1816 and 1857 would show all too well.

Over the next few years Rollo Gillespie ran regiments, speared tigers and bedded women. By the close of the first decade of the 19th century his was one of the most stellar reputations amongst all the military men in India. That he should not be given a prime place in the heady adventure of the Java Expedition was unthinkable. Had the reluctant Dutch defenders at Weltevreeden and Cornelis in August 1811 known just who was leading the advance against them, they might well have surrendered without a shot fired. In the event they did raise some kind of resistance, but given their significant numerical superiority they hardly covered themselves in glory. Rollo Gillespie's most intransigent adversary in Java would not be a Dutch marshal, a Napoleonic governor, or even a Javanese sultan, but an effete young Englishman who liked to fraternise with poets and orientalists, who had never killed a man or wrestled a tiger, and who fought his duels with the pen, rather than the sword.

* * *

The column of soldiers moved out of Old Batavia and headed south in silence towards Weltevreeden at 4 a.m. The Javanese night was at its darkest – thick, hot, velvety and perfumed with strange things. The dark hulks of grand Dutch houses loomed up on either side of the well-worn track, but their doors gaped open and no flickers of candlelight showed in their windows. To the left the great sweep of the Chinese cemeteries opened; a thigh-high forest of headstones silhouetted against a blue-black sky and here and there the glowing orange pinprick of a burning joss stick where someone was making a furtive, late-night obeisance to a departed ancestor. The soldiers trod carefully and quietly. This was a grander advance than the little group that had entered the old town two days earlier. There were 1000 British troopers and 450 Indian sepoys, and somewhere in the darkness to the north the main body of the army was making its way across the Ancol River to bring up the rear. At the head of the advance rode Colonel Rollo Gillespie, pausing every so often to vomit violently at the roadside.

After seeing off the initial Dutch attack the British had spent 9 August sweating in Old Batavia, bolstering their regiments and checking their supplies with an advance to the south planned for the early hours of the following morning. There were still considerable numbers of European, Chinese and native residents in the town; it was impossible to keep word of the planned manoeuvres from them, and there were two attempts at sabotage in the early hours. At 2 a.m. a Malay was caught creeping into a powder store with a blazing firebrand in his hand. Had he managed to set the building alight, the fire would quickly have spread in the cramped alleys and the entire British advance could easily have been roasted alive.

The next attempt came two hours later. As Gillespie and his staff officers gathered in the gloom outside their quarters, whispered a few last-minute instructions, and got ready to clamber onto their horses, the housekeeper they had requisitioned – 'a Frenchman who had been a menial servant of General Daendels' – hurried out from his kitchen with cups of sweet black Java coffee. It was a welcome refreshment, set to sharpen their senses after the sticky slumber of the mosquito-plagued night, and they reached eagerly for the steaming glasses. But the servant was clearly a dedicated and desperate devotee of the Napoleonic cause, for he had poisoned the coffee, and 'it had such an immediate effect, that Colonel Gillespie and every officer of his staff, and others who had tasted it, were all at once seized with most violent pains and vomitings'. If the poisoner thought a stomach upset would be enough to halt an advance led by a man like Gillespie, however, he was much mistaken. Instead the afflicted officers wrestled him angrily to the ground, forced his mouth open and gave him a taste – or rather an entire mug-full – of his own tainted medicine, 'which produced the same effect on him, only a little more powerful'. And with that they climbed into the saddle and the advance headed for Weltevreeden, silent but for the occasional sound of retching. The Malay arsonist was hanged the next day; the Frenchman escaped and fled to America.

It was dawn when they reached the cantonments. The enemy had known they were coming (blue flares had streaked into the night during the march as the defenders tried desperately to figure out where the British were), and they had already fled. As the advance moved through the empty barracks and across the dew-soaked expanses of grass the officers, soldiers and sepoys must have wondered if they were ever going to see any real action in Java. The Dutch had departed the well-contented cantonment in such a hurry that they had left at least 300 guns and plenty of powder behind in the armoury, and it seemed as though they might already have retreated as far as Cornelis. But as the advance pressed on to the south, through a stretch of dense pepper plantations flanked on the right by the Ciliwung River and on the left by a canal called the Slokan ('the Trench') a sudden and furious fire erupted on either side from villages hidden in the trees. The British had been in Java for a week; they were about to fight their first real battle.

The Dutch forces around Batavia in August 1811 amounted to at least 18,000 men – a full third more than the entire British expedition. They were not, however, an army at the peak of their fitness. Some of the original VOC regiments were drink-addled, heat-ravaged ruins who had been posted in Java for years (and who had little loyalty to the French Republican cause), and the longer-standing Napoleonic battalions were fast approaching a similar sorry state. There were other units that had been sent out from Europe more recently – not least those which had accompanied Janssens when he arrived to replace Daendels a few months earlier – but they were a distinct minority, and according to the rather biased British they comprised the dregs of the French Army, hardly fit for service at home. As for the native Javanese regiments, many of them were forced conscripts with very little commitment to the coming fight. But still, in this first engagement amongst the pepper trees outside Weltevreeden they hugely outnumbered the British advance, were well entrenched with deep watercourses on either side, large palms and banyans felled across the road to stall their attackers, and strong cover in the villages. As the sun rose above the ranks of the volcanoes to the southeast they blazed away with a set of artillery guns, and sent a welter of musket-shot whizzing through the bushes in the direction of the redcoats.

Had the British tried simply to slog on through the hail of fire and felled trees they would probably have been annihilated. But Gillespie – still vomiting from time to time – was a fine tactician, and despite the rivers, burnt bridges and thick forest that blocked the way, he had parties head out left and right to attack the Dutch-held villages side-on. Meanwhile, field guns were swung into position on the road, and fired back through the pepper trees towards the defenders. As the main column of the advance nudged its way up the road under furious fire and began to haul the first of the felled trees out of the way, the Commander-in-Chief, Sir Samuel Auchmuty, arrived from Batavia, where he had just seen the rest of the army across the Ancol. He was on the scene as the parties who had stumbled through ditches and hacked through undergrowth to reach the Dutch flanks launched their attacks. It was all over in minutes: the villages went up in flames, the soldiers and sepoys on the main road charged the enemy guns, and Hollanders, Frenchmen and Javanese conscripts were soon fleeing headlong through the forest for Cornelis. Here and there a furious Napoleonic officer demanded that they rally, but to no avail. At one point, Janssens' chief of staff General Alberti, who had lost his own men and was stomping around confusedly through the steam and smoke, ran into a small party of the British 89th. This regiment – which had a fairly bloodthirsty reputation – wore green rather than the usual scarlet. Alberti mistook them for a cowardly clutch of Dutchmen and began upbraiding them angrily for retreating without orders. The British had been fighting for two hours; it was desperately hot and humid; they were exhausted, and now they were being berated in a foreign language. It was more than one private of the 89th was prepared to take: he raised his musket and shot the ranting general in the chest (he survived, fortunately, but was taken prisoner).

It was now an all-out chase through the trees to Cornelis. In and out of the forest, over the rice fields, around the ridges and along the banks of the Ciliwung, Gillespie and a party of dragoons pursued the scarpering enemy. So fast were the Dutch forces fleeing, and so hard were Gillespie's men riding that they carried the advance right to the walls of Cornelis. The Colonel was in half a mind to storm the place immediately, but instead the British pulled back and set up forward batteries in the thick trees, 800 yards north of the enemy's last great redoubt.

By midday everyone was slumped in the shade tending their wounds. Over the course of the morning the British had lost one officer, 16 men and three horses. A further 73 soldiers had been seriously injured. No one was quite sure how many of the enemy had been killed, but judging from the number of battered bodies scattered between the shot-scorched trees it probably amounted to hundreds.

The British were, it must be said, a little taken aback by the speed of their own success. The pre-emptive Dutch retreat from Batavia had been a smart idea: they were 'well aware that the unhealthiness of the town and the noxious climate of the seashore would in a short time destroy our troops and compel the crippled remains of an exhausted army to return without effecting their purpose'. But then, having lured the invaders into this malarial death trap, they had failed to pin them down, had abandoned Weltevreeden without a fight, and had turned tail when the bullets began to fly on the Cornelis road. The British now had a comparatively healthy and modern cantonment of their own at Weltevreeden, and were well-placed for the final decisive engagement. The fortress of Meester Cornelis, however, was a far more formidable obstruction than anything they had seen so far.

The place was named for a schoolmaster called Cornelis Senen who set up an estate there in the mid-17th century (the title 'Meester' was granted to landlords). A minor fort had been built in the 1730s, but it was Daendels who had chosen Cornelis for his great stronghold, setting up sentry posts on outlying ridges, and ringing the whole place with five miles of fortifications studded with 280 pieces of heavy cannon, and bounded by the slithering Slokan in the east and the meandering Ciliwung in the west. Now Daendels' successor Jan Willem Janssens, his commander-in-chief the French General Jumel, and their entire army were settled inside it.

Sir Samuel Auchmuty decided that after the heady early British successes, now was the time to move more delicately, to make careful preparations, and to hold back the final attack until everything was really ready. He did not know at the time, but Janssens and Jumel were already half-expecting to retreat from Cornelis when the British assault began, and had already prepared detailed orders on how to go about it (their men were to 'spike the guns, and to repair quickly, and in good order'). But for now the British set up a siege.

Heavy guns were brought south from Batavia, and the last encampments back at the Cilincing landing point were dismantled and moved forward towards Weltevreeden. The British dug trenches along the tree-line, and all the while the two armies fired furiously at each other in the blistering heat. Whenever there was a lull British scouts did their best to spy out the rear walls of Cornelis and the approach roads through the surrounding trees. It was convoluted countryside, where dirt tracks faded into the forest and what ought to have been a highroad often led only to a Javanese farmhouse.

On 15 August a thunderous salute of cannon rose from within the walls of Cornelis – it was marking perhaps the world's most far-flung celebration of Napoleon Bonaparte's birthday. Four days later the Dutch tried to flood the dry moat which ran in front of the fortress' northern flank, but the water, turned from the Slokan, threatened to bring the walls down, so they redirected it towards the British trenches, prompting wet feet and furious curses. The following evening under cover of darkness the British edged their batteries forward another two hundred yards. From now on a near-continuous cannonade roared in both directions from dawn until dusk, and on 22 August the Dutch launched a desperate – and nearly decisive – sortie from their fortifications. A stretch of low scrub still separated the forward British posts from the walls, and in the night a party of enemy soldiers had crept through it towards the batteries, while another group looped away to the east to attack them from the side. The Dutch plan was to launch a synchronised assault at sunrise, but fortunately for the British, the flanking column got lost in the jungle, and the ambushers had to leap from the undergrowth alone. They were eventually seen off, but it had been the bloodiest encounter yet, and the British lost almost 100 men.

Time was beginning to run out. The forward pickets were not as far advanced as Auchmuty and Gillespie would have liked them to be and no major breaches had been opened by the shelling. But whenever there was a lull in the shooting the Dutch had been busily entrenching their own position, digging ditches and erecting new, outlying batteries of their own. Cornelis might have been a healthier spot than the old town, but it was still a sticky, steamy sump by English or even Indian standards. What was more, two weeks of cannonade had annihilated the covering canopy of the trees. Musket balls had shredded the leaves, grapeshot had stripped the branches, and mortars had smashed the trunks. The weather was 'excessively sultry' and there was no longer any cooling shade for the besiegers. Before long, any advantage they had in energy and determination would be lost. It was time to act. The battle for Meester Cornelis was about to begin; the 'day that was to fix the destiny of Java' had arrived.

* * *

The narrow path splintered left and right in the noisy silence of the forest and in the darkness a group of men came together in a hissing huddle, uncertain which way to turn. It was a few hours before dawn on 26 August, and a long line of troopers were creeping through the dense, damp countryside east of Cornelis on the far bank of the Slokan Canal. They made up the main body of the final assault on the enemy lines, planned for first light. The eastern approaches of the fortifications were the weakest, they had decided. The northern buttress – that which they had been bombarding for the last fortnight – was too solid to attack successfully head on; the western walls were flanked by the unfordable meanders of the Ciliwung, and the rear bastions, facing the mountains, were well defended and out of reach. But still, even on the Slokan side there was scarcely a chink in the Dutch armour. To get at it, the British had to loop out through 'a very difficult country, intersected with ravines, enclosures, and betel plantations, many parts of which could only be passed in single file'. And now, it seemed, they were lost.

Colonel Gillespie whispered furiously at the Dutch deserter who had crossed the lines the previous day and agreed to lead them through the tortuous tangle of paths and track-ways to the point where they could ford the Slokan. It was hardly surprising that he could not recall the way in the steaming darkness, and the terrifying prospect of an angry Rollo Gillespie was unlikely to help him remember. Fortunately, one of the English officers who had reconnoitred the country a few days earlier thought he recognised this intersection, and suggested a path. They started forward again, and soon the nervous guide was nodding with relief and whispering happily over his shoulder: yes, this was it; he remembered these trees and clearings!

The bulk of the British Army in Java were tiptoeing through the forest behind them. They had started out a little after midnight on foot (this countryside was too rough and overgrown for horses). Another party had headed west in the hope of somehow crossing the Ciliwung under Cornelis' western walls; a third group were waiting back at the forward batteries to attack the northwest bastion, and

Sir Samuel Auchmuty would lead a furious diversionary assault on the heavyset, shot-scarred northern battlements. The final advance had been carefully conceived and minutely planned, but ultimately it was still a nerve-wracking shot in the dark: reconnaissance out in the jungle-clogged countryside had been tricky; the local villagers and even the handful of deserters and captives had little useful information to give about the true strength and nature of the Dutch forces, or the internal defences of Cornelis. The whole business could easily have gone horribly wrong – and as the first thin grey light began to filter through the trees, it almost did.

The forward part of the advance – Gillespie, the guide and a gaggle of mud and sweat-soaked soldiers – had arrived on the edge of the thick forest in sight of the outer walls of Cornelis. Away to the east a long saffron stain was beginning to seep out over the serried ranks of ridges that rose towards the mountains; a ribbon of cool mist hung over the oozing waters of the Slokan, and here and there the grey silhouette of a Dutch sentry shuffled sleepily in the half-light. But as the British looked out on this scene of their coming battle a horrible realisation dawned: a continuous file of men should still have been coming up through the trees behind them, but a backwards glance showed no more redcoats making their way along the muddy paths. The rear part of this main advance was nowhere to be seen; they had gone astray back in the forest, either at that same troublesome crossroads or somewhere else. Captain Thorn (who, Gillespie noted, had 'hardly slept since we landed') was there amongst the forward party as they realised what had happened. 'It was', he later wrote, 'an awful moment! One of those pauses of distressful anxiety, which can be better conceived than described'.

Alone, cut off, isolated, and with the full bulk of the enemy army just a few hundred yards away, the horrified soldiers scurried back into the shelter of the forest and huddled together, wondering what to do. Messengers were sent jogging back along the paths to try and find the missing masses, but the light was now streaming into the forest; the Dutch sentries would surely soon spot the dashes of skulking scarlet in the undergrowth, and away to the north and west the other British parties – beyond communication – were about to launch their own attacks in full confidence that the eastern side of the Cornelis fortifications would be coming under furious assault at the same time. There was only one terrifying option – hugely outnumbered, unsupported, and with no idea when the rest of their comrades would emerge from the jungle, Gillespie and his truncated advance party would have to go ahead and attack anyway.

With the little colonel in front and his grim-faced comrades hurrying behind they slipped out of the trees and moved towards the outlying Dutch pickets that defended the Slokan. Twice they were challenged by sentries who spotted the shadowy figures moving through the murky pre-dawn light; twice some talented British impressionist affected a European accent and called out '*Patrole!*' and they hurried past unhindered. But then came a third challenge, from a picket on the embankments of the main Dutch redoubt guarding the canal. There was no hope of sneaking past this one. The sun was about to break clear of the eastern mountains; flocks of screeching birds were clattering out from their roosts in the drooping branches of the banyans, and the skeins of milky haze were thinning over the sagging heads of the palm groves. It was time. Colonel Gillespie raised his sword above his head and roared: 'Forward!'

The morning erupted into noise. Blue flares shrieked skyward from the Dutch positions as frantic gunners struggled to pick out the attackers in the haze, and scorching shot whistled through the sky and crashed into the forest. On Gillespie's cry the advance had rushed forward so quickly that they had completely overwhelmed the first picket, and its startled defenders were all killed or captured. They were in the full, frantic fury of battle now, and knew that if they so much as paused they would be obliterated. They swarmed on, bullets and cannonballs howling over their heads, and launched themselves at the first major Dutch redoubt. Again, momentum and adrenalin carried them into it, through it, and out of it with all the Dutchmen left dead in their wake.

Now there came a furious fight to wrestle the bridge over the canal out of Dutch control. There were solid redoubts, bristling with artillery on either side and four guns facing directly across its creaking wooden spans. Englishmen – privates and officers – began to fall here, but with Gillespie roaring like a bull at their head they thundered across, charged the guns, and hurled themselves at the stocky walls of the left-hand redoubt. They were now deep inside the lines of Cornelis, and that first momentum of surprise had faltered. The attack stalled for a moment under a welter of grapeshot; British soldiers were falling on all sides now, and bayonets and gun barrels sprouted from every corner of the redoubt. But somehow they still surged forward and over the walls – and in a roaring ruckus of hand-to-hand fighting and flashing bayonet blades Gillespie's men took control.

Elsewhere, on the other flanks of Cornelis other battles were now underway. Any long-legged, white-winged cattle egret that had launched itself at sunrise from a roost in the branches where the forest began to rise in stepped tiers towards Buitenzorg, and had then beaten northwards through the warm, still morning air, across the flooded rice fields towards the mudflats of the coast, would have seen the smoke rising from the corners of the Dutch fastness. Had it circled for a moment in the powder-scorched haze it could have picked out Gillespie's bloodied advance, furiously hacking away with their bayonets in Redoubt Number Four. Three-quarters of a mile to the south another party, under Major Yule, were firing with furious frustration across the Ciliwung – they had found the last of the bridges burnt and were doing what they could from the far bank. Taking another turn our bemused egret would have spotted a third bloody fight underway far below: just 500 yards west of the spot where Gillespie was slashing wildly with his sword a column of the Scottish 69th Regiment had forced their way into the northwest bastion. A little way to the north, meanwhile, Sir Samuel Auchmuty could be seen, ordering the gunners in the forward British trenches to reload and keep up a covering cannonade on the outer lines of the Dutch defence, while a party of requisitioned sailors armed with pikes rushed forwards to take them on at close quarters. And finally, as it made a last turn to the east and swooped away from all this strangeness towards its day of foraging amidst the pestilential marshes, the egret would have picked out a huge train of men in red jackets – some of them white-skinned, some of them Indian – emerging from the trees on the east bank of the Slokan Canal: the lost columns had finally found their way through the maze of the Javanese countryside and come stomping over the splintered boards of the bridge to bring up the rear.

There was no time for recriminations. Gillespie ordered the new arrivals to attack Redoubt Number Two, a stone-walled cube brim-full of bayonet-wielding enemy soldiers a short way to the north. They did, and were soon surging over the walls. But as the redoubt was on the very point of falling it erupted in a huge, sky-shaking explosion. Someone had set fire to the powder magazine:

[A] sulphurous blast of mingled ashes, smoke, and fragments of every kind, broke upon us like a volcano, stunning all around, both friends and foes. This catastrophe was followed for a minute by an awful silence. The Captains... and many others, all found death, but few a grave! Numbers of the enemy also were destroyed, and the ground was strewn with the mangled bodies and scattered limbs of friends and foes, blended together in a horrible state of fraternity.

Stumbling through the smoke and scattered limbs the survivors picked themselves up, gathered their battered bayonets, and stumbled forwards once more. The British latecomers were still streaming over the Slokan, and the Dutch were still peppering them with shot. At one point a body of armed horsemen emerged from somewhere in the bowels of Cornelis and prepared to charge the advance, but British guns were turned frantically towards them, and they broke away and retreated. More redoubts fell, and more Dutch guns were taken, and though the morning was strewn with dead British soldiers, something in the defence had indefinably but unmistakably broken: all Gillespie and his men had to do now was to keep moving. They headed south. The Dutch made a brief stand at the original, stocky little Cornelis fortress but it quickly gave way; and then suddenly it was no longer a defence but a retreat, and then before long it was no longer even an ordered retreat of the kind that Janssens and Jumel had planned, but a panicked, hell-for-leather flight through the palm trees. The British had conquered Cornelis.

There was no time for celebration however: if the enemy got away in force to Buitenzorg they could entrench far more firmly than they had done on the steaming flatlands of the coast. The British had to ensure a total rout. Gillespie was by this stage not just exhausted and suffering from several minor injuries; he was also beginning to come down with a fever. As the Dutch defenders started bolting like rabbits into the jungle, he collapsed. Captain Thorn caught him as he fell. The lights were not out for long, however; he hauled himself out of the swoon, cut an abandoned enemy horse from one of the field guns and clambered onto it to join the pursuit through the palms.

It did not last long. Here and there some determined party made a desperate stand, but soon there were only stragglers stumbling along the muddy trails, hopeless of reaching Buitenzorg and with every inclination to throw up their arms in defeat. By the time they had gone ten miles the British had taken some 6000 prisoners. Most of the Dutch amongst them had surrendered quite willingly. One captured Napoleonic officer recorded the scene as he was marched back through forest towards what was now British-held territory:

The nearer I came to our taken retrenchment of Meester Cornelis, the more prisoners I met. With a feeling of shame and indignation I saw more than one [Dutch] officer amongst them trample on his French cockade to which he had sworn allegiance, uttering scandalous imprecations and swearing and assuring the English: 'I am no Frenchman, but a Dutchman.'

By midday there was almost nothing left of the huge Dutch army that had started the morning in a strong defensive position. One small band of mounted fugitives, however, had escaped the rout. Jan Willem Janssens, General Jumel, and a clutch of brother officers had ridden hard and fast, ignoring the sight of their underlings spitting on the French flag in the trees on either side, and pressing for the cool air of the mountains.

The same Captain Robison who had gone blindfolded through the lines two weeks earlier was sent off in pursuit with a summons. The Dutch party had already reached Buitenzorg by the time Robison caught up, and again the answer was 'no'. Robison went back towards Batavia, and in the cool of the following morning the little band that had remained with the Governor-General clambered into the saddle once more, took a last look down towards the plains that they had failed to hold, and at the little upland outpost that they could not hope to defend with so few men, and headed out along the rising switchbacks of the Post Road towards the airy saddle of the Puncak Pass. There were other Dutch garrisons along the coast at Semarang and Surabaya, but Janssens must have realised that he had little real chance of victory now. However, pride and that ominous Napoleonic warning were still playing on his soul. He could not bring himself to surrender.

* * *

With their conquest of Cornelis, the British had won a victory that finally came close to honouring the Javanese name for the old settlement on the banks of the Ciliwung River – Jayakarta, 'Glorious Victory'. But they knew almost nothing about the rest of Java, and the idea of Janssens in the role of the rebel prince, stirring up the hinterlands and perhaps joining forces with the unknown quantities of the Javanese royal courts, was not one they were prepared to countenance. They set off in pursuit.

A fleet headed for Cirebon where the Post Road re-joined the coast. General Jumel was caught here at the start of September. Another little fleet of British boats went further east and took control of the Dutch posts on Madura with hardly a shot fired, and on 5 September Sir Samuel Auchmuty himself sailed for Semarang, the great port town of the central Pasisir where Janssens was rumoured to be regrouping. All the while Auchmuty and Lord Minto were sending demands to the intransigent Dutchman to surrender; he could not possibly hope to defeat the invaders now; he was only delaying the inevitable peace and increasing the suffering of the colonial subjects. Janssens replied in his furious French – 'My Lord! ... I am not insensible to the sufferings of the inhabitants of the Colony, but it is not I who is the cause of their sufferings' – and sprayed the paper, and surely also the desk and any unfortunate lackey standing nearby, with ink as he whipped his signature across the page.

When the British reached Semarang they found that Janssens had already retreated to the hills. On 13 September they came ashore, and three days later they attacked the Dutch positions in the mountains above the town. The positions themselves were strong, but the spirit of defiance was weak. At one point two ADCs managed to chase off an entire lavishly dressed Napoleonic cavalry regiment by 'uttering the wild hunting cries of the English', and Janssens was soon on the run once more, pushing deeper into the green uplands of Java. The old Dutch fort at Ungaran fell next; more Dutch and French officers and men were captured, and finally, on 17 September from the little upland garrison of Salatiga, on the very cusp of the sovereign territory of the Javanese courts, Janssens – who was almost alone by this stage – sent a message to the British requesting a cessation of arms. Still, a flicker of defiant hauteur remained: 'When I applied to treat for capitulation, it was because all my resources were exhausted', he declared; 'as long as I had any left me, I would never have submitted.' But submit he did, and six weeks after they had landed at Cilincing the British were in formal possession of all the former Dutch territories in Java.

Sixty-two Europeans and seventeen Indians had been killed

during the main advance on Cornelis on 26 August, and a few dozen more had fallen in the secondary attacks. Hundreds of others were horribly injured (the casualty lists offer a gruesome tally of officers tagged to phrases like 'lost his arm', 'mortally wounded', or 'wounded, since dead'). Lord Minto, a man of the drawing room and the debating chamber rather than the battlefield, visited Cornelis the day after it fell. He was appalled by what he saw: 'A field of battle seen in cold blood is a horrid spectacle, but is too horrid for description. The number of dead and the shocking variety of deaths had better not be imagined.' But given the challenges the British had faced when first they sailed down the Straits of Melaka and across the Java Sea, it could have been much, much worse.

However, another more insidious enemy was already beginning to make its presence felt long before Janssens signed his grudging capitulation at Salatiga. All of the dire prognoses about the climate of Batavia had proved true. The pestilent miasma, the foul airs and marshy effluvia were indeed a force to be reckoned with. *Coups de soleil* had claimed their first lives on the second day of the invasion; during the siege of Cornelis dozens had gone down with heatstroke, dengue and malaria, and even the most formidable constitution of all had not proven impervious.

The low fever that had seen Colonel Gillespie swoon in the heat of battle on 26 August soon rose to a raging sickness. By the time he reached Buitenzorg the following day he could barely stand up, and no refreshing mountain breeze would revive him. Sir Samuel Auchmuty was without his best officer during the Java-wide pursuit of Jan Willem Janssens – Gillespie was in bed on 'the brink of the grave' for several weeks. Ultimately he vanquished this new sickness just as he had seen off the yellow fever in Jamaica, but elsewhere another constitution less martial and violent, more intellectual and poetic, had already given way.

* * *

During the weeks of fighting Raffles and Olivia had steered safely clear of flying bullets and flashing bayonets. The other civilians too had loitered well back from the front – in their cabins on the ships moored out in the bay in the early days, and then in the salubrious quarters of Weltevreeden once the Cornelis lines were drawn. John Leyden too had fallen back after his first fancy-dress fight with the Cilincing chickens, but he ached to see more of this great green Land of Promise as soon as possible. In the coming years the British – Raffles foremost amongst them – were ever-eager to portray their Dutch predecessors in Java as utter philistines, without the slightest interest in the complex cultures and grand histories of the island they claimed to rule. This was not entirely fair. It was true that by the end the Hollanders in Batavia were mostly far too drunk and depressed to engage in heady orientalist scholarship, and there had never been a concerted official effort to make academic sense of Java. But there *had* been Dutch historians and enthusiasts over the years who had made shift with the local languages, who had gazetted archaeological remains, and gathered flaking palm-leaf manuscripts in Old Javanese. It was the thought of these very manuscripts, mouldering in basements somewhere in Batavia and Buitenzorg, that had sent Leyden pirouetting up the beach in such a state. He had no interest in being shot at, but he could hardly wait to get to a desk.

The British-ruled Java that Leyden and Raffles had fantasised over was an empire of the mind as much as a political entity. Its past could be a playground for their intellects and imaginations, a historical trove of which they – orientalists to their very socks – could take possession. The volcanoes and villages, the palaces and temples were still out of reach in August 1811, but Leyden was eager to engage in whatever academic looting he could as soon as possible.

Once Old Batavia had fallen he hurried along the coast from Cilincing in the army's wake and began his search amongst the burnt-out warehouses and scattered coffee beans. There, somewhere between the crumbling alleyways and pestilential canals, 'Amongst other objects calculated to excite and to gratify his favourite passion, was a library, said to contain a valuable collection of Oriental MSS'. Leyden hurried inside to begin his mission. In the bowels of the building was a shuttered room 'said to contain some Javanese curiosities'. For locals such a chamber would surely have been infested with malevolent spirits, but Leyden wasn't scared:

With fatal inadvertence he entered it, without using the precaution of having it aired, although it had been shut up for some time, and the confined air was strongly impregnated with the poisonous quality which has made Batavia the grave of so many Europeans. Upon leaving this place he was suddenly affected with shivering and sickness, the first symptoms of a mortal fever ...

Leyden himself attributed the sickness to 'the pestilential air he had been inhaling', and declared at once with poetic but entirely accurate melodrama that he would not survive. Locals would have put it down to bad magic or the icy touch of a wicked djinn, but more likely it was either a fresh dose of Batavian malaria, or a recurrence of whatever tropical ailment had plagued him back in his early days in India. He went down hard and fast and was soon producing no more flights of oriental fancy or flowery verses to the Land of Promise, but only the delirious ramblings of a dying man.

John Caspar Leyden died on 28 August 1811, a few weeks short of his 36th birthday, and two days after the fall of Meester Cornelis – though by the end he was too far gone to understand the news of Britain's glorious victory. Raffles was with him until the last. He was buried in the European cemetery at Tanah Abang, west through the fields from Weltevreeden.

Lord Minto was deeply affected by the death of his fellow Scot, and he eulogised him with typical generosity: 'No man, whatever his condition might be, ever possessed a mind so entirely exempt from every sordid passion, so negligent of fortune, and all its grovelling pursuits'.

How Olivia reacted to the loss of her most ardent admirer is not recorded (though it is hard not to suspect that a certain amount of hysteria and a significant quantity of brandy were involved). When word of his demise reached Europe the following year, Sir Walter Scott penned an epitaph in verse and gave his one-time collaborator a walk-on part in *The Lord of the Isles*.[7] But the person who felt the loss of the polymath most powerfully was Raffles himself. Leyden, he wrote, had been 'my dearest friend, and I may truly say that while I looked up to him with all the admiration and respect which his wonderful Talents and glowing Virtues were calculated to command from all who knew him, I felt towards him the most brotherly affection'.

By 28 August Raffles knew beyond doubt that Java – or the former Dutch part of it at least – was to become British territory, and he was also confident that he would be placed at the head of its administration. Whether or not he already realised that there were others on the scene who would object to his ideas and attitudes is unknown, but he had certainly expected to have Leyden on hand as a creative partner for all the grand projects to come. The poet would likely have been appointed his First Secretary. Together with Olivia they would have set up a dreamy *ménage à trois* somewhere in the hills above Batavia; everything would have been perfect.

But now Raffles, aged just thirty, was faced with the daunting prospect of trying to realise alone his vision of British Java – this

---

7 The poem was a potboiler published in 1815 by a cash-strapped Scott. It is a lengthy epic on the subject of Robert the Bruce, and Leyden makes his appearance as an outrageously indulgent anachronism in the 11th verse of the fourth canto:

Scenes sung by him who sings no more!
His bright and brief career is o'er,
And mute his tuneful strains;
Quenched is his lamp of varied lore,
That loved the light of song to pour;
A distant and a deadly shore
Has Leyden's cold remains!

'Other India', this 'Eastern Empire' – and just how very little he, Lord Minto, or anybody else knew about the place was suddenly and painfully apparent.

A Thousand Little Questions

Central Java lay beneath a fine, bluish haze, and the road to the Surakarta Kraton was crowded with onlookers. Shirtless Javanese farmers in grubby white shorts and checked sarongs jostled on the verges with itinerant hawkers balancing smouldering charcoal braziers and bundles of greasy fried cakes in wicker baskets at the ends of sagging bamboo poles. Bulky peasant women with betel-black teeth and coarse, greying hair scraped back into tight buns carried grizzling infants at their hips in cloth slings. On the shadier corners, attended by gaggles of cringing, parasol-carrying servants, stood local aristocrats dressed in elaborate batiks with polished *krises* tucked into their cummerbunds. Here and there a Chinaman with a shaven brow and a long black pigtail peered from the dark recesses of a roadside shop. All of them were straining to get their first glimpse of an Englishman.

The people of the Javanese heartlands had not been oblivious to recent events on the other side of the mountains. News that the Dutch, so long a strange and irksome, if peripheral, part of the Javanese scene, had been utterly routed in their Pasisir possessions by some new group of sweating white men had already passed through the markets and *kampungs* and mixed with gossip and black coffee over late-night card games in flickering lamplight. For the commoners the departure of the Dutch was mostly a matter of mere curiosity; but for the courtiers of the royal palaces it was a potential game-changer, a chance to bring a strange and troublesome episode of Javanese history to an end. No one was more eager for a look at an Englishman than the royals, and now, at 10 o'clock in the morning on 22 September, just a few days after Jan Willem Janssens had signed over Dutch Java to the British, they were about to get their chance. The first emissary of the 'Maharajah Gilbert Lord Minto' was arriving in Surakarta, one half of the bifurcated royal realm of Mataram, the magnificent kingdom that had held sway over the great green bulk of Java for two centuries.

* * *

The story of Mataram had started with a falling star.

In Javanese lore, kingdoms were always transient. The mystic power, the sacred energy that formed the divine right of kings, was constant, but it was a mantle that could travel backwards, sideways or diagonally, and that could depart a royal house of its own accord and find lodging elsewhere with some new dynasty.

The long Hindu-Buddhist centuries in Java had given way in the early 1500s as the mighty Majapahit Empire fell to the nascent Islamic power of Demak, and for much of the following century the regal lustre was hard to discern amongst the warlords and chancers who rattled through the rice fields. But then, sometime in the 1570s, a young Javanese noble called Senopati, the son of the ruler of a minor fiefdom occupying the fertile Central Java country between the fiery peak of Gunung Merapi and the stormy shores of the Southern Ocean, began to seek spiritual powers. Senopati was a Muslim, but even today some Javanese Muslims – peasants, students, businessmen and, it is rumoured, generals and presidents – seek out the places of power, the old temples and hidden springs, where meditation can sometimes bring a shot of *kasekten*, the sacred energy that will win them ascendency.

Senopati, haunting the wilder corners of Central Java, started to practice *tapa*, mystic asceticism, meditating up to his neck in the chilly waters of mountain streams, hanging upside-down from the branches of banyan trees, and going wild and unwashed for weeks on end. The ascetic exercises evidently worked, for one night as he lay asleep atop the holy stone of Sela Gilang, a hunk of black rock thrusting through the sandy soil of the coast, a star detached itself from the great smear of the firmament and tumbled through the perfumed darkness of the Javanese night to hover above Senopati's head. The star brought with it a prophecy: Senopati would found a great kingdom. The light of the prophesying star was bright enough to sink its shafts down through the inky gloom beneath the waves lashing angrily at Java's southern shore. It caught the attention of a figure who would be intimately associated forever more with the mortal royals of Central Java: Nyai Loro Kidul, the Queen of the Southern Ocean.

In the great weedy web of myths that surround her, the Queen of the Southern Ocean was once a flesh-and-blood princess of a long-lost royal court who had retreated to the salty spirit world under a curse after refusing her father's choice of suitor. She is all-powerful and all-beautiful, though she ages with the cycles of the moon. Green is her favourite colour, and she will quickly press-gang anyone foolish enough to wear that shade while bathing on Java's beaches to join her spirit army. Dozens of swimmers and fishermen vanish each year on the fringes of her realm. Her palace is somewhere far below the waves south of Java – close to the spot where the Indo-Australian Tectonic Plate slips beneath the Eurasian Plate to send its own special energy shooting up into Java – and it was there that she now led the star-struck Senopati. For three full days and three full nights she taught him the arts of governance, war-craft and lovemaking, and she assured him that she would not only lend him her ghostly legions for his coming conquests; she would be a patron and a consort for all the rulers of the royal house he founded – provided they did not neglect her. The young noble eventually emerged dripping and dazed, but brim-full of energy, on the beach at Parangkusumo, due south of the summit of Merapi, and in due course he turned his father's little fiefdom – a patch of green land called Mataram – into one of the greatest kingdoms that Java had ever known.

That, at least, was the story.

In truth the historical Mataram rose to its apogee under Senopati's grandson, Sultan Agung, who made the kingdom shine as brightly as the spark that had first burnt above his forefather's head. In the first half of the 17th century he extended his rule to encompass almost all of Java, coming up short only against the western realm of Banten, and the little orange boil of Batavia where the Dutch were digging canals between their bouts of malaria. Agung built his own capital at Karta on that power-charged axis between the Merapi volcano and the sea, and declared himself a sultan towards the end of his reign. But for all his Muslim faith he kept his ancestral link with the Queen of the Southern Ocean strong – invisible to all but the initiated, she nonetheless had a key role in court ceremony and protocol.

This kind of thing was always the way in Java. Though by the end of Agung's reign the island was almost entirely Muslim, much of what had gone before, many of the old reference points, remained. Raffles would later snootily dismiss such phenomenon as 'the accumulated delusions of two religious systems', while one of his contemporaries declared that 'Of all Mahomedans the Javanese are most lax in their principles and practice'. But they and other Europeans had missed the point: by the 19th-century Java was enthusiastically and wholeheartedly Islamic, and being Muslim – especially for the royals and the aristocrats – was very much part of the local identity, even if few people paid much attention to the daily prayer routine. However, most people saw little challenge in being both Muslim *and* Javanese – and the latter badge brought with it a whole other set of ideas and ideals, inherited from both the Hindu-Buddhist centuries, and from the myth-laden epochs beyond.

This Muslim-Javanese duality remained the watchword of the Mataram dynasty that descended from Senopati and Sultan Agung, but though the kingdom endured, over the generations it lost its sparkle. A succession of inefficient and ill-advised rulers, a series of famines and earthquakes, and a sustained volley of rebellions saw the fringes of Mataram begin to fray. Meanwhile, the Dutch VOC had rapidly entrenched in Batavia, and by the start of the 18th century they were routinely pimping out their colonial armies as mercenaries and powerbrokers in Mataram's infernal internal affairs.

In the interests of an auspicious new start the capital of the kingdom had been moved from its original site to Kartasura, a charged spot on the axis between the mighty Merapi and Lawu volcanoes. The shift failed to stem the rebellions however, and a few decades later, in the rainy February of 1746, the court upped sticks once more and was shunted seven miles east to the village of Solo where a grand new *kraton*, a traditional Javanese palace, with a reversed name was built. The sacred banyan trees that pinned the *Alun-Alun*, the Royal Square, were uprooted and transplanted to this new town of Surakarta, a city that would outlast not just united Mataram, but also European rule in Java.

But though the reconstituted court was still in possession of powerful *pusaka*, the energy-laden heirloom regalia that fuelled legitimacy, and as far as anyone knew the successive rulers were still regularly consorting with the Queen of the Southern Ocean, no one could deny that the temporal realm was in a terrible mess. In the middle years of the 18th century a frustrated Dutch administrator declared that the Javanese nation 'is in itself fickle, and by the multitude of princess very inclined to rebellion.' It was not an entirely unreasonable assessment. A useful primer for newcomers on native customs which would later appear during Raffles' rule declared that 'The species of Government which exists among the Javanese, is an unlimited despotism', but this was not entirely true. A king would never have real legitimacy – and never achieve real success – without the advice and approval of his courtiers. In fact, it was often said that the most perfect Javanese king was one who acted as nothing more than a passive receptacle for the sacred energy of the realm, a figurehead who handed the practical matters to his *patih*, his prime minister, and his circle of advisors. It was hardly democracy, but it *did* rely on a kind of assent, and by the time of the shift to Surakarta the then king, Pakubuwono II, had clearly lost it.

A rebel princeling called Mas Said was harrying the borderlands, the coffers were empty, and the Dutch were calling with an increasingly irksome frequency, and had taken away great tranches of the Pasisir in payment for their earlier power-broking. And then the king's half-brother Mangkubumi, disgusted by Pakubuwono II's ineptitude, launched his own rebellion. The war that followed continued for almost a decade.

VOC officials wrote of Mangkubumi's 'well-known hot-tempered constitution' and of his 'habit of answering importunate Dutch requests with an enigmatic smile'. For at least a century the Dutch policy towards royal Java had been one of compromise: though they were ever willing to get involved in Mataram's troubles, their aim had always been to stabilise the throne, and to ensure that its occupant was someone they could work with. But by the middle of the century their own armies were exhausted, and their empire was bankrupt – financially, morally and imaginatively. Mangkubumi was more than they could deal with.

The ultimate compromising solution to the chronic instability in Mataram was one that no one really wanted at the time, but which was to have unexpected consequences. On 13 February 1755 at a misty, murky spot called Giyanti, perched high on the slopes of Mount Lawu, a peace deal was brokered by Nicolaas Hartingh, governor of the VOC's north coast territories, and point of contact with the Mataram court. It saw the realm cleaved in two. From now on a king known as the Susuhunan would sit in Surakarta, while thirty miles west on the site of Senopati's original capital a new palace would be built for a sultan, with Mangkubumi the first to take that crown under the magnificent title of Hamengkuwono I.

As every Indonesian high school history student would have it today, the Treaty of Giyanti was a dastardly Dutch deed of *divide et impera*, but in truth the idea of splitting the kingdom had been as much Javanese as Dutch, and not without precedent. Other rumpled realms had been divided between warring sons as a last resort, long before Europeans arrived in Java. Much later the Dutch would indeed realise with hindsight that they *had* divided, and that they *could* rule, but in the middle years of the 18th century, all that the VOC wanted was to be allowed some peace to crawl away and die. The idea that the original partition of Mataram was the devious deed of a perfidious puppet-master did not emerge until much later. It was first voiced during a bout of energetic anti-Dutch propagandising by a thoroughly partisan historian, a man who would take the concept of divide and rule in Central Java and run with it further than any Dutchman. He was, of course, Thomas Stamford Raffles.

In any case, even if the Dutch *had* been planning to create a permanently hobbled native realm in 1755, the policy would have been a notable failure. For decades, for whole generations, Mataram had been hopelessly unstable; by the end it had become a joke. But the partition had an unexpected consequence: after flickering, fading, guttering and all but vanishing, the light, the lustre, the sacred sparkle, was back on in Central Java. As Mangkubumi, a Muslim prince, was crowned the first Sultan of the half of Mataram now known as Yogyakarta, some amongst the onlookers noted that he looked for all the world like Vishnu, the Hindu god who, in the Javanese telling of the tale, is the saviour of mankind in troubled times. And what was more, he was reputed to have the blessing of the Queen of the Southern Ocean ...

By the time the British arrived in Java there was not one but two shimmering royal courts holding sway over the hinterlands, amounting to what one observer described as 'the Pith, the Sinews, and the Strength of Java'. And now, on 22 September 1811, the initial English emissary was about to make their acquaintance.

* * *

The man who had been deputed by Sir Samuel Auchmuty to carry the greetings of the British Crown and the East India Company to the courts of the Susuhunan and the Sultan, was the same messenger who had gone through the lines at Batavia with missives for Jan Willem Janssens.

Captain William Robison was a young Englishman with a surfeit of ambition and a certain inability to recognise the limits of his own authority. He had trained at Sandhurst and had served in Canada, the Mediterranean and South Africa (where he had married a local Dutchwoman called Cornelia) before shipping out to India. He had volunteered for the Java campaign in 1810, and headed south the following year in Lord Minto's party. Robison had, it seems, rather overstated the extent of his fluency in Dutch to get himself a key role in the expedition, but Englishmen speaking *any* sort of Dutch were in such short supply that he would probably have been pressed into service anyway. Minto lent him to Sir Samuel Auchmuty as an ADC during the operations around Batavia, and then, once the fighting was over, he had been sent to the royal heartlands.

He had travelled south from Semarang in a horse-drawn carriage, with a Javanese translator and a small entourage, passing the great weedy lake of Rawa Pening and the great peak of Gunung Merapi, the most sacred and ill-tempered of all Central Java's volcanoes. '[N]othing can surpass in beauty, richness and picturesque scenery of the country we passed over,' Robison wrote to Minto. He had reached the Dutch residency at Surakarta at first light on 22 September, and after breakfast with the resident, van Braam, who was still at his post despite the fall of Batavia, he headed out for his first royal audience.

Surakarta lay in the basin of the Bengawan Solo River.[8] The city was the biggest in the Javanese hinterland, with craftsmen's quarters full of the best artisans in the country. The ruler, Susuhunan Pakubuwono IV, was usually referred to by foreigners as the Emperor of Java. His name meant 'The Nail of the Universe'.[9]

---

8 Surakarta is often colloquially known as Solo, after the village that stood there before the *kraton* was built.

9 The kings and princes of Java had names that were both convoluted and confusingly similar. Though Pakubuwono IV was referred to as 'the Emperor' by the British this was not really an accurate reflection of his status. To keep things comprehensible he'll simply be called the

The ambitious Robison must have been delighted: less than two months after arriving in Java he found himself the first emissary of England to a fabled royal court, the guest of an emperor. As he and van Braam passed through the great white palace gates into a realm of gilded pavilions, shifting breezes and the transient scents of incense, melati flowers and frangipani, he was filled with pride and excitement.

A Javanese *kraton* was more than just a palace. Wrapped around its ceremonial gateways, its *joglo* roofs, its forbidden women's quarters, its *gamelan* pavilions and airy *pendopos* was an invisible cladding of immeasurable, indefinable power and prestige that meant far more than mere rank or title, but coupled with which were infinite stratum of formality and protocol. For the Javanese deference and respect were vital. Their language had multiple layers with entirely separate vocabularies for each: a commoner would address a courtier in the soft, high-spoken *Kromo*; the reply would come in the cruder, rougher *Ngoko*. The same formula of address applied even between generations of the same family, and acknowledgment of status extended as far as physical comportment. The shuffling, the crouching, the strange dropping of the right hand to the floor that Robison would first have noted amongst van Braam's household staff, and that would have reached truly bizarre extremes as he entered the Kraton, was all in the name of submission to rank. A commoner should always hold himself lower than an aristocrat; a son of a good family should crouch before his father, and everyone should squat humbly on their heels in the presence of a king. Nothing, for a well-bred Javanese, was more offensive than unseemly coarseness of speech or carriage.

An earlier generation of Dutchmen had paid at the very least lip-service to all this protocol when they visited the Javanese courts.

Susuhunan here, and his Yogyakarta counterpart will be the Sultan; their predecessors (and successors) will appear by their official names and regnal numbers.

Those who could speak Javanese usually followed the correct linguistic formulas, and though they baulked at actual grovelling they generally managed to keep their heads below the level of the ruler's. But such sensitivities had recently been cast aside. Robison was being shown the ropes by the haughty van Braam, who had a mutually antipathetic relationship with the court, so it seems doubtful that he crawled on his knees to his audience with the forty-three-year-old Susuhunan. But still, he seems to have made a very favourable impression, for he noted in a letter to Lord Minto that 'the reception I met with was a testimony of joyous satisfaction on all sides'.

In any case, the Susuhunan was so keen for an opportunity to rid himself of the hated Dutch resident that he was prepared to forgive any transgression of protocol. That night he committed his own breach by crossing from the sacred confines of the Kraton to the Dutch residency for a private meeting with Robison in some shuttered backroom, out of earshot of the meddlesome van Braam. In the heavy, scented gloom of the Javanese night the two men huddled together with only Robison's translator and a pair of courtiers present to share the moment.

Susuhunan Pakubuwono IV has been judged harshly by historians. Serious modern academics grumble about his 'unrealistic aspirations and a consistent inability to assess his political environment' and talk of his 'misguided opportunism'. Contemporary commentators were still less kind. The usual negative clichés that 19th-century colonialists liked to attach to 'Asiatic despots' were heaped upon the Susuhunan in almost every Dutch and British account. He certainly seems to have been a conflicted, contrary character, and something of a hell-raiser to boot. He had come to the Surakarta throne in 1788 at the age of nineteen, having already been involved in traitorous manoeuvres against his father during his years as a teenaged crown prince. At various stages of his rule he courted the company and the influence of hard-line Islamic conservatives, revolutionary Javanese mystics, and even, during the dying days of the British Interregnum, Indian

Hindus – and all this while continuing to engage in a certain amount of debauchery. He had been married twice before he even took to the throne – once in defiance of courtly advice to a Madurese princess; once to his own cousin – and was rumoured to have had any number of sordid affairs. Thirty years into his reign, contemptuous English visitors were still reporting similar shenanigans. The last British resident at Surakarta even hinted at homosexuality in an 1815 note about the Susuhunan's 'dissipated, debauched, and I am sorry to add … unnatural habits'.

But all of this negativity, and in particular the comments about his apparent lack of judgement, overlook something important: the Susuhunan had a remarkable ability to cling on to his throne despite repeatedly being involved in the kind of anti-colonialist conspiracy that would surely have seen any other native ruler rocketed off into far-flung exile at the drop of a Dutch topper or the tilt of an English sola topee. Over and over he was clearly implicated in cack-handed attempts to evict the Europeans from his realm and to reassert his own power over Java, and over and over he got away with nothing more than a minor capitulation and an apology by way of recompense. His judgement may have been flawed and his habits debauched; he may never have actually achieved his goals or reasserted his paramountcy, but he was a wriggler and a squirmer, a thoroughly political cat with an inexhaustible supply of lives.

Now, in a backroom of the residency, he embarked on a new series of manoeuvres. Robison had already declared during their formal morning meeting that the British came in peace and were keen for a friendly relationship with the court, but he had realised that with van Braam sneering on the sidelines, a frank political discussion with the Susuhunan was impossible. Now the Javanese royal could speak openly, and the first thing he made clear was just how much he hated the resident.

The Javanese had always regarded Europeans as the oddest of all races. Drawing on the allegory-laden resources of the *wayang kulit*, the sacred shadow puppet shows of classical Java, they tended to regard the Dutchmen as clowns.[10] Everything about them was farcically uncouth. They sweated and got uproariously drunk; when making a formal greeting, instead of bowing politely, they rose bizarrely to their feet as if they wanted to start a fight. They usually spoke the laughably coarse Malay language more readily than proper Javanese; they sat on chairs with their legs splayed, they were lecherous around women, and they wore ridiculous hats. On the surface they were a joke, a comic turn. But the clown in the *wayang kulit* is not the simple light relief of the European circus. Of all the shadow puppet characters the best loved is not a dashing mystic superhero, but the pug-nosed, pot-bellied, bent-backed Semar, the jester. The headline stars of the *Wayang* are naturalised Indian immigrants from the Ramayana and Mahabharata story cycles, but Semar is not found anywhere in Sanskrit texts: he and his bumbling troop are son-of-the-soil Javanese natives from long before Islam or Hinduism. He is, in fact, the guardian spirit of all Java, and though he readily plays the fool and cares little for matters of decorum, he never makes a mistake. In the *Wayang* it is the jester, not the prince, who has the nerve and the know-how to speak up against the gods. By turning the Dutch – and by association all other Europeans – into clowns, the Javanese were both mocking the absurdity of their behaviour, but also paying them a grudging and deeply significant compliment.

---

10 The *wayang kulit*, the shadow play, is the ultimate cliché for foreign writers tackling Java, but it is just as much a preoccupying motif for Indonesians themselves. The Indian Mahabharata and Ramayana epics are the inspirational wellsprings, though with multiple Javanese modifications and additions, and the set pieces and the key concepts of the *wayang* are used over and over as metaphors in discussion of everything from love life to business strategies. The cast of characters – from Arjuna to Semar – runs to hundreds, all rendered mantis-like with jointed limbs and sharp noses in filigreed buffalo-hide, and the man who makes them jump and dance against the screen – the puppet master, the *dalang* – is the most potent and respected of all Javanese figures, in both practice and in allegory.

But van Braam, the Susuhunan told Robison, was no wise clown in the model of his predecessors, most of who had been prepared at least to respect basic court protocol. He was completely intolerable, and the British would be viewed very warmly if they were to get rid of him. He had other concerns too, about his relationship with the colonial power on the coast, and about the amount of money he received in annual subsidies in return for the territories his ancestors had ceded to the VOC.

Faced with all these earnest complaints Robison found himself in a difficult position. He knew that he had been sent to the courts merely to offer greetings; he had no power to conduct treaties or even to make promises, but he realised that for the sake of future British relations with Surakarta he had at least to make friendly noises. The best thing he could do, he decided, was to tell the Susuhunan to put down all his problems in a formal letter to Lord Minto and to assure him that close attention would be paid to his concerns. The letter, when it arrived the following day, amounted to eleven numbered demands, foremost of which was the Susuhunan's 'earnest desire that the Minister Van Braam ... may be removed as soon as possible from Sooracarta ...'

With the royal missive safely bundled in his baggage, and with a few astute observations in his mind, Robison departed from the city on the morning of 24 September, heading southwest to continue his royal progress. Two days had been enough for him to get the measure of van Braam. Without authority or instructions from higher British powers he had had no option but to request that the Dutchman remain at his post and await further instructions, but he wrote to Minto that 'For the honour of my country I hope an honest Englishman with a nobler ambition than that of getting rich may be sent by your lordship to replace this gentleman.' The Susuhunan, meanwhile, had struck him as 'well-disposed and tractable'.

The road from Surakarta to Yogyakarta was a rough one, and they had to leave the carriage behind. Robison rode part of the way, but here and there, where the going was too tricky even for mounted horses, he was carried in a swinging, swaying palanquin, called here a 'djolie'. The Lawu volcano, a great purple hulk rising into murky cloud, fell away behind, and Merapi showed to the north. The countryside closer at hand was rich and green, and the fields were full of women in brightly coloured shawls, preparing the next rice crop. At lunchtime Robison noted what he described as an 'old city' in the trees to the north of the road where 'nothing now remains, but the ruins of several Hindoo Monuments and temples falling to pieces'. Robison was the first Englishman to see the great 9th-century temple complex of Prambanan.

He was in Yogyakarta by sunset.

* * *

The city that Sultan Mangkubumi had founded in 1755 over the bones of Senopati's capital had quickly turned into the most illustrious royal city in Java. Its full formal name was Ngayogyakarta Hadiningrat. Like the Thai town of Ayutthaya, Yogyakarta was named for Ayodhya, mythical birthplace of the Hindu god Rama. It was a classic Indonesian move: they had taken the name of a mythical city from Indian Hindu mythology, stuck the trickiest of Javanese consonants ahead of its initial vowel to make it unpronounceable to foreigners, and then placed a Muslim king (who might just also have been a reincarnation of Vishnu, and who had a mermaid queen for a girlfriend) on the throne. The name alone, not to mention the esteemed location on the Merapi-linked ley-lines and the foundations of old Mataram, made it a city destined for greatness.

Mangkubumi had constructed his court with great energy, throwing up new extensions to his burgeoning palace, and tearing down any project that failed to meet his kingly standards or those of his astrology-minded architects. By the time he died in 1792, passing the throne to his son Hamengkubuwono II, it was a truly magnificent place. The centrepiece of the public city was the northern Alun-Alun, the great grassy square, studded, like that in Surakarta, with a pair of sacred banyans which framed the distant view of Gunung Merapi's smoking summit. Beyond this the inner palace was a maze of gilded pavilions and forbidden quarters, a place of strict ceremony and protocol (the details of some of the ceremonies of the inner court are still guarded secrets even today). Around this sanctum sanctorum was a network of organised quarters, housing artisans, musicians and consorts. The royal family itself was huge, and the wider circle of courtiers and hangers-on ran into the thousands. Five hundred yards southwest of the inner court, was one of Mangkubumi's most intriguing legacies, the Taman Sari, the Water Palace. It was a network of white-walled, red-roofed chambers around a series of spring-fed pools, the water trickling from the mouths of carved *naga* serpents and echoing around cool, flower-strewn courtyards. It was ostensibly the bathing place for the king and his women (who numbered in the hundreds), but a royal sleeping platform islanded by water in an inner chamber suggests that the place had been built with someone special in mind. Taman Sari, it was said, despite the frivolous frolics in the pools above, was first and foremost a guesthouse where the Sultan could meet with his most important visitor: Nyai Loro Kidul, the Queen of the Southern Ocean. Around all of this – the artisans' quarters, the inner palace and the Taman Sari – ran a grand curtain wall, 45 feet high and 3 miles long.

The European part of town, north of the Alun-Alun, did not do well by comparison. The Dutch had never really managed to get the measure of Yogyakarta, and under both Mangkunegara and Hamengkubuwono II they struggled to understand, let alone orchestrate, events inside the Kraton. But still, they had managed to build a rather fine official residence on one side of the main approach road to the court, and a modest fortress with grey walls and shuttered barracks on the other. It was to this residency that Captain William Robison headed when he arrived in Yogyakarta, and it was there, from the ailing Dutch resident, Pieter Engelhard, that he learnt of the slightly irregular state of affairs in the Yogyakarta Kraton. The Sultan, Hamengkubuwono II, had technically been deposed on the demands of Daendels twelve months earlier and replaced by his own son. However, the court did not regard itself as in the business of taking orders from foreigners, and the Sultan had in fact remained in the palace, and in charge, as far as everyone except the Dutchmen were concerned. The Sultan was, Engelhard declared, 'extremely headstrong, and difficult to deal with', but Robison couldn't help but feel that he had probably been unfairly treated by Daendels.

The following morning he met both the ruler and the Crown Prince face to face, and noted that they were 'very jealous of each other'. Again, as in Surakarta, they had complaints about Dutch policies; again, all that Robison could do was assure them of the friendly nature of the British newcomers, and suggest that they compile a letter to the Governor-General listing their concerns. He told Engelhard, sick as he was, to remain at his post for the time being, and in the evening of 26 September he climbed back into the lumbering palanquin and headed north into the Javanese night. By noon the next day he was back in Semarang.

Robison's brief journey had been a heady one, and he was full of ideas by the time he reached the coast. 'There are a thousand little questions every hour arising which require some person to answer', he wrote to Minto. 'I have used your Lordship's name in the temporary arraignment of several matters of more or less consequence, and I doubt not you will approve of what I have done.'

Minto would indeed have approved. After all, Robison had done nothing more than offer assurances of friendship to the Susuhunan and the Sultan, and to take note of their specific complaints. He had also made plenty of other useful observations, including canny assessments about which Dutch officials were trustworthy, and which were otherwise (there was, for example, 'a French Man, by name Van Haak, Drost [Resident] of Japara, a Frenchman in everything, who it would be advisable soon to relieve, and send to his idol Bonaparte'). But Minto would soon return to India, and Robison could have had no idea that by displaying a certain degree of ambition, independence and initiative he was setting himself up for all sorts of difficulties with his new superior.

Raffles, it seems, had taken a profound dislike to Robison from the very first, and it's not entirely hard to work out why: the two men were decidedly alike. Both had ambition, both had ideas and opinions and were quite happy to voice them openly, and both were quite happy to invent authority for themselves whenever circumstances allowed.

Without the deceased John Leyden to back him up, Raffles seems to have retained a gnawing sense of insecurity for all the external bluster. The task of managing Java was an enormous one, and his human resources were minimal. A man of obvious energy and ideas like Robison ought to have had a key role, and a more mature and confident Lieutenant-Governor would surely have given him one. But Raffles seems to have regarded him as an unconscionable challenge. To be part of the team, it seems, you had to be either a committed collaborator or a sycophantic drone. Underlings who spoke their mind and went off-message were not welcomed in the Raffles circle. He was soon making entirely unfounded claims that Robison had caused all manner of problems by making unreasonable promises to the Susuhunan and Sultan, and when Robison was later appointed assistant secretary to the British government of Java, his new boss did his utmost to make life intolerable for him.

Robison was certainly somewhat difficult to handle, but Lord Minto, a canny, time-served sixty-year-old governor-general rather than an insecure thirty-year-old upstart, thought highly of his abilities and remained sympathetic to him throughout the difficult years ahead. The obvious antipathy that Raffles felt for Robison, and the vitriol that he and his immediate acolytes later poured upon him (and which was repeated by Raffles' biographers, one of who called Robison 'a hyena' and 'a miserable, spiteful creature, wholly irresponsible and unfitted for any major degree of authority'), were entirely unfair. And had Raffles been a better judge of character he might have realised that treating a man like Robison roughly was a bad idea: before the British occupation of Java was over he would make noisy efforts to obtain revenge.

But in September 1811 the trouble was yet to brew, and while Robison had been treating with Javanese royals, the rest of the British had been coming to terms with their new Dutch neighbours in Batavia.

* * *

The room was alive with the heat of oil lamps and overdressed bodies. Streamers and banners hung from the heavy wooden beams of the ceiling, and uniformed bearers scurried about carrying trays of drinks. In the corner, with their backs to the dark, panelled wall, the perspiring band were striving to find a tune that might unite the two nations gathered for this first official ball in Batavia since the British conquest.

An official British proclamation had already informed the old Dutch Burghers of Batavia that providence had 'brought to them a protecting and benevolent Government', and that in light of this great good fortune they should 'cheerfully perform the reciprocal duties of allegiance and attachment'. Most of them did seem willing to give the British newcomers the benefit of the doubt, but on the social side things were not going entirely smoothly.

All of the senior British officers and civilians were there for the ball, dressed to the nines despite the humidity. Those wives who had joined the expedition were in attendance too, in all their crinolined finery and overwrought hairdos. Olivia Raffles, a little rosy of cheek perhaps, was foremost amongst them. They gathered on one side of the room, attempting to look at ease as sweat coursed down their brows and dripped into their eyes, and forcing out the occasional merry guffaw between whispered expressions of distaste and disapproving glances at the other guests. The best of Dutch Batavian society had been invited to the gathering, but if the British had been hoping to encounter a civilised European society to match their own standards they were sorely disappointed. The white men of Batavia were largely shabby drunks. The handful who spoke English were seized upon and pumped ceaselessly for conversation, but most attempts at small-talk were in fumbling French. And when it came to the Dutch women – The horror! The horror!

'It is impossible', wrote the appalled Lord Minto, who was ever-willing to pass wry comment on the charms of the ladies, 'to give you anything like an adequate notion of the total absence of beauty in so crowded a hall.' The problem, he explained, was the historical lack of white women in the Dutch East Indies: 'The consequence has been that the men lived with native women, whose daughters, gradually borrowing something from the father's side, and becoming a mixed breed, are now the wives and ladies of rank and fashion in Java'.

By the early 19th century Batavia and the other big colonial cities of Java were home to large communities of mixed race Indo-Europeans. It was from their ranks that colonial wives were usually drawn. Girls were wedded off at shockingly young ages – children of twelve or thirteen were considered marriageable 'if they are but tolerably handsome, have any money or expectations, or are related to people in power'. Foreign visitors who did not stop long enough to feel the need for a wife were generally disapproving of these women:

Many of them can neither read nor write, nor possess any ideas of religion, of morality, nor of social intercourse ... Women of fifty, in Europe, look younger and fresher than those of thirty in Batavia ... Beauties must not be sought amongst them; the handsomest would scarcely be thought middling in Europe ...

The one point that counted in their favour, apparently, was that they had 'very supple joints'.

The discovery of this state of affairs in 1811 left the upright English folk deeply distressed. Though there were still a few British old-timers in India with native *bibis*, the idea of half-castes – heaven forefend! – becoming the women of 'rank and fashion' there was anathema. No one was more horrified by the sight of their swarthy counterparts than the British wives, gathered on the edge of the hall in Batavia that sweaty September evening. Alternately giggling and tutting, they stared at the uncouth couture of these so-called Dutchwomen. They wore what appeared to be a native sarong bound around the middle of their body as high as the armpits, over which was draped a chintzy chemise. From their shoulders hung a fine linen *kebaya* that reached as far as their ankles. Their hair meanwhile – black without exception, of course – was scraped back into oiled buns. It was undoubtedly an infinitely more comfortable get-up for a night on the tropical tiles than corsets and dresses weighing almost as much as the wearer, but it was hardly *dignified*. The older Dutchwomen meanwhile were great quivering slabs of obese flesh in coarse stockings. All of them were distastefully dusky. The bona fide *memsahibs* were still further aghast when they attempted to make ladylike conversation with this new set of sisters. Immaculate, governess-taught French or even Dutch proved largely useless: many of these monstrous mulattoes spoke nothing but Malay! And then there was the problem of dancing. English and Batavian styles were rather different, as Lord Minto reported:

Mrs Bunbury, the wife of an officer, a young pretty English-woman, stood up in the dance; but seeing when the first couple reached her, the Dutch gentleman take his partner fairly in his arms and hug her, as it appeared to her as a bear does his prey, she fairly took to her heels, and could not be brought back again by any means to share such a horror.

Polite conversation and dignified dancing had proved impossible; there was nothing else for it but to drown the sorrows: Lord Minto and 'other great men as well as many of the little ones, got loyally tipsy'. If Raffles was faced with an uphill task in bringing the principles of good British governance to the island of Java, then his wife, tottering from group to group on the fringes of the hall and keeping a ready eye out for the nearest tray-carrying servant, would face no less of a challenge in the setting of a new series of feminine standards.

* * *

Cultural differences aside, the British were already making swift progress around Batavia. Even before Janssens formally capitulated, Lord Minto had battered out the first ad hoc new legislation in the form of a proclamation announcing the British style of doing things. While Dutchman would still be eligible for government posts, there were certain changes that needed to be made at once. The first and most eye-catching of these adjustments pronounced that 'Neither torture nor mutilation shall make part of any sentence to be pronounced against criminals.'

Torture, it was well attested, had been very much part of the VOC's system of ensuring order, and until recently the gruesome process of public impalement had been a favoured Dutch method of disposing of native criminals. It was, as a late 18th-century account reveals, a horrific way to go:

The criminal was led in the morning to the place of execution, the grass-plot, and laid upon his belly, being held by four men. The executioner made a transverse incision at the lower part of the body, as far as the *os sacrum* [the base of the spine]; he then introduced the sharp point of the spike, which was about six feet long, and made of polished iron, into the wound, so that it passed between the backbone and the skin. Two men drove it forcibly up along the spine, while the executioner held the end, and gave it a proper direction, till it came out between the neck and the shoulders. The lower end was next put into a wooden post and riveted fast, and the sufferer was lifted up, thus impaled, and the post stuck in the ground. At the top of the post, about ten feet from the ground, there was a kind of little bench, upon which the body rested.

The insensibility or fortitude of the miserable sufferer was incredible. He did not utter the least complaint, except when the spike was riveted into the pillar; the hammering and shaking occasioned by it, seemed to be intolerable to him, and he bellowed out for pain; and likewise again when he was lifted up and set in the ground. He sat in this dreadful situation till death put an end to his torments, which fortunately happened the next day about three o'clock in the afternoon. He owed this speedy termination of his misery to a light shower of rain, which continued for about an hour, and he gave up the ghost half an hour afterwards.

Well over twenty-four hours of agony could hardly be called a 'speedy termination', but there were cases during the dry season where the impaled criminal survived for over a week. Rain, by all accounts, was the only guarantee of a relatively rapid demise, for 'as soon as any water gets into the wound, it mortifies and occasions a gangrene, which directly attacks the more noble parts, and brings on death almost immediately'.

The ban on torture was certainly worthy of celebration, but Lord Minto expediently avoided mentioning another evil in his September proclamation – slavery. In the early 19th century staunch anti-slavery sentiments were very much *de rigour* for upright British liberals – among whose ranks Lord Minto certainly counted himself. William Wilberforce's decades-long campaign had come to fruition in 1807 with the Slave Trade Act, and during the preparations for the British invasion of Java Minto and Raffles had made a good deal of noise about freeing the slaves of the Dutch East Indies.

But once they arrived in Batavia they discreetly moved the goalposts. They had quickly discovered that *everyone*, not least the government, owned slaves by the dozen. There were 30,000 slaves in European ownership in Java; household staff were largely indentured, and without them the dinners would go unserved and the shirts unpressed. Slavery could clearly not be abolished at once, it was decided, and in any case, the 1807 Act outlawed only the *trading* of slaves in British domains, not the practice itself. Minto reassured himself with the thought that slaves in Java – who had mostly been kidnapped by pirates or sold by their own chiefs in the remote eastern parts of the archipelago – were almost all menial or domestic workers. He liked to believe that they were in fact better off than hard-labouring freemen, and though the whole business was indeed a 'monstrous system', it was 'too general to be suddenly suppressed'. For the time being the British would simply outlaw the import of slaves from other islands, and would stop buying them for use by the state. Outright abolition could come along in good time.

In any case, more immediately pressing than all these earnest sentiments and honourable pledges was the practical matter of how Java would be run in the coming years. The big civilian and military cheeses, Lord Minto and Sir Samuel Auchmuty, had already decided on a return to Calcutta by the end of October; before they sailed away they needed to put some kind of British administration together from the limited financial and human resources at hand.

There were two options for a newly conquered British territory in Asia: it could be made a Crown colony, ruled directly from home and almost always placed under a military administration, or it could be thrown into the pot of the East India Company's possessions, usually with a civilian government in charge. Though there was a clear understanding from the very start that Java might later be transferred to the Crown, and may very well be given back to the Dutch if Holland regained its sovereignty, Lord Minto was too much of an enthusiast to rescind his own role in running the place at once. It would be made a Company territory, and the little man with the limp fringe would be put in charge:

His Excellency has been pleased to appoint the Honourable Thomas Raffles, Lieutenant-Governor of Java, who will aid him in the executions of the said functions until his departure from the island. After the departure of the Governor-General the Honourable the Lieutenant-Governor will exercise in his own name and person the powers of Government, and will be invested with all the authorities appertaining thereto in the fullest and amplest manner.

A scratch legislature had been thrown together: Raffles would sit at the head of a four-man council, made up of his military counterpart and a pair of requisitioned Dutchmen, H. W. Muntinghe the former head of the Batavia Supreme Court and a future close collaborator of Raffles, and the ex-chief alderman, Jacob Willem Cranssen. Meanwhile, Rollo Gillespie, who was up and about once more by the end of September after his weeks of fever, had been made the Commander of the Forces, the chief of the British Army in Java, and the second most important man on the Council.

Lord Minto could scarcely have chosen two less compatible people to head an enormously challenging new administration – one a bruising aristocratic war veteran, the other a wildly ambitious if somewhat insecure young middle class civilian, and neither of them with any real experience of government. He did make note of 'a shade of dissatisfaction in the Military Quarter' at the time, and was eager to make provisions in his instructions 'to prevent collision, disputes, and discontent'. But as he finally set sail from Batavia on 19 October, less than three months after the arriving fleet had dropped anchor off Cilincing, he could never have imagined just how quickly and how drastically things would turn bad in the Java administration.

* * *

As Minto sailed away, Thomas Stamford Raffles must surely have reflected for a moment on all that had come to pass. He was just thirty years old; a year earlier he had been dictating missives in Melaka while the pet orang-utan tripped over its trousers, and a year before that he had been a clerk in Penang. Now he was – in theory at least – in absolute charge of an island the size of England with a population of some 5 million people. Though his government would be based in the council chamber, Lord Minto had actually issued him with extraordinary powers to overrule *everyone* if he saw fit, even when it came to military matters. In short, Raffles had been appointed the uncontested oriental despot of the Land of Promise. If only John Leyden had been there to share the glory.

The first thing Raffles did on coming to power was to head for the hills. Batavia's climate had already killed off his best friend, and the wet season – when, by all accounts, the marshy effluvia and pestilent miasma were at their most poisonously potent – was looming. Fortunately, just thirty miles to the south, there was an airy spot that seemed to offer the perfect antidote to the deleterious heat of the coast. Weltevreeden might have meant 'Well Contented', but there was a place tagged with a still more superlative cliché perched on the slopes of the nearby mountains: Buitenzorg meant 'Without a Care' in Dutch.

Up through the rice fields, *kampungs* and palm groves along a good road beyond Meester Cornelis, over the gradually rising ridges towards a bank of towering purple peaks clad with coffee gardens and deep forest, the air cleared as travellers made their way towards the carefree little hill station. It stood in a bowl of green ground, cut by deep bamboo-clogged ravines beneath a great fan of volcanic mountains. Mount Salak rose directly to the south, while Daendels' Post Road writhed back and forth to the southeast past the double peaks of Gunung Gede and Gunung Pangrango towards Cipanas and the Puncak Pass.

The VOC had established the place as a weekend retreat in 1745, and Daendels had expanded the residency as his own principal home. Now Raffles followed suit. He was never more closely associated with any other spot in Java. The grand white house at Buitenzorg was not quite a palace but was much more than a bungalow, and was modelled – rather loosely – on Blenheim Palace in Oxfordshire. It stood incongruously with its neoclassical columns amongst the terraces and palm trees, and over the coming years it was here that Raffles would collate reports of antiquities and native customs, puzzle over land reforms and pen furious counter accusations to the claims that would before long be made against him. It was also the place where those admitted to the inner circle enjoyed 'the utmost hilarity and good humour'. At centre of that inner circle was Raffles'

ADC, Thomas Otho Travers.

Travers was everything that Captain William Robison was not. The son of a banker from Ballymoney in Ireland, he had come to India as a military cadet, and had fallen in with Raffles in Penang in 1806. He quickly turned into the most slavishly devoted of all his lackeys. He had curly brown hair, a delicate mouth and watery eyes. He was a committed diarist with a decidedly fruity style and an inclination to gushing protestations of emotional gratitude over the patronage of greater men. He enjoyed moments of romantic solitude but also adored 'gaiety and amusement', and seems to have had a tendency to erupt into floods of tears at trying moments. Yet he also somehow combined this flighty air with an uncanny ability to position himself in the first class carriage of the gravy train. And he absolutely adored Raffles. Any slur or slight against the great man was more than Travers could take; no opinion was worth having unless it had been handed to him directly by Raffles himself.

For Travers, Buitenzorg was the finest spot in Java. It was the scene of all manner of fabulous parties with Olivia playing host, and the setting was sublime after the seamy sump of Batavia. 'I shall ever remember the happy days passed at this sweet place', he wrote.

* * *

The view from the Buitenzorg lawn may well have been sublime, but the economic prospect was somewhat more grim, and as 1811 tailed out towards a damp and dripping Christmas Raffles began to take stock of what he was now responsible for. The problem that ought to have caused him most concern was that of money, not least in light of the bare-faced lies Lord Minto had told his masters about the prosperity of Java.

Minto had been convinced that the Board of Directors back in Leadenhall Street in London would see sense and approve when they learnt that he had disobeyed their orders and annexed Java. Just to make sure that they saw things his way he had over-egged the pudding in his early missives explaining what he had done. 'Java will supply resources at the least for its own expenses', he told them, even going as far as to claim that the Dutch had deliberately exaggerated the extent of the crippling debts that their empire had accrued:

We now know from proof that it was the policy of the Dutch to conceal the value and to exaggerate the defects of their possessions, especially of Java. This will account for the inadequate opinion entertained, at least I imagine so, at home of this island. It is now most flourishing; but the field for improvement is inexhaustible.

This was nonsense of course. Throughout the 18th century the VOC had done quite the *opposite*, and even after a decade of direct government control horrified officials back in Holland had still not quite got their heads around the monumental mountain of arrears that Java and the former Spice Islands had accumulated. The British had in fact taken possession of a colony in the grip of the same kind of crippling crisis that would bring the 'tiger economies' crashing into the mud during the Asian financial collapse 186 years later.

In Java the Spanish silver dollar was the currency of choice, but the problem had long been that there simply wasn't enough of this cash in circulation. In an attempt to raise funds for the Post Road and other expensive projects, Marshal Daendels had taken the ill-omened decision to start printing paper money. And then, when there still wasn't enough in the coffers, he printed more. It was a course of action that demonstrated a fundamental lack of understanding of the basic principles of economics. So much for 'quantitative easing', the paper currency had brought the already bankrupt colony to the brink of outright meltdown. By the time the British arrived the notes were so depreciated that one paper dollar was worth barely a fifth of the value of its metallic equivalent.

Clearly something had to be done, but there were simply too many of these useless scraps of paper floating around to declare them void at once. Minto had instructed Raffles to liquidate the paper currency by increments, buying it off the market whenever funds were available and attempting to stabilise it by forcing its use in certain payments. But despite this its value continued to dwindle. Within a year of the British conquest it had depreciated by something like 90 per cent; getting rid of it altogether proved impossible, and attempting to do so prompted some of the stickiest scandals of Raffles' tenure. As the years passed he made efforts to conceal the real extent of the mess from his masters in India, and by the end of the British Interregnum useless, confetti-like clouds of the stuff were still fluttering around Java on the tropical breeze.

And in any case, even had Minto been telling the truth about Java's financial health, it would have done nothing to appease the Company chiefs in London. When first they learned what their Man in Asia had done, they were absolutely horrified. 'We are so strongly imbued in this country with the inexpediency of extending our Colonial possessions in India,' they wrote to him in a very stern reprimand, 'that we shall be very unwilling to depart from the line of policy [that which had instructed Minto to overthrow the Dutch and then hand Java back to the natives]'. Still, the rice was already porridge as the Indonesian saying has it, and there was little that they could do now that their wayward governor-general had actually established a British government in Java. Such circumstances 'may possibly compel us to acquiesce in the limited establishment,' they grudgingly conceded. The palpable lack of enthusiasm for the Java project oozes from the page, and once the financially grim annual returns began to dribble into Leadenhall Street they were even more furious.

But in the rainy season of 1811-1812 the Board of Directors were very far away indeed – it could take six months for a message to reach Java from England. Raffles had been left entirely to his own devices, and before facing up to the facts of finance, he was eager to wrestle with the royals.

* * *

Raffles had already recognised that the double-headed Mataram dynasty amounted to much more than a pair of petty fiefdoms. But from the very start he made it clear that the idea of two courts which regarded themselves as at best equals of the European power, and at worst its betters, was not something he was prepared to countenance. Daendels had harboured similar ideas, but the Thundering Marshal had not been on the scene long enough to push this point through to its domineering conclusion. It was Raffles who would make the decisive move.

His first step was to send competent Englishmen to the courts. Colonel Alexander Adams was sent to Surakarta where he would quickly cause almost as much consternation as his predecessor van Braam with his unseemly conduct. The man who headed for Yogyakarta, meanwhile, was a twenty-eight-year-old Scotsman, a former army surgeon with a furious frown and bushy eyebrows. His name was John Crawfurd.

Crawfurd was another committed orientalist. He spoke Malay well, and rapidly got to grips with the subtleties of courtly Javanese too. Despite Raffles' greater acclaim, by the end of the British occupation Crawfurd was certainly the foreigner with the most detailed and intimate knowledge of Javanese history and culture. It was hardly an admiring intimacy, however, and the Scotsman was spectacularly racist, even by 19th-century standards. His contempt extended as far as the language he had mastered. Reflecting the minds of its owners, Crawfurd theorised, spoken Javanese was a mass of curious contradictions: 'In unimportant trifles, it deals in the most puerile and endless distinctions, while, in matters of utility, not to say in matters of science, it is utterly defective.'

In the later stages of the interregnum Crawfurd managed to rein in his rancour and to respect formalities, and he earned a good deal of popularity in the Yogyakarta Kraton as a consequence. But when he first arrived in the royal city on 15 November 1811 he embarked on a policy of belligerent foot-stomping.

Before Crawfurd's departure from Batavia he and Raffles had

discussed the idea of restoring the semi-deposed Sultan to his original stature as a demonstration of 'British liberality'. The Sultan, however, clearly felt no need to rely on such haughty hand-outs. Sometime between Robison's visit and Crawfurd's arrival he had pre-emptively reinstated himself in totality, demoted the Crown Prince to his original powerless position, and murdered his rebellious prime minister for good measure. For the British this was the most outrageous exercise in Asiatic insolence. Crawfurd made this clear as soon as he had moved into the gloomy Dutch residency, from which the sickly Engelhard had been evicted, and began noisily recommending moves to dethrone the Sultan. Before long he had got himself banned from the inner sanctum of the Kraton for his decidedly rough and distinctly uncouth behaviour.

The situation was critical. It was time for Raffles himself to make a journey to the east.

* * *

The courtiers sensed that the white men were not going to behave as they should in the presence of the Sultan long before they reached the great Bangsal Kencono, the Golden Pavilion at the heart of the Yogyakarta Kraton. It was only a small party that had emerged sweating from the old Dutch residency, home to the ill-tempered Crawfurd for the past month, but they had crossed the grassy sweep of the Alun-Alun, the royal square, and passed between its sacred banyan trees with a certain unseemly swagger. It was late December and away to the north – in perfect alignment with the main axis of the palace – Gunung Merapi was buried in banks of bruise-coloured cloud. A hot breeze, full of the rusty scent of rain, shifted in the foliage and set the cicadas singing, and a smell of cloves and tobacco, tea, wood-smoke and rotting blossoms hung over the red-tiled roofs of the town.

The white men – Raffles and a small bodyguard of redcoat soldiers – strode forcefully through the great ceremonial gateway of the Kraton where it pierced the surrounding sweep of the curtain wall, and clattered up the steps to the Siti Inggil, the High Place, the first of the great *pendopo* pavilions and the spot where the Sultans were crowned. It rose on teakwood pillars to a tiered roof with elaborately carved royal *naga* serpents writhing along the balustrades.

Beyond the High Place Raffles and his men trotted through another gateway and across a pair of oblong white-walled courtyards. Gilded pavilions stood in the corners with the tarnished bronze gongs of *gamelan* orchestras arrayed on their raised platforms. Great crowds of courtiers shuffled on either side. They wore sarongs of intricate ochre-gold batik. Each was barefooted on the scattered black sand of the courtyards, but the heavy wooden hilt of a sheathed *kris* jutted ominously at each of their backs.[11] They did not like the way the white men were carrying themselves; they did not approve of the uncouth speed at which they were moving.

Raffles had reached the threshold of the very heart of the Yogyakarta Kraton. Ahead stood a pair of monstrous *dwarapala* statues, the bulging, bug-eyed guardian figures of classical Javanese temple architecture, and between them a gateway, crooked to confuse wicked spirits – and perhaps also wicked Englishmen. All of this – the gateways, the *nagas*, the *dwarapalas*, the very gilding of the columns

---

11 In Java the *kris*, the tapered ceremonial dagger, was the most potent of all the sacred objects a king or a commoner could possess. The men who forged these blades were not just blacksmiths; they were shamans too, and they knew the secret mantras and incantations that would load the thin, chased iron with unseen energy. Sometimes they would mould the hot metal with their bare hands. As it passed through the generations a dagger's power grew, and there were elaborate annual cleaning ceremonies and offerings that had to be made to keep it secure. A real heirloom *kris* was more than an inanimate object; it was actually *alive*, had its own personal name, and if not properly cared for could become dangerously unstable. Tucked into the sarong of any properly dressed Javanese a *kris* was also an obvious symbol and cipher for masculine potency – so much so that a man's *kris* could actually take his own place beside the bride on the ceremonial dais on his wedding day should he be absent. Stripped of his *kris* a Javanese male was spiritually neutered. Finally, it was also a practical weapon, and a prime tool for assassination and execution.

– was rich in potent symbolism; the scattered black sand itself was a concession to the ever-demanding Queen of the Southern Ocean. The Kraton architecture ought to have intrigued even the most half-hearted orientalist, and it clearly showed that some three centuries after the island had turned to Islam there were still other currents that ran very deep in Java. But all of that would have to wait. Between those bug-eyed guardians and beyond that crooked gateway an oriental despot with an entourage of thousands was waiting. A clash of egos was coming, and Raffles would carry off the meeting with equal measures of arrogance and the kind of reckless bravery that even Rollo Gillespie would have been proud of.

He had set out from Batavia on 28 November with Olivia and Travers in tow, travelling by ship as far as Semarang, and then heading south across the mountains for Surakarta. 'It is impossible to conceive anything more rich than the bounty both in cultivation and in picturesque scenery', Raffles wrote of the journey. He did *not* write – though another member of the party did – of how he press-ganged the inhabitants of this lovely landscape to carry his baggage, nor of how they complained bitterly at this unpaid heavy labour.

Raffles made his entry into Surakarta on 21 December in full formal style. He formed a singularly unfavourable view of the Susuhunan, who he later described as being 'of a weak, unsteady and sinister disposition, devoted to luxury and amusements', and made sure that everyone knew that any problems between the British and the court were all the fault of the unfortunate William Robison.

The Susuhunan's earlier requests were bluntly refused one by one. His complaints about the new resident were ignored, and as for his stated preference for 'My brother the commissary Mr Robison' as his official point of contact with the British, he most certainly would not be getting *that*. Despite his alleged lack of judgement, at this stage the Javanese royal seems to have shown a certain degree of pragmatism. He managed to maintain a façade of courtesy and signed a friendly, if rather prejudicial, treaty. Raffles was delighted; he had successfully bearded a despot in his very palace. He spent Christmas in Surakarta with thunderclouds rumbling over Mount Lawu, and then set out for Yogyakarta where he touched base at the residency to hear the full force of Crawfurd's vitriol against the Sultan, before blustering across the Alun-Alun for that high stakes encounter.

The inner courtyard of the Kraton, beyond the guarded gateway, was crawling with *kris*-carrying courtiers. It was studded with sagging trees, rising in thick canopies to a hot and heavy sky and flanked by yet more pavilions. In the centre stood the greatest *pendopo* of all, the Bangsal Kencono. Its roof rose in tiled pyramids above a forest of columns of fragrant teak, each carved and inlaid with ochre and white. Bare feet and the hems of batik sarongs swished over the marble floor, and beneath the tapering apex of the ceiling, a space had been prepared for an audience. It was here that the trouble began. As the crowd of courtiers parted and the perspiring Raffles came face to face with the Sultan himself, a tall, slanted fez atop his head, his body swathed in enough batik to clothe an entire family, the Englishman decided to take offense at the seating arrangements.

As the patriotic British take on events would later have it, 'The Sultan, to test the sort of man he had to deal with, had deliberately arranged the seats in a way that put the Lieutenant-Governor in a position inferior to himself' – and that, of course, was the most atrocious insolence. This interpretation is by no means reasonable. Crawfurd, fulminating in the residency, had already expressed to Raffles his opinion that the Sultan had reinstalled himself as a test of British resolve, but the truth was that until very recently he had been the legitimate ruler anyway; he was by all accounts reasonably popular with his people, and he, like both his forebears and his Surakarta counterpart, liked to regard himself as an ally rather than an underling of the European power in Java, whether it flew a Dutch, French or British flag. The post-invasion uncertainty had seemed the obvious moment to undo Daendels' meddlesome measures.

And as for the seating arrangements, the Sultan was an invested Javanese royal, his power confirmed by an immaculate pedigree, the possession of any number of sacred heirlooms, and a direct connection with the Queen of the Southern Ocean. Obviously *he* should take pride of place in his own court. Before Daendels, generations of Dutchmen had been quite happy to make allowances for this sort of thing, even if only for show. What was more, reports of the nature of the new European administration in Batavia had led to understandable confusion in Central Java. The royal courts had long been familiar with the concept of a European governor-general, a position they acknowledged as having significant – perhaps even pseudo-royal – status. But this odd little man with the floppy fringe and the wonky eye now making an outrageous and undignified fuss about the positioning of a set of heavy teak chairs was *not* a governor-general. They had already been introduced to the name of the owner of *that* title by the much better behaved Captain Robison: the new equal of Janssens, Daendels and all who went before them was none other than the Maharaja Gilbert Lord Minto. This newcomer was merely Minto's minion, and in the colonial scheme of things as they understood it the next rank down from a governor-general was a resident, a man who might well be nothing more than a petty administrator of a few remote villages. To arrange things so that such an individual would sit with his head higher than that of the Sultan was absurd. Rather than a sinister test of Raffles' mettle, the positioning of the chairs was more likely the only obvious choice available for whichever court functionary had set them up. By having the outrageous audacity to complain, it was Raffles, not the royal, who was behaving in an 'infuriated spirit of insolence'.

Quite what compelled him to act in this way, as he stood staring furiously at the unequal chairs in the centre of the Golden Pavilion, is unclear. If it was the cold-headed move of a tactician, a canny assertion of dominance, then it was one that took serious guts. Raffles was backed by only a small party of soldiers, had no significant reinforcements waiting outside, and was surrounded by quite literally thousands of already unsettled and armed Javanese functionaries of a court where protocol counted for everything. If however, it was the *hot*-headed, spur-of-the-moment tantrum of an egomaniac, then it was a piece of supreme idiocy, and he was incredibly lucky not to have been murdered on the spot.

A murmur of outrage did indeed swell and spread between the carved columns of the packed *pendopo*, followed by the spine-chilling sound of dozens of *krises* being slipped swiftly from their sheaths. Quite how this moment of extreme tension was ultimately smoothed over was not recorded. Much has been made by the imaginative Raffles-worshippers of him 'stilling with eloquent Malayan phrases the storm', but this too demonstrates a marked ignorance about Javanese culture. The Javanese were *not* Malays, and their language was *not* 'Malayan'. Anyone visiting the Kraton should certainly have been speaking decent Javanese, and should have been addressing the Sultan in soft, formal *Kromo*. These people were not unfamiliar with Malay, but for them it was a language that was anything but eloquent. It was the tongue of the market trader, the Chinaman and the vagabond. It was what prostitutes and card-sharps spoke amongst themselves in the hugger-mugger of the Pasisir ports. It was without subtlety, poeticism or even bare politeness; 'the language of chickens'. Any decent Javanese noble who understood it would have been inclined to pretend that he didn't. For Raffles to start griping in Malay over the seating arrangements would have been equivalent to him berating George III in the idiom of a fishwife.

Somehow, it seems, the Sultan managed to show an enormous forbearance – or perhaps a sudden indecision at the crucial moment. The *krises* went back into their sheaths, the seats were shifted and Raffles got to go away with his ego still further inflated. When he later told the story to Minto, he declared that 'if I once had allowed the sword to be drawn or a blow struck, we should have had at this moment, a war ten times more destructive than that of Candy [a notably bloody British failure in Sri Lanka the previous decade]'.

The Sultan signed a treaty of sorts with the British, and on 28 December was officially recognised as having regained his throne. Raffles headed back for the coast, and on the first day of 1812 he arrived in a rain-lashed Buitenzorg telling everyone who would listen that he had definitively stamped his authority on the Javanese courts. In the later official version of events it was claimed that the Lieutenant-Governor really *was* hoping for a lasting peace in Java as he celebrated a belated New Year while the thunder rumbled over Mount Salak. Raffles himself would state that he only came to contemplate violence in the coming dry season when the Sultan treacherously reneged on the new-found friendship. But scattered through his private and secret correspondence from the monsoon months of that first year in Java are clear indications that he was harbouring dreams from the very first of a crushing military defeat of one or other – or possibly both – of the Javanese courts as a 'decisive a proof to the Native Inhabitants of Java of the strength and determination of the British Government'.

It was mere expediency that had stopped him acting in December. It does seem that he left instructions at Semarang to prepare for an unprovoked attack on one or other of the courts early in 1812: a note in the journal of an officer there states that 'Early in the New Year rumours had spread, confirmed apparently by the Depots of Stores and Grain and the Barracks preparing at Salatiga, that a movement of Troops was likely to be made in the vicinity of the Native Princes'. But by the time Raffles returned to Buitenzorg in January news had arrived from the far side of the rain-lashed Straits of Sunda that gave a pretext for a more pressing military expedition to the royal city of Palembang, wellspring of the Malay language and one-time capital of a mighty Buddhist empire, on the banks of a meandering river in the heart of the South Sumatran jungle.

Events that were perhaps the grubbiest in the whole five years that the British spent in the East Indies were about to unfold. In Palembang the stage was set for an episode from which no one emerges smelling of roses, and which future generations of patriotic Dutch historians, howling in contradistinction against the flood of Anglophone adoration, would use in their attempts to prove that far from being a glowing paragon of liberal virtue, Thomas Stamford Raffles was a very bad man indeed ...

Hearts of Darkness

The boat, a little open schooner rising to a high prow, slipped out of Palembang on the evening tide. The high, earth-coloured walls of the fortified palace and the wrecked and ransacked Dutch compound on the opposite bank fell behind, and the mass of thatched hovels built on platforms of raised bamboo along the muddy shoreline began to give way to the forest. The surface of the river was slick and white in the thickening twilight, moving uneasily, filled with strange boils and dark eddies. Here and there the long, low blade of a native canoe cut across the murky flow, a dark figure silhouetted in the stern. Away upstream a last livid stain of dying daylight showed beyond the lost fringe of the sodden hinterland and the evening prayer call echoed out from the Arab *kampung* downstream from the gloomy palace – '*Allaaah uh akbar, Allaaah ...*'

Huddled, bruised and bloodied in the belly of the boat were two dozen Dutchmen, and one sobbing white woman. Equally bruised and equally bloodied were the 63 native servants, slaves and soldiers who until that morning had been under their command. They shuddered and moaned softly in the dense, velvety gloaming. The prayer call fell away – '*La ilaha il Allaaah ...*' – and the boat found its path in the steadying downstream current. The black walls of the Sumatran jungle rose on either side.

It was mid-September 1811, and there had been woeful whispers of descending doom for some time amongst the weary, fever-wracked occupants of the lonely Dutch compound on the southern bank of the Musi River, across from the palace of Sultan Badruddin of Palembang. They had always been far from their nearest European neighbours, but it was weeks now since they had last had news from Batavia, and there had been gossip that, some months earlier, a huge fleet of warships flying Union Jacks had sailed south towards Java through the shallow seas that lay beyond the mouth of the Musi, sixty miles to the northeast. In recent weeks the Chinese junks and Arab dhows that anchored in the coffee-coloured channel had started to unload dark rumours that Holland's empire in Asia had ceased to exist. If that was true, they wondered, then what would become of a forgotten community of Dutchmen and their sickly wives and children deep in the forest and now at the mercy of a native court with a reputation for violence?

The critical moment had finally come earlier that same September afternoon. A party of senior Sumatrans had crossed the river to the Dutch compound. Malay soldiers with long lances walked with them. They brought the news that had long been looming: Batavia had indeed fallen to the British; any agreements that the vanquished Dutch government had had with the court of Palembang were now null and void, and the few dozen Dutch citizens left in the territory were to be evicted with immediate effect.

The size of the armed party that had entered the compound and the very manner of the men who delivered the message must have let the Europeans know that they were now in deep trouble. There had long been tensions; Palembang was not a soft-edged place of protocol like a royal Javanese city. It was an island adrift in an infinite ocean of tiger-haunted forest; the only way out was by river, and the floodtide sometimes brought strange men and dark influences. At night weird shrieks rose from the bamboo *kampungs*; the Chinese traders who kept their dwellings close to the Dutch quarters had long whispered their fears of a massacre, and always the oppressive enormity of the forest bore down on the place.

The horrified Dutch resident pleaded with the courtiers. Where could they go? He had no boat at his disposal; there were women and children. Would they let him at least have three days to prepare for departure?

The reply from the lance-carrying locals was that the orders came directly from Sultan Badruddin; if the resident had any requests then they should be made on the other side of the river. With the afternoon light lengthening they ferried him to the far shore along with his assistant and secretary, and the commander of the miniscule Dutch garrison. The inner palace across the river was forbidden to foreigners, but another local chief met them at the gate with an ominous declaration: they had no need to prepare a ship for their own carriage; there was a boat already waiting. And with that they were dragged away, and ordered roughly aboard the waiting schooner. Back across the river in the compound the remaining Dutchmen and their native staff were similarly overwhelmed and manhandled to the water's edge. The wives begged and pleaded, but they were roughly shoved back amongst the shrieking children as their horrified husbands were hauled away. One woman, however, howling and clinging, made it to the muddy shoreline. They trussed her up and threw her aboard the schooner too, and she was there amongst the men as they slipped seawards through the gloom. The River Musi was a pale ribbon through the roaring darkness of the forest.

What exactly happened aboard the little ship as it crept downstream through the night is not known; what exactly happened when it reached the shallows over the mud-bank that marked the river-mouth in the milky, salmon-pink mists of the dawn is a mystery too. But the next tide carried some 86 corpses, including that of a much-abused Dutchwoman, away between the mangroves and into the deeper water.

* * *

It took many weeks for news of the massacre to reach Batavia. If Raffles experienced a gut-crunching moment of panic when first he heard that something awful had happened in Palembang, and went frantically flicking through his mountains of old correspondence, desperately trying to remember exactly *what* he had written to Sultan

Badruddin from Melaka all those months ago, he gave no hint of it in his initial letter to Minto on the subject. On 13 January 1812 he wrote of the rumours that had greeted him on his return from Yogyakarta: 'It appears that the Sultan [of Palembang], as was expected, allowed the Dutch factory [trading post] to remain until he heard of the fall of Java, and then like a villain (most unexpectedly) ordered them away. A report, too true I fear, says [he] allowed them to be cut off and murdered, for no soul of them has ever reached a European port.'

That bracketed 'unexpectedly' was the one minor attempt that Raffles made to cover himself. There was nothing remotely unexpected about the occupants of the compound having been 'ordered away', or even murdered. Twelve months earlier, sweating and scribbling in Melaka, Raffles himself had done his very best to encourage Sultan Badruddin to 'drive the Dutch from Palembang.'

Palembang lay deep in Sumatra, inland from the mangrove-crowded eastern coastline where a strip of stuttering islands formed a southward continuation of the Asian mainland, an ellipsis beyond the final syllable of the Malay Peninsula. The British knew little about the town itself beyond what they had picked up in second-hand accounts from the Dutch, who had a treaty with the place. It was very remote; it lay in the original heartland of the Malay language and its natives were indeed Malays. The royals, however, were of Javanese extraction and some kind of debased Javanese was still the language of the court. But high, Yogyakarta-style ceremony and pre-Islamic traditions were not the order of the day here. The Sultans made as much of a legend of descent from the family of the Prophet Mohammed as of their claim to the blood of Hindu Javanese kings. They had long taken Arabic names; it was reported that the locals were 'zealous and superstitious Mahomedans',and that among the residents were 'a number of Arab Priests who have acquired an ascendant power on the natives'. The palace had mighty fortified walls; the surrounding jungles swarmed with tigers, and there were pagan tribes in the deep interior. Roads counted for nothing, and the meandering sixty-mile course of the lower Musi was the only highway. It was exactly the kind of imaginative setting – and indeed the kind of characters: the Malays, the Arabs, the decaying court – that Joseph Conrad would make his own later in the century.[12]

During his hectic months in Melaka the previous year Raffles had employed a pair of local agents to carry messages up and down the Musi River. Their names were Tunku Raden Sharif Mohamed and Sayyid Abubakar Rumi,[13] and on 10 December 1810 Raffles opened the correspondence with a deliberate attempt to scare Sultan Badruddin:

I have heard with much concern of the approach of a Dutch force to the mouth of the Palembang River, and I lose no time in dispatching this letter to put your Majesty on your guard against the evil machinations of the Dutch, a Nation that is desirous of enriching itself from the property of your Majesty as it has done with that of every Prince of the East with which it has had connection ...

---

12 In the centuries straddling the dawn of the Second Millennium Palembang had also been the heart of one of early Indonesia's greatest realms, the Buddhist entrepôt state of Sriwijaya. In the 19th century, however, even local folk memories of Sriwijaya had been lost. It wasn't until the early 20th century that scholars rescued its history from Chinese manuscripts and a handful of other obscure sources.

13 Though the messengers were reportedly Penang residents, they probably had connections amongst the 300-strong community of settled Arabs in Palembang, as both their names strongly suggest Middle Eastern antecedents. Abubakar was a *Sayyid*, a descendent of the Prophet, with a last name – Rumi – that also hinted at Turkish blood. The other man too had decidedly Arabic appellations, but they were preceded by honorifics – Tunku and Raden – that also hinted at an aristocratic Malay or Javanese connection. When earlier discussing possible messengers Raffles had written of 'the syeds and principal natives [of Palembang] who are in the habit of trading in Malacca and Prince of Wales' Island [Penang]', and mentioned 'a Malay Prince born at Palembang and connected by blood with the leading men if not the reigning family, and who married a sister of the present King of Keddah'. This is presumably Raden Mohamed, though he was not actually a prince.

I would recommend your Majesty to drive them out from your country at once, but if your Majesty has reasons for not doing so, and is desirous of the friendship and assistance of the English ... I have power over many ships of war and if I think proper to do it, I can drive the Dutch out even were they 10,000 in number ...

This rumoured Dutch fleet does seem to have existed, but if it had military concerns on the Musi it was probably only there to reinforce the existing Dutch garrison rather than to overthrow Badruddin, and in any case, before long it upped anchor and vanished away to the south. Raffles may not have been inciting murder at this stage, but he was certainly inciting hatred. The next letter he sent to Badruddin declared the Dutch 'a bad Nation' and wondered why the Sultan still allowed them 'to reside in Palembang'. Later he called them a people with a 'sinister disposition, want of faith, and rapacious spirit of aggrandisement'.

Replies from South Sumatra were never as regular or as fulsome as those that were mailed from Melaka. For a start Sultan Badruddin seems to have been a little suspicious of the status of Raffles' messengers (and indeed, Raden Mohamed and the Sayyid were later accused of being untrustworthy adventurers). They were clearly not fully invested emissaries of an empire, and for all Raffles' wild claims of his power to drive out 10,000 men, there had been little real display of British strength. It made perfect sense for Palembang to hedge its bets for the time being rather than risk Dutch wrath should the English promises prove empty.

But still, over the coming months as 1810 turned into 1811 and preparations of the fleet got underway in India, letters continued sporadically to shuttle back and forth between Melaka and Palembang. Badruddin gave assurances both of his friendship for the British, and his dislike of the Dutch, but still he was inclined to play for time. He also seemed to show a certain flicker of a guilty conscience: the Dutch had been let into the realm on proper terms by his ancestors, and they had brought certain benefits to the court over the years, he noted.

Raffles, however, was increasingly frantic in his attempts to make some definite arrangement and to hear that the Dutch had been removed. In March he sent an actual treaty across the Straits for Badruddin to sign. It was full of yet more harsh words for the Hollanders, declared that the Palembang court would immediately upon signature cancel all treaties and agreements with the Dutch, would in effect declare total independence, and would then agree 'never to re-admit such a Residency, or that of a similar agency from any foreign power whatever with the exception of the English, who shall be at liberty to establish such Factory or Factories as may be hereafter agreed upon'. Most pressingly of all, the second clause declared that 'His Majesty the Sultan hereby engages to dismiss from his Territories the present Dutch Resident, and all Persons acting under the authority of the Dutch Government'.

Much mileage has been made by patriotic and angry Dutch historians over the way the phrase 'to dismiss from his territories' was rendered in the native scribe's Malay version actually sent to Sultan Badruddin. The original has vanished, but in a rough copy that later came to light the words appeared as '*buang habiskan sekali-kali*'. There has been unnecessary debate over how exactly to translate this very simple phrase which most Malay or Indonesian speakers would explain as something along the lines of 'throw out [literally] and finish utterly' – decidedly ominous, but still ambiguous as an instruction.

Rival Anglophone historians on the Raffles team later dismissed as unreliable the rough copy of the translated treaty, although very similar phrases – full of 'throwings out' and 'strikings' – certainly do crop up in the surviving Malay originals of Raffles' other letters to Palembang. This is all fairly simple stuff, and even if Raffles' Malay wasn't as strong as some like to claim, he would still have got the gist, and indeed the inference, when the translations of his English originals were read back to him.

Raffles also attached an explanation of the clauses of his treaty for Sultan Badruddin, telling him that if he valued his independence in any way he must throw off whatever Dutch yoke he laboured under, no matter how light – *before* the British seized Java. Regardless of the actual circumstances, Europeans regarded Palembang as a vassal of Dutch Java; as soon as Batavia fell it would become the property of the British, and there would then be no room for renegotiation of terms with the new landlords. Raffles sat back and waited, but a month later in April no response had arrived from Palembang. He fired off another note warning Badruddin that the British fleet was beginning to gather in the Straits; the adventure to Java would soon be under way, and by then it would be too late for a friendly agreement.

Sultan Badruddin was in fact busily working out his own, much less belligerent, treaty. Once he had read Raffles' proposed agreement he had scribbled a note to the messenger explaining that he was 'entirely unwilling to be involved in the hostilities between the Hollanders and the English'. For all Raffles' bravura, the conquest of Java was still by no means certain; if the Sultan prematurely 'threw out and finished utterly' the Dutch community he could cause terrible troubles for himself. His prevarications were perfectly understandable. He wrote a letter which he felt sure would please the Englishman across the water, stating that he had in effect already broken with the Dutch and that 'I have accordingly sent to Batavia that they may take away those Hollanders with all speed who are in Palembang and if they are not speedy in taking them off, some misfortune will befall them and the blame will not be mine'. But his own version of the treaty stated that 'while Batavia is not yet taken, as this might occasion some distress to his Majesty, the Hollanders shall continue to occupy [the compound in Palembang]'. But that treaty was sent to Melaka too late for Raffles to sign or to quibble over its clauses: the British fleet was already departing for Java.

Raffles had been despairing of the slow progress of the negotiations with Palembang, but he had at least made Badruddin aware of his desires, had hammered home the truly evil nature of the Dutch, and stressed just how happy the British would be to hear that they had been removed from the town. He had also offered Badruddin a very clear explanation of the limited nature of his future sovereignty if he *didn't* evict the Dutch before Batavia fell. And then, on the eve of embarkation from Melaka in June, Raffles sent another missive to Palembang, and with it a portentous gift: 'As the Dutch are at Palembang I send four cases of 80 muskets in all as well as 10 baskets of cartridges filled with powder and shot'.

Thomas Stamford Raffles may not have actually *asked* for the lonely little European community to be annihilated; he may not even have *wanted* it (though the shipment of arms is a tricky charge to answer). But through a combination of avarice and naivety he had sold them down the Musi River.

* * *

But why exactly had Raffles been so desperate for Sultan Badruddin to destroy the Dutch outpost and declare independence *before* the British reached Java anyway? The answer was indeed avarice, and it showed all too clearly just how devious a schemer he could be. In his explanation of the terms of his proposed treaty Raffles had tried to convince Badruddin that 'The English holding such immense Territories and Power on the Continent of India ... cannot in their proceedings Eastward be actuated by the rapacious and greedy conduct that has distinguished the Dutch'. But in truth those were *precisely* the motives that had drawn British attention to Palembang in the first place.

Much of Sultan Badruddin's realm was uninhabited jungle, and it was not a land with the greatest of economic prospects. But even as he was opening his correspondence from Melaka Raffles had written to Lord Minto that 'the Sultan of Palembang is one of the richest of the Malay Chieftains and is literally said to have Godowns [warehouses] stored with Dollars and Gold hoarded by his Ancestors'. That alone was enough to set the more piratical inclinations of the colonialists abuzz, but what Raffles was so keen to obtain was not those dollars themselves, but the bounty that had provided them. The Palembang interior might have been mostly jungle, but its sultan was also the ruler of the rough, hundred mile-long hulk of offshore land that sheltered the mouth of the Musi. Its name was Pulau Bangka, and it was the richest source of tin in all the Indies.

Locals on the island – and on its smaller neighbour Belitung – had always panned for the black ore in the muddy streams that flowed through the stony hills, and in the previous century an organised mining industry had been set up by Chinese migrants. Most of the tin they harvested was shipped to China anyway, where, amongst other things, it was used to make the gilded spirit money, burnt in temple offerings. Sultan Badruddin's grandfather had paid the VOC to help him out in a succession struggle against his older brother, and once he took the throne he signed a treaty with the Dutchmen, allowing them a plot for an outpost opposite his palace, and a contract for a fixed annual delivery of tin at a prearranged price in silver coin. It was an arrangement that for once was genuinely beneficial to both parties.

Raffles knew about the tin; he was determined to seize Bangka from Palembang, to make it a directly administered British territory and to take control of all the income from the mines. As early as the summer of 1810, back in Calcutta, Raffles had written to Minto of Sultan Badruddin and his tin that 'He knows the facility with which the English might in the event of any misunderstanding take possession of Banca [sic] ... and when he reflects on the probable loss of the immense treasure stated to be in his capital, and which might ensue from any misunderstanding, he will no doubt consider seriously of such terms as may be made to him'.

It is clear that by the time they actually reached Batavia, long before they heard anything of the massacre, Raffles and Minto were absolutely determined to seize Bangka and its mines from Sultan Badruddin. In his October 1811 notes to the Company's Bengal Secret Committee, written up as he was preparing to leave Java, Lord Minto had scribbled under the column headed 'Miscellaneous' that

'Palembang is to be occupied as soon as possible ... With regard to Banca and the tin, the Lieutenant Governor knows my sentiments'.

A warren of lucrative tin mines and an established China trade might just convince their masters in London that the whole rogue Java project was worthwhile. As for the attempts to get Badruddin to evict the Dutch and declare independence ahead of the invasion, it was both mightily Machiavellian and full of foresight. Raffles was not lying when he stressed to the Palembang Sultan the nature of his sovereignty, and declared that the only way to void pre-existing treaties would be to act *before* Batavia fell. But he had long-term British, not Sumatran, interests at heart when he pressed this point.

Even before the first British soldiers came ashore in August 1811, both Raffles and Minto already realised that if ever Holland regained its sovereignty from France, Java would probably have to be handed back. They hated the idea. 'All that I fear is the general peace', Minto had written as he left Batavia in October. They were desperate for the British to hold some kind of tangible, guaranteed legacy in the archipelago, even if the Dutchmen were back in the Javanese jewel itself. What better souvenir to take away from the interregnum than the island of Bangka, which was not only a valuable mining concession, but which also had a rather useful location near the mouth of the Straits of Melaka? If they seized it *after* Janssens capitulated, with Palembang still nominally treaty-bound to Batavia, then it would likely count for nothing, and they would eventually have to give it back along with everything else. But if Palembang was altogether independent at the time of the conquest, then there would be a case – a shaky one, but a case nonetheless – to argue for its British retention.

This is why Raffles had been so frantically trying to induce Sultan Badruddin to throw out the Dutch and sign some new voiding treaty in the early months of 1811. In doing so he had entirely lost sight of the very real danger he was placing the little European community there under.

A commission had been sent to Palembang at the same time as Adams and Crawfurd were dispatched to the Javanese courts. The commissioners arrived at the mouth of the Musi in the middle of November. They were treated with a certain amount of cheerfully evasive prevarication, informed that the Dutch had been 'sent away' several months earlier, shown a number of potentially incriminating letters from Raffles, and offered an apology to their request to take control of the Dutch compound: it no longer existed; the locals had obliterated even the foundations. There was not much more the commissioners could do. They returned to their little cruiser and headed downstream. Between the stands of low jungle they spotted half-clad Malay labourers erecting bamboo palisades and fortified rafts.

Meanwhile, the gallivanting messengers, Raden Mohamed and the Sayyid, had turned up with a terrible tale to tell. Their signed depositions, written in Melaka, reached Batavia on 1 January 1812. On 14 September, as soon as news of the fall of Batavia reached Palembang, they had declared under oath, the Dutchmen and their native staff had been separated from the women and shipped off downstream to be murdered somewhere near the mouth of the Musi. Sultan Badruddin, eager to make it look as though he really *had* made himself independent long before the British conquest, had then had the Dutch compound razed to the ground. When someone suggested that this might be unlawful he furiously responded that 'I am not like other Native Princes, I dread nobody, I fear no nation'. The two mortified messengers had been forced to swear that they would never reveal the truth lest all their relatives at Palembang should be murdered. They then fled without their baggage, and, showing a decided lack of concern for their supposed kinsmen, they spilled everything to the first Englishmen they met.

Raffles responded remarkably coolly to all of this, writing to Minto that 'there can be but one opinion on the policy we ought to pursue. We evidently, I think, must break with him [Sultan Badruddin], block up his River which we can do with three or four cruisers, and establish ourselves on Banca.' Instead of suffering pangs of guilt at the fate of the Dutchmen (what had become of their wives was still a mystery), Raffles was delighted to have been handed a perfect pretext for a project that had been planned all along.

As the wet season rolled on and the mildew sprouted on the white walls of the Buitenzorg residence preparations were made for another military adventure. Gillespie, who had been cooling his heels and doubtless beginning to see things he disliked in the way that the young Lieutenant-Governor was running the show, was delighted. A river, a jungle, a tyrannical Asiatic despot in a blood-soaked palace: only the prospect of a delicate young damsel on horseback was likely to leave the little colonel in a more heightened state of arousal.

Raffles wrote to Minto again on 10 March to explain what he was planning. He was, he realised, acting without any higher authority by organising an invasion of a Sumatran principality, but believed he was doing 'what is right and best for the British Interests', and that 'the present opportunity of obtaining Banca should not be passed by ... I am inclined to contemplate the present state of affairs as fortunate for the eventual security of our interests in that quarter'. Two dozen Dutchmen might have been murdered, but everything was perfect. Raffles even remembered those rumoured warehouses full of dollars and bullion: he had instructed Gillespie to levy a fine on Sultan Badruddin to cover the cost of the expedition. He perhaps had an inkling that the correspondence of the previous year might one day come back to haunt him, especially if the Dutch ever returned to the East Indies and started asking questions about the massacre of their countrymen. It was a little unfortunate that the Sultan had so promptly presented his letters to the commissioners back in November, he wrote, and had 'to serve his own purposes, grossly perverted the meaning and intention of the same'. But what mattered now was the expedition.

Several hundred men and eleven ships were prepared as the rain rattled down over Batavia Bay. Raffles told Gillespie to dethrone Badruddin and replace him with his brother. But in case the fiery little soldier's blood got too hot, and the thought of avenging butchered white men led him to lose sight of his real aims, Raffles reminded him that the punishment of the Sultan for what he had done was not the most important task; in fact, if it proved too costly, dangerous or difficult, he wasn't even to bother trying: 'The possession of Banca is to be the *sine qua non*, whether the same is to be obtained by cession, or by the mere act of settling there.'

And with that, on 20 March 1812, Gillespie and his men set sail under a stormy sky, bearing northwest as best they could in the squally seas, heading for the heart of darkness. Raffles watched them go. '[W]hen we negotiate with arms in our hands, the slightest circumstance will give rise to actual hostilities', he wrote to Minto the following morning.

* * *

They raised their anchors at sunset. The murky boils bubbling over the bar showed that the tide had changed and was beginning to flood upstream into the jungle. The sky was the colour of bruised flesh. Slowly, uncertainly, wallowing in the flow, the fleet began to move south along the Musi, away from the sea. No trails of pale cooking smoke rose from the little bamboo-and-thatch village of Sungsang on the muddy promontory to the right; no dug-out canoes slithered through the shallows. The place was deserted, and beyond it the forest was vast and dark. It was the evening of 18 April 1812.

It had taken them a month to get this far. Gillespie's fleet had had to battle against bad winds and contrary currents all the way from Batavia. Afternoon rain squalls had lashed the rigging, and the short, choppy swells of an island-filled sea had slapped against the hulls. The sloops, cruisers, and lumbering transport ships had finally slipped into the calmer waters of the channel between Bangka and the blank Sumatran shoreline at the start of April. For a week they had anchored off the little outcrop of Pulau Nangka, Jackfruit Island, a place of wild pigs and pirate hideouts.

From Pulau Nangka it took them another five days, creeping up the channel, to reach the mouth of the Musi, and another two days after that for the whole fleet to leapfrog the muddy bar on the peak of the transient tides. All the while the enormity of the green emptiness of Sumatra loomed to the west. On the night of 17 April another violent storm lashed its way out of the hinterlands and ripped the awnings of the open boats to shreds. They had still had had no word from Palembang or the dark personage of Sultan Badruddin. A few open war canoes, bristling with spear-carrying Malays, had showed on the cusp of the first bend of the river at one point as the British were waiting for the tide, but they had vanished upstream as soon as a posse of longboats set out in pursuit. The fishing hamlets on the foreshore had all been abandoned.

Everything about the place seemed dark and strange and unsettling, and as they began their upstream journey into the dusk on the evening of 18 April the British soldiers must have peered out nervously at the land around them. The river here was a great brown smudge, 600 yards across. The walls of the forest were black and forbidding, and the cries of strange animals and the lingering whistles of weird insects carried out across the water. The tide took them ten miles upstream and they anchored at midnight, deep inside Sumatra. Far away to the south, towards Palembang, lightning flickered against a blank sky.

They rode in the same spot throughout the morning of the following day. There was no wind; there was precious little oxygen it seemed. No more war canoes showed upstream; no message came from the Sultan. A whisper of a mud-and-salt-scented breeze rose in the afternoon, and they crept on upstream on a feeble flood tide. The river was beginning to narrow now, the walls of the forest closing in on either side, and several times the masts of the boats got tangled in the low branches during the night. At dawn they were at anchor once more, and a native longboat was slicing towards them from upstream, the Malay oarsmen oily with sweat as they paddled. The boat was carrying a messenger from the court. What, he requested to know, did Gillespie want?

This business of a creeping advance by ship, dependent on a dwindling tide, was not what Gillespie was used to. There was no chance for a headlong and heroic charge here, and even he must have been unsettled by the surrounding forest. But still, he managed to tell the messenger that he would not go into details until he met the Sultan face-to-face. Badruddin was to remain in his palace until the fleet arrived, and if he tried to flee he would 'be pursued by the British force with fire and sword, to the utmost extent of his empire'. The messenger's longboat retreated upstream, and an hour before sunset Gillespie's men hauled up the mud-smeared anchors and crept on towards Palembang on the vestiges of the flood.

Over the next two days the fleet inched up the river, the jungle drew closer, and several more messages were borne up and downstream in native canoes. A note from Badruddin was full of friendly sentiments for the commander, and expressed the hope that 'may he enjoy long life and prosperity in this world!' Gillespie was unimpressed and sent back a stern warning to the palace and an assurance to the common people that he was 'happy to announce to the inhabitants of Palembang, the most friendly disposition on the part of the English Government towards them'. In the afternoons great columns of purple-grey rain marched out of the forest and turned the surface of the river into a dancing carpet of droplets. The British soldiers alternately shivered and sweated under the tattered awnings of their little ships. In the steaming sunrise of 22 April, Gillespie and his men passed the first villages they had seen since the abandoned hamlets at Sungsang. These were miserable places of drunken huts and skinny chickens, but around a crooked bend in the river they spotted the great bamboo palisades, the readied fire rafts and the rugged batteries of Borang. They were twenty miles from Palembang and the skies were growing darker by the day.

This far up the river the flood of the incoming tide did little more than bring the flow to a stagnant standstill, but a fleet of British longboats pulled upstream to take a closer look at the fortifications. It was a strange and threatening spot. A murky tributary ran into the Musi here, and there were bamboo barricades along the banks of the little promontory it formed. In the shallows before them sharpened branches had been fixed to baffle any would-be landing party, and most ominously of all, long strings of fire rafts were moored in midstream, great bundles of kindling on wallowing bamboo platforms that could be set alight and cut loose to drift down towards an advancing fleet. Malay soldiers with muskets and spears were clambering all over these defences, and armed war canoes were strung along the shore.

The rain went on all afternoon that day, and long into the night thunder crackled over the forest. The next day was dark and wet too. There had been another message from the Sultan, requesting Gillespie to proceed to the palace unarmed – and a sensible refusal from the little commander in response. There was a strange quibbling with a messenger over the batteries, a little waterborne scuffling between longboats and war canoes in midstream, and then, for all the formidable palisades, for all the sharp spikes poking out from the muddy water, on April 24, Gillespie and 'a small but formidable array of the British advance' paddled up to the Borang fortifications and found that they had already been abandoned.

It ought to have been a moment of celebration, but somehow it only set the Englishmen still further on edge. What exactly was going on? Why had the defenders fled, and what on earth was happening twenty miles further up the Musi in Palembang itself? Captain Thorn, Gillespie's friend and future biographer, was in the advance, and in his account of the journey he hinted at the frightened frustration as they edged towards their dark destination. 'Where the chiefs of a nation act with so much treachery, and where the breach of faith uniformly marks their character, it is a most unpleasant and difficult task for a generous mind to counteract and oppose their proceedings', he wrote.

That night there were lights flickering in the forest on either side, and several burning rafts did come floating down the river, the flames doubled up in reflection on the oily surface of the Musi. These rafts were 'extremely dangerous, when once in a blaze, to ships coming in the opposite direction', and British rowboats criss-crossed the flow frantically trying to cut them apart and to sink them before they crashed into the ships of the advance. In the smouldering morning, here and there a burnt-out fire raft lodged in the overhanging branches of the banks, two Arabs arrived amongst the British boats. Word had reached the town that the British had passed the amphibious barricades, they said, and in the strange, flame-lit hours of the night Sultan Badruddin, along with his inner circle and the women of his harem, had fled to the forest. Palembang had descended into anarchy.

'Upon this, Colonel Gillespie resolved to lose not a moment,' Captain Thorn reported, 'but to hasten by the quickest possible manner, to put a stop to the scene of horror, and by his immediate presence, prevent the execution of the massacre, which it was reported the Sultan's adherents meditated to perpetrate the very next night, upon the wealthy Chinese and other inhabitants'. These may indeed have been the honourable motivations in mind as Gillespie, a clutch of officers and seventeen grenadiers clambered into the Arabs' canoes, and another gaggle of flustered redcoats scrambled into the fastest of the British launches, but the thought of gold-filled godowns falling to the looters must surely have proved a powerful imperative too.

The four little crafts cut upstream, native paddles and English oars gulping into the oily brown water. Here and there a local dugout fled into some hidden creek at their advance, and by nightfall they were sliding between the first of the riverbank *kampungs* that lined the approach to Palembang. Any hint of a sunset over the forest was lost behind great walls of black cloud, crackling with angry electricity. A single gunshot echoed out through the trees ahead; fires began to flicker through the *kampungs*, and as the rain began to patter down like falling bullets a chorus of weird shrieks and feverish yells rose on either side. The eyes of the men in the boats must have flashed fearfully in the gloom. As one of them wrote 'every thing around us tended to excite suspicion of some treacherous design being in agitation'. The launches had fallen behind the swifter Arab canoes, but now the English oarsmen began to pull more frantically, desperate to bring themselves closer to the reassuring presence of Rollo Gillespie. If they were about to enter some kind of unhappy underworld then the little colonel might be the only talisman that could keep them safe.

They came ashore in the torrential rain at 8 o'clock, under the towering black walls of the Palembang Palace. Seventeen sodden grenadiers, a clutch of bedraggled officers, and a few exhausted rowers clambered from the canoes and launches and passed 'through a multitude of Arabs and treacherous Malays, whose missile weapons, steeped in poison, glimmered by the light of torches'. Palembang had, it seemed, succumbed to carnage:

To paint the horrors of the scene that presented itself to our view in proper colours, or to attempt an expression of the sensations it was calculated to excite, would be a difficult task. Romance never described any thing half so hideous, nor has the invention of the imagination ever given representations equally appalling, with what here struck us in reality.

The rain was roaring out of an inky sky; the crowd around them seemed on the edge of violent hysteria, and everything was lit by the slow strobe of the lightning. The way from the water's edge to the grim gates of the palace presented 'the frightful spectacle of human blood, still reeking and flowing on the pavement'. Even Gillespie must have felt his courage falter – this was all weirder, wilder and darker than anything he had seen in the Caribbean or in India. But he still had his wits about him, for as they edged through the shifting crowd he spotted a Malay *kris* in the hand of a man who had sidled up alongside him. A flash of lighting had shone for a moment on the blade as the would-be assassin slipped it into his sleeve: 'The Colonel's eyes caught the object, and instantly turning round, he had the fellow seized, totally regardless of the crowd'. The *kris* clattered to the blood-splattered cobbles; its owner somehow wriggled away into the liquid night, and the British party pressed on into the once-forbidden palace, which now looked more like a slaughterhouse. The rain was roaring down, sheeting from the battlements; 'the place was completely ransacked, the pavements and floors were clotted with blood', and 'In every direction spectacles of woe caught our sight, and [were] rendered particularly awful by the glare of the surrounding conflagration, and vivid flashes of lightning, amidst loud peals of thunder.' Palembang was going up in flames. The lengths of hollow bamboo that made up the walls and floors of the native houses were popping and crackling like gunfire in the heat, despite the downpour, and a great seething mass of unsettled humanity was at large in the darkness. The circumstances, wrote Captain Thorn, 'altogether gave our situation a most appalling prospect'.

Gillespie ordered them to barricade themselves in the heart of the looted palace. There was, it seemed, no trace of the fabled treasure; Badruddin had carried it all off into the jungle, but at this stage no one really cared. The British had contrived to take control of the Palembang Palace without having fired a shot, but all that the little advance hoped for now was to survive the night. Whether they would have made it until morning unsupported cannot be guessed, but many others outside the palace – Chinamen and locals, and the crews of visiting vessels – would surely have died had another party of British soldiers not somehow made it upstream through the rain on what remained of the tide. They came ashore at midnight and joined Gillespie. The sight of the sixty soggy soldiers was enough to send the huge mobs of rioters heading homewards through the darkness. There had been no battle for Palembang – at least none that the British had fought in – but the town had fallen.

* * *

Gillespie had seized a city that was on the verge of vanishing into the void of anarchic oblivion. Just what unseen tensions and unrequited hatreds had been unstopped by his advance and Sultan Badruddin's retreat cannot be known, but a large portion of the inhabitants had gone on the rampage – and those who hadn't had either fled, or were dead. As well as the demise of the Dutchmen and their servants Raffles' incautious letters of the previous year had indirectly and inadvertently led to the deaths of untold others in Palembang.

The embittered Badruddin – who would later protest, letters in hand, that the Englishmen had only got exactly what they asked for with the annihilation of the Dutch – was somewhere far away in the forest, and for all Gillespie's earlier threats to pursue him, he and his treasure were out of reach. The town itself was a weird and bloody ruin. The rest of the British advance dribbled up the Musi over the coming days. In his glowing public account of the adventure, Captain Thorn mentioned the 'feeling regard for the interests of humanity which always distinguishes the British character' and claimed that it had such a soothing effect that 'the inhabitants assumed confidence, and many who had fled into the woods returned to their homes'. This is contradicted somewhat by the records of Gillespie's actual letters and proclamations. On 27 April he was compelled to declare that 'It is with pain the General commanding the British Forces observes that the natives are alarmed, and have no confidence in the English, and are flying in all directions.' He tried to assure them that 'their property will be safe, and their wives and families will be respected, and nothing but hostility on their part can provoke it on ours'.

The accounts of those first days as the British took stock of the blood-soaked palace are patchy to say the least. But it seems fairly clear that many of the natives were still steering very well clear of the town, and very few people were telling the truth. Messages were sent to Badruddin's brother, the Prince Adipati, who was now destined to rule, whether he liked it or not, as Sultan Najmuddin, telling him to come out from wherever he was hiding, and to treat with his new masters.

Meanwhile, Gillespie set about the hopeless task of trying to find out what exactly had gone on back in September when the massacre took place. 'I have been occasionally so bewildered by falsehood, guilt, and prevarications, that I have experienced considerable difficulty in selecting the evidences most worthy of attention', he wrote. But eventually he latched onto a tall tale that made not Sultan Badruddin himself, but his grotesque son, the Pangeran Ratu, the Crown Prince, the true villain of the piece. Gillespie seems never actually to have met the Crown Prince, who was sensibly skulking in the jungle along with everyone else, but he nonetheless declared him to be 'one of the most abominable and unprincipled villains that ever disgraced humanity'. He was an 'iniquitous monster' who liked nothing better than 'spearing the unhappy and defenceless wretches whom he accidentally encountered in his lawless excursions, or of sacrificing their wives and daughters to his abandoned cruelty and passions'. According to the tale that Gillespie's informants spun, the Crown Prince had ordered the Dutch community destroyed after they intervened to stop him raping a Chinese woman.

It was certainly a dramatic tale, and it made no mention of inciting letters from an Englishman. But it was unlikely to be true. For one, there was no hint of it in the eyewitness depositions from Raffles' messengers, and if, as Gillespie claimed, the Crown Prince was popularly held in Palembang with 'one common sentiment of horror, hatred, and indignation' then he could hardly have wielded the influence to command such a comprehensive annihilation of not only the Dutch themselves, but even of every last foundation stone of their compound. He almost certainly *had* been involved in the massacre, but then so had everyone else, including the 'mild and beneficent character' that Gillespie was planning to place on the gore-splattered throne – the Prince Adipati. It seems likely that those courtiers still on the scene had simply decided to let the despised Crown Prince – who probably *was* a lecherous libertine – take the flack.

On 28 April a Union Jack was run up the flagpole above the palace – where the pools of blood had turned to black stains between the rainstorms – and the hapless Adipati came out of hiding to meet with Gillespie the same day. But what exactly the British themselves had been doing in the interim is unclear. Despite Captain Thorn's protestations of British humanity, when a native palace fell to the redcoats in the 1800s, looting – and sometimes worse – was very much the order of the day, as we will see when we get back to Java. Rumours that Gillespie himself personally embarked on certain outrages worthy of the Crown Prince eventually came to light many months later – stories carried out of the Sumatran darkness by a troublemaker we have met already and will meet again. There are no records, and no eyewitness accounts of course, but judging from everything else that had gone on there, Palembang in the wet season was certainly a place that brought out the worst in people.

* * *

On 1 May a rumour did the rounds of a fresh conflagration: 'various reports were circulated of a body of Malays having resolved upon running a Muck, which is a desperate custom peculiar to this people', wrote Captain Thorn.

'Amok' is part of the tiny pinch of spice that Malay has added to the bubbling semantic stew of the English language, and the concept – of native Southeast Asians, individually or en masse, going on a frenzied, *kris*-wielding rampage – was one that preoccupied many a 19th-century colonialist. Though most of the contemporary accounts of people running amok appear to be nothing more than a description of a conventional alcohol or drug-fuelled rage or the last stand of a desperate party of professional soldiers, and while it is perfectly obvious that the practice was by no means unique to Southeast Asia (the only perfect synonym for *amok* is drawn, not from the exotic East, but from chilly Norway – *berserk*), the idea quickly became one of the most potent in all the negative European impressions of 'the Malay races', along with their alleged 'laziness'. The very word 'amok' was enough to leave an Englishman or a Hollander trembling in his boots.[14]

The planned outburst of 1 May, however, did not come to pass. Precautions were put in place, and though fires flickered in the distance and 'a considerable uproar' was heard in the hours of darkness from the eastern edge of the town, major mischief was prevented. Palembang was still smouldering between the rainstorms, and much of it was still uninhabited, but preparations were underway for a coronation. The miserable Prince Adipati came and went from the palace, the window frames from the demolished Dutch compound were discovered stacked up in a garden a couple of miles upstream, and other traces of recycled Dutch masonry were detected in a half-built harem behind the Sultan's ransacked quarters.

The unfortunate female refugees from the September massacre, meanwhile, had been retrieved from the jungle. They had, Gillespie wrote to Raffles, been 'sent as slaves up the country, and the relation of

---

14 Amok, or amuck, is the anglicised version of the root of a proper Malay verb, *mengamuk*, which means, quite simply, 'to run amok'. 19th-century descriptions of the practice were certainly bloodcurdling:

When the cry 'amok! amok!' is raised, people fly to the right and left for shelter, and after the blinded madman's kris has once 'drunk blood,' his fury becomes ungovernable, his sole desire is to kill; he strikes here and there, he stabs fugitives in the back, his kris drips blood, he rushes on yet more wildly, blood and murder in his course; there are shrieks and groans, his bloodshot eyes start from their sockets, his frenzy gives him unnatural strength, then all of a sudden he drops, shot through the heart, or from sudden exhaustion, clutching his bloody kris.

In VOC Batavia the police were even issued with special equipment – a kind of spiky cleft stick – with which to restrain such maniacs. However, despite its enduring association with Southeast Asia, there is considerable evidence that the word and the idea comes originally from southern India, and in its four pages dedicated to the subject, *Hobson Jobson*, the great dictionary-encyclopaedia of the British Empire in Asia comes up with more examples of the practice from non-Malays than Malays: everyone was running amok from Sikh soldiers in the Punjab to Spanish sailors in Liverpool ...

distress, starvation, and misery they encountered in their bondage, is calculated to excite such sentiments of horror and indignation against the whole race, that at times I can with difficulty hold intercourse with people allied to such monsters of barbarity.' Unsurprisingly they were rather pleased to have been rescued, and Gillespie was making arrangements to ship them out to civilisation.

Despite the simulacrum of British order, Palembang was still in an unsettled state. On 3 May an unfortunate misunderstanding almost brought the bamboo walls crashing down once more. Stomping around the town, a patrol of British soldiers happened to spot a certain number of spears being carried from a boat into a rather grand native house. Still understandably unsettled by the petrifying prospect of amok, and doubtless brim full of 'horror and indignation' against the entire Malay race, they burst into the house, where a party of rather well-dressed natives were engaged in a very serious discussion. Predictably startled – not to mention greatly offended – by this sudden and boorish intrusion, the men leapt to their feet and 'one of the chiefs drew his criss and struck a blow at the Officer who commanded the party'. He missed, but one of the British soldiers stabbed him through the stomach with a sword by way of recompense.

Clearly all natives looked alike to the redcoats: the men they had attacked included the Arab who had kindly conducted them into Palembang on the night of 25 April, and the man they were about to place on the throne, Prince Adipati. The gathering was a meeting to discuss the unenviable challenges of the coming administration; the spears being carried from the boat were the royal regalia. Fortunately the Adipati himself had escaped through the backdoor and fled, as had the Arab, who dashed to the palace to tell Gillespie what was happening. Meanwhile, the patrol began liberally relieving the rest of the Malay nobles of their 'spears richly gilt and crisses set with diamonds, as trophies of their triumph'. The bayoneted chief was quietly bleeding to death in a corner.

As a result of this monumental blunder, of the kind that still seems to occur all too often in occupied countries today, 'the result of several weeks anxious solicitude in the settlement of a permanent government, was rent asunder'. Mortified messengers came running from the palace within minutes; all the loot was handed back, and a medic even arrived just in time to watch the wounded man die. But if the Prince Adipati had been a reluctant heir assumptive from the start, he had now altogether had enough and had retreated once more to some outlying house in the forest. The handful of commoners who had crept out of hiding, meanwhile, were now entirely convinced that claims of English humanity were barefaced lies, and had vanished again amongst the trees.

Gillespie sent a grovelling letter to the Adipati and actually went into the forest to say sorry in person the following day. He also hammered out a lengthy public apology to the locals. It had all been a horrible mistake, he assured them; it couldn't possibly happen again: 'every precaution will be taken to prevent similar mistakes in future. Such of the inhabitants as may have left their houses in consequence of this unfortunate affair are invited to return, and may rest assured, that a repetition of the same cannot possibly occur.'

The coronation finally went ahead eleven days later. In the morning, before the black rainclouds had time to roll in, the Adipati and the un-bayoneted members of his entourage arrived at the palace by boat. He was led up the steps from the water between columns of redcoats at arms (he must have glanced nervously at their gleaming swords). Inside the gates, until recently unsullied by the presence of Europeans, a gaggle of white officers in full uniform were standing on a stage hung with royal yellow banners while a frightened audience of press-ganged locals sat cross-legged on the floor at their feet.

The dazed Adipati was tugged and prodded to a couch covered in red cloth where he was seated alongside Gillespie. A proclamation was then read, declaring that:

The Commander of the British Forces, in virtue of Powers vested in him by the Government of Java, hereby declares the said Mahmoud Badruddin, to be deposed from the Throne of this Kingdom. And the Commander of the Forces, in consideration of the virtues of Pangerang Adipati, and of the love, esteem and veneration with which he is regarded by the Natives, Inhabitants of this Country, as well as the Arab and Chinese colonists, has, in pursuance of his instructions, selected the said Pangerang Adipati, to fill the vacant Throne of this Kingdom.

According to the watching Englishmen, the Adipati 'was evidently much affected by the notice taken of his brother's crimes': he was spotted dabbing the corners of his eyes with a handkerchief during the proclamation. He may have been mourning the massacre; more likely he was actually mourning his own prospects. Neither the British nor the Dutch ever seemed really to appreciate the true nature of kingship in Indonesia, to realise that simply handing someone the crown meant nothing if a sense of legitimacy that might well be connected to supernatural forces was missing. Palembang lacked the refinement of Java, and royal legitimacy there might not have been rooted in the ownership of sacred, power-charged ancestral heirlooms. But it still required courtly ascent. It also required the particular mystical energy – and financial clout – provided by possession of the royal treasure, and Badruddin had buried *that* somewhere in the jungle.

Snivelling slightly, the new sultan was led by the hand and plonked on the throne by Gillespie himself. A 21-gun salute thundered out over the forest from the British artillery lined up outside, and the Union Jack came down and the Palembang Royal Standard went up the flagpole. The Adipati was not allowed to move into his palace immediately however. The British weren't quite ready to leave the town, and they certainly weren't going to vacate their quarters for a mere native. The coronation over, he was bustled back down the steps to the river and sent back to his old house on the outskirts.

Gillespie and his men eventually got underway three days later, their little fleet rolling off down the Musi and leaving what was left of Palembang behind. The Adipati had begged them to stay, fearing that his rule might be over before his vanishing benefactors even reached the sea, but Gillespie had made soothing noises and left him 'in the most confident assurance of his safety and strength'. He also left him with a signed treaty. It declared, amongst other things, that whenever the Adipati managed to recover Badruddin's treasure, he would promptly forward fully half of it to the British. This seemed a little unfair, as the principal clause of the treaty had already deprived the Palembang palace of its main means of replenishing its coffers. The eternally grateful, ever tearful new sultan had been obliged to cede 'full and unlimited Sovereignty to His Majesty the King of Great Britain and the Hon, English East India Company, the islands of Banca and Billiton [Belitung]'.

The whole grubby business had been a great success, the inability of Gillespie's men to get their hands on the fabled royal bullion notwithstanding. In fact, even while they were making their strange and unsettling journey up the Musi, several hundred Bengal Sepoys and requisitioned Dutch Indonesian troops had been left behind at the river mouth to pre-empt the treaty. By the time Gillespie reached open water they had already done their work; Bangka was now called Duke of York's Island, and Muntok, the little capital where the tin boats docked and the Chinese miners gathered to drink and gamble of an evening, had been renamed Minto, 'in honour of the Right Honourable Governor General of all India ...'

Raffles was delighted when he heard the news. He issued a formal statement congratulating Gillespie on his efforts and declaring that 'The successful termination of these operations, in a manner so highly beneficial to the interests of humanity, and to the security and advantage of the British possessions in those seas, must be entirely attributed to the prompt, judicious, and politic measures adopted under the personal direction of the Commander of the Forces'. The tensions between the two men that would before long turn into a protracted and bitter war were already in play – brought to the fore over the question of the military budget for the most part – and Raffles had already written to Minto about the Commander of the

Forces to tell him that 'It is quite unnecessary that I should inform your Lordship that I have rather a strange character to deal with'. But the Palembang expedition was precisely what he needed a soldier like Gillespie for. Raffles could decide like a Roman emperor that some far-off king must fall; he could point the undersized Commander of the Forces in that vague direction with perfect confidence, trouble himself not at all about the actual business of flying bullets, and knuckle down to plotting land reforms – or coming up with some new military project to test Gillespie's skills.

Raffles might not have succeeded in his earlier plan to incite Sultan Badruddin to oust the Dutch from his realm ahead of the British advance, but with that same chieftain now unceremoniously ditched on the grounds that the men he had killed were de facto British subjects and that if 'those occurrences are allowed to pass over unnoticed or unpunished, the British character would be compromised', he now continued to engage in a series of mind-bending mental gymnastics. No other European nation, he declared, had ever laid claim to Bangka (regardless of the fact that it was always a legitimate territory of the Dutch vassal Palembang). There was therefore no need whatsoever to regard it as an indirect dependency of Java; Britain could retain it for ever more, whatever happened to the former Dutch territories in the future. Unsurprisingly, no one else was ever able to follow his logic on this point.

Palembang in 1812 had not been a pleasant episode. It was not just a reflection of the ruthlessness that Raffles himself was sometimes capable of; it was a manifestation of all the ugliness, all the twisted motives and crooked logic that European colonialism could at times muster in its quest for lucre. Schools, railways, traffic regulations and cricket ought to count for something – and they do. But they do not excuse or outweigh the fact that for more than three centuries in Asia, hearts of the utmost darkness often beat behind civilian buttonholes and military medals.

* * *

Palembang had been yet another episode of bravery, blood and guts for Colonel Rollo Gillespie. He set sail from Bangka on 22 May in a schooner called the *Wellington*. The rest of the advance – those left behind to keep possession of the newly acquired islands excepted – would lumber along in his wake in the transport ships. It was another stormy passage. The wet season was already coming to an end, but stray squalls and pistol-crack cloud-breaks still stalked the Straits of Sunda. A little wobbly on his feet, Gillespie reached Batavia on 1 June 1812 to find that his erstwhile future enemy was not at home in Buitenzorg, and that the troops he had left behind were not in their barracks in Weltevreeden. An urgent message was waiting for him. He was to proceed as quickly as possible along the Post Road to Semarang, and to bring his battle gear. Palembang, it seemed, had been just the dress rehearsal: while Gillespie was gone Thomas Stamford Raffles had resolved to run amok in Central Java.

* * *

While Gillespie had been gallivanting in Palembang, Raffles had been pacing his office in Buitenzorg, dictating like a demon and demanding that everything be written out in triplicate as the warm rain thundered down outside. Watching doe-eyed from the sidelines Otho Travers was enthralled by his master's energy – 'As a public servant, no man could apply himself with more zeal and attention to the arduous duties of his office'. Another observer was somewhat less enamoured, however.

When Lord Minto left for India, Captain William Robison had been appointed Assistant Government Secretary, but the antipathy that Raffles seems to have already felt for him made his job a difficult one. What was more, Robison claimed that the chaotic working practices of the Lieutenant-Governor left him at a loss to know how to continue. A jealous inability to delegate was a major part of the problem: 'He took so much in hand himself and appeared to place so little confidence in me that I was frequently at a loss what

I should and what I should not do', Robison complained. Raffles' own take on all this was that it was the secretary who was at fault, for he 'considered his appointment as a simple reward' rather than a job that actually needed doing. Robison was clearly not a man who responded well to being bullied, and as their relationship deteriorated further he doubtless became less and less inclined to knuckle down. But his version of Raffles at work is echoed in the Dutch accounts of the administrative chaos they encountered when they eventually returned to Java. Raffles, they conceded, had been spectacularly prolific, with reports, projects, accounts and proposals piled ceiling-high in the government offices. The problem, however, was that there was very little discernible method in the madness.

In any case, by the end of 1811 Robison had had enough: 'the most marked displeasure was shown me by the Lieut. Governor,' he wrote to Lord Minto, 'and his proceedings became such towards me as to put it out of my power to continue in the office of secretary with any degree of credit to myself'. He resigned from his post and took a job in the translation department.

While office politics were at play in her husband's workplace, Olivia Raffles was busy too. In January she had written a gushing letter to Lord Minto telling him in a strange, slanting hand full of emphatic underscorings that she could 'only assure you in the simple language of the heart that it throbs with affection as dear and as tender for you as ever a child's did for a father':

You my Lord gave me a right to call you so when at Malacca you desired me to consider myself your Daughter, happy me, and this right, this dear right, I will only resign with my last breath. I am proud and selfish enough not to make distinction in favour of those, your Daughters excepted, who now engage you to the exclusion of me from the place you said I should have in your memory ...

Students of the new science of Freudian psychoanalysis later in the century would have made much mileage out of all *that*. Minto himself was rather touched, especially by Olivia's desire 'to see your Lordship once again before you leave India ... I shall hope to see you here one day in <u>your country</u>, this beautiful Java ...'

Olivia was also still reeling from the sight of all those ghastly Dutchwomen at the first Batavia ball, and as First Lady of European Java she had appointed herself Trend-setter Number One. Tottering from gay gathering to gay gathering and doing her best to ignore the niggling pain in her liver that would drag her down before many months had passed, she led by example. A lady of fashion should most certainly *not* be out and about in some kind of hideous semi-native get-up, and as for the repulsive business of chewing betel nut, long an afternoon pastime for the wives of Dutch Batavia, it needed to stop at once!

Though the interdiction against the betel was reportedly a matter of some consternation and debate on Dutch verandas, Olivia's ideas about clothing do seem rapidly to have caught on. By May 1812 sarongs and *kebayas* were thoroughly *passé*, as a report from the newly launched *Java Government Gazette* reveals:

At the entertainment recently given at Batavia it was remarked how great an improvement has been introduced in respect to the attire of the Dutch Ladies, since the British authority has been established. The Cabaya appears now generally disused and the more elegant English costume adopted ...

The *Gazette* had first rolled off the presses and been sent out to subscribers in February 1812. It appeared every Saturday for the rest of the British Interregnum in Java, under the management of one Amos H. Hubbard, the second son of a Connecticut newspaper-owner. The paper was a broadsheet, printed on coarse, creamy paper, and it usually ran to only four pages. It was an official government mouthpiece, of course, but there was more to the *Gazette* than propaganda. Its front page was dappled with bizarre advertisements for everything from pickled herrings to domestic slaves, and the correspondence columns were filled with proudly patriotic poems and bloodcurdling accounts of native customs on outlying islands. The back half of the paper was usually filled with six-months-old European news, but there were also various titbits on local happenings – in April 1812, for example, a pair of Indians had robbed their English employer in Surabaya and gone on the run:

One of them is a robust looking man, about 35 years of age, and has lost many of his front teeth; he speaks the Malay language tolerable fluently, and has rather an effeminate voice. The other is a very tall, thin, black, miserable looking creature, has no one good quality to recommend him and may be easily known from his great stupidity which approaches nearly to idiotism ...

The *Gazette* also had a strong editorial line of its own, and it celebrated the news of the dethronement of Sultan Badruddin of Palembang in fulsome language. It was marvellous, the editor felt, that 'such a monster should be deposed and hurled headlong from an authority which he has so barbarously and outrageously abused'. Before long the *Gazette* would have another victory and the unseating of another Asiatic despot to report and to editorialise over, for by the time the reports of the Palembang adventure went public Raffles was already swinging hard for Yogyakarta.

* * *

That Raffles had already decided that he needed to extract absolute submission from the Javanese is obvious. Back in January, after his first testy visit to Central Java, he had written to Minto that 'the importance of these Courts in every thing which concerns the arrangements in Java, is much more than I contemplated at first or than I believe was contemplated by your Lordship'.

There were probably several motivations at play in his desire for dominance. Practicality certainly came into it: Raffles' plans for Java were broad and ambitious, and having to tiptoe around a pair of jealous, protocol-bound kings would likely interfere with sweeping – and potentially antagonistic – reforms. There was also the issue of national pride. 'Strange as it may appear', Raffles wrote to Minto, 'the Sultan [of Yogyakarta] decidedly looks upon us as a less powerful people than the [Napoleonic] Government which proceeded us, and it becomes absolutely necessary for the tranquillity of the Country that he should be taught to think otherwise'. Far from the liberal reformer of biographers' legend, this is Raffles as a swaggering imperialist of the first order, and a man rather enjoying imbibing from the cup of unlimited personal power.

And by the time the 1812 wet season dribbled to a halt, Raffles also had a thin pretext for violence. Way back in October 1811 a secret correspondence had opened between the long-estranged Javanese royals, fragrant missives in refined courtly language shuttling back and forth between Yogyakarta and Surakarta. It was the slippery Susuhunan who had sent the first letter. Those unrealistic aspirations were in play once more, and he had embarked on Machiavellian machinations that rivalled Raffles' own earlier incitement of Palembang – and that would ultimately have equally catastrophic consequences for the recipient. The Susuhunan was trying to encourage the Sultan of Yogyakarta to rise against the British, offering hollow promises that the Surakarta legions would follow his lead if he did so. His motives were obvious: Mataram had been divided for almost six decades; the partition had been a humiliation for the Susuhunan's own father, Pakubuwono III. Now, he believed, if he was able to provoke a situation which would make Yogyakarta a *kraton non grata* with the European power of the moment, then perhaps there was a chance that he, the Susuhunan of Surakarta, could become once more the paramount, unrivalled royal of the Javanese universe, whether as an English vassal or a truly independent chief.

The British seem to have been made aware of this correspondence sometime in early April 1812 by an ambitious and unpatriotic junior

Yogyakarta prince called Pakualam, a half-brother of the Sultan with an eager eye on a possibly soon-to-be-vacant throne, and a mutually beneficial working relationship with John Crawfurd.[15] Of course, it should by rights have been Surakarta which received the full brunt of any chastisement, and indeed, Raffles noted that the Susuhunan was 'far from deserving of the consideration he met', and that 'both Courts require a lesson which may impress upon them the Character and power of our Government'. But it was the younger, haughtier, more luminous court that really rankled with the Lieutenant-Governor. It didn't really matter who was the guilty party in the conspiratorial correspondence, for Raffles had already decided what he would do: 'I shall immediately adopt decisive measures with regard to Djocjocarta'.

* * *

On 23 May Raffles, Olivia and a full entourage headed east along the coast to Semarang to set up a forward base for the coming attempt to cow the courts. Semarang was an old town with a huge Chinese quarter and a burgeoning colonial district of sturdy homes and warehouses with hipped red roofs. On 4 June the British marked the 74th birthday of King George III at the residency there with a party of epic proportions. Things kicked off in the middle of the afternoon, and the members of the 'gay and fashionable assemblage' were still going hard nine hours later when they were called in to a midnight dinner. Predictably it was Olivia Raffles who was the focal point of the orbiting partygoers. She was 'an amiable and animated Hostess who on this particular occasion exerted to the utmost her well-known affability and pleasing manners which we never remember to have seen equalled by anyone', the Gazette recorded. Favourite amongst

---

15 Pakualam was actually known by his given name, Notokusumo, at this stage. Pakualam – meaning 'the Nail of the World' – was a title he took later on.

the energetic dancers was a recently composed hit tune, 'The Fall of Cornelis', and after the witching hour a grand display of fireworks burst over Semarang, startling the fishermen plying the dark waters offshore. The dancing 'continued until long after the glowing sunbeams of the morning had made the remaining night grow dim and reminded the party that it was time to retire.' The hangovers had scarcely subsided by the time Gillespie turned up, eager to flex his muscles in what Captain Thorn called 'a new field of glory... for the display of British valour, in the very heart of Java.'

As Lieutenant-Governor, Raffles was once again seriously overstepping the limits of his remit by unilaterally launching another war. His hierarchical equals amongst the British residents in the Indian provinces would never have organised – would never even have *considered* – such a move without first seeking direct approval from Calcutta. But isolated on the other side of the Indian Ocean, Raffles could always plead the difficulties of distance. He penned a note of apology to Minto claiming that he had no other option but to proceed. 'I regret to state that the conduct and disposition of the Sultan is so unfavourable and unsafe that his removal becomes necessary,' he declared; to do otherwise would be a poor 'reflection on my administration'.

But if he was untroubled by the lack of superior sanction, Raffles perhaps ought to have been rather nervous about the practicalities of the undertaking in hand. Most of Britain's military manpower in Indonesia was still floating around somewhere between Bangka and Batavia; just one company of grenadiers from the 59th Regiment had arrived back from Sumatra and the remainder of the advance for the Yogyakarta campaign was made up of odds and ends, the leftover companies, Indian sepoys and European redcoats, who had remained in Batavia. It was a bubble-and-squeak army, and it amounted to no more than 1200 men. The only extra support they had was from a little army-for-hire belonging to one of Surakarta's strangest inhabitants.

Shortly after the bifurcation of Mataram in 1755, the original rebel princeling, Mas Said, had come in from the cold in the hope of getting a piece of the partition action. Despite his years of treachery he had been installed in a miniature *kraton* on the outskirts of Surakarta as the independent ruler of 4000 households under the title of Mangkunegara. Though Mas Said himself had been renowned as a zealous xenophobe, his successor, Mangkunegara II, had taken to speaking Dutch, wearing European military uniform, and pimping out his private army to the colonialists. He had been the only man in Central Java that the Dutch could rely on, and now in Semarang he offered the same support to the British. Gillespie, however, seems not to have been entirely keen on having Javanese soldiers in the front line, and the 400-man Mangkunegaran Legion was given a relatively unimportant role in the adventure.

But despite the lack of manpower, and the formidable nature of the enemy, on the eve of departure from Semarang south into the heartlands, Raffles seemed to exude an air of perfect confidence. As it was later presented to the British public 'The existence of the European power on the island of Java was at this time in imminent danger of being annihilated'. This claim is decidedly hyperbolic and doesn't stand up to much scrutiny – not least given that the Susuhunan was never very serious about joining in the mooted uprising – and there is no sense of panic or impending doom in Raffles' private letters of the period: he was an adventurer on the brink of triumph.

An orientalist-cum-military engineer by the name of Colonel Colin Mackenzie had been sent on ahead to Yogyakarta to join John Crawfurd in the residency and to plot a plan of action. Crawfurd himself had managed to get the Crown Prince secretly to sign some kind of pre-emptive treaty based on hypothetical post-conquest conditions, and everything was as ready as it would ever be. On 16 June, the red-coated column snaked its way into the mountains of Central Java. Olivia – who was feeling decidedly liverish, perhaps thanks to the excesses of the King's birthday party – was installed at the halfway staging post of Salatiga, and the following day Raffles, Gillespie and the advance reached Yogyakarta and moved into the

Dutch fort beside the residency, 800 yards north of the Kraton. It was time to send in the clowns.

* * *

The guns fell silent at three in the morning.

For two days a near continuous barrage of cannon-fire and grapeshot had roared back and forth across the northern Alun-Alun of Yogyakarta. The British had barely kicked off their boots on 17 June when the trouble started: mobs of the Sultan's horsemen were thundering through the countryside north of the city, burning bridges and ripping up the roads, and in the steamy hours of darkness there had been minor skirmishes as Gillespie and a posse of 50 dragoons – with Crawfurd on hand to translate – tried to stop them. By morning a British soldier had been killed.

There had followed a charade of negotiation, with Raffles sending a messenger into the Kraton with a demand for capitulation. Given that there were at least 11,000 Javanese soldiers peering through the loopholes of the Kraton walls and priming their muskets, and some 100,000 hostile civilians armed with sharpened bamboo staves in the surrounding hamlets, no one was surprised when there were 'no symptoms of concession' and the messenger was promptly ejected from the court with a firm 'no' by way of an answer. Yogyakarta was the hub of the Javanese universe, after all; its ruler was hardly likely to hand it over without a fight. In fact, in a subsequent 'act of arrogant exultation' the Sultan actually sent his own messenger to the British, demanding *their* unconditional surrender. The request was met with derision, and the cannonade continued. Any local civilians who crept out of their houses and found some safe vantage point amongst the palm trees from which to watch were greeted with a view of what one military observer described as 'the singular spectacle of two contiguous forts, belonging to nations situated at opposite extremes of the globe, bombarding each other'.

The Javanese may not have realised, but the British were stalling for time: much of their heavy firepower was still stuck somewhere on the road down from the little upland fortress of Salatiga, halfway between Yogyakarta and Semarang, under the command of a colonel named Alexander McLeod. Until McLeod arrived all they could do was to keep up a covering fire. At one point the northeast corner of the Kraton was rattled by an enormous explosion: a huge heirloom cannon, one of the defenders' heaviest weapons, had quite literally backfired, sending a rain of hot iron shards down into the palace. Shortly afterward an ill-secured powder store in the Dutch fort also erupted and a section of that building went up in flames leaving several young British officers with horrific burns.

Eventually, before either invaders or defenders had further opportunity to blow themselves up, on the morning of 19 June, McLeod and the heavy guns turned up. Gillespie and Colin Mackenzie ordered the sepoys to set fire to the network of bamboo *kampungs* that flanked the Kraton walls; at sunset a bugle sounded and all the British troops still out in the field were called back into the fort, and then, at 3 a.m. on 20 June 1811, Gillespie ordered the gunners on the ramparts to cease fire.

A few stray musket shots, fired by the distant Javanese defenders, whistled out of the darkness; a few slugs of hot metal thumped into the scarred and pitted walls of the fort, and then there was silence. Other sounds, long lost beneath the noise of battle, reasserted themselves: the ticking and creaking of cooling gun metal, the startled whiny of an unnerved horse, a fugitive breeze moving through the sagging leaves of the tamarinds, and the stifled coughs and whispers of tired men. Inside the grey barracks the lamplight shone on sweat-greased faces. Bengali sepoys, their tight white jodhpurs stained with mud and blood, slumped against the damp walls, while their English comrades fiddled with the blades of their bayonets or caught a moment's repose over soggy tobacco and dirty drinking water. But this was merely the briefest of respites: they had stopped firing only to put the Javanese off their guard. Away to the east, beyond the serried black hills of the hinterland, a faint white stain was beginning to show on the edge of the night. It was time.

The plan that Mackenzie and Gillespie had contrived was simple but precise: they would attack the great fortified cube of the Kraton from all sides. A column of infantrymen headed silently out into the gloom at 4 a.m. They were to make a wide circuit out into the rice fields before cutting back to assault the southern gate. A few minutes later another party crept out, slipped between the columns of trees and headed across the dusty expanse in front of the fort to launch a diversionary attack on the main entrance, the ceremonial gateway that faced due north towards Gunung Merapi. And then finally, with thin grey daylight spreading like milky liquid over the Yogyakarta rooftops, the main attack force – a column of the Bengal Light Infantry Volunteer Battalion – hurried out and bore left across the burnt-out *kampungs* to launch their desperate assault on the northeast bastion of the Javanese fastness.

Raffles was left behind to watch from the battlements with a turbulent mix of pride and awe. The Dutch had spent two centuries in Java, yet they had never even considered doing anything so audacious or so outrageous. Raffles, meanwhile, had been here for less than twelve months. But now, on his orders, the British Army was set to do something that would have an earth-shattering impact on the local aristocracy, and that would change the balance of power in Java forever. They were about to storm the sacred space at the very heart of a mighty Javanese kingdom.

* * *

Raffles, on the morning of 20 June 1812, is a man a very long way from the pedestal that was later constructed for him. Amateur botanist, gardener, gentleman scholar, liberal, visionary founding father of a multicultural city-state, and acceptable exception to the ugly rule of European imperialism, he is *not*.

The two preceding centuries of British colonialism had been in many instances shamelessly piratical, but, as with the rival Dutch project, money, not glory had been the motivation. But with a new century opening that was all about to change. Far from standing in contrast to the arrogant and aggressive side of the British Empire, Raffles was actually one of its pioneers.

Much has been made of how singularly awful the VOC had been in their rickety Indonesian empire – and awful they often were, as those accounts of torture attest. But even so, Java had consumed and digested the earlier generations of Dutchmen, modified their habits and got under their skin – quite literally – in a way that Raffles and those who came after him would find abhorrent. There were the native consorts, and those legions of mixed-race women in sarongs and *kebayas* for a start. The shuddering disgust of Olivia Raffles and the other English wives at all this was symptomatic of new social attitudes towards native people and native customs that would dominate in the coming decades. The aggressive compunction to crush and humiliate the Javanese courts displayed by her husband, meanwhile, was symptomatic of the equivalent political attitudes that would drive both the British during the rise of the Raj, and the reinvigorated Hollanders once they returned to Java.

Raffles, looking out from the pockmarked grey walls of the Dutch fort, across the Alun-Alun with its shot-scorched banyan trees, to the great gateway of the Yogyakarta Kraton, was a new kind of European. The Javanese, peering out across the Alun-Alun in the opposite direction, had had their first unsettling, unbalancing, unnerving glimpse of such a man in the person of Daendels, but it was Thomas Stamford Raffles who was about to turn their world upside-down. Nothing in Java would ever be the same again.

A New Field of Glory

The guns fell silent at three in the morning ...

The four princes looked uncertainly up at the night sky with its low-slung moon and its smears of jaundiced cloud. Calls of query from the defenders manning the artillery on the Kraton's outer ramparts echoed back and forth in the darkness. What was happening? Had the British really stopped firing? And then, for the first time in two days, a kind of exhausted calm descended. It was 20 June 1812. But the four royals did not relax. They had spent the night out of doors in one of the pavilions of the Yogyakarta Crown Prince's shell-scarred quarters in the northeast corner of the Kraton. They had not slept. They had prayed and mumbled incantations, fingered their amulets and wondered nervously what was coming next. They had heard from the watchers on the walls that the British had pulled their men back inside the Dutch fort at dusk, but unlike the foot soldiers, they could not believe that this marked some kind of real retreat. Now in the uneasy silence their sense of foreboding only deepened.

Foremost amongst the little princely quartet, sitting cross-legged in the gloom and fiddling nervously with the handle of his *kris*, was the Crown Prince himself. The heir to the Yogyakarta throne was a man in his early forties with the long, tumbling black hair of a Javanese nobleman. The other men were his uncles, the closest of his supporters from amongst the Sultan's legions of half-brothers. The great Mangkubumi had been a virile king with a multitude of wives and concubines, and he had still been siring sons in his final decades: the youngest of the three uncles – a bumbling hunchback called Diposono – was actually younger than his nephew the Crown Prince.

The other two were his near contemporaries – a rather pompous man who liked to be known by his recently self-applied new name of Muhammad Abubakar, and the calm, collected and refined Arya Panular.

Arya Panular was the child of one of the first sultan's many unofficial consorts. A kidnapped Hindu noblewoman from the far east of Java, she had, as Panular himself told it, been given to Mangkubumi in the aftermath of the Treaty of Giyanti as a token of friendship by the Dutchman Nicolaas Hartingh (who had first got his hands on her during negotiations with a minor eastern chieftain). The king had plucked a fragrant beauty from his harem to serve as Hartingh's own concubine by way of reciprocation. If the story is true – and it seems likely that it is – it is a clear indication of how, corrupt and usurious though they often were, the VOC Dutch could be close to the Javanese royals, both in their friendships and their lifestyles, in a way which the British newcomers would never countenance. The idea of Raffles or John Crawfurd accepting a native concubine as a gift from a Sultan would have been unthinkable; what on earth would Olivia and her coven of English wives have thought of such an enormity?

As at best a semi-legitimate son, Panular had grown up without a chance of candidacy for the Yogyakarta throne, but he had made himself a Javanese nobleman of the first rank. He was steeped in the arts and literature of the court, had a fine line in *wayang kulit*-inspired metaphors, and could quote chunks of both local epics and the Holy Koran (though he would never have considered cutting off his hair and assuming an affected Arabic appellation like his brother, Abubakar). He was refined and upstanding and pretended not to understand Malay, but he also had a sense of humour. He had been close to the Crown Prince since their youth, and now his own oldest daughter was married to her half-cousin, making the heir to the Yogyakarta throne his friend, his nephew and his son-in-law. A certain degree of self-interest was probably involved in his chivalrous loyalty to the Crown Prince, but Panular was, it seems, a good man.

He is also the best source of information about what happened within the Kraton walls in June 1812, for he wrote a detailed and anecdotal account of the earth-shattering events, full of acute observations, wry opinions and lively turns of phrase.

The penning of *babads*, courtly chronicles, was a skill that any Javanese aristocrat worth his *kris* ought to cultivate. But the gilded manuscripts they produced on royal history were often mired in allusion and myth-making. Arya Panular, however, has left us his first draft, written out in tight fences of Javanese script on tree bark paper in the immediate aftermath of the events. Like all such *babads*, it was designed to be chanted aloud amidst the incense smoke and clashing gongs of late night gatherings, but it is full of the kind of deliberate details and indiscretions – and points of cross-reference with the British accounts – that inspire confidence. And given that the British were very obviously lying through their teeth in certain sections of their own write-ups of the Battle for Yogyakarta – as will become clear later – there is absolutely no reason to trust them above a cultured and erudite Javanese prince about what happened on 20 June.

And the first thing that Panular's *babad* makes clear is that since the British arrived in Yogyakarta the Kraton had begun to descend into chaos. For all the might of the Javanese forces and for all those gestures of defiance and haughty refusals of Raffles' demands, no one was exercising a clear command. Long-standing tensions between the Sultan and the Crown Prince had re-emerged, and a plethora of vested interests were nudging for attention. As the shells fell the threads of the great web of courtly rigmarole had begun to fray and snap; the rhythms of the daily dance performances in the inner courtyards were thrown off kilter, and the tumbling scales of the royal *gamelan* orchestras were knocked out of tune. It was hard to pay the correct obeisance to your betters when cannonballs were shrieking out of the sky and landing all around you.

Some units of the Yogyakarta army were formidable and professional – not least the Sultan's corps of black-trousered Bugis mercenaries – and some of the individual commanders and princes, including Arya Panular himself, were honourable and brave. But the Javanese had no Rollo Gillespie to rally the troops and lead the charge, and no Colin Mackenzie to plot an orchestrated defence. As soon as the firing started on 18 June everything had gone to pieces. Men abandoned their posts; that huge heirloom cannon, possessed of its own sacred energy, had exploded on the battlements, and the defenders who did remain steadfast usually ended up blown to pieces.

Uncle Abubakar had briefly attempted to organise the stand-off as an Islamic Holy War, but he seems already to have been something of a laughing stock amongst his various brothers, and the idea did not go down well. Two years earlier Abubakar had shaved his head, taken a new name, and declared that he was about to depart on the Muslim pilgrimage to Mecca. Whether the haircut and travel plans were due to genuine religious sentiment or misguided political machinations is unclear, but he lacked the means, motivation and the organisational skill actually to make good his ambition. He never left Yogyakarta. Still, he had taken to strutting about the palace in the manner of a pseudo-Haji – with people sniggering at him behind his back. As the first shots were fired in 1812 he had dressed himself in the white robes and turban of a mujahedin and taken to the battlements full of zeal. Alone amongst the earthy brown batiks of the other Javanese he made an excellent target for the sepoy snipers. Abubakar came rapidly scrambling back down into cover with a bullet hole in his turban, explaining that a Holy War was no longer practical under the circumstances.

The Sultan himself, meanwhile, who for all his swagger was clearly no Mangkubumi, was camped out in the *Bangsal Kencono*, the Golden Pavilion at the locked heart of the inner palace where he had had that unseemly argument over the seating arrangements with Raffles six months earlier. He was surrounded by his amazon corps of female bodyguards, was doing an awful lot of praying, and was regularly joining with his companions in the endless repetition of the first half of the Islamic *Kalimah – La ilaha il Allah*, 'there is no god but God' – which Javanese mystics like to use in their ecstasy-inducing ceremonies. He was also making tentative steps towards replacing the Crown Prince with a more compliant younger son, was failing to send any competent commanders to the most vulnerable quarters of the Kraton, and was taking ill-considered solace in the most misleading reports of Javanese success. When the British powder store exploded on the second day of hostilities and black smoke was seen pouring into the pale sky from the direction of the Dutch fort cheers erupted in the Inner Kraton, only to be abruptly replaced by ever-more fevered chanting as the cannonade resumed.

The Sultan had never believed that a European army would actually attack him. This was not the way the VOC had been doing things in Royal Java for the past 200 years. Posturing and brinkmanship had always been the way the game was played; European musket-balls had never before pattered onto the red tiles of the *Bangsal Kencono* roof like heavy hailstones. The Sultan had absolutely no idea how to respond. Far from being the devious despot 'at the head of a general confederacy of all the native Courts' as he is presented in the British propaganda, in June 1812 the Second Sultan of Yogyakarta seems like the embodiment of tragic incompetence.

His son, the Crown Prince, was showing a little more verve and a little more nerve. He had, of course, been treating with Crawfurd in recent weeks, and seemed to be the British first choice for the future throne. However, since the shooting started he had been bearing the brunt of the bombardment – and doing the most to resist it.

The forty-five-foot-high outer wall of the Kraton formed a great square, opening in front of the Alun-Alun in the north and boxing in the entire warren of the greater Kraton city with its stately residences, pleasure palaces, open grassy squares, humble retainers' quarters and forbidden women's sections. The walls themselves were some ten feet thick with a broad inner ledge to accommodate guns and gunners. They were pierced at the cardinal points by royal gateways where the walls swelled around an arched entrance, and at each corner was an armed bastion, a skewed square of masonry projecting outwards like an arrowhead. The bastions were some fifty feet across, and defended with cannon. At the outer edges there were domed structures the shape of birdcages, each pierced with half-a-dozen tiny loopholes for musket barrels (a feature borrowed from the Dutch). The whole Kraton sloped gently, almost imperceptibly, downhill towards the Southern Ocean, away from Gunung Merapi.

The Crown Prince's personal residence, his own palace-within-a-palace, lay in the northeast crook of the fortifications with its own direct gate through the northern walls, close to the very bastion on which the British redcoats and sepoy gunners were concentrating the full force of their firepower. Cannonballs had crashed through his *pendopo* roofs; crude cluster-bombs – shells that exploded on impact and scattered hot stones – had walloped into his courtyards, and his entourage of highborn ladies and royal retainers had taken the worst of the trauma. Whenever he or his messengers entered the delusional bubble of the inner sanctum, with its chanting amazons and scurrying flunkies, to ask for orders or assistance in organising the defence, they met with prevarication and confusion.

By the time the guns fell silent in the early hours of 20 June the Crown Prince and the trio of uncles gathered in his battered quarters knew only too well that whenever the British chose to launch their decisive assault, the Kraton was almost certain to fall. Peering up at the night sky they made plans for that eventuality. The Crown Prince himself was bound by filial loyalty, he said, despite his father's ineptitude and apparent hostility. He, his women, his infant children and his fiery twenty-six-year-old son Diponegoro would attempt to retreat to the secure recesses of the Inner Kraton to join the Sultan in a last stand whenever the main defences gave way. But he made no demands of his uncles should they choose instead to flee to the safety of the villages in the green countryside beyond. Upright Arya Panular, the aspiring Haji Abubakar (who had by now shed his pious white robes), and the grizzling hunchback Diposono all agreed that they would try to stick together come what may. They did not have long to wait to test their resolve.

* * *

Dawn was threatening in the wild country to the east when the firing started once more. The defenders on the ramparts, who had wrapped themselves in their sarongs and curled up to sleep under the cannons, came awake in a panic, stumbling and tripping as they hauled themselves upright, fumbling for powder and shot to prime their own guns. But as they peered out into the half-light, across the smouldering stumps of the burnt-out *kampungs* beneath the walls, they realised with horror that this was not just the opening of another round of long distance duelling. Sweeping across the Alun-Alun at a steady jog-trot, bayonet blades jutting before them, were hundreds of Englishmen and Indians. They came, Arya Panular recalled, 'with their eyes screwed up and their heads down as though impervious to death'.

Frantic warnings echoed between the explosions from the walls. The first bamboo ladders were being slapped up against the battlements from the ditch below and the first angry-faced Bengali sepoys were shimmying up and over and into the Kraton. To the Javanese defenders they looked like demons from the *wayang kulit*. In the Crown Prince's quarters terrified women were grabbing bundles and babies and fleeing for the inner court. The northeast bastion had already given way, and now the Prince's Gate was under attack; batik-clad soldiers were bolting through the alleyways below, and the British troops were manhandling the Javanese artillery pieces, humping them around through 180 degrees and firing them back *into* the Kraton.

If he had not realised it before, Arya Panular now recognised that something had gone badly awry in the balance of mystical power. Talk of the illustrious past, of the laurels of Senopati, Sultan Agung and Mangkubumi, of powerful *pusaka* and the Queen of the Southern Ocean, had amounted to nothing more than the burying of aristocratic heads in the black sand of the Kraton courtyards. The attacking foreigners, he understood, had the stronger magic:

In battle they were irresistible; foreign and Javanese rulers alike had been conquered by them. Awe-inspiring to behold, they were as though protected by the very angels and they struck terror into men's hearts. Facing them the lustre of the Javanese had vanished for they had been visited by the Holy One's anger on account of the magnitude of their sins.

The light had gone out.

That the unseen forces were not on the Javanese side was obvious even this early in the battle: in the first confusion and panic as the Crown Prince's household was abandoned, the uncles' earlier resolution to stick together had come to nothing. Arya Panular and his immediate retainers found themselves cowering under fire in the courtyard without their compatriots. The Crown Prince had gone on ahead towards the Inner Kraton; the hunchback Diposono had hobbled off somewhere out of sight, and Abubakar had vanished. Shells were exploding on all sides, and the redcoats were now tossing the Javanese cannons over the walls into the outer ditch and sweeping south along the walls, firing as they went. The sun was slipping up into the morning, and it was every man for himself.

The only thing Panular could do was to try to follow the Prince's party (which also included his own daughter, the young royal wife). They had slipped out through the gateway that connected the Prince's quarters – which were now collapsing under the plummeting shells – to the first of the narrow anteroom courtyards of the Inner Kraton, the *Kemangdungan*, which opened through the ceremonial Srimenganti Gate to a second courtyard, and then to the inner core, the walled fastness that held the Golden Pavilion and the person of the Sultan.

But the rain of shot and shells was thickening. There was broken masonry everywhere, and the crumpled corpses of those defenders who had tried to make a stand lay in their blood-stained batiks. A dead horse had fallen against the door to the escape route. Sweating and gasping, with shot whistling all around, Panular and his retainers managed to haul the horse clear enough to clamber over its carcass and to scurry down the white passageway beyond, but when they reached the Srimenganti Gate they found its solid door – a great hulk of riveted timber – bolted and guarded by a lance-wielding trooper. The Sultan had barricaded himself inside with his women, and no one – not even the Crown Prince – was to be allowed in.

In the princes' urgent discussions the previous night the suggestion of seeking refuge in the Taman Sari, the Water Palace, with its warren of damp chambers and underground passageways, had been raised. If nothing else it would make a fine place to hide the most sacred of the heirloom treasures. The Crown Prince had been set on joining his father at the critical moment, but with the way blocked to him, Panular guessed, he must have remembered the earlier suggestion and headed southwest for the Taman Sari. Panular hurried off in the same direction, forcing his way through another guarded gateway beyond which, to his relief, he met his hunchbacked younger brother Diposono who had made it this far by another route. Behind them they could hear the roars of close combat; wounded Javanese soldiers were still fleeing in all directions, and the rising heat of the morning was thick with the smell of gunpowder.

The two princes scurried though narrow passageways and shell-shattered courtyards. Here and there a tamarind tree had been felled by a cannonball and they had to scramble through the branches, their sarongs catching amongst the leaves. Finally the creamy walls of the Taman Sari came in sight, towering from its grove of mango trees and palms. The thought of its shaded chambers and cool water, and – just perhaps – of the soft, *melati*-scented breeze that shows that the Queen of the Southern Ocean is in residence, must have seemed like a dream of paradise. It would be a place to wait for the inevitable in cool, calm dignity.

But it was not to be. Milling in confusion outside the eastern gateway to the Taman Sari – a pyramid of masonry sporting the flat, leering face of a guardian ogre – was the party of the Crown Prince. This gateway too was shut and bolted, and they had been unable to force their way in. There followed a moment of despair. There was firing from all directions now, and they could see the scarlet splashes of jacketed sepoys and English soldiers all along the outer walls. Someone suggested heading south to the secondary Alun-Alun, smaller than the main square, but within the walls. Perhaps they could make a stand there between the sacred banyans, the optimist said in a bright moment, before succumbing to hopeless sobs. It was Arya Panular who staved off the mounting hysteria: they could not stay where they were, he said, but they would keep together; they would defend the Crown Prince, and they would move south, looking for a place of refuge.

The little party bore away through the more open quarters of the southern Kraton, passing shot-shredded banana plants and abandoned artisans' quarters, coming together again with the royal women of the Crown Prince's household, who had somehow gone astray in the initial retreat. These were all ladies of high birth, the daughters and the mothers of princes, but now they were travelling like itinerant beggars. They had gathered the most valuable of their possessions and the most potent of their charms before they fled their quarters, and were carrying them in cloth bundles, with their children slung at their hips in knotted sarongs. All of them were terrified, and as everyone hurried on together at the shambolic pace where walking gives way to running in fits and starts, servants, masters, princesses and handmaids were no longer separated in posture or in person. Everyone was jumbled together, as Arya Panular put it, 'like winnowed rice'.

When this sorry harvest of royal refugees reached the far southeast corner of the greater Kraton they turned north along the walls, traversing the edge of the humblest quarters of Inner Yogyakarta. At the great West Gate hordes of terrified courtiers were trying to flee to the fields, and in the melee Panular spotted the missing uncle, Abubakar. The hapless would-be Haji had had the ride of his life since splitting from his brothers at first light. In the confusion as the shells began to shower down on the Crown Prince's quarters and the shrieks of warning rose from the battlements he had found himself a horse. Backing the whinnying beast into the shelter of a gateway for a moment he had scanned around for his brothers and nephew, but they were nowhere to be seen and he could not go on horseback through the doubled doorways and crooked alleys of the inner court. Instead he had wheeled for the eastern bastion – now firmly in the hands of the invaders – and then gone frantically cantering away to the south along the inner line of the walls, sepoys taking pot-shots at him from above as he went. He must have been muttering praise to whichever power seemed most appropriate that he was no longer wearing his snow-white mujahidin's robes. Close to the southern Alun-Alun a locked doorway had blocked his way and stopped his horse, but he had eventually found his way on foot to the western gate, dodging parties of marauding Englishmen.

British soldiers were approaching from all directions now and columns of dark smoke were rising from all over the Kraton. This was the last moment for an escape out into the villages and palm groves, the final chance for the kind of exile amongst jungles, volcanoes, tigers and spirits that the old *babads* told of. Many chose to go that way. Taking a hurried leave of his brothers Abubakar squeezed out through the gate as the sepoys closed in, heading for the old Mataram cemetery at Imogiri. At this desperate moment he had chosen for his refuge a place of profoundly Javanese power, not some white Haji's prayer room. Diposono too, hobbling and exhausted and hardly able to keep up with the more able-bodied courtiers, had also decided to head for the villages. Instead of jostling through the crowd in the gateway, his retainers hauled him piggy-back up onto the walls and dropped him down to the other side. He landed with a thump in the ditch. His *kris* tumbled away into the long grass, but he did not even have time to reclaim it – British bullets were flying all around – and he too hurried away to the south, un-knifed and unmanned.

But the Crown Prince, his sons, the royal women, and the loyal Arya Panular would not flee Yogyakarta. They were now to the west of the Taman Sari; they could see its red rooftops rising through the scorched trees 500 yards away. Perhaps if they doubled back they would find the door on this side of its walls unblocked. Leaving the milling, terrified crowd in the Western Gate they hurried south for a way, but parties of sepoys – who seemed to be materialising djinn-like at every corner by this stage – blocked their way, and they cut northeast again. Snipers on the ramparts were firing directly on the royal party now, and the hysterical wives and concubines were bobbing around like a herd of terrified sheep. Arya Panular ordered them to stay calm, but to little avail, especially when one of the wives was hit by a bullet in her delicate foot.

There was no relief when they reached the walls of the Taman Sari. The western door too was bolted from the inside. Perhaps it was the Queen of the Southern Ocean herself who had blockaded the way to her watery guestrooms. She had, after all, decided to play no part in this battle, nor to lend the support of her spirit legions to the Sultan; that much was obvious from the way things were going.

The Crown Prince and the women and children huddled in the arched gateway as the last of the loyal retainers struggled without success to force open the locked door. The sepoys were closing in now, and bullets were smacking into the masonry around them. Shouts and angry orders in unknown languages – Bengali, English and Hindustani – were echoing in all directions, and the figures of the advancing Indians were taking terrifying shape through the smoke. They were dressed like ballerinas in skin-tight white jodhpurs, but they swung curved cutlasses, touted long-barrelled rifles and shouldered sharp staves. Their eyes blazed beneath sandal paste-daubed brows and their wild moustaches extended in oiled twists from firm upper lips. The royal women whimpered.

There had been precious little heroism all morning; Arya Panular felt he had to do something. He grabbed his most powerful weapon from one of his retainers, the heirloom lance that formed part of his own collection of *pusaka*, a spear with a personal name and – he had always believed, and now profoundly hoped – a power all of its own. Clinging to its shaft and praying for divine assistance he jostled to the head of the cringing cluster of courtiers and stood at the opening to the blocked recess in which they were sheltering. Shots smashed around him. The sepoys were coming at a run now. It was the final moment.

And then a new voice came through the chaos, a new accent, and a new set of orders, and suddenly the shooting stopped. Wheeling on a whinnying horse, a white man, a British officer, had appeared, yelled at the sepoys to cease fire, and now he was saying something to Arya Panular.

Clinging to his sacred lance, a gaggle of petrified princesses and the royal nephew to whose fortunes his own future was tied cowering at his back, Panular must have been on the brink of emotional collapse. He was a man who had lived amongst court dances and *wayang kulit* shows. His generation had known none of the battles that had raged in Java before the Treaty of Giyanti; he had no training for this sort of thing. Yet in the short and shocking hours since dawn he had manhandled a dead horse, had his passage blocked by guards who should have shown him deference, watched the sacred walled city in which he had lived his whole life begin to go up in smoke, been shot at repeatedly by uncouth foreigners, and was now the last line of defence between the heir to the throne and a legion of apparently divinely driven demons. To hear an understood and reassuring phrase from the mouth of a member of the fearsome army that had been harassing him and his companions all morning must have been a heart-breaking relief. For a moment Panular was happy to forget his haughty pretence of ignorance of the undignified language of itinerants and market traders: the Englishman on the horse had called out to him gently in curiously accented Malay, 'Don't be angry, come here!'

Their flight was over.

* * *

While Arya Panular had been leading frightened princesses through the falling shells, Rollo Gillespie's men had been charging – with their heads down and their eyes screwed up – for a victory destined to 'ever shine conspicuous in the Annals of Java.' The main column of the attack had snuck out across the Alun-Alun at first light. One party headed due south for the central gateway, passing between the twin Banyan trees in the middle of the grassy square. Anyone who can pass blindfolded in a straight line between these trees with their dreadlocked mass of trailing roots is destined for success, they say. The soldiers and sepoys were not blindfolded, but they bore as straight as an arrow for their destination.

The rest of the group cut away towards the Northeast Bastion, behind which lay the Crown Prince's quarters. This was the place that had been chosen for the focal point of the attack; it was here that the British would hurl themselves with all their strength at the Javanese fastness. They had crept right to the marshy ditch below the walls before the dozing defenders above realised what was happening. As the Javanese fumbled for their guns the first of the bamboo ladders were raised against the walls and the first sepoys went scuttling up them like spiders. Snipers back across the ditch picked off the enemy soldiers through the gaps and loopholes of the bastion. The defence of this northeast corner of the Kraton lasted mere minutes as more and more redcoats swarmed over the ramparts. The bayoneted Javanese bodies were tossed down into the ditch below.

At the head of this first assault party was a lieutenant-colonel called Watson. With the bastion fallen Watson now turned his back to the sunrise and charged along the inner ledge of the walls towards the gate that led directly into the Crown Prince's quarters, 300 yards to the west. A party of sepoys had waded across the ditch and were scurrying along the slope immediately below the ramparts in the same direction. The Javanese had already gone spilling off the fortifications above the gate like lemmings and vanished into the interior of the Kraton, but the gate itself was strongly barricaded. While sappers laid charges to blow it open, the sepoys scrambled up on each other's shoulders to join Watson on the ramparts. As soon as the explosives went off and the gate fell they doubled back at a jog and went running along the ledge to the corner bastion where they lugged the Javanese guns around to fire them back into the Crown Prince's residence and the buildings beyond. If the British had had more men they would have left soldiers in possession of these captured guns, but their force was far too small to take a place with three miles of ramparts by conventional means. After a few inward shots they tossed the guns over the walls and bore south en masse.

The Kraton walls here formed a long, straight line, angled gently downhill for three-quarters of a mile, and with the full, tree-studded sprawl of the walled town opening to the right with its tall, tiered roofs and its maze of bone-white and earth-brown walls. To the left the Javanese countryside stretched away southeast to a bank of dark hills. New sunlight was streaking through the palm groves and lying in a thin golden patina over the fields, but Watson and the sepoys were not interested in the picturesque landscapes of a tropical morning at this stage. From the network of buildings below a steady barrage of bullets was whistling: the defenders had not held the walls, but they had not yet given up the fight. As they jogged on south, ducking and diving to avoid the sniper fire, the British party must have spotted a Javanese man in princely dress on a horse, galloping frantically ahead at the inner foot of the walls. Some of the sepoy sharpshooters paused for a moment to take a shot at him.

The southeast bastion – a mirror image of its northeast counterpart at the bottom corner of the Kraton – was still full of Javanese soldiers, and with only the narrow ledge of the main wall for access. Watson urged his men on and they scrambled onto its cobbled platform with bayonets forward, stabbing and hacking away at anyone who resisted. This bastion too fell quickly, but as they continued their advance, along the southern ramparts now, the defence seemed more desperate. There was hand-to-hand fighting all the way along the walls to the South Gate, the portal that led to the small southern Alun-Alun and the back door of the Inner Kraton.

Above the gateway itself – a narrow, arched tunnel – the walls swelled to some fifty feet thick, armed with cannons, and crawling with defenders. There was an all-out battle here for a few minutes, before this place too fell to the British. Another column of redcoats – that which had departed the Dutch fort at 4 o'clock to loop away to the south – were clamouring outside the gate, having already fought their own battles in the outlying villages. Their compatriots let them in, and the redoubled force charged on, swept the southwest bastion and then went jogging north. They had made a three-quarter circuit of the Kraton by now. The smoke rising to the right showed that the artillerymen back in the fort had kept their aim on the inner palace true; failing sniper fire from the *kampungs* and courtyards below showed that the wider defence was giving way, and the sound of fighting and firing to the north showed that the main gateway was coming open too. Little units of sepoys started to scramble down from the ramparts into the Kraton itself and began sweeping northwards through the laneways.

Outside the walls meanwhile, parties of mounted cavalry were thundering along the dusty tracks with swords swinging, cutting down or driving back anyone who tried to flee to the fields beyond. A great mass of panicking Javanese were crowded in the arches of the West Gate. Many of them fell to British bullets as the redcoats approached. The invaders were, it seemed, possessed of an 'impelling force, which, like a whirlwind, swept everything before it'.

Gillespie himself was a Commander at Large throughout all of this, charging around the outside of the Kraton and popping up whenever some skirmish started. This was, once again, the stuff he lived for. There was a formidable fortress, a manufactured sense of outrage, an under-gunned but over-brave body of Britishers, and an enemy who could safely be viewed as faithless barbarians and therefore cut down without qualm. And there was also, of course, the promise of untold Asiatic riches to be plundered once the shooting stopped. His eyes must have blazed and his little legs carried him with unbounded energy.

But there *was* one man who needed to be saved from the rampaging sepoys. The Indian troopers now pushing into the interior of the Kraton were annihilating anyone who raised a whimper of resistance, and were hardly likely to stop to ask if their victims had a notable royal pedigree. Somewhere amongst the fallen trees and the batik-clad bodies, the dead horses and the burning pavilions, was the person who the British were expecting to place as a cowed vassal on the dented throne of Yogyakarta once they had finished their demolition work. It would be decidedly unfortunate if in the heat of battle a Bengali sepoy inadvertently took a dagger to the Crown Prince. A British officer by the name of Dennis Dalton who had picked up a little pidgin Malay in the months since the conquest of Batavia cut into the Kraton from the western gateway on horseback to seek out the royal refugee, and within minutes he found him, cowering in a locked gateway a few hundred yards to the east.

There was no resistance once Dalton had convinced a rather overwrought man in a batik headdress who was clinging to an antique spear at the head of the gateway to stand down. Englishmen and Indians clustered around the little group, the sepoys leering lasciviously at the trembling women of the party. They stripped the men of their *krises* and pikes, relieved the ladies of their bundled jewellery, and made off with the Prince's royal *pusakas*. At this point Gillespie, who had been swinging his sabre and leading his men in a chant of 'victory or death' on the walls nearby, arrived on the scene with the Malay-speaking secretary of the Yogyakarta residency, John Deans (who seems to have been thoroughly enjoying himself as a bloodthirsty amateur soldier) to tell the Crown Prince that he was wanted by his new master the Lieutenant-Governor in the Dutch fort. The prisoners were led away and Gillespie went back to finish the fight.

The great thousands-strong mass of the Javanese forces that had started the morning had been pared of its cowards and incompetents, and whittled down to a kernel of determined fighters now, and the final northwest bastion held out longer than any of the others. But it could not resist forever, and soon sepoys and Englishmen sloshed up over the walls and sent the survivors fleeing to the north. The tattered remnants of the 11,000-strong army of Yogyakarta made its last stand in the Royal Mosque, a colonnaded cube with a pyramid roof outside the Kraton walls on the western side of the Alun-Alun, parallel to the twin banyans where the Merapi-Southern Ocean axis intersected at a right-angle with the *kiblat* alignment towards Mecca. They barricaded themselves inside the House of God and prepared for a siege. Gillespie and his men surrounded the building, firing from behind a low outlying wall, but this was a stronger fastness than the open bastions; the Javanese had small apertures to fire through and thick masonry columns to hide behind. Low shots fired by the besieging soldiers made little impression, and portable field artillery pieces could not be lined up from the safety of cover.

Full of the fury of battle, however, a sepoy of the Light Infantry Battalion called Meerwan Singh clambered up into full view on the corner of the defensive walls. He was 'instantly saluted' with a shower of shot, but he held fast and sat 'bolt upright' while his companions hurriedly loaded musket after musket and passed them up for him to fire coolly and calmly into the mosque, sending many of the Javanese scurrying for cover.

At this point, at another spot on the defensive wall behind which the British forces were crouching, the great commander himself took a direct hit. Hoping to match the audacity of Meerwan Singh perhaps, one of the Javanese fighters had scurried out from the mosque with a gun, found a loophole in the outer wall, leaned through it and taken a pot-shot at the nearest foreigner. That foreigner happened to be Rollo Gillespie. The ball hit him in the arm. Swearing furiously and clamping a cloth to the gushing wound he abandoned any kind of forbearance and commanded his men to annihilate the last defenders. The audacious Javanese sniper had by this stage popped his head out of the loophole for a second shot, but he had had no chance even to choose a target. A sepoy called Bhoop Narain Singh 'put his musket to his head and blew his brains to the devil'. Gillespie later had Singh promoted for exacting this instant and outright revenge. The rest of the riflemen now stood up and unleashed volley after volley, riddling the mosque with bullet holes and putting an abrupt end to any lingering resistance.

Cursing and bleeding Gillespie stomped away. It was 9 o'clock in the morning and the conquest of Yogyakarta was complete. Just 23 members of the British party had been killed, and a modest 76 had been wounded, including, at this late moment, the Commander of the Forces himself. All along the battlements meanwhile, tumbled in the ditches, abandoned in the alleyways and heaped in great steaming piles in the broken gateways, were thousands of dead Javanese.

* * *

In the main building of the Dutch fort an Englishman with absolutely no inclination to risk even a flesh wound was presiding over his own conquests.

While the fight for the northwest bastion was still underway the Crown Prince, his sons and wives, and his uncle Arya Panular had been briskly marched across the Alun-Alun to the British headquarters. The Prince's heart felt 'like water in a white bowl', Panular recorded, and borne along in the hot sun amongst a jangling, clattering mass of armed white men in red jackets, he surrendered himself utterly to the will of God. At the gateway to the fort those sepoys who had already retired from the battlefield came clustering around the royal Javanese women, grinning, sniggering and making lewd gestures. Unable to do anything to stop the humiliation, Panular himself could only mutter prayers for preservation, and to note proudly how his own daughter maintained a cool dignity in the face of the ogling onlookers.

They were led into the courtyard of the fort where they were met with the shocking vision of minor Javanese princes in European military dress. One was a man that they did not know by sight. He was babbling in Dutch and Malay and heartily engaging in backslapping and ribald laughter with the British soldiers. He was, of course, Mangkunegara II, Surakarta's mini-king and Europhile mercenary whose little legion had joined in the assault on the *kampungs* south of the Kraton. But the other prince in trousers was someone Panular knew well – it was one of his own older half-brothers, Pakualam. The man who had traitorously told the British of the correspondence between the Sultan and the Susuhunan was clearly attempting to follow the example of Mangkunegara – he wanted to join the circus; he wanted to be one of the clowns.

Pakualam had realised that committing himself utterly to the British was the best way to gain power, even if it was only of a compromised sort. He and his sons had spent the morning enjoying a grandstand view of the wanton destruction of their own great city in the company of Thomas Stamford Raffles on the battlements of the Dutch fort. Though he didn't yet look entirely at ease in his clinging, itchy new clothes, Pakualam made a point of greeting his brother and his nephew the Crown Prince not with the correct soft Javanese formulas, but with a self-conscious and ill-practiced European handshake. As far as Arya Panular was concerned, it was all faintly obscene.

The Crown Prince, Pakualam, the other men of the party were now called by Crawfurd to come inside the dark hall of the main fort building where Raffles was waiting for them. The Javanese remembered Raffles from his uncouth earlier visit to the Kraton of course, but now the thought that this rather limp little man, hardly as impressive as the ogre-like redcoats or the flamboyant Indians, was the great chief who had called down this catastrophe on Yogyakarta must have been galling. Arya Panular, the Crown Prince and his sons were all struggling to restrain upwellings of tearful emotion after everything that had happened in the recent turbulent hours. Though Raffles made an attempt at a polite Javanese salutation this was not a moment conducive to casual conversation, and after a few uncomfortable minutes he and Crawfurd retreated behind a closed door.

What the two orientalists wanted to talk about is unclear, but Arya Panular claimed that they were arguing about the succession. Raffles, he would have it, had taken a shine to Pakualam, and felt that he would make a perfect British vassal sultan. He had a shrewd mind, spoke Dutch and Malay and would surely soon master English. And he was seemingly rather taken with European culture – he had put on a pair of trousers to impress his hosts, after all. What better choice of loyal lickspittle for the Yogyakarta throne could there be? This, of course, was exactly how Pakualam himself had been hoping things would pan out.

John Crawfurd, however, already knew much more than his superior about Javanese courtly culture. The only realistic candidate for the throne, he explained as Raffles frowned and chewed his lip, was the Crown Prince. He was the legitimate heir; if the kingdom was given to someone else it would be hard to convince the great mass of courtiers and secondary princes to give their assent. And if the Crown Prince then decided to go into rebellion – as he was quite likely to do – he would find ready support. What was more, there was simply no precedent for placing *someone else* on the throne if a properly anointed and still-legitimate crown prince was at hand. Raffles saw sense, but he still felt concern and sympathy for Pakualam. How could they reward him for his loyalty to the European power, if not with the throne? Crawfurd suggested giving him his own autonomous territory within the kingdom, making him to Yogyakarta what Mangkunegara was to Surakarta. Both men wore trousers, after all.

This section of Arya Panular's *babad* is rather hard to assess. Even if he could have listened in on the closed-door conversation in the Dutch fort on 20 June, he could not speak a word of English, so could never have understood it. But there is something in his account of the debate that rings true. John Crawfurd was the one man who routinely stood up to Raffles, who never signed up to his cult, and who was quite prepared to state his disagreements openly. Considering Raffles' treatment of men like Robison, this ought to have prompted an aggressive reaction from the Lieutenant-Governor. But the truth was that Crawfurd was simply too useful for Raffles to sideline. He was the only member of the British party who ever truly got to grips with Javanese culture, and who really knew how to deal with the courts. What was more, he was a formidably capable administrator. Raffles needed to feed off his scholarship, to utilise his skills, and even, much as it probably galled him, to take his advice.

After the battle for Yogyakarta Arya Panular became a close acquaintance of Crawfurd (in fact, he seems to have presented his first draft of the account of the fall of the Kraton to the resident as a parting gift towards the end of the British Interregnum), so perhaps he eventually got to hear a first-hand account of the early arguments that decided the succession, straight from the resident's own mouth. Whether or not the conversation he describes actually took place behind that locked door in such fast-forwarded form is not something we can ever know; neither Raffles nor Crawfurd ever made any record of it if it did. But that such a debate, over such issues, and with the two men taking the opposing positions outlined in Arya Panular's *babad*, did take place – perhaps over a period of several days – seems entirely feasible.

Whatever the Englishman and the Scot were really talking about, there was precious little conversation on the other side of the door. The ambitious Pakualam and the emotionally exhausted Crown Prince were sitting very still and very upright, and concentrating as if their lives depended upon it on ignoring each other. They looked, Panular recorded, 'like women with their new co-wives who have just been abandoned by their menfolk'. The space vacated by those absent husbands – the empty chairs of Raffles and Crawfurd – was all that separated uncle and nephew, but they would not talk. That both men were in the running for the possibly poisonous throne was clearly in their minds. Pakualam had offended protocol with his clownish handshake, and the Crown Prince was wondering whether *any* of this should be happening while he still had no idea what had become of his father, the Sultan.

It was the younger man who finally broke the frosty silence. Clearing his throat and speaking with some strangled difficulty, the Crown Prince asked if Pakualam was well. Without turning Pakualam nodded slowly and half-whispered a reticent affirmation that yes, he was indeed well.

Another aching silence passed before the Crown Prince tried again. It was, he suggested, pointless for them to continue as enemies in this fashion.

Pakualam nodded but did not speak. He did not turn towards his nephew, and there was nothing more to say until one of the Crown Prince's young sons began to sob quietly in a corner. The little boy had been hauled along with his mother during the terrifying ordeal of the flight through the Kraton. He must have been utterly traumatised, and he was certainly thirsty. The Crown Prince, the man who as a result of the discussion apparently going on behind the door, was about to be raised to the fabled throne of whatever was left of the great Kraton city to the south, was utterly helpless. He could hardly go in search of water for the child himself and nor could he make such a request of the watching Arya Panular. But his servants and retainers were all fled, dead or captured. He was utterly alone. Sick with shame he turned once more to the suited and booted Pakualam to ask humbly if he would send one of his own staff to fetch water. For a royal Javanese heir it was a profoundly humiliating moment. There had been many such moments already that morning, and there were still more to come.

* * *

Sultan Hamengkubuwono II, son of the mighty Mangkubumi and second scion of the dynasty that claimed the mantle of Mataram and with it that of all the great Javanese kingdoms back to Majapahit and beyond, had been fiddling while Yogyakarta burned. All around the Inner Kraton smoke was rising; shells were still landing amongst the courtyards and the sound of fighting was drifting in over the tops of the tamarind trees. But the Sultan was still idling on the cool tiles between the gilded columns of the *Bangsal Kencono*. The amazons were still chanting, the court women were becoming more frantic, and all manner of hangers-on were offering all manner of useless advice. At one point, in a moment of sudden energy, it was decided to send out an armed party to organise the defence and save the city, but the moment they left the sanctuary of the Inner Kraton they saw sepoys swarming everywhere and went hurriedly scuttling back to shelter. A rumour did the rounds that the Crown Prince had been killed, prompting tears from the Sultan, and gleeful hand-rubbing from the younger son who had been angling for the post since the bombardment started. Lookouts peering over the high white walls declared that the whole city seemed to have fallen and that the British were now working their way through the courtyards, heading for the sanctum sanctorum.

With the sun edging into a hot mid-morning sky, and the tattered leaves of the remaining trees rustling in a fiery dry season breeze, the hard reality of what was happening seems finally to have dawned on the Sultan: Yogyakarta had collapsed. Some of the men around him urged a last stand, but clinging to one final delusion – that the British might enter his presence with correct respectful formalities – he gave miserable orders to run up a white flag. The last of the guards around the pavilion were ordered to go out through the crooked doorway between the *dwarapala* statues and to pile up their weapons in the Srimenganti Courtyard. Seats were arranged in the pavilion for an audience as if the coming conquerors were merely on a formal diplomatic mission, but lengths of white cotton were also hauled out from some storeroom and torn into lengths which every member of the royal party, women included, hurriedly wrapped around themselves as a mark of surrender.

Sepoys had now forced their way into the Srimenganti courtyard where they opened fire on the Javanese troops who were in the middle of piling up their abandoned lances and swords, sending the survivors scattering with shrieks of terror. And with that the British came sweeping into the heart of the Kraton, paying not the slightest heed to the fearsome guardian statues, and remaining completely unbaffled by the crooked gateway. Beefy white men in shiny black boots came swaggering over the black sand towards the pavilion, and

Indians with flying moustaches and black hats went jogging to the peripheries to guard any hidden escape routes. Evidently no one was going to observe correct formalities after all.

John Crawfurd, who, debate with Raffles over, had ridden down across the Alun-Alun to oversee the seizure of the Sultan, arrived on the scene. Sepoys moved in and roughly disarmed the courtiers of their *krises*. None of them protested; no one ran amok. A burly officer of the 78th Highland Regiment had the sniggering honour of arresting the Sultan himself. This 'turbulent and intriguing' despot, alleged head of a great confederacy of native princes bent on annihilating every European in Java, had his arms roughly pinned behind his back by a grinning foreigner with oversized hands and broad shoulders. The prisoner, stripped of all his accoutrements, no *pusaka* on hand, no royal parasol to shade his sacred head, and looking absolutely *nothing* like a reincarnation of Vishnu, was marched on foot across the Alun-Alun.

In the grainy sepia photographs of later generations of Javanese royals posing beside Dutch residents and governors-general the most striking thing is almost always how very small they are. Even in the presence of a man like Gillespie they would have seemed delicate, dwarfed by roast beef physiques and barrel chests. Hurried along in the heat, surrounded by giants and with his arms still pinned behind him, the Sultan must have cut a pitiful figure. There was no relief when he was jostled and prodded into the inner hall of the main building of the Dutch fort. As soon as they saw him, Pakualam and the Crown Prince – who were still sitting uncomfortably side by side – made to slip down from their chairs. Pakualam might have been lately engaging in outrageous treachery; the Crown Prince might well be aware that he himself was about to become the preeminent royal in Yogyakarta, but both men were hardwired with the modes of deference that were the very underpinning of the court.

Regardless of royal status the Sultan was a father and an older brother; for high-born Javanese it was essential to show kneeling respect to such a man. But Raffles – who was eyeing the Crown

Prince closely – was having none of it. He barked angrily at the two princes as soon as he saw them make their move. They froze, half-off their seats, looking up in confusion, startled by the coarse Malay imperative. Raffles had ordered them to stay sitting; no one would be showing the Sultan respect any more. This, wrote Arya Panular (who, unobserved in a corner, had managed to slip from his own seat as form demanded), was the moment when the Crown Prince truly realised 'that none other than the Lieutenant-Governor had real power in Java'. The sobbing Sultan was hauled away and locked in a little backroom with a guard at the door. Back to the south meanwhile the sepoys and the English soldiers had embarked on a victorious rampage.

In the official celebratory statement that the wounded Gillespie issued the following day, he declared that 'The person of the Sultan has been secured, and the circumstances attending his seizure, reflect so much credit upon the troops in general, that the Commander of the Forces cannot sufficiently express his admiration and applause. In the heat of the storm, his person was respected, his family was placed in security and protection, and no part of his property was either pillaged or molested'. Such statements were intended for governments and publics back in India and England – and for future patriotic historians. But those on the scene in Yogyakarta must have grinned and raised knowing eyebrows when *they* read the proclamation. It was complete nonsense.

The British forces – both Indians and Englishmen – had already engaged in energetic looting of the abandoned aristocratic residences outside the Kraton walls in the run-up to the assault. Now they went absolutely berserk. Though there had been occasional opportunities to pocket some small souvenir during the Batavia campaign the previous year, there had been no great hordes of treasure there, and what items there were had to be regarded as the property of the new British administration. Those who had been to Palembang meanwhile had been bitterly disappointed after all the unfounded talk of gold-packed warehouses. But now they finally had a chance for proper plunder.

In the inner court the royal women were running about in terror and the amazons were acting nothing like amazons. Though the Englishmen looked decidedly like ogres, the Javanese had seen Europeans before, and beyond their uniforms there was nothing to distinguish these newcomers from the Dutch; it was the Indians who were truly terrifying. Throughout the British Interregnum in Java the sepoys seem to have left ripples of unease in their wake. They had magnificent moustaches or full beards of the kind that few soft-skinned Javanese men could muster. These, and their swaggering stance, were scary enough, and their weird yet strangely familiar cultural practices – all joss sticks, *sindoor* paste and petals – were decidedly unsettling too. They also seem to have had a tendency to bully the Javanese, and many English officers noted that the sepoy regiments had such an effect on the natives that in Java they were every bit as useful as battalions made up entirely of true-blue Englishmen – a rare compliment indeed in the age of imperialism. 'It is a fact that the natives look upon a Sepoy with more dread than upon a European', Raffles noted. And above all else, it seems, for the Javanese the Indians exuded an ominous air of sexual threat. The sepoys, as professional soldiers far from home, probably deliberately played on this, and the Javanese women were absolutely terrified of them.

But despite this air of lechery, on 20 June in Yogyakarta both sepoys and Englishmen do seem to have left the women largely unmolested: the lust for wealth had overridden the lust for sex. There was no raping, but there was plenty of rapine, and when it came to the latter they ran completely amok. All around the *Bangsal Kencono* princesses and concubines were manhandled and stripped of all their jewels. Their sarongs and *kebayas* were torn open – not in the name of sexual assault, but to get at whatever treasures they might have hidden about their persons – and throughout the whole walled city an orgy of looting erupted. Residences were ransacked, doors were kicked in and everything was taken. The British redcoats seem to have become completely unhinged in their quest for plunder: they dredged ditches, smashed up cabinets, clambered down wells, and even took to digging up floors, lest any small treasure should escape their attentions.

The only fatality of the entire Yogyakarta campaign amongst the British officers took place not during the initial fighting, but in the midst of this wild eruption of looting. In his effusive official orders Rollo Gillespie made note of Lieutenant Hector MacLean of the 14th Rifle Company as having been 'zealous and meritorious', but in truth there was nothing heroic about MacLean's demise. He had, it seems, gone one step beyond and decided to add a beauty to his booty. Rampaging through the ransacked women's quarters of the Inner Kraton he had chanced upon a trembling royal lady, alone and vulnerable, and decided to have his wicked way with her. She was carrying a *kris* in the folds of her sarong. As he flung himself upon her she stabbed him in the neck, saved her honour and ensured that MacLean got a hero's send-off as the first British internee of Yogyakarta's little Christian cemetery.

Far from attempting to stop the looting, the senior members of the British party took enthusiastic part. Gillespie and the other top brass had staff pillage on their behalf; the Colonel's personal booty was valued at £15,000 in gold, jewels and hard currency (something like half a million pounds sterling in today's money). Raffles paid in cash for stolen artefacts, and he and Crawfurd embarked eagerly on grand academic larceny, the Indiana Jones approach to historical research: they stole the entire contents of the Kraton archive, every bound manuscript, every lontar-leaf chronicle, every *babad*, every last text in Kawi, Jawi, Arabic and Sanskrit. Princes and courtiers were turned into porters and ordered to lug the loot across the Alun-Alun to the fort.

* * *

On Sunday 21 June the Crown Prince was officially appointed as the new British-approved Sultan of Yogyakarta. A proclamation to that effect, prepared in advance, had been pasted up all over town the previous afternoon while the looters were still at work. 'The Sultan Homongkubuana the 2nd has by his crimes and violations of treaty, shown himself unworthy of the confidence of the British Government, and unfit to be further entrusted with the administration delegated to him', it declared. He had reduced his country to 'a state bordering upon anarchy', and was to be replaced by his son.

Any lingering doubts over who was now in charge had vanished, and the coronation ceremony seemed more like a ritual humiliation than a moment of divine royal ascendancy. It was afternoon when the princes and courtiers were ordered to gather in the main hall of the residency, across the road from the fort. Chairs had been lined up on a raised platform, and sweaty, red-faced Englishmen – looking like demons who had just feasted on unfortunate humans, according to Arya Panular – were seated around the edge of the room. The Javanese were instructed to sit cross-legged on the floor. A proper coronation should have taken place on the *Siti Inggil* pavilion, the High Place at the head of the Kraton, with the smoking cone of Gunung Merapi presiding to the north and the Queen of the Southern Ocean in invisible attendance. But correct ceremony counted for nothing now.

There were proud statements of British military triumph and declarations of the justice and mercy of their government, read out in English and translated into Javanese, and the proclamation explaining the dethronement of the old sultan (who was still locked in the fort, and all set for an exile in Raffles' old stomping ground, Penang) was repeated. The Crown Prince was placed on a seat on the dais beside – not above – Thomas Stamford Raffles. He was declared to have become Sultan Hamengkubuwono Senopati Ingalaga Ngabdurahman Sajidin Panatagama Kalipatulah the Third, and the golden items of the royal regalia – which had somehow been retrieved from the soldiers' loot – were handed to him. Raffles gave the new sultan a formal kiss of congratulation. To Arya Panular, sitting amongst the rest of the cross-legged courtiers below the dais, the two men's pecking at one another looked like the effete fighting of a pair of quails.

The senior princes were then called up to pay their respects to the king and his English sponsor. The new sultan sat passively, drained of any visible emotion. Raffles was upright like a Roman emperor. Crawfurd was stalking the dais like some belligerent master of ceremonies, and his purpose became clear when the first of the royal uncles rose to the platform. As a brother of the deposed sultan this prince was quite correct to employ the salutation of an equal to the new ruler, but Crawfurd wanted total submission to the new British vassal. Looming over the man he ordered him to kneel and to kiss his nephew's knees as if *he* were the older man. A ripple of unease flowed like a passing ghost through the batik-clad crowd on the floor of the hall, but it was what happened next that left them reeling.

Having completed this inappropriate act of humility the baffled prince rose creakily to his feet and turned to Raffles. Bowing respectfully he extended a hand for a European greeting, but Crawfurd, standing watchfully behind him, snarled angrily. He gripped the nape of the prince's neck, forced him down onto the floor and thrust his face onto the Lieutenant-Governor's trouser-clad knees. In two centuries no member of a royal Javanese court had ever made such a humiliating gesture of obeisance to a European, let alone been roughly manhandled into doing so.

One after another the princes of the Yogyakarta court, uncles, brothers and cousins of sultans, rose to the dais like men approaching the gibbet. Outside a 19-gun salute thundered from the fort (two fewer shots than the much less grand Sultan of Palembang had merited), and a military band began to play. The sun was slanting away westwards, its light turning coppery against the walls and blazing on the polished swords of the sepoys. All the regiments – foot soldiers, cavaliers, artillerymen – were lining up for a pointed and triumphal show of British military might to underscore the coronation. Inside the residency it was almost dark, but the reluctant princes were still lining up, trembling and sweating, to approach the king and the lieutenant-governor. Raffles kept his eyes haughtily raised to the dark and dusty heights of the hall. One by one the princes shuffled before him, and one by one Crawfurd ordered them to go down on their knees for the humiliating act of homage, pushing them physically to the floor when they hesitated.

Each left the stage and took his seat once more, aching to flee out into the evening, to find some private place to bury his shame. Their eyes flared and flickered in silent turmoil. In the darkness of the room, Arya Panular recalled, even above the racket of the band stomping around on the road outside, you could hear the confused, traumatised, and profoundly humiliated princes panting for breath like wounded dogs. If any of them were capable of mustering a single clear thought at that mortifying moment it would have been this: the Queen of the Southern Ocean was *not* in the room.

* * *

Raffles left Yogyakarta at daybreak on 23 June. He had spent less than a week in the city. He headed for Semarang at full tilt, pausing only for a roadside conference with the Surakarta Resident, Colonel Adams. Just what Raffles intended to do about the Susuhunan at this stage is not entirely clear. After the glorious sensation of haughty princes kissing his knees, the thought of bringing down similar destruction on Surakarta too must have appealed. The Susuhunan had, after all, been the real guilty party in the exchange of letters that was the main pretext for the sacking of Yogyakarta, and he had also, in a very tentative move, placed a unit of his troops across the British line of retreat once they entered his rival's capital on 17 June. As soon as the likely outcome of the battle there became obvious he had pulled them back and started practicing his most fulsome apologies instead, but on the precedent of what Raffles had just done to the Sultan, the Susuhunan ought really to have suffered the same fate.

Indeed, reading Raffles letters from the immediate aftermath of the Yogyakarta campaign, it does seem as though he was actively considering swinging next for Surakarta. On the eve of his departure on 22 June he had penned a note to Gillespie asking him to have troops 'concentrated at Souracarta in about 20 days or a Month from this date for reasons which I have confidentially stated to you'. Whatever those reasons were, Gillespie was stated to 'entirely accord' with the plan. In the end however the Susuhunan wriggled, squirmed, signed a decidedly prejudicial new treaty, gave up large chunks of his outlying territories to direct British control, and thereby saved what remained of his treasure and his dignity.

Raffles had left the practical business of putting the shattered Yogyakarta court back together and drafting a suitable treaty there to Crawfurd, who approached the task with enthusiasm. The new contract, explaining very clearly the revised nature of relations between the European power and the Javanese court, was signed a few weeks later. The script of the English version is furiously marshal, full of violently angled arrows; the letters of the Javanese version rise across the page like bubbles in water. The abject humiliation of the court is emphasised from the very first passage, which reminded everyone – as if they were likely to forget – of the 'utter extinction of his [the old sultan's] power and unconditional submission of his people'.

There were twenty-three articles covering everything from the timber trade to road building (on the former, the new sultan had lost the right to the income from his own teak forests; on the latter he had to build a network of new roads for the transport of British troops and trade goods – at his own expense). The common crooks of the country could take heart to hear that 'every kind of torture and mutilation and the combat of criminals with the Tiger shall be abolished in future', but peasants should know that they could now be called upon at any time to labour for the Europeans. Chunks of the Sultan's realm were to be hived off, and he was to have no further intercourse with any foreigners except the British. Articles 16 and 17 explained that Raffles and his cronies were free to think up unilateral new clauses to add to the treaty whenever they saw fit, and reminded the new vassal that 'His Highness promises to pay strict attention to any advice which the British Government may occasionally judge it necessary to give him'. But it was the 15th article that really drove the nail of the new reality deep:

His Highness acknowledges the supremacy of the British Government over the whole Island of Java and the right of interference on their part wherever the situation of the Country may demand it.

Pakualam was, as Crawfurd had suggested, turned into another mini-king. A 3000-household chunk of Yogyakarta was handed over to him wholesale and his title to it declared hereditary. Raffles had already made much of the devious Dutch division of old Mataram, and would press the point still further in his future writings. But that instance of *divide et impera* had been a fortuitous accident; this new one was downright deliberate, as even the ever-present propagandist Captain Thorn was willing to state in his public explanation of events:

The more effectively to prevent any future attack, a third power was established, by creating Nunga de Suma [Notokusomo, i.e. Pakualam], brother of the late sultaun [sic], a sovereign prince, with considerable estates. Thus the once potent and extensive Empire of Mataram, formerly enjoyed exclusively by the Soosoohoonan, is now divided into three separate principalities [sic: there were *four*, of course, including the Mangkunegaran]; and the favourite project of the native chiefs to destroy the European settlement in Java terminated in the full and apparently permanent establishment of that dominion over the island.

Raffles, rattling for Semarang in thirteen brisk hours, was full of swagger. The Crown Prince – now the third sultan – 'was a prisoner at the time he was placed upon his throne', he noted with relish:

The blow which has been struck at Djocjo Carta, has afforded so decisive a proof to the Native Inhabitants of Java of the strength and determination of the British Government, that they now for the first time know their relative situation and importance ...

Semarang, with its extensive European quarter and its coarse Malay lingua franca, was a world away from Yogyakarta, and as Raffles settled down in the residency there on 24 June, the six-day interlude over the mountains must have taken on a dangerously dreamlike quality. At the time Crawfurd was still attempting to codify the complexities of the new arrangements, and to ease the traumatised Javanese back into the shattered Kraton, but Raffles was unconcerned with nation building in this instance. Someone else could take care of that; shock and awe had been his specialities.

On 25 June he wrote a celebratory letter to Lord Minto. He apologised for not seeking official clearance before embarking on the adventure, but, 'Necessity having compelled me to resort to actual hostilities', he was happy to proclaim everything a great success. Lord Minto could take comfort in learning that 'the loss to our side [was] very inconsiderable, and comparatively nothing; on the part of the enemy [it was] dreadful'. It had all, in fact, been a most magnificent business: 'A more splendid event than the fall of the proud and haughty Court of Djocja never graced the annals of any Country, and Java will long have reason to remember with gratitude the events of the 20th of June'. The victory had been absolute, Raffles wrote, and 'The European power is now for the first time paramount in Java'.

In the short, sweaty space of less than a year, across just two changes of season – from dry to wet and back to dry again – Britain, in the person of Thomas Stamford Raffles, had conquered the Land of Promise. The Dutch had been routed and their Napoleonic sponsors sent packing. Sultan Badruddin of Palembang had been turned into a jungle refugee and his city drenched with blood, and now, best of all, the most fabled kings in the entire archipelago, the Susuhunan of Surakarta and the Sultan of Yogyakarta had been trampled beneath Raffles' feet; the courtiers had literally kissed his knees!

The British had triumphed; there were no more foreigners left for them to fight, and from now on they would have no other choice but to turn viciously and bitterly on each other. But sitting in Semarang with a smile on his face, Raffles was thinking less about the future than about the past. The garden of the residency there was full of ancient statues, prised from the old temples of the hinterland by an earlier Dutch administrator. Raffles' next adventure would be backwards into history.

Making History

The man hurried across the muddy track and picked his way through the undergrowth. It was 9 o'clock in the morning, and already the fine lavender chiffon of the first haze was thickening to a heavy blanket of bruised cloud. It was the height of the wet season, and Java was at its greenest. Away to the north Gunung Merapi rose dark from the flatlands, trailing vertical columns of smoke into the flaccid air. There was a faint smell of jasmine.

It was 19 January 1812; six months later and ten miles to the west Colonel Colin Mackenzie would plot the troop movements that would lead to the downfall of the Yogyakarta Kraton, but today he had another kind of surveying in mind. He could hardly contain his excitement as he made his way through the bushes and looked out on the tangled, overgrown countryside before him. Everywhere – at his feet, wrapped in the roots of the banyan trees, supporting the irrigation canals of the little rice fields – were blocks of intricately carved black stone. Sometimes a tilt of his head or a change of his position resolved a jumble of relief-work, half buried in the deep volcanic soil, into the figure of a stately, full-bosomed women or a cross-legged ascetic. Broken columns lay in the undergrowth and here and there the flat grinning face of a demon leered behind a furring of green moss.

But the most exciting prospect lay ahead. A series of great stumps, many times taller than a man, rose from the infestation of greenery, towering up to the height of a palm tree and beyond. Creepers knotted around their flanks; trees sprouted drunkenly from their ledges and birds nested in their crevices, but as Mackenzie hurried closer, stumbling over the riot of fallen blocks and sweating in the heat, their seemingly natural, half-melted hulks began to show lines of monumental masonry and panels of great intricacy. He was looking out on the ruins of a civilisation.

Coming this way at the end of September Captain William Robison had also noted those 'ruins of several Hindoo Monuments and temples falling to pieces', but Robison was much more interested in the present than some long-forgotten past. Mackenzie however, was a very different man, and when he made *his* first journey along the Surakarta road ahead of Raffles' bad-tempered visit to Yogyakarta in December he had been absolutely tantalised by the great piles of greening stone he had spotted through the trees. Then there had then been issues at hand so pressing that he could not even pause for the briefest of explorations, but now he was back. He and his companions – a Dutchman called Johan Knops who lived in Semarang, and an Anglo-Indian draughtsman from Madras called John Newman to sketch their discoveries – had left Surakarta before dawn. By 9 o'clock they had reached the little wayside village of Prambanan where they had arranged to lodge in the house of the richest inhabitant – the Chinaman who controlled the tollgate. They had travelled thirty hot and bumpy miles, but Mackenzie was so utterly abuzz with excitement at this new field of antiquarian glory that while his friends slumped in the shade beneath the fearsome ancestral statue in their host's hall and waited for refreshing glasses of sweet black tea he rushed out alone into the morning without waiting for a guide, ducked beneath the tollgate, dodged through the bushes, and plunged into the past:

The vast mounds covered with Trees and Bushes, the statues placed close to the road, the Fragments of richly sculptured stones that showed the way and lay about the Houses would naturally attract the notice of every Traveller; but when it appeared now that the mounds were in fact the vestiges and Debris of so many once beautiful Temples, little known to Europeans, curiosity was so much excited, that while the usual arrangements for refreshment were making [sic] by the hospitable Chinese, I crossed over the way without waiting for my Conductor to explore the field of Antique Research that lay displayed before me ...

Of all the motley and at times disreputable crew who make up the *dramatis personae* of the British Interregnum in Java, Colonel Colin Mackenzie is perhaps the most sympathetic. He was much older than the other key players – approaching sixty – and mature enough to know that forced ambition would earn as much animosity as success. He was without the insecure egoism of Raffles, was not an over-compensatory bruiser like Gillespie, showed few signs of Crawfurd's snarling racism, and managed to be neither an impolitic hothead like Robison nor a snivelling sycophant like Otho Travers. He also had interests far beyond those of accumulating money, was by no means jealous of his own scholarly work, and seems to have managed to maintain friendly and respectful relationships with both Raffles and Gillespie throughout. But what makes him most attractive of all is his sheer boyish enthusiasm for the down and dirty business of practical archaeology. A few lumps of chiselled basalt on some high mountainside or a blunted and broken statue rumoured to lie somewhere deep in the jungle – Mackenzie, a man who ought to have been approaching retirement, would go rushing out to take a look without pausing for a lunch-stop.

Mackenzie did not have the most likely of origins for a first-class orientalist adventurer. He was the Gaelic-speaking son of a postmaster, born in 1754 amongst the cold grey seas of the Outer Hebrides, and he started his career as a customs officer in Stornoway, overseeing the maritime trade of an archipelago a world away from Indonesia. In 1782 he set sail for India to serve as a military engineer in Madras, and there, between mapping native fortifications – and working out how best to blow them up – he first took an interest in the temples of old Hinduism. Mackenzie spent all his spare time and all his spare money in studying the sacred architecture of southern

India. After the fall of Tipu Sultan's Mysore in 1799 he had surveyed the whole interior of the Deccan, sketching and measuring its ruins and recording its languages. He seems to have been remarkably free of the kind of effusive – and at times absurd – romanticism of other orientalists like John Leyden. Mackenzie simply collected temples in the way that other men might have collected guns, or books, or dogs. In his portrait he appears standing very upright in full uniform (Mackenzie was 6 feet 2 inches tall), backed by a trio of white-robed Brahmins with manuscripts in hand. He has thick blond hair, a long nose and sky-blue eyes. He looks very Scottish indeed.

He had been called away from his post as Surveyor-General of the Madras Presidency to come to Java with the invasion force as head of the Engineer Corps. He was a little perturbed by the interruption of his Indian researches, but was doubtless delighted by the rumours of Hindu ruins amongst the green jungles of this far-off Muslim island. Indeed it seems that his seniors had Mackenzie's well-known hobby in mind when they selected him. Both the Commander-in-Chief and the Governor-General left him with direct instructions to make the most of his time in Java. In 1813 he wrote to Lord Minto to tell him that 'The general and verbal Instructions under which I was left by the Commander in Chief Sir S Auchmuty, I considered as much of an act of indulgence to my habits, with a degree of confidence, highly pleasing to my feelings, and when your Lordship added your sanction, I conceived it particularly incumbent on me to strain every nerve to make my stay generally useful'.

And useful he was. Though Mackenzie left Java well before Raffles' administration came to its depressed and dreary end, he probably managed to see more of the island than anyone else. Once he had surveyed the fallen fortifications at Cornelis (they were far bigger than was necessary, Mackenzie noted, and difficult to defend as a consequence), he set out at the end of November 1811 to make a preliminary survey of Java. He went everywhere: the settlement of Bandung, where there were bamboo barracks, morning markets and general tranquillity; to Surakarta where there was 'a bustle and activity... different from the other native towns of Java', and where 'the quantity of meat daily exposed to sale shew [sic] how far the habits and the manners of the Javanese are removed from the strict Hindoo observance of food, of casts [sic] and religion'; and even to the smoking summit of Gunung Merapi where 'I experienced an intense degree of cold equal to any I ever experienced in Europe'. And now he was to get his first proper look at those crumbling structures, rising through the trees at Prambanan.

He wandered on alone through the ruins, 'unattended by any guide', following the course of a narrow river, 'hopping over large blocks of cut stone' and becoming more excited by the minute. Lying here and there amongst the long grass like the fallen warriors of some great battle were statues he half-recognised from his travels in India, and as he drew closer to the great vine and banyan-covered 'pyramids' the scattered statuary grew thicker. This was not an abandoned landscape however. There were fields between the stands of mango trees, and peasants at work, up to their knees in the muddy water planting rice saplings, or padding along the raised pathways carrying loads on bobbing bamboo yokes. An oddly dressed white man wandering alone in this world will always attract attention, and by now Mackenzie was being followed by 'two or three natives'. None of them spoke anything except Javanese (he had already noted how few commoners in rural areas knew Malay), but they 'seemed desirous of cultivating an amicable understanding'.

They led him between the biggest of the buildings. These were magnificent ruins, huge hulks of crumbling block-work wrapped in a mesh of roots and creepers. Swifts darted out from cracks and crevices and flickered overhead in the damp, heavy air. There were three large buildings, each faced by a smaller stump across a field of fallen masonry. Trees had sprouted all over them, and their upper levels had given way to a chaos of collapse. But closer to ground level there was much that remained remarkable. Here and there the crowned head of a royal *naga* serpent projected at a crooked angle. Blaring guard lions, Chinese-style with broad mouths and ringletted manes, stood stiff-limbed between the blocks, and trios of *dewis* with tilted hips huddled in the recesses like sharp-tongued socialites. Panels fallen from the friezes lay about the place as if on some celestial cutting room floor.

Mackenzie's would-be guides pointed out the central building, bigger than all the others, and seemed to be telling him its name. It was known locally as *Candi Loro Jonggrang*, the Temple of the Slender Maiden – and they wanted to show him the goddess herself. Peering nervously at the teetering blocks above, some of which seemed to be held in place by nothing more than the roots of the invading vegetation, Mackenzie followed them into a chamber in the northern flank of the building, almost like a cave in a natural cliff face. As his eyes adjusted to the gloom inside a statue took shape before him. Despite her supposed name she was not exactly slender; she was positively voluptuous. She stood atop a crouching calf, the stone black and greased with age and specked with bat droppings, and her smooth but sturdy legs rose to slanted hourglass hips, a full midriff and a levitating bosom. Her left hand crushed a demon with contemptuous ease while she looked away in the other direction beneath finely arched eyebrows. A whorl of secondary arms sprouted from her back, waving swords and shields, and a scattering of petals and turmeric powder at her feet suggested that someone – perhaps the men who were guiding Mackenzie – still made some small daily obeisance here.

Mackenzie ought to have recognised her at once as the goddess Durga, wife of Shiva in her more belligerent incarnation, but he seems not to have done so. As for the locals, the name Durga would have meant nothing to them; they *knew* who she was: she was the Slender Maiden, the woman whose fate explained the very existence of these strange buildings amongst their fields and bamboo huts. But the story could wait for later; Mackenzie had more exploring to do. Picking his way over the masonry like a mountaineer he found another chamber in the western wall. Durga's identity might have eluded him, but there was no mistaking her son, the elephant-headed Ganesha, even if his vehicle, the rat, was missing.

'From there', wrote Mackenzie, 'I clambered higher, over vast heaps of the stones'. He scrambled down into a dark cavity on the southern side of the building. It was scented with the musty, unwashed odour of bat droppings and full of tumbled blocks, standing amongst which was a statue of 'an aged Chief ... remarkable for the Majesty and Gravity of its aspect, for its flowing Beard and for the raised aquiline nose and European Countenance ...' Though Javanese temple conventions were certainly different from those of the Deccan, Mackenzie might also have been expected to recognise this figure as the Vedic sage Agastya, but perhaps the sheer excitement of exploring was preventing him from making cool assessments.

After an hour of wandering he returned breathless and voluble to the Chinaman's house. He took a brief rest and a slurp of cold tea before he and his two companions headed back out amongst the ruins riding 'in chairs provided with canopies of leaves each carried by men on bamboo poles'. The pace of these rustic palanquins was not one suited to men so energised by the sight of such 'tantalising ruins' however, and they kept leaping out of the chairs to race ahead on foot. They headed north through the rice fields, Mackenzie noting that many of the water channels were reinforced with pieces of magnificent masonry robbed from the temples. A mile from the road, beyond the buildings that Mackenzie had already explored, they came to *Candi Sewu*, the Thousand Temples. The trees around this complex were so thick that they saw nothing until they came upon 'two gigantic figures of porters, apparently resting on the knee on pedestals facing each other resting on clubs held in each hand'. They had curly hair, flying moustaches, and 'eyeballs starting out'. Beyond these dramatic *dwarapala* doormen they passed through an avenue of hundreds of ruined temples, some with archways which Mackenzie felt looked vaguely gothic in style. Here and there amongst the stones lay the delicate statue of a mendicant, cross-legged in meditation and startlingly lifelike. The main temple was a fabulous ruin with trees sprouting like mould all over it, but Mackenzie was baffled by the apparent lack of Hindu symbolism here, and he and his companions searched in vain for some hint of writing, some revelatory scratch of Sanskrit amongst the friezes.

It was growing dark and rain was threatening by the time they returned to the village, 'much fatigued tho' highly gratified'. Dinner was ready – 'The Chinese here were very polite, civil and accommodating and with cordial smiles and the most obliging aspect came forward to tender every offer of hospitality' – and they ate in the central hall of their host's Javanese-style house under the furious glare of a statue of a Chinese household deity. Afterwards they worked on their notes and sketches by candlelight, and listened to the legend of the temples, told by a villager and translated by the Chinaman. Mackenzie was disappointed: it was 'rather a confused mixture of local stories from which as little Historical truth can be elicited as from the generality of vulgar traditions', but it was a good story.

Long ago, before Yogyakarta, before Mataram, before Islam and *long* before the Dutch, there was a great but brutal king in these parts. He ruled from a palace on a promontory of the hills that rose to the south of the modern village, and his name was Ratu Boko. He had a beautiful daughter known as Loro Jonggrang (though she was in truth rather more buxom than slender). Another kingdom, further away to the northwest in Kedu, was ruled by a man called Damar Moyo, and one day the two rulers went to war. The northern troops were led by the Crown Prince, Bandung-Bondowoso, and they vanquished the southern army and slaughtered Ratu Boko. As he and his men took possession of the fallen palace Bandung-Bondowoso caught sight of the grieving princess. One glimpse of Loro Jonggrang's heaving bosom was all it took: he fell madly in love and asked her to marry him. He had not really chosen his moment very well (having just murdered her father) and she refused, saying that she would only ever countenance such a connection if her suitor was able to build one thousand temples in the hours between sunset and sunrise – the eternal herculean task of the fairy tale.

This being the age when such things were possible, Bandung-Bondowoso raised an army of djinns to render the impossible possible and by midnight great towers of magnificent stonework were sprouting all over the Prambanan plain. The terrified princess called her handmaids together, had a fire built in the east to mimic the dawn, and set them to work pounding unhusked rice, as Javanese women always do at sunrise. The ghost army, hearing these portents of the coming day – and just one temple short of the total – downed tools and went home to the underworld. Bandung-Bondowoso, unsurprisingly, was rather annoyed when he discovered the ruse. He had the faithless beauty turned to stone and installed in a final, thousandth temple, where she has stood, keeping watch over the surrounding villages, ever since ...

And with the bedtime story finished, it was time to sleep. Mackenzie, Knops and Newman settled down in the chambers off the main hall. Outside the rain was sheeting down, roaring on the roof and cascading off the leaves of the banana plants. The porters who had travelled with them from Surakarta were gathered under the dripping eaves smoking and drinking coffee and frittering away their wages over card games, but the Europeans 'enjoyed a profound repose undisturbed by any fears or want of security or any noise'.

It was still raining in the morning, but at 9 o'clock they went out anyway, heading south this time with 'a venerable Javanese' leading the way. The wobbling bamboo palanquins were rolled out again, but the paths were so narrow that all too often Mackenzie had to get down and wade through the mire himself. The downpour was intense, and everyone was sodden in seconds, but they marched enthusiastically on, slipping and slithering, thunder crackling in the distance. They passed another monstrous, grinning *dwarapala*, 'rather like a negro'. Its tightly curled locks made Mackenzie think of the profile reliefs of Zoroastrian kings at Persepolis in Persia.

Another temple in a clearing had a huge banyan growing from its very summit, but the explorers still picked their way into the inner chamber: 'it is not without awe that on looking up one perceives a thousand heavy blocks retained by little visible force just ready to tumble in and crush and overwhelm the curious Beholder', Mackenzie wrote, also noting with wonder that centuries after the work was done 'the marks of the Chipping knife was visible on many of the stones'.

Mackenzie was pressed for time; he still had the rest of Java to survey, and was hoping to make a quick visit to Bali too, and other political duties were piling up. He stayed out amongst the ruins most of that afternoon, and continued to explore most of the following day too. The female statues, he noted, not least Loro Jonggrang herself, were 'singularly striking, delicate and beautiful, in no manner resembling the Physiognomy, habits of costume of the present Inhabitants of Java'. Finally, after a third night with the hospitable Chinaman, Mackenzie headed back towards Surakarta, utterly exhausted. Gunung Merapi showed clear to the north, and the road was lined with little bamboo stalls 'where Tea and Coffee, Rice boiled in heaps, Soups, Vegetables, Fruits, Nuts, Betel, the eternal Tobacco and the never failing Opium are prepared ready for the nourishment, comfort or intoxication of the weary traveller'. But the mind of this particular weary traveller was already abuzz without the help of artificial stimulants. 'It was not without reluctance I left these interesting ruins, and while I was surveying them with mixed emotions of regret and pleasure' wrote Mackenzie. He couldn't stop wondering at the origins of the people who had built them – they surely couldn't be the same race as the shabby farmers who lived around the temples now! And what were the cultural influences that had played upon them? Should he start hunting for links with Gujarat, with Siam, or with eastern India?

The conclusions which Mackenzie did draw about Prambanan were ultimately rather slipshod. He had mistakenly identified several of the statues as belonging to the Jain religion, and, confused by the original stylistic touches, he believed that 'the Brahmin or Vedantic system of mythology' had less importance there than Buddhism (the next serious British visitor to Prambanan took the sensible measure of asking an educated high-caste Indian from one of the sepoy regiments to accompany him. Thousands of miles from his Bengali home, and hundreds of years after the carvings were made, the sepoy was nonetheless able to clear up many of these confusions with his first glance at the stonework). Mackenzie might also have done well to listen more closely to the myth of Loro Jonggrang, with its talk of two rival kingdoms and a marriage between them.

* * *

Long ago, before Yogyakarta, before Mataram, before Islam and *long* before the Dutch, there *were* two kingdoms in Central Java. One – which may or may not have been ruled at some point by a brutal king with a buxom and beautiful daughter – was based somewhere in the vicinity of the Prambanan temples; the other seems to have had its capital away to the northwest. One was Hindu; the other was Buddhist.

Indian religions, Indian vocabulary and ideas, and Indian arts had begun dripping into Indonesia, and especially into Java, sometime early in the First Millennium. The religion arrived much the same way as Islam would centuries later – amongst the boxes and bundles of traders in the Pasisir ports, and then in the late-night stories of wandering sages, men half-saint, half-lunatic. There was no great conquest by armies sweeping out of the Subcontinent, and no great influx of Indian immigrants. But individual travellers – many of them probably nothing but chancers, claiming to be learned Brahmins the way later Arab charlatans would claim to be Sayyids – arrived in the rustic villages of local chiefs, and there amongst the palm trees and chickens they espoused stories of Shiva, Brahma and Vishnu, and of the enlightenment of the Buddha. Temples began to sprout here and there amongst the folds of the green volcanoes, in places of older power usually – a high plateau or a sacred spring – and as villages coalesced into fiefdoms, and fiefdoms into royal realms, Javanese was written down on strips of palm leaf, or carved into celebratory stone columns, in a script based on Sanskrit.

The first of these old Javanese dynasties to take some kind of clear shape on the photographic paper of history is the Sailendra, the Kings of the Mountain. They were Buddhists, it seems, and they ruled from somewhere in Kedu to the west of Gunung Merapi, from the 8th century. At the same time another dynasty, the Sanjaya, rose in the eternally power-charged vicinity of the future Yogyakarta. These rulers were not Buddhists but Shaivite Hindus, and it was they who built the temples at Prambanan. There were certainly wars between these two powers, and at some point Sanjaya seems to have been made a vassal of Sailendra. There were later rebellions, and there was also a marriage between the kingdoms. Whether the bride was willing or not is unknown, but it seems that a flurry of temple building was probably involved in the wedding celebrations (though perhaps not all between the hours of dusk and dawn). It was unsurprising that Mackenzie could find no Hindu imagery at Candi Sewu – unlike the neighbouring Loro Jonggrang complex a mile to the south, the Thousand Temples were dedicated to the Buddhist faith of the new in-laws.

Later the two kingdoms and the two faiths seemed to melt into one, and though many dynasties would rise and fall in Java there would never again be a clear dividing line between Buddhism and Hinduism. At the end of the First Millennium the shining, shimmering centre of royal power shifted east out of Central Java to the basin of the Brantas River near Surabaya. Kingdoms bubbled up and rose briefly to the surface like boils in the lava cauldron of a volcano, often lasting only a few generations before popping, and releasing the power to rise elsewhere – Kahuripan, Janggala, Kediri, Singosari, and then, finally, in the 14th century, the biggest bubble of all, Majapahit. But by that time the merchants rolling into the Pasisir ports when the trade winds blew from the west had brows unmarked by *sindoor* and sandalwood, and were touting Arabic texts, not Sanskrit epics.

The Hindu-Buddhist centuries had left Java studded with temples. Those at Prambanan were amongst the most dramatic, but there were hundreds of others out amongst the jungles and rice fields, high on the mountainsides or in between the villages. They had been built without mortar, and the seeds of the island's rampant vegetation lodged in the cracks and sprouted, sending roots down between the friezes. Sometimes the villagers – nominal Muslims now – took the stone away to edge roads and line ditches, but as had always been the way in Java, domestic architecture was built of wood and thatch, and for the most part they left the old places to fall of their own accord.

A tower of black masonry might stand in a grove of trees amongst their fields. They would build a story for it and fill it with djinns and other bad spirits, but if its location was one with unmistakable energy they would not avoid it altogether. Those seeking power or enlightenment would slip out along the field boundaries at sunset to spend the night meditating on the platform of some vanished idol in a crumbling chamber, or if a statue remained they would give it a new name and would bring *sajen* offerings of flowers to place at its feet. They had, in fact, made the temples their own again, democratised them. Though the stones were crumbling and the friezes vanishing under the moss, they had been stripped of allegorical foreign mythology and renamed in a language that the villagers understood. The ersatz ceremonies of usurious priests had given way to a pinch of petals, left at dawn. These places, these hulks of ancient masonry, had been consumed by the island, they had been made wholly Javanese.

But now a new body of foreigners had arrived, touting a new language and carrying a whole new set of ideas.

* * *

Thomas Stamford Raffles had already conquered and humiliated the courts of the Javanese present; now he wanted to conquer their past. He wanted to annex the island's history, to make it his own vassal state.

The idea of European scholarship in Asia as an act of possession and domination is one that can be taken *much* too far, but in the case of

Raffles in Java it is entirely apt. 'Knowledge is power,' he once wrote, 'and in the intercourse between enlightened and ignorant nations, the former must and will be the rulers'. He and his contemporaries sent military engineers to survey ancient temples as though they were reconnoitring a fortress ahead of battle; they moved from district to district, epoch to epoch defeating the massed armies of myth and misinformation, and rendering the latter-day inhabitants as ignorant degenerates, unworthy of their own heritage. It was an invasion; the white men were the winners, and Raffles did it all without his guru, without his sage.

Throughout the British Interregnum in Java the absence of John Leyden aches like an empty wall niche in an old temple, the statue stolen by looters. The versifying Scot was supposed to have been Raffles' partner in academia, his collaborator and guide in these attempts definitively to dominate the Javanese past. His own development as a scholar had only just begun when the fever felled his friend, and a sense of inadequacy and loss clearly remained, for over the coming years Raffles often seemed to try slotting some other idol into the vacant niche, until finally he reached the stage where he was inflated enough to clamber into it himself. The first and most obvious Leyden-substitute was William Marsden, the godfather of British scholarship in Southeast Asia, who had collected the material for a monumental slab of history, ethnography and general observation entitled *The History of Sumatra* while serving in the singularly insalubrious hardship posting of Bengkulu in the 1770s. Raffles had corresponded with Marsden during his first tentative scholarly steps in Penang, and the letters continued long into his career. When finally he produced his own hulking two-volume magnum opus on the Land of Promise, the year after the British Interregnum ended, in a nod to Marsden, and with the same arrogantly definite article, he called it *The History of Java*.

Its hundreds of pages amount to a curious compendium of history, anthropology and hearsay, a discourse on Javanese literature, a gazetteer of temples, a dash of anti-Dutch propaganda, and a howl of frustrated self-justification. It was also by far the most significant work to emerge from the minor publishing boom that came of the Java campaign, and it presented for the first time ideas about the history of Indonesia that would remain pervasive – and at times pernicious – throughout the colonial era and beyond.

Clearly, with all his other business to attend to, Raffles did not have time to go stripping the creepers off temples himself, and in many ways *The History of Java* is simply a grand exercise in sanctioned plagiarism. Though the book itself contains plenty of claims that the Dutch had taken no interest in the history and culture of Java before the British arrived, Raffles made liberal use of accounts and manuscripts he found in the Buitenzorg library; the translations tagged on as footnotes were often simply translations of translations, and he sometimes turned to the expertise of time-served, fever-wracked Hollanders when hunting out obscure cultural details. But more importantly, Raffles employed his own legion of mini-Leydens to do the footwork.

Mackenzie was the first, and a captain in one of the Bengal regiments called George Baker was employed to make a more complete survey of Prambanan and the other ruins in Central Java. And then there was Dr Thomas Horsfield, the most unlikely of all the foreigners in Java. An American medical doctor from a strict Moravian upbringing in Pennsylvania, he had come east in 1800 and discovered botany to be more rewarding than either medicine or Christianity. He had been based in the Susuhunan's city ever since, pressing flowers, climbing trees, and setting up what could probably be regarded as the first zoo in Java. Horsfield had already explored much of Java. He claimed apologetically that he now spoke Dutch better than English, but was quite happy to head for the hills once more in search of history and horticulture at Raffles' behest. He soon became a fixture of the reconstituted Batavian Society, a group of Dutch and British gentlemen who would gather of a steamy evening in the colonial capital to hear readings on topics ranging from the interior regions of Borneo to the 'chemical analysis of a volcanic sand

and iron ore', and to discuss such pressing matters as 'the most proper food for young children, who are not suckled by their mother'.

* * *

Horsfield dealt mostly with the natural world; the most celebrated of all the work that Raffles ordered was done by the energetic young Dutch surveyor, Hermanus Christian Cornelius. He had already explored many of Java's temples on behalf of his own countrymen (he had made a preliminary survey of Prambanan for the Dutch authorities in 1807, for example); now he continued the work for his new English master. Though his own name has been largely forgotten, the discoveries he made remain a high point of the whole British administration in Java.

It was in Semarang, sometime in 1814, that Raffles seems first to have heard a story of a huge monument, somewhere in the forests of the rugged green district of Kedu, taken into British control as part of the loot of Yogyakarta Treaty. The garden of the residency in Semarang was full of statues and friezes collected by a former Dutch inhabitant. Amongst the flowerbeds there were seated Ganeshas in weathered stone, panels lifted from the Ramayana epic, and many-limbed goddesses. There were probably also a few mendicant Buddhas, cross-legged in contemplation amongst the bougainvillea. Perhaps it was these particular graven images which caught the Lieutenant-Governor's attention; perhaps some of them had been taken from the very spot, close to the junction of the Progo and Elo Rivers where the forested hills formed a bowl of green land, and where there was said to be a great man-made mountain of stone, even bigger and even less well-known than the towering ruins of Prambanan.

Cornelius – who almost certainly already knew of the place, and who is in fact a logical candidate for Raffles' initial informant – was dispatched to investigate. The young surveyor took the well-trodden and picturesque road south into the mountains, branched right before Salatiga, passed between the fiery Merapi and its western twin,

Mount Sumbing, and came to the place, twenty-six miles northwest of Yogyakarta, where in the 9th century the long-forgotten Sailendra Dynasty had overseen the construction of a spectacular mountain of stone.

Today Raffles often receives the credit for 'discovering' Borobudur, as if the Lieutenant-Governor had waded through the swamps and tugged aside the creepers himself. It is a fairly obvious misrepresentation and one that all but the most credulous of sightseers would likely see through. But two other tales about the rescue of this mighty monument from obscurity are rather more enduring. The first is that it was completely 'lost' when Raffles dispatched Cornelius to look for it. It wasn't; everyone in Central Java knew it was there. It even had a taboo attached to it – crown princes of the Mataram line were recommended to avoid the place (a youthful Yogyakarta royal who ignored this good advice was said to have died vomiting blood after he went to take a look in 1758). It wasn't even entirely unknown to the earlier generations of Dutchmen. The first European record of the place comes courtesy of a man named Frederik Coyett who stole some statues in 1733. And the fact that all these people already knew that Borobudur was there clearly negates the second myth – that the whole 100-foot high hulk of masonry was buried deep beneath layers of volcanic ash.

It *was* in a bit of a mess, however. Borobudur was already a thousand years old and the whole place had fallen out of repair when the focus of Javanese Hindu-Buddhist royal power shifted east towards Surabaya in the 10th century. Cornelius had to command the labour of 200 men from the nearby villages to strip back the clogging vegetation and dig out some of the ash, the accumulated debris of ten centuries of volcanic eruptions from the surrounding peaks which had clogged the terraces, if not covered the entire building. It was not a full restoration attempt by any means; it was just a little gardening work ahead of a preliminary survey, but it still took a fortnight, and it revealed a clearer view of an epic in stone than anyone had enjoyed for centuries.

When the work was done Cornelius would have looked out on a magnificent piece of architecture, a million-and-a-half blocks of grey andesite rising between great heaps of sawn branches and slashed creepers. The air would have been thick with the sticky, sweet scent of newly cut foliage and trampled earth, and the exhausted labourers would have been reclining in the shade to smoke as the surveyor made his way around the levels. The whole thing formed a huge, squat, four-sided pyramid, rising through ten levels to a single crumbling *stupa*. From a distance it was strangely blunt, little more than the coarse cladding of the natural hill that formed its core. But once Cornelius came closer the true scope of the place became apparent: every wall was faced with remarkable bas-relief friezes; the inner and outer sides of the balustrades were lined with scenes of Buddhist legend in narrative order. It all amounted to a sublime three-mile-long cartoon strip. Above the preliminary levels were three shrinking circular platforms arrayed with latticed, bell-shaped structures, each capping a seated Buddha. And at the very top was that slumped *stupa* in the same form. The whole thing was slowly coming to pieces; the paved floors had warped like a rumpled blanket, and the latticed *stupas* had slumped drunkenly or toppled inwards, leaving their Buddhas exposed to the temporal world. Stairs had collapsed, and trees had sprouted all over the terraces, but it was still a masterpiece.

Neither Cornelius in his first glances, nor Raffles in his later musings were able entirely to untangle the true history of Borobudur, but we now know that the Sailendra kings had it built over a period of some seven decades, starting in around 780 A.D. It was put together without an initial plan, each new generation of kings, architects and masons building upon what had been done before until it reached its ultimate apex. What it was actually *for* is still not entirely clear – unlike the buildings at Prambanan it is not really a temple, for there is no inner sanctum to house a deity and to receive prayers. More likely it was meant as an epic of educational pilgrimage, visitors circuiting the levels in order and climbing ever higher towards enlightenment. It was, and it is, the biggest Buddhist monument in the world. For

Raffles it was simply another archaeological conquest.

But whatever the motivations – and whatever the misinformation created by later tour leaders and guidebook writers – Raffles and his collaborators really *had* been the first people to bring Borobudur to the attention of the European world. Though Cornelius' two weeks of hacking and slashing were nothing to the epic restoration efforts – almost matching the original Sailendra work in scope and scale – that began under later generations of Dutchmen and that were not completed until the 1980s, they did amount to the first tentative steps in the right direction. They quite literally cleared the way for those who would follow. And the first brief and somewhat perfunctory overview of the statues and carvings in *The History of Java* (Borobudur got much less attention from the British than Prambanan), let the world know that this place existed. The book let the world know of many other places too, other heaps of chiselled stone on high hillsides: Sukuh, Penataran, the temples of Dieng and Singosari, epic monuments forgotten by everyone – except the people who had lived around them ever since they were built, of course. The concerted cataloguing of the temples of Java was ultimately the most benign and admirable of all the British conquests in Indonesia.

* * *

While Cornelius was surveying, other source materials were called in to Buitenzorg. Native translators slaved over looted manuscripts, and draughtsmen's copies of old inscriptions were routinely delivered up to a prince of Sumenep in Madura who, it had been discovered to Raffles' delight, was something of an expert on the archaic languages of the archipelago. Even the Susuhunan himself was ordered to compile an account of the history of Mataram from the venerable old sages of the court. The work of these unknown, long forgotten men provided the foundations on which Raffles's *History* was built – and provided later hagiographers with the opportunity to infer that he himself was a master not just of 'eloquent Malayan phrases' but of the grammar and scripts of all the eastern tongues.[16]

Raffles was also drawing on the work of another swaggering orientalist, the one man he couldn't quite sideline. John Crawfurd, the Yogyakarta Resident, was busily working on his own great treatise, and the scholarly rivalry between the two men was starting to spark. Raffles ultimately beat Crawfurd into print by three years, but the sour-tempered Scotsman had plumped for an even more ambitious scope, and an even greater glut of pagination: his *History of the Indian Archipelago* (no definitive 'the' here) ran to three volumes when it finally appeared in 1820. It took in the whole sprawling galaxy of islands between the Malay Peninsula and Papua New Guinea. In doing so it amounted to probably the earliest academic assessment of the region as a single entity, and the name that Crawfurd chose for

---

16 The first volume of *The History of Java* contains a rendering of the Bharatayudha, a lengthy episode from the Ramayana cycle, written in *Kawi*, Old Javanese, the archaic language of high literature with its own specialised script. Raffles' first biographer (who also happened to be his second wife, and who had never visited Java) claimed that 'he passed the greater part of every morning and evening in reading and translating with the greatest rapidity and ease the different legends with which they [native informants] furnished him, particularly the Brata Yudha'. Raffles could not even *speak* colloquial Javanese (as is made clear by Yogyakarta court accounts about the embarrassing difficulties of his meetings with those from the Kraton who knew no Malay), let alone read, understand and translate the archaic literary form of the language. The version of the Bharatayudha in *The History of Java* may have been drawn from a pre-existing Malay translation with the help of a reader, or done as a simultaneous double translation with a Javanese scribe from either the original or one of the modern Javanese re-writes. It may even – whisper it! – have been done by someone else entirely. But one thing is certain: Thomas Stamford Raffles did *not* sit alone at his desk skimming over the wriggling, squiggling squirms of the text in the original manuscript and rendering it directly into purple 19th-century English 'with the greatest rapidity and ease'. Incredibly, however, biographers from later, more sceptical generations were perfectly prepared to swallow this line from the second Mrs Raffles, and to give credulous credit to Raffles for doing it all himself. They approached the founding of Singapore in much the same way.

this watery world – the Indian Archipelago – prefigured the Greek compound later used for the independent nation that would spring from it: *Indonesia,* The Indian Islands.

Crawfurd's book was more firmly rooted in personal experience – especially when it came to the chapters on language – and he suffered less chronically from literary appendicitis, inserting far fewer undigested chunks from the works of other men. This all made for a decidedly lighter read, but many of Crawfurd's conclusions were rather lightweight too, and the whole tome is monumentally racist. In his comprehensive assessment of the native characters of the various islanders, he explained to interested readers in English drawing rooms, 'I shall consider the more civilized races only, for the habits of the mere savages of all climates are nearly assimilated'. Still, he made it very clear that he was using the term 'civilised' in only the most relative of senses with his assessment of the people he knew best of all in Indonesia, the Javanese:

All the faculties of their minds are in a state of comparative feebleness; their memories are treacherous and uncertain; their imaginations wanton and childish; and their reason, more defective than the rest, when exerted on any subject above the most vulgar train of thought, commonly erroneous and mistaken. No man can tell his own age, nor the date of any remarkable transaction in the history of his tribe or country ...

He regarded them as 'semibarbarians'.

This kind of thing makes it easy enough to laugh at Crawfurd, and to dismiss him as the bigoted archetype of a mercifully long-forgotten past. It also, by way of contrast, makes it easier to take Raffles more seriously, for he is rarely so crude, and despite the longueurs his literary tone is rather more refined. But a close reading of *The History of Java* reveals that the difference between the scholarly rivals was more of style than of substance, for rarely is there an idea posited that is not contradicted in a later chapter.

Raffles was desperate to view himself as a liberal in the Wilberforce tradition, and he was eager to disavow the received Dutch view of the Javanese in which they were innately 'indolent and insensible beyond conception'. If the natives were at times a little dozy, Raffles declared, it was not because of some inherited racial inferiority, but as a result of centuries of bad government by local despots and the VOC. Under a liberal British administration they would flourish as well as anyone – or at least that's what he *wanted* to believe. But Raffles was a 19th-century Englishman; there were certain ideas hardwired into *his* genes, and they emerged most often in his writing on the antiquities of Java.

'The grandeur of their ancestors sounds like a fable in the mouth of the degenerate Javan', he wrote. And Raffles had a simple explanation for this alleged ignorance and degeneracy: Islam.

Raffles often wrote of his contempt for the Muslim faith – 'I abhor and abominate the tenets of Mahometanism' he once noted in a letter to his cousin – and he blamed it for the decline and fall of Java. Before conversion, Raffles would have had it, everything was perfect (as it would be again if he ever got a chance to put his administrative reforms into full practice). There had been no hunger; there had been art and intellectualism of the highest order, and it was only conversion from the noble, civilised Hindu-Buddhist faith that had brought the 'distraction of internal war and the division of the country into petty contending sovereignties'. Raffles can almost – *almost* – be forgiven for nurturing these ideas: he gave by far the greatest part of his attention to the pre-Islamic past of Java. Its ruins and its stories of empire made for the instant classics of a fallen civilisation in the Greek and Roman mould, and he deliberately snubbed the monuments of more recent history – the modern Muslim-built palaces, where he would have found plenty of impressive old Javanese conventions had he bothered looking. And when Raffles himself visited Prambanan and Borobudur he did so in the company of local peasants. Watching them move slack-armed, loose-shouldered through the ruins with limp footfalls, hearing them speaking amongst themselves in low *Ngoko* Javanese – a language like a mouthful of hot pebbles – and then turning once more to the bounteous glories and immaculate craftsmanship of the bas-relief panels, the idea that this was a fallen people was irresistible. A Javanese prince would have felt much the same way if he had visited St Paul's Cathedral in the company of paupers from the East End slums.

If Raffles had dug a little deeper into the chronicles he would have seen that the 'distraction of internal war' had been just as much a feature of Hindu-Buddhist Java as of its Muslim reincarnation; Mataram had lasted as long and had shone as brightly as Majapahit. Raffles failed to realise that these great temples were likely built using forced labour, and he connected the well-fed figures on the friezes to a reality, as if those rice bellies and ample limbs represented an actual prosperity, as if those beatific smiles demonstrated a genuine contentment rather than the obvious propaganda of a despotism. This was a serious failure of imagination, a naivety which, blended with cultural hostility, became something else, a blunt turn of intellect with all the finesse of the most brutish *dwarapala*.

As for his own motivations for all this scholarship, Raffles explained them in a letter to William Marsden towards the end of his time in Java. The energy he and his collaborators spent on hacking through creepers to view crumbling ruins and on translating ancient texts left many members of Batavia's older European community bemused, he wrote: 'The Dutch colonists accuse us of folly; and the only answer I can make to them is that I am ambitious of the title of Bitara in after days.' Bitara (or Batara) was a royal title taken by the kings of Majapahit. Raffles had embarked on his all-conquering historical research to crown himself emperor of a mythical Javanese past.

But before you make history, you have to deal with the present. As the first full year the British had spent in Java drew towards its damp and dripping close Thomas Stamford Raffles had plenty to be worried about. He had a sick wife and an administrative migraine, and the second most powerful man in Java was rapidly becoming his worst enemy.

* * *

Any casual visitor who arrived in Java in the months after the fall of Yogyakarta might have been forgiven for believing that all was well. As far as the British public was concerned, there was 'evident tranquillity and general prosperity', and the first foundations were being laid for a new colonial society. In October they had held the first annual Salatiga Races in the uplands of Central Java. Posses of ponies ridden by hot-blooded young officers thundered across the fields; there was a cricket match, the opening meet of a new pack of staghounds, and a sublime view of the mountains, as recorded in the *Java Government Gazette*: 'The long continued dry weather had given the woods and downs the russet tint of autumn. The huge mountain of Salatiga [Merbabu] wrapped her head in mists and clouds, and her giant volcanic brother of Boyalillie [Merapi] hid his craggy cliffs in the same fleecy mantle'

As the year turned the *Gazette* continued to carry the kind of news to be expected of a remote British colony going quietly about its business. A Mr Watt had come into possession of 100 cows, and wanted to sell them; there was 'Superior French Claret, Newly arrived' on sale for '18 Spanish dollars per dozen'; the Batavian Society was hosting regular meetings for the first time in several years, and Weltevreeden now had a venue for socialising – Raffles had organised the completion of a half-finished club house, the Harmonie, a place for drinking, dining and dancing. There were little glitches here and there of course. People died of fever with depressing regularity. Frequent front-page 'wanted' notices suggest that Indian servants had a tendency to go AWOL (often having first raided their masters' cash boxes). Low-ranking soldiers had been caught selling their uniforms in the market in Batavia and were threatened with a fine of ten times the value of the clothes in question if it happened again, and literary bickering under pseudonyms in the correspondence columns of the

Gazette had gotten out of hand, prompting the editor to issue a stern notice to the offenders, reminding them that 'General satire is both amusing and useful, but we are averse to admitting any remarks that can be considered personal.'

There was another concern, not covered in the Gazette, and that was the health of the First Lady of British Java. Olivia Raffles had not been feeling herself. Back in Central Java in the dry weather in the aftermath of the Yogyakarta campaign, it had been six weeks before Raffles was able to prise her out of bed in Salatiga to make the journey back to Buitenzorg. She seems to have been very ill indeed, for at one point Raffles wrote to Minto in a genuinely overwrought state at his wife's condition:

I am concerned to state that Mrs Raffles is labouring under a very severe illness ... an abscess burst in the Right Lobe of the Liver, and the quantity of mercury which it became immediately necessary to throw into the liver, to save her life, has so effectually reduced her strength and shaken her constitution that I am at this moment under the most serious alarm. At the time I am writing my nerves are so unsteady and my ideas so confused that I hardly know what I say ...

Olivia was by now advancing into her forties. In the early 19th century, even in England, that would have made her a decidedly mature woman. In the fever-haunted ranks of a European community in Southeast Asia it made her of an age where a collapse in constitution would have been quite normal. Raffles himself attributed her recurrent illness to the after-effects of 'a fall while dancing' in Penang several years earlier, an accident which he claimed had led to some kind of internal haemorrhage. Of course, in steamy Java she could have been suffering from all manner of ailments: repeat dengue or malaria, chronic dysentery – or mercury poisoning for that matter. But given the repeated allusions to her liver, and to 'fits of gout in her head and stomach', as well as the hints, whispers and rumours, it does have to be considered that 'a fall while dancing' – a dizzy, spinning stumble in the midst of a jolly crowd – may well have been more of a symptom than a cause: Olivia certainly enjoyed a party. The crisis of the dry months seems to have passed by the New Year, and a relieved Raffles wrote to Minto that his wife was 'herself again'. In truth her health would always be fragile from now on, but there was no keeping the good woman down and she was soon presiding over gay gatherings at Buitenzorg once more.

The couple lived in some style in the white house in the hills above Batavia. Though Raffles would later make strident claims about his own frugality, he did not stint when it came to hosting parties, and he did not stint when it came to domestic staff. Besides the Lieutenant-Governor's relatively modest tally of 3 European servants and 23 salaried Indians and Indonesians, there were 77 slaves at Buitenzorg, including 9 indentured musicians, 7 cooks, a saddle-maker and a cowherd. Raffles also kept 8 slaves to attend upon him personally.

Translators had by this time plodded through the cascade of clauses attached to the existing Dutch laws on slavery. These ran to ninty-seven articles, and they governed every aspect of the buying, selling, beating and burying of slaves (on the latter matter, you were not allowed to inter a dead slave in your garden). Religion was dealt with (all Christian masters were to 'instruct their slaves in the principles of the Christian Religion and to have them baptised'; the children of slaves belonging to Christians were not under *any* circumstances to be circumcised). Article 38 declared that 'No slaves male or female are allowed to walk on the pavements of the streets, except when obliged to do so to avoid carriages', while Article 45 stated that 'slaves are not permitted to ride horses, whether saddled or not, on pain of being flogged'. It was a crime to sell alcohol to a slave, or to let one in to a gambling house, and slaves were strictly forbidden from gathering together after sunset, 'even should they do no mischief'. Article 35 declared that 'Executors of estates are prohibited from disposing of such female slaves as have borne children to their masters', a common enough occurrence by all accounts. When it came to punishments for bad behaviour you were quite within your rights to use 'domestic chastisement', and any slave who abused his master was to be whipped. If, however, you wished to clap your slave in irons you did have to apply to the magistrate first.

Raffles had decided to leave most of these clauses on the statute books, particularly those dealing with the thrashings. Slavery in Java, he liked to believe – as a benevolent slave-owner himself – amounted to nothing more obnoxious than 'regulated domestic servitude'. However, 'it is to be considered that slaves in general are led to the good conduct, which universally characterises them on this island, in a certain measure by this long established law, and any serious alteration therein might lead to the most serious consequences'. A firm hand, apparently, was required to make such a mild system work. The import of fresh slaves from outlying islands had been banned, in accordance with the liberal zeitgeist of post-Wilberforce England, with one exception: Raffles was ready to allow some low-level interisland flesh trade to continue, as long as the slaves were 'under fourteen years'. At such a tender age, he believed, 'the change cannot be felt and the misfortune is not remembered'.

While the slaves did all the menial work, at a rather more elevated level of employment there was a decided element of jobs-for-the-boys in the Raffles establishment. British Java was chronically understaffed and underfunded, and outlying residencies and unglamorous departments were usually manned by poorly paid skeleton crews. If, however, you were part of the Raffles clique then you could usually be found a lucrative position close to the centre. This had all started back in the early days of the occupation with a certain Captain William Flint. Flint was married to Mary Anne, Raffles' younger sister who had come out from England to attach herself to her brother's household back in his Penang days. In the aftermath of the fall of Cornelis Flint had been given what was essentially an honorary position as head of the prize agents, the men sent out to assess and catalogue the seized Dutch assets. Flint did no scrambling around in clove-scented warehouses himself, and filled in no lengthy tables of takings, but, much to the chagrin of the other prize agents who had actually done all the work, Raffles allowed him to take a hefty commission on the prize. This kind of thing seems to have been very much the way Raffles worked, and makes it abundantly obvious why he could always find strident attack dogs from his own circle to fight his cause whenever opinion turned against him. But it also helps explain why so many *other* people took violently against him and made accusations of corruption and self-interest.

The person who seems to have done best of all from his seat in the Java gravy train was Otho Travers. The year 1812, he noted in his journal, had been 'the pleasantest and most profitable since I left my "own dear native land" '. Pleasantness and profit always seemed to go hand in hand for Travers. As well as working as Raffles' ADC he had been appointed town-major of Batavia, a post which gave him the responsibility of disposing of the estates of all those who died without leaving a will – and the right to claim a commission on this macabre duty. As the Batavian climate tended to fell Europeans in sudden swathes Travers was a busy man, and 'Although it was a very troublesome job, the profit of my 5 per cent was an ample compensation.' Travers managed to take up plenty of other lucrative positions too, and within two years of arriving in Java he was declaring that he had made 'enough money to go home with', by which he meant enough money on which to retire – at the age of twenty-nine.

* * *

For all the merry money-making in the inner circle, however, Raffles was actually presiding over a colony on the brink of total financial collapse. The cursed paper money was still fluttering all over the place (it was now worth a thirteenth of its original value), and plans to get it out of circulation were crippled by the continuing and chronic lack of real money in Java. Meanwhile, the financial projections which Raffles had cooked up in the first months of his rule had proved to be the wildest of fantasies. He had told the East India Company that

Java would make three-quarters of a million Spanish dollars profit in the first twelve months. It had done nothing of the kind.

Raffles had banked on various dubious sources of income. He had expected a steady procession of American cargo ships to arrive in Batavia to buy coffee, but Britain and the United States were technically at war from 1812, and no such ships arrived. He had also shut down the local cottage industry which manufactured cloth for everyday wear. This, he reasoned, would open a slot for imported British fabric, while the disenfranchised Javanese weavers could find work elsewhere in the burgeoning economy he was all set to create. A shipload of cheap chintz did arrive from England; the locals did buy it at a reasonable price, but on the first wash the dyes ran, and later shipments were ignored by the sceptical public and piled up unsold in government warehouses. Even the fabled tin mines of Bangka – the El Dorado that prompted Raffles to show his ugliest side – had not turned out as much tin or as much profit as expected. And then there was another failed gamble – opium.

The poppy was a cornerstone of the East India Company's economy, and the first cases of the stuff had actually been pre-emptively shipped in to Java aboard the troop ships in August 1811. Raffles had expected to make the drug a government monopoly in Java, and he spent agonised hours pondering 'the best possible means of keeping up the price of Opium in the market' while at the same time 'preventing an improper and injurious consumption of that Drug amongst the Inhabitants of the Country'. But it turned out that there was markedly less demand for opium in Java than the British had expected. Believing the stuff to be 'extremely detrimental to the society', the VOC had allowed only a modest 500 cases to be imported each year, and had sold them at an eye-wateringly prohibitive 5000 Spanish dollars apiece. In any case, even before Raffles had chance to exploit this limited luxury market the all-powerful opium barons of Calcutta had done their lobbying and had the ports of Java thrown open to unlimited free private trade in the drug. Opium use would indeed increase exponentially during the British Interregnum, but none of the profits went into the government coffers.

Besides all these basic failures, the single most significant reason why Raffles' predicted 750,000-dollar budgetary surplus for Java in 1812 had turned into a crunching loss had been his military adventures. Raffles had expected his plotted battles to pay for themselves: there were those fabled hordes of gold in Palembang, and Yogyakarta too was clearly a court with cash to spend. But Sultan Badruddin and his treasure had vanished from Palembang, and the cost of the entire expedition had to be borne by the budget. When it came to Yogyakarta, meanwhile, Raffles seems to have forgotten to make preparatory provisions for the plunder. It was on this point that he and Gillespie – who had clearly had a prickly relationship from the start – first turned violently against each other.

* * *

In the immediate aftermath of the conquest of Yogyakarta, Raffles had written to Lord Minto that 'The Craton having fallen by assault, it was impracticable to make any provision for Government to cover the Expenses of the Undertaking. Consequently the whole Plunder became Prize to the army'. At the time the Lieutenant-Governor was clearly still buzzing from the excitement of it all, and he declared that the loot 'could not have fallen into better hands. They richly deserved what they got.'

For the British Army to plunder a palace as the defences gave way was very much the order of the day at the turn of the 19th century, and treasures prised from Asiatic palaces contributed to the enduring fortunes of many a stiff-lipped war hero. It was a perk of the job. Quite why Raffles ever thought things would be different when he directed Gillespie to storm Yogyakarta is unclear, especially as he had issued no specific advance instructions about the windfall. But once he had had a month to brood, and to realise that by charging the whole business to his budget any last, lingering hope of ending the year in the black would vanish, he began to wonder if the soldiers really deserved their gains so richly after all.

In July he had written to Minto that 'I should mention that in the immediate distribution [of the loot], they [the army] took more upon themselves than I think was justifiable'. According to convention they were quite justified in taking it *all*. But Raffles, with his capacity for curious logic, seems to have decided that a retrospective reinterpretation of events was needed. While the Javanese were still mounting a defence he had been quite happy to defer entirely to the Commander of the Forces. However, he now seems to have concluded that the moment the Kraton fell – at around 9 a.m. on 20 June – the war was over and his own supreme authority was reasserted. The plunder of Yogyakarta, then, should have gone to the government. It was a very weak argument indeed, and Gillespie reacted predictably. The business of the loot was no business of the civilians, and what the army did with it and how they divided it was up to them. The first shots in a protracted battle had been fired.

Gillespie – who had been promoted to major-general in light of his recent triumphs – had gone down with a fever, possibly from the infected bullet wound in his arm, after the battle, and once he had touched base back in the Weltevreeden barracks he had gone in search of a cooler climate. Heading further uphill from Raffles' seat at Buitenzorg, he had set up house at Cipanas, just over the cusp of the Puncak Pass. Like the aging Middle Eastern businessmen who rent villas in the same place today, he had also obtained an attractive young local female to keep him company. While the civilians were largely blazing a trail towards a later colonial age where such indiscreet behaviour would be considered an outrage, the army were rather more old-fashioned. Plenty of officers took native concubines for the duration of their stay in Java, and Gillespie is reported to have produced his own Indo-Irish additions to the already-significant mixed race population of Java.

Throughout the final months of 1812, across the New Year and into 1813, a triangle of cranky correspondence came into being between Gillespie in the lofty heights of Cipanas, Raffles in

Buitenzorg, and the official seat of government in Weltevreeden. The question of the plunder was only the start of it. With the last of his planned battles fought, Raffles wanted the scale of the British military presence in Java drastically reduced. He was desperate to cut costs – and almost certainly also eager to reduce Gillespie's consequence – and he wanted men sent back to India as soon as possible. Though there were reports from Crawfurd that things were not yet entirely tranquil in Yogyakarta, and though there were worrying whispers from the badlands of East Java, Raffles in his eagerness was happy to claim that there was not 'a wandering banditti, much less a Chieftain from one end of the Island to the other who can give cause for the least apprehension'. Gillespie, meanwhile, pulled in exactly the opposite direction. He was an army man to his boots; the world of barracks and bayonets was the only one he cared about, and any cut in military funding was something he would rail against without ever stopping to examine the circumstances. If Raffles was quite happy to overstate the tranquillity of Java, then Gillespie – up in the clouds of Cipanas, a delicate Sundanese girl preparing a dressing for his aching arm somewhere in the background – was perfectly prepared to go the other way. He claimed that he had it on 'undoubted authority that General Daendels will not fail of recommending to Bonaparte to send out an Expedition under his direction for the recovery of this valuable Colony'. The Dutch and the French had been effectively evicted from the entire Indian Ocean by this stage; such an expedition was decidedly unlikely, and Gillespie must have known as much.

Then there was an issue over delayed payments and new barracks. Gillespie's record in the Caribbean makes it clear that he cared deeply about his men, and wanted the best accommodation and services that money could buy. It was, he would have argued, a false economy to run an army on a shoestring, especially in a place with a climate as morbid as Java. Raffles prevaricated; Gillespie responded furiously:

In fact every representation to you Honourable Sir on the subject of the Colonial Corps has been attended by so many changes and differences of opinion on your part and want of decision, that I have been frequently at a loss to know how to act ... To conclude – I again repeat that you are at liberty to act as you please as you have very frequently indeed made me know the little power I possess here, by repeating to me that your voice is decisive and having crippled me in many military points even when I have given way to your opinions to avoid any unpleasant discussions.

The fight had turned petty and personal. The two men, quite simply, hated each other. In separate shadowy rooms in separate misty mountain residences both hunched angrily at their desks writing petulant missives and rude responses. Raffles was prepared to sanction nothing that Gillespie wanted; Gillespie was reluctant to give his assent to any proposals that Raffles raised. The whole business was a mess, and it must have been deeply embarrassing for those on the scene, especially the bemused Dutchmen who had signed up for roles in this new government and who must by now have been wondering just what kind of people these bickering Britishers were. So much for turbulent princes and the 'distraction of internal war'; Raffles and Gillespie were making the Javanese look like a model of peaceful cooperation. They were, one visitor noted, 'at daggers drawn and constant variance'.

Otho Travers was particularly distressed, for he seems to have found Rollo Gillespie rather dashing. In January 1813 he expressed exasperation to his journal that the pair were 'not being on those cordial terms of intimacy, which a well wisher to both parties would desire'. It was all quite simply awful:

The unhappy differences and misunderstandings between our Chiefs seemed rather to increase than diminish. Every day brought with it some new point of contention, and those immediately connected with either party had to lament the length which matters had gone and which now precluded all hope of reconciliation.

Lord Minto, back in India, seems to have been profoundly embarrassed by the arguments, and though he was ever willing to accept Raffles' side of the story, he urged restraint. Restraint was *not* forthcoming. In April 1813 Raffles wrote to Minto that 'I regret much to inform your Lordship that the conduct of the Major General continues decidedly hostile to my administration, and that it is not now merely in a spirit of annoyance that he acts but from a real desire to injure and distress.' There was, Raffles continued, 'no measure of my Government, no proposition or consideration which arises with me, but is opposed by him, and in his demeanour and correspondence he avows himself to be what I have reason to believe he is, my decided Enemy'. Gillespie, meanwhile, had had enough. Unbeknownst to Raffles he had already sent a request to the Commander-in-Chief in India, General George Nugent, requesting to be removed from his post and set to work in the Subcontinent where the civilians were less troublesome. He would be replaced, sometime in late 1813, by the decidedly tame, if not dozy, Major-General Miles Nightingall.

Even before this news was made public, Lord Minto seems to have run out of patience: a letter from Bengal was already on its way to Batavia to tell Raffles that 'the differences between him and you, as having risen to such a height, that it has become absolutely necessary that you should be separated'. Two grown men, the most senior figures in colonial Java, one of the brightest of Britain's military stars and one of its most noteworthy civilian administrators, needed to be split up like a pair of bickering toddlers.

The Buffalo and the Tiger

One afternoon in mid-May 1813 a party of strangers arrived in the little village of Ngadas in the mountains of East Java. It was a damp, misty place of bad coughs and cold mornings in the forest high on the western slopes of the huge Tengger Massif. Colin Mackenzie had passed this way on his epic tour of Java the previous year, but these newcomers were not foreigners.

There were six of them, lean, long-haired young men with angry eyes and sharp *krises*. They moved into the village with an air of rough confidence, speaking of Holy War. Their leader called himself Kyai Mas. He said he was a prince. The villagers of Ngadas knew exactly what kind of man Kyai Mas was. His sort had always wandered the wilder parts of East Java with their little bands. People called them *jago*, after the strutting, preening fighting cocks. They touted amulets, strong words and sharp knives and they trod the line between hired goon and romantic rebel. In good times a party of *jago*, swaggering uninvited out of the forest meant petty extortion and trouble with the teenage girls. Someone with money and a grievance might pay for their services, but for the most part they were a nuisance. But in times when the whole village had cause for complaint, they could quickly turn from petty gangster to rabble-rouser, and from rabble-rouser to visionary hero. And in May 1813 the people of Ngadas certainly had a grievance.

They were tenants of a Chinese landowner called Han Kik Ko. He ruled these forested slopes and the sweltering coastal flatlands far below from the settlement of Probolinggo, and he milked the villagers for all they were worth. Fifty per cent of any crop they raised was taken in tax, and the rest was bought by Han Kik Ko at a paltry rate. There were arbitrary taxes on everything; funerals were taxed, buffaloes were taxed; even people were taxed. And now they had had enough.

Kyai Mas, cross-legged and wagging his index finger on a bamboo platform, dark hair tumbling to his shoulders, henchmen looking on, said he was from Ampel, the Muslim quarter of Surabaya. He had learnt allusive phrases of misunderstood Arabic from the Yemenis there, and he talked of claiming all of East Java in the name of Allah. This meant little to the villagers, but Kyai Mas also proclaimed himself the *Ratu Adil* – the Righteous Prince – the messianic hero who was always out there, somewhere on the fringes of the Javanese imagination, ready to appear in times of trouble. He talked of slaughtering every last Chinese usurer in the province. *This* they certainly understood.

Over the coming days whispers that a new leader had appeared in Ngadas passed down from the mountains and into the other villages of Han Kik Ko's territory. A dead buffalo appeared in the road in the middle of the country overnight as some kind of ominous portent, and men armed with bamboo staves began to arrive in Ngadas to meet with Kyai Mas, to see if he really was the Righteous Prince. Those who agreed to join his cause slipped away with yellow ribbons tied to the handles of their *krises*. In less than a week a ragged band of half-a-dozen chancers had swelled to a hungry army of hundreds. On the morning of 18 May they headed downhill through the forest under a yellow banner. In every village they passed farmers left their fields, collected their staves and pikes and cutting knifes, and fell in behind them. By the time they reached the edge of the plains near Probolinggo they had 2000 men.

At about this time a dusty carriage containing five Scotsmen and a single white woman pulled up outside Han Kik Ko's mansion. They were answering an invitation to a party …

* * *

Raffles' rule in Java was all about land. As he sat at his desk in Buitenzorg the great green swathes of the stuff that extended on all sides beyond the shuttered windows seemed to turn into some abstract asset, as did the men and women who lived upon it and worked its black basaltic soils. The ownership, value, management and taxation of land became the obsessing motif of the British Interregnum, and the source of almost all the subsequent debate and contemporary controversy. Four months before Kyai Mas' ragged band of *jagos* descended from the mountains at the other end of Java, Raffles had presided over the episode that was to provide the most persistent of all the claims of corruption levelled against him. It was not the trampling of a sultan, or the instigation of anti-Dutch violence; it was a dodgy land deal in the hills behind Buitenzorg.

Up through the great sweeps of the Post Road beyond the Lieutenant-Governor's little white mansion, across the Puncak Pass and down through the pine trees, lay a village called Cianjur. The hillsides around it were cloaked with dark, glossy-leaved coffee bushes. The hundreds of thousands of bitter words that have been attached to the sale of four lots of government-owned coffee land there in early 1813, both in the immediate accusatory aftermath, and in the two following centuries, have made it almost impossible to make sense of what really happened. Raffles' adoring biographers have poured gallons of obscuring verbiage onto the bare facts in their chapters on the subject, and tossed in a few reticent allusions to 'errors of judgement'; aggressive Dutch witch-hunters later raised a hue and cry so shrill as to be impossible to listen to, and Raffles himself churned out page after defensive and increasingly angry page on the issue.

The bones of the matter are these: late in 1812 the Government of Java decided to sell a certain amount of public land as a means of raising hard cash to liquidate the crippling paper currency. The 'government' consisted, of course, of Raffles, Councillors Muntinghe and Cranssen, and Gillespie. When the proposal was debated and decided upon Gillespie was out of town in Cipanas. Selling a chunk of state assets was a radical measure in any circumstance, and was *particularly* radical in a colony with a future as uncertain as that of British Java. Lord Minto was approaching the end of his term as Governor-General; a new chief was unlikely to share his romantic dreams about holding Java for ever more, and would possibly want the place transferred to the Crown under military rule. What was more, the whole place was likely to be handed back to the Dutch at some point in the not too distant future. For the governor of a subordinate British territory of uncertain status to sell major state assets without asking permission from Calcutta was unprecedented insubordination – a house-sitter is not generally expected to sell the garden, after all. But Raffles had already launched two wars without higher sanction, so to him this must have seemed the merest trifle, and there was always his extenuating plea of difficulty and distance, not least in the wet season.

The land to be sold was chosen on grounds that remain unclear, but it was conveniently close to the colonial capital, and likely to prove lucrative to a canny landlord. It was assessed ahead of the sale by a shady character called Thomas McQuoid, an old friend of Raffles from his Penang days. He was resident of the Buitenzorg district, ran a shoddy banking house and held an unseemly number of other posts in the British administration of Java. McQuoid came up with a guide-price for the land that was significantly *below* the value on which its previous tenancy leases had been based. A public auction was fixed for the means of sale, but no time was allowed to forward notices for the attention of interested investors with ready capital in Penang or Bengal. In the meantime a separate chunk of government land was sold directly to a private buyer for a fixed price. On 26 January 1813 the Cianjur plots were sold at public auction in Batavia. Interest was limited. They sold for markedly more than McQuoid's paltry estimates, but still for much less than what most would have considered their true value. One of the buyers was a Dutchman called Nicholaus Engelhard; his investment partner – whose identity was kept secret until the auction day – was one

Thomas Stamford Raffles. A one-sixth share of the same lot went to Thomas McQuoid; a further one-sixth share went to a Mr de Wilde who had already been chosen to manage the land. The recipient of the earlier private sale had been one Councillor Herman Muntinghe.

This much no one ever disputed, and this much alone makes it perfectly clear that the whole business was highly irregular. Raffles himself responded with angry indignation to the very suggestion of impropriety when the storm broke twelve months later, but he must surely have understood that the idea of selling a chunk of public property as governor, and then buying it for below its true value as a private investor was no way to make yourself look squeaky clean. That he ought not to have sold the land at all – to anyone, at any price – was something upon which almost everyone later agreed. When Lord Minto found out he responded in his usual patient tone of gentle admonition. He did not, he wrote, doubt Raffles' motives (Raffles claimed that he had simply been trying to raise funds, and had bought in himself merely to generate confidence amongst would-be investors). But Minto had gently to point out that 'I should not, I confess, have thought an extensive alienation of the public domains advisable in itself, under the particular circumstances of the Colony at the time'. And of course, it all really 'ought to have received the previous sanction of the Supreme Government'.

That something shady was going on is obvious, though the aggressive acrimony of the later argument makes it hard to say exactly *what*. Raffles' protestations of innocence were so noisy that they are almost convincing, and though he made many highly questionable decisions as a Lieutenant-Governor, in terms of his private behaviour the Cianjur land sales do seem somewhat out of character. In a world where just about everyone was pocketing significant sums of public money, Raffles – as far as can be judged at such a distance – seems to have been relatively straight. As Lieutenant-Governor he was on a salary of £8000 (well over quarter of a million in modern terms), but he seems to have been so profligate in his personal finances that he took no great fortune home with him at the end of his career, and even had to borrow the cash to partake in the Cianjur auction. However, those around him – from Otho Travers to William Flint – were *not* squeaky clean, and in light of this perhaps the most likely explanation for the land scandal was that Raffles had been taken for a ride by a cabal of dodgy Dutchmen, steeped in the old ways of Batavian society and in collusion with the murky McQuoid. They knew how critical the currency crisis had become but had their own silver dollars to spare; they knew how to make a tidy profit from coffee, and they had talked a naive lieutenant-governor into unwittingly setting the whole scam up, and – the best joke of all – actually coming in on the deal as an innocent investor.

If this *is* what happened, then the issue cuts suddenly through the air of arrogant egoism that hangs around Raffles' character, and leaves him seeming rather pathetic – a dupe and a dreamer, a man to be taken advantage of. The crowd of hangers-on suddenly seem less like stooges than vultures, and the Lieutenant-Governor begins to look like a lonely, if far from sympathetic, figure. Raffles had not exactly risen from the gutter, but in a world where men like Rollo Gillespie – men who grew up on country estates and who thought of class as though it was an ethnicity – had much of the power, his middle class ambition would always labour under a chronic disadvantage. The sons of sultans had kissed his knees, but upper-class Englishmen laughed at his background and made rude comments about his wife. At around the time that the land sales were decided Raffles had written to a friend in England: 'I am here alone, without any advice, in a new country …'

* * *

With one lot of land hived off, Raffles quickly added another huge swathe to the British territories – organising the outright annexation of the remaining territories of the old kingdoms of Cirebon and Banten. And he was soon focusing once more on the question of taxation.

The method that the Dutch had long used to earn an income from their Javanese possessions was one of monopoly. Cash crops could only be sold to the colonial government at a fixed price, and cultivators were obliged to pay their taxes in kind. This system, Raffles and Minto had repeatedly declared with excessive hyperbole, was the root of all evil in Java. The place ought to have been a paradise, but, in Minto's words, 'the mischievous deteriorating and grievous maxims of a narrow, monopolising, harsh and malignant policy' made it anything but. From the start Raffles had been determined to set up a new form of land revenue collection, one that would be, to his mind, fairer, more efficient, and – most importantly – more lucrative.

Raffles had called on the wanderlust of Colin Mackenzie in his quest for information on which to base his new system. After his breathless romp through the ruins at Prambanan, Mackenzie had continued his explorations, making a detour whenever he caught a whiff of a temple, examining rice fields, and questioning peasants. Mackenzie was never one to overstate the value of his own work, and he pointedly drew attention to the difficulties he had had in 'rendering through three different languages, Javanese, Malay and Dutch, into English', and stressed that 'It may be imagined with how little effect any enquiry could be managed in this way'.[17] But on the basis of his report, and on those of a handful of other overstretched surveyors,

17 Mackenzie went back to India shortly after completing his report to become Surveyor-General. He took an unusual souvenir back to India with him from Java – a wife. After decades as a committed and very busy bachelor, he had astonished his friends by marrying an Asia-born Dutch girl forty-three years his junior. Her name was Petronella Jacomina Bartels. As the youthful bride got used to the Indian scene, Mackenzie went back to his temple researches in the Deccan, but he was already suffering from a chronic 'weakness of the stomach'. In 1821 he died, while travelling up and down the Hooghly River on a boat in search of a climactic cure. In his will he had made generous provisions for many of the native surveyors who had worked with him over the years; the rest of his inheritance went to his widow.

Raffles now claimed to have created a brand new system of land management designed specifically for Java. That it bore a striking resemblance to the very system used to gather land revenues in the East India Company's Bengal territories was entirely coincidental, he insisted.

In short, the system would see the abolition of almost all forced production and monopolies; in all but a few crucial coffee areas people would be free to grow what they liked. Mackenzie's report made it clear that all land in Java was traditionally viewed as belonging to the Sovereign. That may once have meant some haughty sultan, but it now meant the British Government, and the people would pay tax on the value of their land, not on their crop.

In the notes that Raffles presented to the tame commission he set up to examine the matter he wrote that 'It now becomes necessary that the Government should consider the inhabitants without reference to bare mercantile profits and to connect the sources of the revenues with the general prosperity of the Colony'.

And there it is. It sometimes seems that Raffles' entire reputation as a liberal reformer, as a man who cared deeply about the peoples of Asia, has been built on that one sentence. His biographers indent it, they italicise it; they wave it wildly above their heads and use it as a brush with which to sweep away the mounds of dead Javanese from the gates of Yogyakarta as if the very concept of saying one thing and meaning another is inconceivable. But it was only ever a throwaway line, and it contained as pointed a reference to 'the general prosperity of the Colony' as it did to the need to 'consider the inhabitants' anyway. For as far as Raffles was concerned, 'wellbeing' seemed simply to mean working hard and paying taxes in cash, rather than growing just enough rice to live on in the back garden, having as little to do with the authorities as possible, and spending your days smoking and drinking coffee.

In most of the villages of Java there had never been a significant cash economy. Here and there a few old Chinese copper coins changed hands for cigarettes or a roadside meal of sticky rice wrapped in banana leaves, but large payments in currency were unknown. But for Raffles this needed to change and he wrote that 'It appears to me beyond a doubt that the introduction of a money rent would bring forward a large proportion of coin which at present lies unemployed'. The happy people of Java were about to be raised up – literally. It was time to start digging.

By May 1813 the new system was being put into practice wherever possible around Batavia. But in another corner of Java another sort of land management had primed the powder keg of discontent, and a group of Scots partygoers and a rabble of Javanese *jagos* were converging on the house of a Chinese landlord from opposite directions.

* * *

The head of the little British party that headed for Probolinggo on 18 May was Lieutenant-Colonel James Fraser. With him were his wife, along for the ride, and four other officers – a Captain James McPherson, a Lieutenant Robertson, and a pair of Camerons, Captain and Lieutenant. All were attached to the 78th Highland Regiment, stationed in Surabaya. As they rolled through the yellow flatlands on the outward journey perhaps they had noticed the way that some of the local men, loitering at the roadside in ragged clothes, watched them coldly as they passed; perhaps they even noticed a scrap of yellow cloth tied to some of their cane knives and *krises*. But perhaps not. The British certainly knew that all was not well in Probolinggo. As far back as December 1811, a helpful Dutchman from Surabaya had written to the new government to warn them that 'If there be a place where rebellion may be apprehended, it is at Probolinggo', and it seems that Lieutenant-Colonel Fraser may have accepted the party invitation as an excuse to pass on a quiet warning to Han Kik Ko about the treatment of his subjects. But Fraser could hardly have known just how explosive the situation had become: he would never have asked his wife to come along for the ride otherwise. As the group stepped down from the carriage and stretched their limbs, brushed themselves down, and moved towards the shady veranda of an ample Chinese country mansion where slaves were serving snacks, they had no idea what horrific experiences the next few hours would bring.

Their host was the forty-seven-year-old scion of one of East Java's most important Chinese clans, the Han, and the epitome of a third-generation émigré made good.

For hundreds of years poor Chinese immigrants had headed south on trading ships and stepped ashore in the Pasisir ports of Java. Most of them were young men, and like the VOC Dutch they married local girls and spawned their own legions of mixed race children. They called these second generation Indonesian-Chinese the *Peranakan,* the mixed-bloods. They developed their own creole culture, and gave the Javanese noodles and meatballs, foul-tasting tonics and a morbid belief that drinking cold water was bad for your health. And before long they were doing most of the work in the economic engine room of the colony. The VOC had licensed out as much of the state apparatus as possible to the Chinese. They ran toll gates and bazaars, and organised customs and opium sales.

Han Kik Ko's brother, Han Chan Piet, had long held the lease on the neighbouring territory of Besuki and Panarukan, but in 1810 the family's grip on the unfortunate peasants had tightened: Thomas Stamford Raffles was not the first man to sell government lands to get himself out of a financial bind. Daendels, struggling to find collateral to float his endless issues of paper money, had sold Besuki to the landlord, and then, rather pleased with the sudden income of 400,000 Spanish dollars, he hived off Probolinggo too. Six months before the British arrived in Java, Han Kik Ko had agreed to pay a series of biannual instalments of 50,000 dollars on the land. In return he was granted outright title to Probolinggo, and a free rein to treat the tenants however he saw fit.

By 18 May 1813 he knew that they were unhappy, but he had clearly dismissed any reports of *jagos* and Righteous Princes, for once his Scottish guests had refreshed themselves he invited them to join him on an evening ride through the rice fields. They had not gone far from the house when they ran into a party of alarmed informants. Cringing submissively to the Chinese chief they begged to tell him that a large mob of armed men had appeared in a village just a few miles to the south. They had camped out in a coffee plantation and 'had declared that they came to take possession of the country by command of Mahomet'. As Captain Cameron later told it, the soldiers were unconcerned by the news, and believed these strangers 'to be nothing more than a parcel of religious enthusiasts'. Han Kik Ko and the guests rode off 'to inspect them personally and to ascertain their intentions'. It was almost dark when they reached the coffee plantation. There were armed men everywhere amongst the glossy green bushes. A group of nervous servants were sent scurrying forward to ask these people what they wanted, but before there was chance to parley a furious shriek rose over the plantation; the rebels attacked, and an uprising had begun.

Han Kik Ko's servants fled in every direction, and Kyai Mas and his righteous rabble came swarming out of the bushes. Captain Cameron and Captain McPherson, armed with nothing more than a shotgun and service revolver, found themselves abandoned. They fired a few feeble shots and then fled, catching up with their Chinese host and the rest of the party on the road back to the house. Night had fallen by now, and they tried to make a stand, but they had little ammunition and no heavy weaponry, and they were outnumbered by a factor of hundreds. A pleasant outing from Surabaya had turned into a terrifying ordeal; their horses had bolted along with the servants, and soon they were fleeing on foot through the angry darkness with Kyai Mas and his men close behind them. Somewhere in the melee, gasping for breath, dripping with sweat and utterly exhausted, Colonel Fraser, Captain McPherson, and Han Kik Ko fell behind. Robertson and the Camerons faltered, glanced over their shoulders, half-started to go back for their comrades, and then, seeing a furious *kris*-wielding horde sweeping out of the night, they ran on.

It was 10 o'clock by the time the exhausted surviving soldiers reached the Chinese mansion where the terrified Mrs Fraser was waiting with a handful of panicking servants. They spent the night under siege. Out in the darkness angry shouts echoed, and figures flickered amongst the trees, but there was no outright attack on the property. Captain Cameron had managed to get a message to the outpost just across the Probolinggo border in Pasuruan, and at dawn a small party of sloppily armed native policemen turned up at the mansion. It was hardly an army, but Cameron now tried to organise a rescue party to go in search of Fraser, McPherson and Han Kik Ko. Before he could muster the men, however, a messenger arrived from Kyai Mas. The white men and the Chinese tyrant were dead, he said, and the Righteous Prince was demanding that the remaining foreigners show the courage to come out and fight. At this point Cameron decided that it was time to flee.

The frantic survivors of Han Kik Ko's household said they knew of a boat on the beach to the north, and so the soldiers hustled the unfortunate Mrs Fraser along with them through the countryside to the coast. The boat was just a little open *perahu*, with a ragged sail and no shade, but it was a means of escape. Mrs Fraser clambered aboard. The officers jogged back for a last look at the house, but all of the servants and Chinese had gone now, and the front veranda was full of rebels. They doubled back to the beach, scrambled into the boat, and pushed off, just as a huge and angry crowd came flowing out from between the palm trees onto the shore, waving their weapons and jeering furiously at the fleeing foreigners. It took them all day to wallow up the hot coastline to Pasuruan.

A relief column arrived from Surabaya the following night. They stopped for a hurried dinner by lamplight in Pasuruan, then pressed on into rebel territory, and after a pitched battle on the main road at first light on 20 May, the rebellion broke apart and melted away as suddenly and as strangely as it had arisen. The bodies of Han Kik Ko, Colonel Fraser and Captain McPherson were found tied up in sacks in the forest. Captain McPherson had been hacked to pieces. As for the Righteous Prince, Kyai Mas, his Kingdom of Islam came to nothing, but he had proven himself no coward. In the final stand-off with the British troops he had thrown himself headlong at their lines, charged through the ranks of gunners with eyes blazing and *kris* flailing, taking four hits without faltering and passing right through as far as the rear of the regiment before 'he was secured, and breathed his last'.

* * *

There was predictable outrage when news of the Probolinggo incident reached Batavia, not least over the sufferings of 'the disconsolate Mrs. Fraser'. But John Crawfurd was dispatched to investigate, and while others fulminated predictably about 'base murder' and 'atrocious acts' and howled for retribution, he quickly decided that the locals had already suffered enough.

The Scotsman's refined Yogyakarta-style Javanese was far-removed from the earthy dialect spoken here, but he eventually convinced the terrified villagers to talk. 'The cry against the oppressions and mal-administrations of the Chinese proprietors is ... so loud and so uniform, that it seems beyond the reach of doubt', he wrote. Han Kik Ko had squeezed at least one quarter more out of the peasants than 'what could be demanded, consistent with an attention to the tranquillity of the country'. In neighbouring Besuki, too, things were every bit as bad. As for the rebellion itself, Crawfurd quickly discovered that Kyai Mas was 'a man of low birth' and no sort of prince. 'He appears to have been a bold and resolute fanatic', but Islam had been little more than 'a rallying point' Crawfurd noted, and 'The Javanese are in general so ignorant, so simple and so credulous, but above all have so little to lose by any change of fortune, that an adventurer must be contemptible indeed who will not at any time find many followers amongst them'.

There was one aspect of the uprising that he seems pragmatically to have left unexamined – those mysterious yellow ribbons and banners. Yellow was the royal colour of the Susuhunan. Before it was ceded to the Dutch, Probolinggo had been Surakarta territory, and no one was naive enough to suppose that a network of agents and informers there were not still reporting back to the Kraton. A few scurrilous whispers suggested that Kyai Mas had been acting on the orders of the slipperiest of all Javanese royals when he took up the mantle of the Righteous Prince. But some closets, Crawfurd must have decided, are not worth opening.

The whole wretched business had been entirely Daendels' doing Crawfurd declared, and 'The very sale of the lands alone may in some measure be considered a violation of natural right aggravated by the circumstances under which it was done'. To this he added a further line – perhaps with a certain mischievousness, for it seemed deliberately designed to sting his superior: 'It is true that the lands were disposed of on terms similar to those on which lands have been sold to Europeans in the vicinity of Batavia ...'

When Raffles received the reports he read them closely, ignored the last line, approved of Crawfurd's conclusions, and took a great deal of interest in his observations that both Probolinggo and Besuki looked like potentially very fertile territories indeed. Han Kik Ko might have squeezed a little too much out of the farmers, but a more enlightened landlord could still turn a good profit there. In short, it sounded like the perfect place for Raffles' new land rent system. Instructions were sent to Crawfurd, still camped out in East Java. The Government should annul Daendels' sales, and take back the land for itself. Crawfurd was instructed to bully and threaten the unfortunate Han Chan Piet and his associates, who had been placed in temporary charge of his dead brother's property; 'you will not fail to point out to them most forcefully the personal danger to themselves and their families by the possible recurrence of similar tumults', the instructions stated. That Han Chan Piet had already made the full payment for his own Besuki lands ought not to stand in the way. Britain wanted the country. By 24 June, Crawfurd had done as he was asked. Probolinggo and Besuki belonged to Britain, an English resident had been installed, and Raffles' land reforms were being hurriedly put into practice. Han Chan Piet went back to Surabaya and bought a sugar farm, and thirty local markets. His family's experiment in petty dictatorship was over, but he wouldn't go hungry.

* * *

For Raffles, far away in Buitenzorg, the abortive uprising in Probolinggo could all be dismissed as a little local difficulty in the provinces. But there was more trouble closer to home. Gillespie was still at his post awaiting relief, and the council chamber arguments were continuing apace. And then, on 30 July, another ill-omened messenger emerged from the heart of Palembang darkness. His name was William Robison.

After resigning from his post as secretary Robison had kept a low profile, labouring away with his Dutch-English dictionary in the translation department, and happy to remain 'quiet as I am for the present'. But Raffles was chronically short of men, and after grudgingly conceding that Robison hadn't actually made any rash promises to the Sultan and Susuhunan during his pioneering visit to the courts, he seems almost to have forgiven him. When the post of resident in Palembang came open early in 1813 Robison was promoted to major and shipped off up the Musi. At first all seemed to be going well, but now, suddenly, unexpected and unannounced, Robison had returned to Batavia, stepped ashore on the dockside with a smile on his face, a clutch of Malay princes at his back, 200,000 dollars in his pocket, and not the faintest clue that anyone might have reason to be angry with him. On the basis of his enquiries up the Musi River he had made a move of positively Rafflesian insubordination: he had unilaterally reinstated the fugitive Sultan Badruddin.

As soon as Robison had arrived in the gloomy town, surrounded by its endless forest and still smarting from the upheavals of the previous year, he discovered that Gillespie's puppet sultan, Najmuddin, the former Prince Adipati, was a miserable man. Without the royal treasure he had little authority – and little spending power – and everyone harked back nostalgically to the days of his deposed brother. And once Robison began asking questions about the massacre of the Dutch, he rapidly uncovered the inconvenient truth: no one was innocent; everyone was guilty. A pair of royal princes had protested to him that 'both the reigning Sultan, and they themselves were as much guilty of it as the old Sultan. They all understood, it was what the English desired that they should get rid of them [the Dutch] from Palembang'.

When Robison continued deeper upriver into the darkness and reached the old king's camp, he heard the same story, and with a staggering simplicity he wrote to Raffles to explain: Badruddin had evicted the Dutch 'because it was what the English had often desired him to do, as he could shew [sic] by several letters in his possession, and that ammunition … had been sent up to him, to get rid of them by force of arms, if he could not do so by remonstrance'. That these were exactly the kind of details that Raffles might have expected a pragmatic resident to leave unmentioned – details that were meant, in fact, to be buried as deep as possible in the jungle – seemed not to occur to Robison. What was more, he was rather impressed by Badruddin. He declared that 'there was nothing atrocious, nothing of the assassin in the character', signed a treaty with him, returned him to a throne which the puppet Najmuddin seemed delighted to vacate, managed to organise a payment of 200,000 Spanish dollars to the British Government from the reinstalled king, and set out for Batavia to tell everyone the happy news.

Major William Robison's character and motivations have been so thoroughly mauled by Raffles' champions over the years that trying to make sense of what kind of man he was is difficult. But he was clearly not a 'hyena', and there does not appear to be any reason to believe that he was corrupt. That he responded very badly to slights and insults will become clear, but in his dealings with native kings Robison's only discernible motivation was that of guileless fairness. His early recommendations about the Javanese courts had been based on the same ideals, and years later, in India, he would get himself in yet more trouble for striking another stance of principle. He certainly does not seem like the sort to incite a massacre and topple a sultan to get his hands on a tin mine, to bully a royal house to satiate personal and national egoism, or to use a little local unrest as an excuse for a land-grab. But he was nothing if not naive. For a start, he had been completely taken in by Badruddin – who affected tears and wrung his hands and pleaded innocence when Robison met him in his jungle hideaway. Most of the royals of Palembang must have been complicit in the killings; to suggest that the foremost amongst them knew *nothing* of what was being planned is just silly. Robison's bigger naivety, however, was in believing that playing straight and eschewing pragmatism in *any* overseas British territory, least of all in one with a single, dominating personality at the top, was advisable. He was not cut out for colonialism.

Instead of being congratulated for his sterling work once he reached Batavia, Robison found himself in disgrace. Gillespie went berserk, and Raffles retreated in a huff to Buitenzorg to figure out what to do. People hissed at him in the street; he was under investigation, and for a while even under arrest. A charge sheet was being prepared for the courts in Calcutta with the hope that he would end up in jail. A commission had been hastily shipped off to Palembang to put the hapless Adipati back on the throne, to evict Badruddin once more, and to come up with whatever evidence the murky pool of Palembang could provide to prove that Major William Robison was a slimy, slippery little specimen of the lowest rank. As for the 200,000 dollar payment Robison had so proudly presented to the Government, Badruddin had made it in good faith, so he really ought to have got it all back when the rogue treaty was annulled. But money was something Raffles was a little short of: he decided to keep half of it. Meanwhile a story was doing the rounds – quite possibly with official encouragement – that Robison himself had been paid by Badruddin, that he was corrupt, and that he was, in the words of the huffing, puffing, outraged Otho Travers, 'the most troublesome and least creditable servant in the service of this Government'.

And at this point the put-upon Robison seems to have lost his cool altogether.

He clearly believed in his own capabilities; he clearly believed he had done the right thing, and he was clearly incapable of conceding that he should have asked for permission first. And now the same sleazy set who seemed to have had it in for him since he first arrived in Java were actually trying to have him charged with a criminal offence! His career in Java was obviously over; he might as well speak his mind. He said very bad things about all sorts of people; he went about, in the words of the appalled Travers, 'addressing the Government in the most improper manner accusing them of tyranny and oppression towards him'. He also began plotting his revenge.

Travers was particularly disgusted by Robison, and worked himself into a veritable lather on the topic, not least once he heard the scurrilous slander plucked out of Palembang which the disgraced resident was spreading – with its talk of the beloved Raffles inciting murder, and the dashing Gillespie behaving in an entirely ungentlemanly manner. 'What story he can make out hereafter to clear himself, or what defence he can attempt, I am at a loss to conjecture,' Travers wrote, 'but this I am certain of, I shall ever consider him a dishonest corrupt man'. For Travers to call Robison corrupt was rather rich, for he had somehow contrived to do very well indeed out of the whole scandal. The princes Robison had brought back from Palembang as diplomatic witnesses had required a guardian; Travers had stepped forward, and had requested an ample monthly allowance for the care of each of his royal charges. Such a request, from a man as well-connected as Travers, was bound to be forthcoming. The princes 'were under my charge from July, and I drew about 3000 Spanish dollars for their subsistence, a good portion of which I was, of course, able to pocket ...' And Travers had another reason to be grateful to Robison: at long last the Lieutenant-Governor and the Commander of the Forces had found something to agree about.

For Gillespie the idea that Sultan Badruddin was back on the throne was an outrage, but there was worse. Once Robison realised that the whole world had turned against him, he abandoned all restraint and noisily repeated the very worst of the dark rumours he had heard on the banks of the Musi River. In April 1812, infected by the swirling swampy atmosphere perhaps, pushed to the edge of amok in the wet gloom of the blood-soaked palace, no lesser man than Rollo Gillespie himself had done *something* very bad in Palembang. Exactly *what* Robison accused Gillespie of having done during the earlier expedition is unclear. There may well have been talk of looting and unnecessary brutality – such practices would have been nothing unusual. But from the way Raffles himself later alluded to Robison's claims it seems that he probably accused Gillespie of something altogether more outrageous, something of a sexual nature.

But whatever it was, as the dry season rolled on, as news from India came of Lord Minto's replacement – the staunch, soldierly Lord Moira, Marquess of Hastings – and as Gillespie's own departure for Calcutta beckoned, it really did seem, incredibly, remarkably, astonishingly, that the two big chiefs of British Java, the scarred and celebrated military man, and the fey orientalist civilian, had made up their differences. Gillespie danced with the ailing Olivia at balls (the Lady Governess was still going hard, despite those frequent 'fits of gout'); there was 'perfect union and cordiality', and if a flicker of bickering ever sparked it needed only for someone to say the name 'Robison' and all would be outraged agreement once more.

On 24 August, two days before grand celebrations to commemorate the second anniversary of the glorious victory at Cornelis, Raffles, Travers and the rest of his hangers-on headed down from the hills to Weltevreeden. They had a private invitation to dinner at Gillespie's residence there (the army man, on better terms with the civilians, had now descended from his Cipanas hide-out). There must have been a little residual stiffness as the black-coated party emerged from their carriages and assembled in the hall with Gillespie's burly, be-medalled cronies standing by, but it didn't last long. 'A little wine, it is said, opens the heart,' wrote Travers, all aglow, 'and from the effects of a great deal a most unreserved conversation took place between those two chiefs, the result of which was reiterated professions of unlimited friendship and good will'. Everyone, it seems, got uproariously drunk. 'The utmost hilarity and good humour prevailed throughout the evening'; wine glasses tumbled, backs were slapped, crude jokes were made at the expense of one William Robison, toasts were drunk, slaves went scurrying, sweat coursed down glowing faces, crickets chirped outside in the hot Batavia night, cigar smoke spiralled, and 'few of the number witnessed before so drunken a scene'. Raffles and Gillespie, stumbling and slurring, ended the night with inevitable protestations of brotherly love. It was all almost *too* divine for the overwrought Travers: 'to a person unacquainted with preceding events these two characters would have appeared a second Castor and Pollux,' he wrote, though which of the two men he considered the immortal is unclear.

Incredibly, the consequent headaches seemed to do nothing to dampen the new sense of fraternity. As September rolled by and October began, bringing with it the threat of another wet season and another tally of fever victims, and with Travers 'obliged again to have recourse to a milk and vegetable diet in consequence of a violent pain in my chest' (quite possibly as a result of too many parties), Gillespie's departure drew closer. His replacement was already on the way from Penang, a ship was ready, and without waiting formally to hand over the command, he departed for Bengal on the steamy evening of 12 October 1813. Raffles had already gone back up to the green hills and damp mornings of Buitenzorg, but Travers was in town to see the little hero off. As the final bundles were being packed in the Commander's official residence, as boots were clattering down hallways and slaves were scuttling to the waiting luggage carts, Travers picked through the chaos, and knocked politely on the door of Gillespie's private room. 'He took me by both hands and swore eternal friendship towards me' then departed for the docks with an escort of Hussars, leaving Travers wallowing in a deluge of tears in his wake.

Elsewhere in the capital, William Robison and his wife were awaiting their own, much less effusive send-off. Mindful of Robison's accusations, it seems that Gillespie had asked for a head-start to Calcutta. He most certainly did not want to share a ship with the detainee (Robison would surely have ended up with a demolished nose at the very least if he *had* gone aboard with Gillespie), and the disgraced former Palembang Resident would be shipped out a few days later, along with impeachment documents accusing him of corruption. The outgoing commander did have one fellow passenger for his journey across the Bay of Bengal, however. A man named Charles Blagrave had replaced Robison as secretary at the start of 1812, but he had proved even less pleasing to Raffles than his predecessor. He had sacked him after a year and installed a compliant character called Charles Assey. Blagrave had been hanging around in Batavia since his ousting, and only now decided to make his escape.

As the good ship *Troubridge* weighed anchor in the Batavia roads, turned slowly in the tide, and lumbered away towards the sunset, Gillespie's staff and officers waved enthusiastically from the beach and Otho Travers made futile attempts to stifle his sobs. The mountains of West Java were buried beneath the dark clouds of a coming storm.

* * *

The buffalo stood at the edge of the enclosure, its head low, swaying slowly from side to side. Its breath came in short, angry grunts and its hooves were planted firmly into the dust of Yogyakarta's southern Alun-Alun. The enclosure – a palisade of posts – stretched in a wide circle across the bleached grass from the shade of the twin banyan trees, a pair of great shaggy eminences at the centre of the square. Courtiers and servants peered through the gaps, eager for the coming spectacle. The Kraton had been patched up since the carnage of the previous year; roof tiles smashed by cannonballs had been replaced, and floors hacked up by rampaging looters relaid. It was the morning of 9 December 1813, and the cloudbanks of the afternoon storms were already piling up over the mountains. Raffles, Olivia, Crawfurd, and the new Sultan – seventeen months into the job – sat on chairs on a raised platform, looking down into the enclosure. Servants in full courtly dress stood around with parasols to shade their heads; court women with oiled hair and bare shoulders were ranged cross-legged behind them.

The buffalo grunted, shifted its great blue-grey haunches, and rolled the crescent of its heavy horns. Thirty yards away on the far side of the ring a bamboo shutter was pulled open, a commotion of clattering and shouting arose, and with an angry snarl its opponent was goaded out of a holding cage. It was a tiger. It was huge, with shoulders rising in great blades of muscled bone, but it was frightened, and it breathed furiously, crouching low and scanning the long line of the fence for an escape route. Across the ring the buffalo still had not moved, but it had fixed its gaze now, and lowered its head towards the flash of flaming fur. The crowd shifted and murmured expectantly. On the side-lines a *gamelan* troop began to play, cymbals clashing and gongs chiming out across the treetops. The Sultan and John Crawfurd smiled passively; both wondering exactly how the fight would pan out. Raffles and Olivia, sweating in the heat and still weary from the earlier round of festivities and formalities up the road in Surakarta, waited for the action to begin.

But the buffalo did not move, and the tiger did not move. On the far side of the ring a gaggle of minders jostled their way to the palisade with bunches of stinging nettles at the end of lengths of bamboo. It was not exactly sporting, but they needed to get things going: they poked the poles through the fence, and smacked the buffalo with the nettles. It bellowed furiously, pawed at the soil, and then launched itself towards the tiger. A heavyset beast weighing a ton can move at a terrifying speed when it wants to, and there was a panicked commotion amongst the spectators behind the fence at the spot towards which the buffalo was heading. The tiger shifted and tensed, then started forward, a tentative crawl giving way to a scurry and then opening to a full charge in all of two seconds. The crowd cheered. The buffalo, tail in the air and a trail of dust streaking behind it, came on, and with a dull thud the two animals came together. The tiger had slipped over the horns and was now hanging at the muscled neck, hugging furiously with its great padded paws. The buffalo bucked and reared; the tiger tumbled clear and went backing away, still primed for a second pounce. Bright blood was streaking down the buffalo's neck now, and the hot, musky smell of sweating, frightened animals was rising over the Alun-Alun. Raffles and his companions looked on.

The buffalo thundered forward again; the tiger sprang again, and again dodged the horns and slashed at its opponent's neck. The first mumble of disquiet passed through the batik-clad crowd. Again the same manoeuvre repeated, and again the buffalo came off worse. John Crawfurd was smiling openly now, and perhaps casting sly glances at the Sultan. Again the tiger had fastened onto the buffalo's neck, and had torn a long gouge through the leathery grey skin. Blood was dripping down its flanks.

The fight went on for an hour. The buffalo continued gamely charging, and the tiger kept leaping clear, until finally the great hulking bovine faltered. Its forelegs crumpled under it; its pink tongue lolled from its blue lips, and with the slow, ceaseless certainly of a huge forest tree coming down it toppled sideways into the dust. The response of the Javanese crowd to this feline victory was strangely muted.

Fights between wild buffaloes and tigers had been a favourite entertainment for guests at Javanese *kratons* for centuries. In the inner palace it might be all intricate *gamelan* scales and refined dance performances, but out in the great square it was blood and guts. But the tiger fights too were supposed to be a formality. Like the epic battles of the Pandawa brothers in the story cycles of the *wayang kulit*, the eventual outcome was a foregone conclusion: the buffalo was *always* supposed to win. From the visit of the first VOC officials to the old Mataram court at Kartasura this epic struggle had been the entertainment of choice laid on by Javanese kings for European visitors. But the Dutch seem never to have understood that the whole thing was a sly joke at their expense. In the great symbolic scheme of things, the buffalo – slow, steady, but ultimately unbreakable – represented the Javanese. The tiger – with a hot temper and a tendency to lash out violently – represented the Europeans. Generations of black-coated Dutch officials, clapping approvingly from the viewing platform as tiger after tiger was tossed in the air with a fatal horn wound in its belly, had had absolutely no idea why the Javanese around them were smiling so broadly.

By the time he wrote *The History of Java* Raffles understood the significance of the fights – it was almost certainly John Crawfurd who explained the symbolism to him. Whether he already knew in December 1813 is unclear, but for the watching Javanese the unusual outcome of this particular fight was *not* how they liked things to go. In an attempt to repair the damage – and thoroughly unfairly to the exhausted victor, panting confusedly in the middle of the ring – a fresh buffalo was hustled through a gap in the fence. It vanquished the worn-out tiger in a few short minutes, and rapidly dispatched a second, much smaller cat too. But the discomfiting embarrassment of the unexpected outcome of the main event must surely have reminded the princes of their abject humiliation the last time they met Thomas Stamford Raffles.

Raffles had set out on a glorious royal progress across Java as soon as Gillespie's mild-mannered replacement, Major-General Miles Nightingall, was installed. With his bitter military rival safely shipped out (and with the wretched Robison transported too), the Lieutenant-Governor must have felt that finally he had achieved outright and unchallenged dominance in Java. He realised that Lord Minto would be gone from India before Christmas and he knew that peace in Europe was increasingly likely. Given the communications delay, for all Raffles knew Napoleon might already have been vanquished, and the return of Java to Holland already agreed. But for the moment he was going to enjoy himself.

For Raffles this trip was meant to be a defining statement of his dominance, and a deliberate reminder to the Javanese courts of their own subservience. He had entered Surakarta on 5 December, with Mangkunegara's troops firing salute after salute into the hazy sky, royal *gamelan* orchestras clanking away under the trees, and an accompaniment of British and sepoy soldiers in all their regalia jogging behind. There followed three days of royal socialising, a good deal of drinking (no problem at *this* Muslim court), performances from dancing girls and magicians, a visit to Thomas Horsfield's private zoo, and all sorts of military pomp. During the evening dancing Olivia led things off as usual, with the Susuhunan for her partner. No one mentioned those suspicious yellow banners that had fluttered in the hot, angry air over Probolinggo seven months earlier.

On 8 December, with cannons booming and Javanese soldiers saluting, the whole party rolled out of Surakarta and trundled southwest towards Yogyakarta for banquets, parades, and the grand spectacle of the tiger fight. If the victory of the big cat had left the princes unsettled, perhaps they paused to reflect on the turbulence of the past year – because for all Raffles' cheery tales of tranquillity, Yogyakarta had been anything but quiet.

The bazaars had been rife with rumours that the old sultan, now exiled in Penang, was on his way back with an army of Frenchmen to seek revenge, and whenever the stories reached a certain hysterical pitch most of the residents would pack up and head for the villages, fearing another round of looting. Inside the court too there had been all sorts of intrigue and backbiting. A royal wife had been thrown out of the Kraton, Abubakar had started threatening to go on the Haj again, and Arya Panular had been having bad dreams about goldfish. Even Pakualam, the British-made puppet, had been causing headaches for Crawfurd, grouching about his maintenance payments, and reportedly plotting an armed rebellion.

On some occasions the new Sultan was reassuringly remarked to have taken on a Vishnu-like countenance, but there were definitely courtiers of dubious loyalty gathering in dark corners from time to time. The succession had taken place in such irregular and undignified circumstances it was little wonder if confidence was lacking in some quarters. And when Raffles and Crawfurd engineered the appointment of the eight-year-old Raden Mas Bagus as the new Crown Prince, the disquiet deepened. As far as the British were concerned the new Sultan was young and healthy man, and with any luck his infant heir could be subjected to half-a-lifetime of subtle domination and English lessons before he ever took to the throne.

Whether Crawfurd had chosen to downplay all the recent headaches in the royal city, or whether the complexities and subtleties of Javanese politics had simply been beyond the ken of the Lieutenant-Governor is not clear, but Raffles does not seem to have been particularly concerned. There were dinners and more royal audiences over the coming days. Raffles did his best to encourage the Sultan to marry the tiny little Crown Prince to the daughter of a former royal minster as soon as possible. When it was mentioned that the girl in question was a good two years older than the heir to the throne, Raffles smilingly pointed out the significant age difference between his thirty-two-year-old self and Olivia – who was looking a little wan at this stage. The Lady Governess was not far off her forty-third birthday. Eventually, on 11 December, with great pomp and a commotion of clashing cymbals and saluting troops, Raffles headed back for the Pasisir.

On the same day, far away beyond a stormy sea, a weary Lord Minto left India for the last time. He was sixty-two years old and his health was beginning to fail. For all Olivia's fervent wishes neither she nor her husband would ever see their smiling patron again, in his own beautiful Java, or anywhere else for that matter. From now on Raffles would be without a patient benefactor. The new incumbent as Governor-General, Lord Moira, was already settling into his post, and attempting to take stock of all the various financial leaks in the addled hulk of the East India Company's empire. Of all the obscure and costly outposts that the Company controlled, there was one that Moira found particularly irksome. Early in the New Year he noted tetchily in his diary that 'Java is a still worse drain than the others':

Instead of the surplus revenue which, for giving importance to the conquest, was asserted to be forthcoming from that possession, it could not be maintained without the Treasury, as well as the troops of Bengal. Just now, in the height of our exigencies, we receive an intimation from the Lieutenant-Governor that he cannot pay his provincial corps unless we allow him 50,000 Spanish dollars monthly in addition to the prodigious sums which we already contribute to his establishment ...

Dubious decisions, outrageous overspends, and budgetary blunders would no longer be met with sympathetic sensitivity at the highest levels, and Java would be viewed not as a romantic land of promise, but as an obscure dot in an irrelevant ocean under the command of an ill-qualified incompetent with no respect for the Army, the Board, or the economy. Raffles might have been feted as a great lord in Central Java; the tiger might have vanquished the buffalo, but an almighty catfight was about to begin.

* * *

At dawn on 26 February 1814 a ship called the *Streatham* docked in Batavia. Amongst the usual packets and papers it had brought from Bengal, the bundles of dog-eared English newspapers for the editor of the *Java Government Gazette*, the books and journals for Thomas Horsfield, and the money bags for the army pay division, there was something altogether out of the ordinary. It was an official letter from the Supreme Government in Calcutta which amounted to 'no less than the impeachment of Mr. Raffles by Major-General Gillespie'. All those fulsome handshakes in October had counted for nothing, it seemed, for as soon as Gillespie disembarked in Calcutta in December he had lodged an official report with the Supreme Government, declaring Raffles a corrupt incompetent, a cad and a liability.

Otho Travers could not have been more appalled. 'Never shall I forget the morning when my worthy patron sent for me to his private office to mention the particulars of these dispatches,' he wrote, with characteristic melodrama. How to explain such treachery? Travers still had fond and emotional memories of that last glimpse of Rollo Gillespie, the epitome of an undersized gentleman, all verve, dash and swagger, and he had looked back happily on the final weeks of brotherly love between the soldier and the civilian. How on earth could the little hero have now done *this*? Raffles was apparently similarly bemused for he asked Travers for his opinion. The hyperventilating ADC, however, was 'altogether unable to answer when he asked me how I could account for such villainy and duplicity in my friend Gillespie'. The only thing Travers was sure of was that Gillespie was *not* his friend any more: 'how much and sincerely I regretted having ever experienced the patronage and favour of a man, whom from that moment I could no longer call a friend or look upon in any other light than a treacherous and false-hearted villain.'

There were seventeen separate charges, dealing mostly with that dodgy land deal at Cianjur. The Council in Calcutta had demanded straight answers from the Lieutenant-Governor: had he *really* bought the land himself? Had it *actually* been valued by one of the other investors? But there was more – serious questions were being asked about the general approach to the absurd paper currency, about Raffles' policies towards the military, about his dealings with the native chiefs, and above all about the wisdom of his land reforms. There was also the issue of how he had personally behaved towards Gillespie. These were all decidedly uncomfortable questions.

Secretary Assey went to work at once, going through each point, paring the whole matter down to its central accusations. Raffles high-tailed it for Buitenzorg to begin preparing his furious defence, and Otho Travers attempted to get his turbulent emotions under control. He was in a state of utter horror, flouncing and huffing, but he had begun to come up with an explanation for Gillespie's beastly back-stabbing: it was all down to jealousy. Gillespie had wanted control of Java; he had resented 'Mr. Raffles superior talents', and his pride had been wounded when his request to be removed from his post – which Travers now believed had been merely a bluff – was so readily accepted. This was obviously the explanation given most credit by the outraged Raffles clique as they gathered in gloomy hallways in Batavia in February 1814, shaking heads, muttering, mumbling, huffing, puffing, spitting, swearing and calling down calumny on the head of Rollo Gillespie.

But Gillespie was supposedly a gentleman of the first order, who 'despised trick and subterfuge'. He was also exceptionally brave. Had he really been still raging in his final weeks in Java, then he would surely have still been speaking his mind too. He had once battered a man to a pulp for refusing to remove his hat, after all. The handshakes with which he had left back in October were almost certainly sincere, regardless of whether or not he had vague aspirations of one day returning to an army-run Java. But a lengthy voyage in tropical seas is the perfect setting for quiet reflection, and the *Troubridge* had stopped off in Penang too, where catty comments about the man they remembered as a jumped-up clerk with a ghastly wife were still current. And most important of all, there had been the company of Charles Blagrave. If Gillespie had been intending to let all that had made him angry in Java lie, perhaps Blagrave had things to reveal that brought everything bubbling back up. Perhaps he had tales of practices in the Buitenzorg office, of the grasping hands of the Travers, the Flints and the McQuoids, which suddenly made Raffles' tight-fisted approach to military finance seem particularly hypocritical. Perhaps he had the full back-story to the Cianjur land sales, or perhaps he simply acted as a reminder of *everything* that had grated for the past two years. Whatever it was that changed his mind, by the time Gillespie reached Calcutta he was very angry indeed. Finding a new administration in place, and scant sympathy for Lord Minto's romanticism and Raffles' expensive indulgences, he decided to speak.

From the moment the impeachment documents arrive it becomes obvious that Raffles' Java was always doomed, and the Lieutenant-Governor starts to cut a decidedly shabby figure. That a youthful clerk with scant experience and a huge ego had somehow ended up with free rein over five million people no longer seems a heartening success story, the cheery tale of the nobody made good; it looks like an indulgent oversight, a critical lapse in judgement, a *mistake* of the kind that cost lives, ruin careers and change history for the worse. Regardless of whether Raffles was actually guilty of anything that could ever be brought before a court, it had suddenly become clear that he was not a man to be left in charge of *anything*, least of all a large, isolated, complicated and above all *temporary* territory.

Not that Raffles himself saw things that way, of course. The arrival of the malevolent February missive did not prompt him critically to consider exactly how he had behaved and what he had done in the previous two and a half years. Raffles might have been nervous; he might have been lacking in confidence in certain sorts of company, but by the age of thirty-two he was a man whose utter absence of self-doubt had passed beyond the point of return. For a month he huddled at his desk while the rain sheeted off the roofs of the Buitenzorg house and the stream down in the ravine below churned over the boulders in cataracts the colour of creamy coffee. His fringe flopped limply and his round shoulders hunched over sheet after sheet of pale paper as he scrawled out response after response to every sentence of the charges from India. The Council in Calcutta had requested 'the fullest explanation respecting your own conduct, in those instances in which it may at all appear to be impeached by the facts stated, or the opinions expressed by Major Gillespie', and Raffles would certainly give them what they wanted. Reading his replies – which run to hundreds of pages in looping, arching script – there is not a hint of a pause, of a moment of reflection, of even the barest concession. He had done *nothing* wrong, he was sure, and anyone who dared to suggest otherwise was engaging in nothing but 'effrontery'. Gillespie's conduct in raising the issues, Raffles stated publicly, was 'most extraordinary, unjustifiable and disgraceful'.

It clearly did not occur to him that cool replies would likely sit better with upright men in government chambers. Some of the charges seemed to rest on questions about his personal character, and in light of that, spitting fire about 'injurious aspersions' was perhaps inadvisable. As the weeks passed and the rain rumbled on, more notes came from India making it clear that public opinion had been 'flowing like a torrent' against Raffles. He continued to hack away at his desk, draining inkwell after inkwell, and delving deep into the minutia of each charge. He could answer every one. He approached even the trickiest as though it were a puzzle designed to encourage lateral thinking, as though a demonstration of devious logic would win a round of applause from the high-ranking officers of the Honourable East India Company. What he seems never to have understood was that Gillespie's charges were not ever really likely to have seen him stand before a judge, and therefore they were not to be approached as if that was where he already stood – with an acquittal on a technicality as good as any other. Though the points that Gillespie raised were in places exaggerated or ill-informed, he had not made this stuff up, and it amounted to but one small squall in a much bigger storm system. It was not the precise chronology of events pertaining to a land auction, or the ephemera of colonial economics that were really in question; it was Raffles' overall competence, his character, and the advisability of the very *existence* of Java as a British colony that was under scrutiny. And nothing he scribbled in the wet weeks of 1814 could convincingly answer any of *that*.

He had also lost control of his anger. It had been claimed that he had shown an unbecoming sort of disrespect and 'indelicacy' in his behaviour towards Gillespie. Instead of simply ignoring this particular charge – which was the only thing he could sensibly have done – Raffles plunged headlong to the bottom of the filthiest, most fetid and malarial gutter in all Batavia. If they wanted indelicacy, Raffles would show them indelicacy:

Let me then ask Major General Gillespie, where was the indelicacy of my conduct towards the Commander of the Forces, when a virgin was forcibly demanded by his orders from the Orphan School in Samarang [sic] – where was it in a similar outrage, perpetrated by Military Force in the House of a Mr. Sluyter in Batavia – both of which instances were reported to me and others may be adduced – or where after the return of Major Robison from Palembang when that Officer openly accused Major General Gillespie, and did not scruple to mention charges of a most serious nature unofficially[?]

Here was the allusion to whatever it was that Robison had claimed Gillespie had done in Palembang, and 'which never came officially before the Government', and here was slanderous tittle-tattle of the kind which should never have appeared in any sort of official correspondence. The tale of the Semarang virgin was an old one: at some point, it seems, a local troublemaker had turned up at the gates of the orphanage there making lecherous enquiries about one of the more comely teenage residents. He had been promptly sent packing. The suggestion that this reprobate had been demanding the girl on Gillespie's behalf was positively outrageous, and where Raffles heard this rumour is hard to imagine. Perhaps the most likely explanation is that he had misunderstood a ribald joke doing the rounds of the Semarang mess halls. As for whatever was alleged to have happened in the house of a 'Mr Sluyter' in Batavia, this was not the kind of topic that the *Java Government Gazette* routinely covered on its front page, and no trace of such an incident has ever turned up. But anyway, even allowing for the possibility of dark deeds done far from home in the murky gloom of Palembang, the idea of the most famous soldier in Java committing nocturnal outrages by force in the middle of the colonial capital seems decidedly silly. By signing off his reply to all the charges levelled at him with this filthy counteraccusation

Raffles had done himself no favours at all. However the Council in Calcutta viewed the rest of his responses, they would always be convinced of one thing – that Thomas Stamford Raffles, as well as being highly unreliable as an administrator, was a shockingly vulgar little gossipmonger, and absolutely *no* sort of gentleman.

And Gillespie's charges were by no means the last of it. The Supreme Government was now asking pressing questions about *everything* Raffles had done, and if he thought that Blagrave would prove to be the only embittered former secretary to seek revenge he was sorely mistaken. Back at the start of November, Raffles had shipped William Robison to Calcutta with a wad of confused and contradictory evidence that he hoped would see the disgraced former Palembang Resident convicted of corruption.

This kind of approach is perhaps an indication that Raffles and his immediate entourage had long since lost any sense of perspective when it came to assessing their own powers and their own significance. Raffles had stuck firmly to the letter of old Dutch laws about respect for the person of the Governor-General (even though he was *not* a governor-general himself). Javanese and Chinese had to dismount from their scrawny ponies or scramble respectfully out of their carts whenever Raffles' carriage rattled past, and no one was allowed to overtake him on the roads of Java. He had once had a coachman who had committed that particular crime flung in jail for a month. With that kind of arbitrary power Raffles had perhaps forgotten that his word was not law *everywhere*, and that he could not blithely toss the most worm-riddled case across the water to the Calcutta courts and expect them to acquiesce to his conclusions. Robison was cleared of all charges.

What was more, when the Calcutta authorities discovered that Raffles had kept half of the 200,000 dollars that Sultan Badruddin had paid as a term of Robison's rogue treaty, they were appalled. This was exactly the kind of behaviour that would bring an empire into disrepute. They ordered him to pay it back at once. But that was not all. The acquitted William Robison was clearly still in a rage, and he decided to float his boat on the tide of public opinion. He lodged his own accusations against Raffles in a paper entitled 'Some account of the general manner of proceeding of the Java Government'. It was at times rather silly, and also decidedly personal – though Robison never stooped so low as to accuse Raffles of raping orphans. He told tales of Raffles' 'Splendid overgrown Establishments and general waste and profusion', and of Olivia gallivanting about Batavia on shopping trips with a full escort of European hussars forced to gallop along beside her carriage 'under a noon day sun' with 'the poor fellows ready to drop from their horses'. Silliest of all – and it really *was* silly – was Robison's claim that the Susuhunan of Surakarta had been 'obliged to submit to the indignity, as impolitic as it was cruel, of travelling from his capital to Samarang [sic] in order to be taught the game of whist with the Lady Governess'. But like Gillespie's charges Robison's report contained just enough of substance, particularly on the matters of Raffles' annexation of the lands of the Sultan of Banten and Han Chan Piet, to call down serious questions.

When a copy arrived in Batavia, Raffles declared it to be 'a mass of absurdity and trash', and scarcely worth answering. But Robison had been an irresistible irritant to the Lieutenant-Governor from the very start, and answer his charges Raffles most certainly did – with vitriol dripping from the nib of his pen. His response ran to thirty-two acidic pages. The point that irked him most was that Robison had gone as far as to make unkind comments about Raffles' friends: the prime jobs in the establishment had been given to 'needy adventurers taken out of the fifth Class of Society', he claimed. Flint, McQuoid, Travers: they had been slandered. 'His effrontery is much on a par with his ignorance' wrote Raffles, and 'so devoid of all shadow of truth that I hardly know how to answer it'.

Raffles signed off his furious replies by declaring that he had deployed 'as much patience as I was master of, and as much temper as I could command'; he may occasionally have been a little caustic, but when it came to his general standards of conduct, the Council 'may be assured that these will never be lowered by the despicable effusions of a man such as Major Robison'.[18]

* * *

The trouble continued as 1814 advanced. Accusations, charges and responses passed back and forth from Batavia to Bengal, and still the tide was flowing hard against Raffles. He decided to send his most trusted lieutenants into the breach. Charles Assey would be shipped to Calcutta, and Otho Travers would be sent to England in an attempt to clear their master's name.

Travers set sail at the end of March. It was a bittersweet departure. He was delighted at the prospect of seeing his family for

---

18 After acquittal on Raffles' corruption charges, and after penning his own revenge, Robison returned to active service. He fought in the Ghurkha War of 1814-16 and was later made a lieutenant-colonel and placed in charge of a regiment for his efforts. But he still had a problem with authority, and he still had a tendency to rage at anything he thought was wrong with the colonial government. In 1822 he published an angry letter in the *Calcutta Journal*, a rather feisty rag with a decidedly strained relationship with the East India Company authorities. The letter, ascribed to 'a Military Friend', congratulated the paper for its campaigning journalism, and condemned the 'fining, flogging, cheating' and corruption of Company-ruled India. The authorities were furious; Robison took public responsibility for the piece to save the staff of the *Journal* from trouble, and ended up arrested and court martialled 'for traducing the Government under which His Majesty's had placed him'. Robison reacted every bit as badly to the censure as he had to Raffles' moves against him the previous decade; it was 'an unwarrantable, tyrannical exercise of authority, which reduces every officer in India to a state of slavery equal to that of the gentlemen in the Russian service'. After the hearing he set sail for England in a parlous state of health intending to clear his name and to present to the British public irrefutable evidence of outrageous abuses by the authorities in India. He had written to supporters at home telling them that he was bringing an accumulated bundle of documents detailing all of the worst things he had seen done by Englishmen during his years in India, but he died as the ship was swinging in towards the Cornish coast. When his friends came aboard at Falmouth and searched Robison's cabin they found no sign of the papers.

the first time in almost a decade, but the thought of all the money-making opportunities he would miss in Batavia had broken his heart. But still, how could he possibly say no?

'For no other man living but Mr. Raffles would I undertake what was before me', wrote Travers. He had collected a remarkable 125 letters of personal thanks and recommendation from the good burghers of Batavia, sold his furniture and dismissed his slaves in a deluge of tears, and then made the hardest parting of all. Raffles was teary-eyed too as he clasped his devotee's hands. As Travers remembered it, the Lieutenant-Governor had declared that 'You have my life, my honour in your hands. I feel they cannot be in better. You know my innocence and I am not able to say more'. Predictably the ADC subsequently 'required a few hours to bring me to myself' before going aboard the *Morning Star* with a resolute heart – and a little gold dust he had picked up cheap at the last minute. He would be gone for more than a year, and by the time he returned the storm of Gillespie's accusations would have begun to subside, but the British Interregnum itself would be slipping slowly beneath the warm waves of the Java Sea, and some of the people Travers loved most dearly would be dead and buried alongside John Leyden and all the others that the Javanese climate had claimed for its own.

Mutiny and Mangos

There was more to the Indonesian archipelago than just Java. East of the lodestone the great green arabesque of islands swings on through a stuttering string of small worlds for another thousand miles. The Dutch had never held all, or even much of this; in the outer limits of Indonesia their presence was patchy – a resident here, a rotting fort there, and then whole clusters of islets where they had never even set foot.

The easternmost extremity of the main chain was Timor, an angled lozenge of land floating 300 miles above Australia. In the mountains there were kings descended from the birds who ruled over hilltop villages, but on the coast there were the great-grandchildren of Portuguese sailors playing worm-riddled guitars and drinking vinegary wine. Portugal had once laid claim to the whole island, but for two centuries the Dutch had held sway over the western half from the steamy little town of Kupang. It had a low-walled fort on a stony headland and a community of Mestizo Portuguese. Dark hills rose to the north across a white bay, and ships from strange places sometimes anchored in the channel. A sun-scarred Captain Bligh had come ashore here in his open boat in 1789, 47 days and 3618 nautical miles after the Bounty mutineers ordered him down the ropeladder off Tahiti. More recently it had been an entrepôt for slaves and sandalwood under the command of 'an old and opulent widow of a former Dutch Resident' who had 'for a long time monopolised all the indulgence and authority of that place'. Britain had seized Kupang in late 1811.

To the north lay the tiny island of Alor – just fifty miles in length, but with a different language spoken in every valley. It was 'inhabited by a fierce and treacherous people, which renders it dangerous for ships to touch there'. Further west was a string of tiny islands, a dappling of irregular shapes nestling against each other like the spots of a clouded leopard. Offshore volcanoes smoked in the dawns here, and tumble-down Portuguese forts stood under banks of green hills. Here and there a mildewed church waded in the greenery and dark children with ponytails raised their brown eyes to a white Virgin and mouthed unknown Latin phrases on hot Sundays. The wriggling, snaking line of Flores came next – still in theory governed by the Portuguese, though by the start of the 19th century their presence amounted to little more than a few feverish friars, fast forgetting their catechism in damp mountain villages with ancestral shrines between the houses.

After Flores came a fistful of tiny brown islands, rising like knuckles from a boiling sea. On the biggest of these outcrops – Rinca and Komodo – there were dragons, real dragons, but it would be another century before Europeans came to know that.[19] Next was Sumbawa, an island even more tormented in form than Flores, whipping itself into contortions like a Chinese serpent. This was as far east as Islam had reached with any confidence, and as far east as Javanese influence had ever stretched with certainty in the days before the Dutch. There was a sultan in a wooden palace in the town of Bima, and a recently installed European resident in a gloomy villa on the outskirts. Bugis sailors traded sea cucumbers and slaves out of the deep natural harbour, and some of the best horses in Southeast Asia – small but strong and carrying their Arab bloodlines lightly –

---

19 The Komodo dragon, the world's biggest monitor lizard, was first recorded by Dutch travellers in the second decade of the 20th century. Local people – who called the creatures *ora* – had always known about them, of course. Today there are around 2000 of them left on Komodo itself, some 800 on neighbouring Rinca, and a few hundred more on the tiny hillock of Gili Motang and in the forests of western Flores. They can grow to ten feet in length, and can, on very rare occasions, eat people …

were raised in the nearby hills. Over the whole island loomed a huge volcano. Its name was Tambora.

West of Sumbawa, propped by its own vast peak, was Lombok, a blot of an island under the harsh sway of the Balinese kingdom of Karangasem. And then there was the deep gouge of the straits, before the dark hills of Bali itself rose, lavender-black and wet as a rotting plum, holding bad weather in the belly of the island. There was no Dutch outpost here, and no British presence either, though an early correspondent of the *Java Government Gazette* had informed titillated readers that in Bali 'the wife burns herself with the body of her deceased husband, she ascends the funeral pile, adorned with flowers, and holding in her hand a dove, which she liberates. On the bird's flying off she leaps voluntarily into the fire'.

In early 1814 there had been a little trouble with Bali. The Raja of Karangasem, strongest of all the island's kingdoms, had crossed the western straits to Banyuwangi at the tip of Java. This region had old and deep links with Bali and had remained Hindu long, long after the fall of Majapahit. But as far as the British were concerned, trespassers would be prosecuted. In his first action as the new Commander of the Forces Miles Nightingall had sailed east along the Pasisir, dropped anchor off Bali's northern coast, where the mountains drop sheer into deep water, and occupied the fort at Buleleng. This place was a separate fiefdom from Karangasem, but the threat was enough to extract a capitulation.

There had been more trouble away to the northeast too, in the second rampart of the archipelago. In the great southwest promontory of Sulawesi – then known as Celebes – there had long been powerful kingdoms run by Bugis chieftains. They had always been the greatest challenge to European maritime power throughout the archipelago, and though the VOC had made the fiefdom of Bone its nominal vassal, Bugis pirates still haunted river mouths and mangrove swamps everywhere from the Straits of Melaka to the Spice Islands. In 1814 there was unrest. 'The restless and ambitious dispositions of the native Chieftains of Celebes had long been a source of annoyance and trouble to the former Government of this Colony', wrote Raffles; 'The recent conduct of the Raja of Boni [sic] at once hostile and insulting demanded an example'. He could do little about the calumnious disrespect of Rollo Gillespie and William Robison, but at least Raffles could still unleash chastisement on an insolent native ruler. Once Nightingall had dealt with Bali he sailed north. In early June he reported back to Java that he had successfully cowed Bone; he had burnt the Raja's house to the ground (without qualms, because he judged that it 'was of trifling value') and sent the Bugis soldiers fleeing into the hills. Another tranche of territory had been subjugated.

And then there was Borneo.

This great green thumbprint – the third biggest island in the world – had always been the trickiest puzzle-piece in the entire archipelago. It still is.[20] The interior was a mass of thick forest, veined by deep rivers running from unknown headwaters. There were rhinoceroses, orang-utans and proboscis-nosed monkeys like sad old men. There were diamonds and gold too, according to the Arab and Chinese traders. And there were people. Borneo was one place where there really were head-hunters. The Dayaks, the people of inner Borneo, lived in smoky longhouses high up the rivers, or travelled on foot with blowpipes and bows and arrows in the deep forest. Their wars were played out beneath the thick canopy far from prying eyes, and their religions – of ancestors and hornbills – were unknown to theorising foreigners. Raffles (who had never been to Borneo) declared the Dayaks 'a race scarcely emerged from barbarism'; they could 'not

---

20 The name 'Borneo' is a corruption of 'Brunei', and was extended to the whole island, according to John Crawfurd, 'by the Mohamedan navigators who conducted the carrying trade of the archipelago before the advent of Europeans'. Today Borneo is divided between three nations. Malaysia holds most of the top tranche, split between the states of Sabah and Sarawak. Tiny Brunei nestles within the latter, while the vast southern bulk of Borneo is Indonesian territory, under the name of Kalimantan.

be worse', and had 'no sacred institutions handed down from their forefathers'. Where there was no mosque, church or temple, Raffles believed, there was no faith at all.

Just as a lack of water saw European settlements form a thin patina around the edge of Australia, too *much* wet greenery had kept the outsiders to the Borneo foreshore. At river mouths and promontories settler states sprang up, a flaking lacquer of Malay language and Islam tacked on to the island's outer fringe. On the slanting slope of the northwest coast the Sultanate of Brunei had grown strong, and on the sagging underbelly of the island other fiefdoms under Malay kings had sprouted – Sambas, Pontianak, Banjarmasin, Balikpapan. The VOC had repeatedly tried – and repeatedly failed – to gain a steady toehold somewhere on this shore. Their demands for treaties and firm agreements lacked the easy fluidity of the Arabs and Chinese who had come before them, and in 1809 Daendels had pulled the last Dutch posts out of the island.

Borneo had caught Raffles' attention for two reasons – first there were the pirates who haunted its murky inlets, and then there was the fact that the Dutch had abandoned the place. From the very start with those inciting letters to Palembang he had been feeling for ledges on which to settle a British presence that would *not* have to be handed over whenever peace finally came to Europe. If the Dutch had abandoned Borneo, he reasoned, then whatever he managed to set up there would remain standing even if Java belonged to Holland once more. This driving desire to found a lasting British settlement, no matter how small and no matter what his masters actually wanted, *somewhere* in the archipelago, was already the kernel of Raffles' ambition. By the end it would be all that remained.

The first attempt to deal with the pirates of Borneo in 1812 had been a catastrophe. Raffles had sent a fleet to the little fiefdom of Sambas at the furthest western snub of the island. The ruler there – Pangeran Anom – was the man who had sent Raffles the gift of the trouser-wearing orang-utan in Melaka, but that kind of friendship counted for nothing, and Anom did have an atrocious reputation as a pirate king. He was also no pushover, for the initial expedition to Sambas returned swiftly with its sails riddled with bullet holes. The commander – Captain James Bowen – died promptly on his embarrassed arrival in Batavia, 'under great depression of spirit'. Another expedition the following year was more successful. Pangeran Anom vanished upriver and a British outpost was established.

But the main British foothold in Borneo lay further east at Banjarmasin on the blunt southern arrowhead of the island. In 1813 Raffles had announced to a meeting of the Batavian Society that in Banjarmasin 'Much valuable and interesting information has already been collected by Mr. Alexander Hare, the present Resident, a gentleman whose desire after useful knowledge and whose zealous exertions in the cause he has undertaken, are perhaps unrivalled'. This Hare, Raffles continued, was doing a very fine job of upholding British standards on the southern shores of Borneo, and 'Under his enlightened administration the country subjected to Banjer Masin has been already reduced to order and regulation'. For this statement from Raffles to be considered in any way truthful a radical reassessment of the meaning of words would be required: 'enlightenment' and 'order and regulation' would need to be regarded as synonyms for unhinged despotism, flagrant disregard for British colonial law, and outright sexual excess. The place was a disgrace.

Hare's outpost at Banjarmasin prefigured the later stories of Joseph Conrad – a European 'lord' with a shady past ruling a little riverside community in the great green blank of Borneo. But if Hare was a Conrad character he was no Lord Jim; Banjarmasin was far from the Congo, but its resident Englishman was unmistakably a kindred spirit of Mr Kurtz.

* * *

Alexander Hare was an adventurer in the very worst sense. He was born in London sometime in the early 1780s. His father was a watchmaker. He had started his career on the docks of Lisbon, but had soon drifted to Calcutta before heading further east. Raffles first met him in Melaka where he was already head of a highly irregular household with barely post-pubescent Asian women of various races tumbling out of every bedroom. This did not, apparently, perturb the young clerk in the least, and Raffles was eager to bend the rogue trader's ear – for by this time Hare was running ships in along the pirate shores of Borneo and speaking rather fine Malay, of the kind usually learnt in the boudoir. He had some kind of working relationship with the Sultan of Banjarmasin, the king who ranked second after Brunei amongst all the Malay rulers of the Borneo littoral, and as soon as the conquest of Java was complete Raffles had appointed Hare British resident there.

What Alexander Hare did when he got to Banjarmasin late in 1811, women in tow, ought to have prompted a howl of outrage from Batavia, for it was in direct contravention of both wider East India Company policy, and Raffles' own regulations for British residents at native courts. A resident was not supposed to accept any kind of gift from a king. But Hare accepted a gift – of 1400 square miles of territory, not as an accession to British domains, but as a *personal fiefdom* in his own name, a place six times the size of Singapore. Raffles should have sacked him at once, of course – or at very least demanded that he hand the territory back to the Sultan, or across to Batavian control. But he did not, for by now the two men seem to have become rather firm friends. There was vague talk of economic potential in the Banjarmasin jungle, and what was more, a little English sultanate might well one day provide the foundation for the kind of British bastion against resurgent Dutch power that Raffles dreamed of.

The land that Alexander Hare ruled was a swampy morass. It never had many native inhabitants, and Hare's habits seem to have scared off the last of the locals as soon as he moved in. As for the promised profits, there were none at all, though as the official resident of the district Hare was able to charge the running costs of his petty despotism to the Batavia treasury – which he did with impunity for the entire duration of the British Interregnum. By 1813 when Raffles made his fulsome speech to the Batavian Society the tranquillity and order of Alexander Hare's realm amounted to a half-built palace on stilts, already rotting before it was finished. A hundred men had slaved on it for over a year, trying to meet the unhinged resident's demand that his dwelling should stand higher than the tallest tree. Hare had minted his own tin coins, but all of his staff were unpaid slaves. All around the ramshackle palace were the filthy huts of Hare's legion of native concubines.

But there was more. Hare was a frequent visitor to Java, where he owned property, and he was doubtless a perfect gentleman whenever he stopped by in Batavia. In this respect Raffles could almost be forgiven for keeping the funds flowing to Banjarmasin, and believing that the resident really was laying out a land of milk and honey in the middle of the jungle. But as well as asking for money to run his outpost, Hare had also asked Raffles for *people*. And the Lieutenant-Governor, great stalwart of anti-slavery, had given them to him.

In early 1813 Raffles had signed an order that all convicts who could legitimately be sentenced to transportation in Java were to be shipped to Banjarmasin for Alexander Hare to do with them as he saw fit. Hare even received a subsidy of 25 rupees a head for every criminal he received. The power of sentencing in Java rested with the Lieutenant-Governor; Raffles ratified every conviction himself. However, the supply of convicts was not enough for Hare. Many of them died; many of them fled into the forest. He wanted more people, and in particular, he wrote to Raffles, he wanted *women*. He was especially interested in women of 'loose morals'. These were easily identified, he suggested, and he would be happy to take as many as could be found without the need for a subsidy payment. Raffles sent them.

Firstly the Lieutenant-Governor began signing sentences of transportation for people who were 'arrested as vagrants or found guilty of petty theft or repeated trifling offences'. An instruction penned by Secretary Charles Assey made it clear to British residents in the east of Java that these people too were to be sent at the public expense, but Assey's instructions also explained that Alexander Hare himself would cover the cost of a third class of 'colonists'. These were not criminals at all, but those who 'proceed either voluntarily, or are removed from temptation to crime and placed in a situation in which they may be induced to earn an honest livelihood'. Unsurprisingly there were few volunteers willing to swap the green fields of Java for the swampy morass of Banjarmasin; instead people were *preemptively* arrested for crimes they had yet to commit, and delivered up to the docks where Hare's ramshackle ships would arrive to collect them.

The only indication of Raffles' famed liberal sensitivities in these instructions lay, perhaps, in the line that stated that 'The Lieutenant Governor in Council therefore directs that preparatory to embarkation they be allowed, under a Guard, to revisit their families'.

And as it was essential 'to the tranquillity and improvement of a new Establishment that the Population should bear a due proportion of both sexes, the Lieutenant Governor in Council desires that the native authorities be directed to assist in procuring young women to proceed voluntarily to Banjar by a small consideration or by release from debts, and when such may have agreed to go, they should be held in readiness for embarkation.' This was blunt and unequivocal stuff by the usual delicate standards of 19th-century administrative instructions. The meaning would have been clear to every resident from Surabaya to Banten: they were quietly to instruct the local regents that women – women with a certain sort of reputation – were to be rounded up. If there was some kind of debt or threat that could be used to make them go quietly, then all the better, but that they were to enjoy one last sobbing visit to distraught families 'under a Guard' and that they should then 'be held in readiness for embarkation' makes it clear that these were a strange sort of volunteer.

Just how many people Raffles had shipped out to Alexander Hare's festering fiefdom over the course of his administration is unknown. For very obvious reasons he did not talk particularly loudly about the business himself in later years – interisland slave-trading, which in other instances he had done a good deal to stamp out in Indonesia, was a crime in British territories, itself punishable with deportation. Talk of 'volunteers', meanwhile, would never stand up to much scrutiny. The deportees certainly numbered in the thousands.

In the very last days of the British Interregnum, with Raffles already off the stage, the appalled incoming British administrators attempted to make sense of what had gone on. The Kurtz-like Alexander Hare, still surrounded by women in his half-built wooden palace, wearily totted up the totals at their behest and decided that there were 907 men, 462 women, and 123 children still sheltering from the rain in his decaying jungle village. An unknown number had already died or fled. All those who had been shipped under sentence – be they murderers or mere vagrants – brought their conviction papers with them for administrative purposes when Hare claimed his 25-rupee rebate. Of the surviving women, Hare stated, 80 were criminals; 137 had tagged along when their hapless husbands were shipped out. The remaining 245 had 'not brought lists of sentence, but have been sent for bad conduct'. There were apparently no volunteers.

The 'Banjarmasin Enormity' has become the filthy little secret of the British Interregnum in Java. Although outraged Dutch historians later howled as loudly as they could against the Anglophone tide, you will find the phrase listed in the indexes of none of Raffles' English biographies. His biographers – who had used weasel-words when it came to the unavoidable issue of Palembang – simply made a headlong dash and leapt clean across the question of Banjarmasin without looking back. By the wider standards of European colonialism it was pretty small beer, of course. But by the standards Raffles set for himself, and which those who have eagerly propped his legend have so loudly proclaimed, it is hypocrisy of the highest order. The only way to deal with it, it seems, has been to ignore it.

But the Banjarmasin story *did* unfold over those five, strange years in the history of Java. All the while that the fine gentlemen of the Batavian Society were gathering for readings in the Harmonie Club in Weltevreeden; all the while that merry gatherings were going on in the halls of Buitenzorg, and Olivia Raffles was leading off the first dances in a whirl of frilly lace; all the while that the *Java Government Gazette* was going out each Saturday to subscribers with its poems of England and its adverts for fine French claret; all the while that enthusiastic surveyors were clearing the creepers from the old temples and English dignitaries were watching tiger fights in Yogyakarta, small tragedies were taking place here and there. In villages or market towns between the volcanoes, or in the sordid brothel *kampungs* of the ports, girls who might, perhaps, have owed an unpaid debt to a moneylender or a bazaar owner, were taken away by native policemen. No one ever recorded the sobs of their widowed mothers and grubby, fatherless children in any journal or column as they were dragged off to Borneo at the behest of Thomas Stamford Raffles.

An 'error of judgement' it may well have been, but the reason Raffles was so ready to let Alexander Hare remain as a mad despot in the feverish jungle became clear two years after the Dutch had returned to Java. He wrote to the new Dutch Governor-General Baron Van der Capellen 'to inform your Excellency that an offer has been made by Mr. Alexander Hare, tendering to the British Government the tract of land and territorial rights alienated to him by the Sultan of Banjermassing on Borneo'. Raffles, camped out in Bengkulu at the time, was excitedly awaiting news of the official decision, and was hoping to have the pleasure of telling Van der Capellen that there would soon be a permanent British outpost deep within what the Dutch had always regarded as their sphere. Much to his chagrin, however, the Supreme British Government had no more interest in taking possession of Hare's seamy cesspool than they had of causing a diplomatic crisis with their allies in Holland.[21]

* * *

While the occasional kidnapping of prostitutes and vagrants for Alexander Hare went on out of sight and out of mind in the Javanese hinterland, for Raffles 1814 had been a miserable ordeal. Throughout the dry months in the middle of the year more accusations and angry questions came from Calcutta, and notes from Charles Assey on damage limitation duty brought word that the general current was still against Raffles and all he stood for. Worse yet, in May there was news that Napoleon had been defeated at Leipzig and that Holland had regained its independence. Britain and the Netherlands were

---

21 Alexander Hare was subsequently kicked out of Banjarmasin. He drifted for a while around the archipelago, trying to get back to his properties in Java, but the Dutch refused to let him in, and he shipped out across the Indian Ocean to South Africa instead. Neither the church nor the civil authorities there looked kindly on his domestic arrangements or his irrepressible habit of contravening laws on slavery, and he was eventually evicted. What Alexander Hare really wanted was a desert island on which to live out his dreams of debauched despotism undisturbed, and in 1826 he hauled his household to one of the most isolated spots on the planet, the tiny clutch of uninhabited coral atolls called the Cocos Islands, a thousand miles west of Java in the middle of the Indian Ocean. He had first heard of the place from a Scottish sea captain called John Clunies-Ross, who had worked for him at some point, and who had passed the islands on one of his voyages. Hare reassembled what was left of his fiefdom on the scorching white sand there, and for a year there was no one to interrupt his excesses. But then John Clunies-Ross himself turned up, with his family and a plan for a more civilised settlement. There were two dozen islands, and plenty of room for both men, but Hare's brutalised slaves and put-upon women were in the habit of fleeing across the lagoon to seek shelter under the auspices of the markedly more benign Clunies-Ross. After five years of bitter quarrels, and with only a few withered old concubines left, Hare departed and headed east once more. He died in Bengkulu in 1835 after falling off his horse.

no longer in a state of de facto conflict. The British threw the usual birthday party for their own king the following month, but it lacked the sparkle of previous years, and the halls of Government House in Batavia had been hung with Dutch flags as well as Union Jacks for the festivities. During the dancing Olivia collapsed.

A sick wife, a reputation on the cusp of ruin, and a decidedly uncertain future; and still the censure and accusations continue to float in from Bengal. The weight of it all pushed Raffles even so far as to admit the possibility of some small fallibility – though strictly in private. On 2 October he wrote to the last man of real influence he felt sure he could count on – the retired Lord Minto. 'Some of our measures are of rather doubtful policy, and that in the course of an administration so extended, and I may add so difficult, some and many errors may have been committed, I am ready to admit', Raffles conceded; 'But the universal censure that has been heaped upon all our measures, plans and expectations is too general to be just'.

But by 2 October 1814 Lord Minto had already been dead for more than three months. The accumulated effects of the Asian climate had suddenly unloaded themselves on his aging frame as his term in office came to an end. By the time he reached London for debriefing he was a very sick man indeed. He had died on 21 June in Hertfordshire, trying to make his way back to his wife and home in Scotland.

Lord Minto would not be the only significant figure associated with Java to pass away in 1814. As the wet season loomed it was as though the vulgarity and the indignity of everything that had happened since August 1811 – the insulted princes, the looted palaces, the kidnapped prostitutes, the misappropriated history, and the infantile arguments – had finally pushed the Queen of the Southern Ocean to reap a terrible retribution. She had had enough, and she would send her spirit army far beyond Java in the name of revenge. If she could reach as far as Hertfordshire, then she could easily reach India.

* * *

On 31 October 1814 Major-General Rollo Gillespie was shot through the heart by an unidentified Ghurkha defender as he tried to storm a little rock fortress called Kalunga in the foothills of the Garhwal Himalayas.

If it had sometimes seemed to Raffles that his nemesis was personally leading the charge against him from Calcutta, he was mistaken. Gillespie had already presented his accusations, been questioned by the Council on the details of Raffles' bad behaviour, and had then gone back to doing what he loved before the first letter even reached Batavia in February. He was almost forty-nine, but he was still in fine health, and he was still in the field with a new fight threatening: the British were going head to head with the Nepalese Ghurkhas for control of the cow county of north India. The Ghurkhas were, it seems, quite unlike any people that Gillespie had ever met in his long life of soldiering. Frenchmen, Hollanders, Malays, Javanese, Irish theatre-goers: none of them had fought like *this*, and when Gillespie tried to overwhelm the little stronghold at Kalunga he found that it was a tougher task than that of taking either Meester Cornelis or the Yogyakarta Kraton. Every attempt was beaten back by the hill men in a hail of bullets, and as Gillespie led one last desperate attempt to breach the walls a shot found its mark. He went down face-first and was dead before he hit the ground.

They gave him a hero's burial in Meerut, of course. But in private, over a glass of evening brandy, senior officers muttered darkly of a needless death. Kalunga, they said, was a place that could *never* have been taken in an all-out assault by escalade (it was a further month before the British finally conquered the fort, and that only after shelling it to rubble). Rollo Gillespie's enormous personal bravery had, perhaps, crossed the line into catastrophic recklessness. Like a Javanese warrior, wielding a magic *kris* in the army of a Righteous Prince, he had believed himself invulnerable. He had forgotten that it was possible to die.

Three days later, and four thousand miles to the south, the Sultan of Yogyakarta collapsed in his private bathroom. He had been ill for a month, with bronchitis and diarrhoea. It should have been a happy time, for the city was quiet for once. Crawfurd had gone away on his wanderings, but he had left the capable Robert Clement Garnham in his place as acting resident. Garnham, who was rather self-conscious about a large birthmark on his left cheek, and who had also served alongside Otho Travers as Raffles' ADC, was well-liked by the Javanese courtiers. The greatest cause for celebration, however, was that the Sultan's youngest wife, the daughter of Arya Panular, was seven months pregnant. The arrival of any new child in the royal household was a happy occasion. But the ruler had coughed and shivered with fever during the elaborate ceremonies that attend the seventh month of pregnancy for a Javanese woman, and by the beginning of November he was very sick indeed. What exactly was wrong is unclear, but perhaps the rattle in his chest had deepened to pneumonia.

He had taken a weary walk on the ramparts on the evening of 1 November with his women and flunkies in tow. There were few signs left now to show where the sepoys had stormed over the walls, and the outlying *kampungs* had been rebuilt. Perhaps Gunung Merapi had showed for a moment through the purple dusk, looming sheer and ominous to the north, before the concerned courtiers drew the shivering Sultan back to his quarters. He did not appear in public the next day, and then, before dawn on 3 November, he woke and told his minders that he needed to urinate. They supported him as he hobbled to the bathroom, but once he had relieved himself he fainted. Calls of alarm echoed through the courtyards of the sleeping Kraton, and soon all the queens and concubines were on hand, and the weeping had already begun. They carried the unconscious king to a platform under a pavilion of the inner court, and sent messengers running for the herbalists, the witchdoctors, and the priests. Robert Garnham came running too with the residency doctor, but as soon as they saw the royal figure, thin and already corpselike on the batik blankets, they knew that there would be no remedy.

As dawn broke over Yogyakarta all the princes gathered in the

Inner Kraton, to sit cross-legged around the Sultan as he lay, breaths coming in thin, fading whispers. The women wailed and the little Crown Prince sobbed; the men prayed, and thought about their own futures, a forest of *kris* handles jutting from the waistbands at the base of their bowed backs. Arya Panular, wiping his eyes, rocking slightly and thinking of his pregnant daughter, repeated line after line of Arabic incantation, and then switched tack to hope for a royal reincarnation in the form of the coming baby. The Queen-Mother, chief of the women's quarters and wife of the exiled king, bent to whisper the Islamic last rites in her son's left ear, while one of the princes came forward to make other, less orthodox preparations for the Sultan's soul to slip out through his navel.

At 6 o'clock in the morning on 3 November 1814, Sultan Hamengkubuwono III died in the Inner Kraton of Yogyakarta. He was forty-five years old. It was little more than two years since Raffles had appointed him, and now the Lieutenant-Governor was faced with the prospect of a ten-year-old on the most important throne in the Indies. Robert Garnham's urgent message, telling Raffles that the Sultan had already been interred alongside his grandfather Mangkubumi and all the other kings of the Mataram line right back to the greatest of them all, Sultan Agung, on the sacred hilltop of Imogiri, reached Batavia within a few days. But before Raffles really had time to make firm plans for the future of Yogyakarta the British in Batavia would have to hold a royal funeral of their own.

* * *

On 21 November Raffles wrote to a friend in England that 'Olivia is far from well but in good spirits'. She died five days later.

Perhaps whatever it really was that had long been wrong with her liver had at last proved fatal. Or perhaps the Queen of the Southern Ocean had finally had enough of a mere mortal – and a foreigner to boot – claiming the crown of First Lady in Java. They brought her coffin down from Buitenzorg, and buried her on 28 November in the cemetery at Tanah Abang, alongside John Leyden. It was an affair with almost as much pomp – and almost as much demonstrative grief – as that other royal funeral at the other end of Java three-and-a-half weeks earlier. Not *everyone* was entirely impressed, however. A young Scotswoman called Carline Currie, married to the assistant surgeon of the same 78th Regiment whose officers had got into a mess in Probolinggo the previous year, wrote to her sister in the Highlands to tell her about Olivia's passing:

Mrs Gregory and I were the only Ladies in the Cantonment that did not attend the funeral, and I am very glad I did not, as I am told they all made themselves very ridiculous by weeping aloud when the Corpse was taken from the Government house and when it was put into the grave and all this for a woman whom some of them had never seen above once or twice ... People who knew her seemed to like her very much and said she was a very good hearted woman but she had one great failing and that was being too fond of a glass of Brandy and when she had taken too much of it and got her Aid De Camps about her, I am told that no modest woman could sit in her company ...

As the first rains of his third Javanese monsoon opened over Mount Salak and the Puncak Pass, Thomas Stamford Raffles was completely alone. Travers and Assey were still away; news would arrive in January of Lord Minto's death, and soon, sometime, *anytime,* word would surely come that Britain had agreed to hand Java back to the Dutch. And Olivia was dead.

For a moment all the overbearing conviction seemed to fail. For a moment land reforms, devious schemes and historical projects seemed no longer to matter. His health began to give way, fever creeping out of the shadows when he had sat too long at his desk. He moved uphill away from Buitenzorg to a higher, cooler place on the green mountain slopes – in search of a better climate, it was said, but probably also to get away from the hollow echo of the empty halls.

He was, he wrote to a friend in England, 'a lonely man, like one that has long since been dead, but whom activity and the cares of public responsibility are now almost necessary for existence'. In the age of stiff upper lips it was a striking admission of depression.

If news had come in the first weeks of 1815 that he was to leave Java at once, perhaps Raffles would have welcomed it. But it did not come. He would rule the island for another year; there would be much work to do, and the very earth of Indonesia itself was all set to unleash its own fireworks.

* * *

On 5 April 1815 the crew of an East India Company cruiser called the *Benares*, anchored off Makassar in Sulawesi, heard what they thought was the sound of distant gunfire, rumbling in from the south. It could only be a party of pirates coming in from the Bone Rate Islands, they thought, and the *Benares* set sail to take them on. For three days they scouted out through the offshore islets, peering through spyglasses and questioning Bajo fishermen. But they found no pirates, and they cut back in to Makassar.

Then, on 11 April came more explosions, 'in quick succession, sometimes like three or four guns fired together'. They sounded so close that the captain of the *Benares* sent a crewman up to the crow's nest to see if he could make out what was happening. The man could see nothing on the horizon, but the whole ship was shaking on the slick waters of the harbour. The next morning a portentous darkness was hanging away to the south, as if a whole slice of the world had sheared off; 'it was apparent that some extraordinary occurrence had taken place' and with a certain trepidation the captain of the *Benares* set sail once more, heading out across the Flores Sea. If the gates of hell had really opened, then it was his duty to survey them and to prepare a preliminary report.

As they edged away from Sulawesi across a transient easterly breeze, the darkness ahead rolled steadily towards them, taking on an infernal reddish tint. The sea was oily around the hull. It grew darker still. By 10 o'clock they could see no further than a mile, and by 11 a.m. there was only a thin clipping of clean light, far away on the eastern horizon. Ash began to fall out of the leaden sky, and at last it became clear what had caused the concussions: somewhere to the south a volcano had erupted. By midday it was pitch dark. 'I never saw any thing to equal it in the darkest night; it was impossible to see your hand when held up close to your eyes', noted the captain. They had only their watches, held up to guttering candles, to tell them that the real night had fallen that evening, and the fine ash continued to descend, working its way into every crevice of the ship, catching grainy between the back teeth of the sailors, and forming a greasy film in the water vats. There was no dawn the following day, but by 8 a.m. a low, dirty light was beginning to seep through the murk. It revealed layers of ash a foot deep on the deck of the *Benares*, and a thick coating on every sheet of the flaccid sails. They scraped it off with shovels.

It took them the best part of a week to pick their way south across the Flores Sea. There was only the thinnest of breezes, and the sky was still a filthy grey smear, uncut by sunlight. On 18 April they first sighted the ravaged coastline of Sumbawa, that snaking island of horses between Lombok and Flores. The *Benares* had to cut through great banks of floating pumice matted with broken trees to reach the mouth of the deep cleft of Bima Bay the following morning. This was a natural harbour that had been well charted, but as they nosed into its sheltered pool they nudged onto a shoal where there had been no shoal the last time a European ship called by. 'The anchorage at Bima must have altered considerably', the captain wrote, with a certain understated irrelevancy: it was not just the anchorage – the whole of Sumbawa itself had changed almost beyond recognition.

The booms and bangs they had mistaken for the cannons of pirates had been coming from Gunung Tambora, the great mountain that towered from a broad peninsula on Sumbawa's northern shore. On the night of 10 April 1815, and into the morning of the following day, after sending clouds of ash and gas booming out of its crater for five days, and after smoking ominously for much of the previous year, Tambora had simply exploded. Looking west from Bima Bay the crew of the *Benares* could see a mountain that had had its top third completely obliterated. On 9 April Tambora's summit had been almost 14,000 feet above sea level; by the 12th it had shrunk to a mere 9000 feet. It was the single biggest volcanic eruption in recorded history. The much more famous explosion of Krakatau – a fiery island in the Straits of Sunda between Java and Sumatra – sixty-eight years later sent a paltry eighteen cubic kilometres of detritus up into the sky; Tambora, in one monumental concussion, spat *150 cubic kilometres* of rock, dust and gravel into the atmosphere.

They had heard the explosions 600 miles away in Java too, and on 5 April the British commanders in Yogyakarta had sent a column of fast-moving relief troops up the road to Klaten in the belief that the fort there was coming under attack. Over the coming days a strange and ominous atmosphere had descended over Java. A fine rain of ash – like dust kicked up in an old hayloft – drifted across the island, giving everything a careworn, antique edge. On 10 April, the day of the final, catastrophic eruption, houses everywhere in East Java had trembled; books and bowls toppled off shelves, rafters rattled and timbers shivered. On the morning of the 12 April Carel van Naerssen, the resident in Gresik, a town of tombs and saltpetre works north of Surabaya, woke 'after what seemed to be a very long night, and taking my watch to the lamp, found it to be half-past eight o'clock; I immediately went out, and found a cloud of ashes descending'. By 9 o'clock it seemed as though night was falling; an inch of ash was lying on the residency terrace, and the resident took his breakfast at 11 a.m. – by candlelight. The gloom did not begin to thin until late that afternoon, and down the road in Surabaya John Crawfurd, who was in town on secondment, reported that 'for several days after I transacted all business by candlelight'.

In Sumbawa itself, meanwhile, there was unimaginable devastation. In the capital Bima, forty miles east of Tambora, the crew of the *Benares* found native schooners tossed up high above the tide line, and houses with their roofs caved in under the weight of the ash. The resident – a Dutchman called Pielaat – had survived, but his house was a wreck. He said the sound of the eruption had been like 'the report of a heavy mortar close to his ear'. Two small kingdoms on the slopes of the volcano – Pekat and Tambora – had been utterly annihilated. Their rajas Muhamad and Abdul Gafur, their fields, their villages, their culture, their language, and all their inhabitants, had been vaporised. Some 10,000 people had vanished from the face of the earth.

The entire rice crop was destroyed in Sumbawa, and within days famine and dysentery had broken out. Over the coming months some 37,000 people died and wild pigs came out of the forests to chew at the corpses left unburied at the roadsides. In Dompu people took to eating leaves; in Bima they killed and cooked their best bloodstock. People started selling themselves as slaves to traders from Sulawesi and Maluku just for the chance to be carried away from their ravaged homeland. Over the course of the coming year as many fled as had died. The population of Sumbawa had been halved.

But the effects of the Tambora eruption stretched much further afield. In East Java cows died and crops were ruined, and here and there a roof collapsed under the weight of the ash. But the worst suffering was on the islands that lay beneath the immediate flight path of the ash – Lombok and Bali. Every rice field there was devastated, and in the coming years the famines killed thousands of people. Perhaps as much as half the population of Lombok died of starvation and disease, and in Bali too the death toll was horrific. Three years later visitors still reported bodies lying abandoned on the beaches with no one left to organise even the most modest of cremation ceremonies. In all something like 100,000 people died in the Tambora eruption and its aftermath in Indonesia.

And the slow shockwaves stretched still further: up in the high atmosphere those 150 cubic kilometres of detritus had lifted on the thermals and slipped into the jet streams, bent their way through the spirals of tropical depressions, and filtered out across the globe, watering down the sunlight, changing the weather patterns, stirring up the seasons. In Europe the following year there were frosts in June; the French grape crop withered on the vine and there was famine in Ireland. In Switzerland people had nothing to eat but stray cats and wood sorrel. In India the monsoon failed, and far, far away in America snow fell in New England in July. They called it 'the Year without Summer'.

For many Javanese people meanwhile, the mighty explosion in the east at the end of the wet season had been an irrefutable sign of a shift. A major volcanic eruption was always a punishment or a portent. The resident in Gresik had reported that amongst the locals 'Some look upon it as typical of a change, of the re-establishment of the former [Dutch] government; others account for it in an easy way, by reference to the superstitious notions of their legendary tales, and say that the celebrated Nyai Loroh Kidul [the Queen of the Southern Ocean] has been marrying one of her children, on which occasion she has been firing salutes from her supernatural artillery. They call the ashes the dregs of her ammunition ...'

* * *

A change was indeed coming. At about the time that Tambora erupted the Board of Directors in Leadenhall Street in London were putting together the final draft of a dispatch to Java demanding a halt to Raffles overreaching land reforms. They felt a great 'uneasiness lest the new system of land revenue, so hastily introduced by the Lieutenant-Governor of Java, should have served to alienate the minds of numerous individuals whose long established authority has been subverted by it'. But Raffles would be all set to leave Java by the time the missive arrived, and the haphazard application of his new rent system continued all over the island. It had not worked.

The monopolies and system of prescribed crops had been dismantled and people were allowed to grow what they liked. So they grew the only thing they had ever wanted to grow – rice, for local consumption, instead of cash crops. But they needed cash to pay their rent to the British, and at times the rates were set cripplingly high. The taxmen who travelled the island on Raffles' behalf were supposed to value each and every plot afresh every year, but it was a task of herculean proportions, even without the heat, the muddy pathways and the mosquitoes, and the ever-present urge to spend the afternoon catatonic in a fine slick of sweat, prostrate on a sagging bed in the shuttered backroom of a remote government bungalow. The inspectors often simply invented arbitrary values for the land, and knowing how eager Raffles was for income, they invented them *high* …

But the farmers simply didn't have the money to pay their rents. In Banten in 1815 only half of the revenue assessment was collected; the following year they were hardly able to collect anything at all, and where they did gather some cash from the struggling peasants, the tax collectors and their local advisors often helped themselves to a significant cut before heading back to Batavia. Elsewhere, where the collectors were more rigorous in their efforts, they pushed the people into penury. The values of the lands around Surabaya had been set fantastically high in 1814. Most of the farmers, however, had never possessed a single silver dollar in their lives, and they had to go into the towns to submit to the Chinese moneylenders to find the cash to pay the British Government. Without collateral they had to borrow against the value of the next year's harvest, but in 1815 the rice crop failed – probably in part due to the Tambora ash. The rents, meanwhile, had been raised even *higher*. The farmers had to go back to the moneylenders.

Everyone who had travelled beyond Batavia already knew that the system had broken down before it even began to run. John Crawfurd was scathing of Raffles' attempted reforms. The Lieutenant-Governor, he wrote, was not much of an original thinker, and not much of an expert, and 'Thus, without much time for examination, seeing it lauded by its partisans, he adopted, and at once carried into execution among the then five million inhabitants of Java, the fanciful and pernicious Indian revenue system … and saw it break down even before he had himself quitted the administration of the island'.

Raffles himself, however, simply refused to see things this way. He had proclaimed the system a great success from the very start, and sent letter after letter to England and India to declare as much to the doubters. Whether Raffles was actually *lying*, or whether he was simply incapable of accepting the truth of his failure, his own version of what was going on in the green provinces of Java under his administration was utterly unhitched from reality. In 1815 he claimed that 'the grand work of establishing the detailed system has been perfected; that every acre of cultivated ground has been measured, assessed and brought to account; that a body of information the most complete, the most valuable perhaps that any Government can boast of, has been collected; and that the revenue has been considerably enhanced, whilst the most liberal consideration has not only been paid to the rights, but to the feelings, the vanities, the wishes of those whose interests might be affected by the change'.

When the Dutch returned to Surabaya in 1816 they found the people in the surrounding countryside in a state of grinding poverty, dressed in rags, and owing a lifetime of future harvests to the Chinese moneylenders.

* * *

By 1815 everyone knew that British Java was doomed, though news of exactly when the Dutch would return was still not forthcoming. For Raffles there was a moment of excitement when he heard in August that Napoleon had escaped from his exile in Elba and was in the field once more. 'The wonderful and extraordinary change in the politics of Europe by the reappearance of Buonaparte [sic] has with all its horrors showed one consoling ray on this sacred Isle; and Java may yet be permanently English', he wrote breathlessly. But the end *was* coming. By the time Raffles heard of Napoleon's return from Elba, in Europe it was all already over: the Battle of Waterloo had been fought and won one wet day two months earlier.

The British Interregnum was entering its dog days, and if the

Englishmen, fever-wracked and exhausted, had started to take their eye off the ball then it was hardly surprising. But at this latest of stages the mistakes and the mismanagement almost had catastrophic consequences: as 1815 trundled towards its termination trouble was brewing in Central Java. The people that everyone seemed to have forgotten about, the third party in the conquest of Java – the Indians, the sepoy soldiers – were about to make themselves heard.

* * *

The five Indians knelt together on the clammy stones, eyes closed, palms pressed. They were deep within the network of pools and grottoes that formed Yogyakarta's Taman Sari, the Water Palace where Arya Panular and the Crown Prince had tried to seek refuge three years earlier. The place had been damaged by the shells of 1812, and had been largely abandoned by the courtiers. It had become a realm of birds' nests and unpicked fruit, sudden unsavoury stenches, and sordid assignations. It was the perfect place for a conspiracy.

The men praying fervently on a stone platform in a secret cloister were non-commissioned officers of the Light Infantry Volunteer Battalion, a division of the Bengal Presidency Army which had been raised in 1810 especially for the Java campaign. They had been recruited far from Bengal, and further still from Java – in the hot, hard desert states of Rajasthan and northwest India.[22] The leaders

---

22 Several contemporary sources refer to the men as 'Bengalis', as do the very few modern publications that deal with this episode. However, the names of the sepoys in question are strongly indicative of non-Bengali origin. A gaggle of high-caste Hindus called Singh, including a declared 'Rajput', would almost certainly have been from Rajasthan. The other identified conspirators have names that could indicate a homeland anywhere in northwest India, including Rajasthan, but none of them have appellations suggesting Bengali origins. The Bengal Presidency was recruiting soldiers from a great swathe of the Indian heartlands at the time, including Oudh and the Northwest Provinces, and Rajputana (Uttar Pradesh and Rajasthan respectively, as they are today).

of the group were called Matta Deen and Dhaugkul Singh. Time-served soldiers, they had been in the thick of the charge at Meester Cornelis, and they had been in the van of the attack that forced open the Prince's Gate, just half a mile from where they now knelt, in June 1812. But since then there had been no fighting, and they had done nothing but shuttle back and forth between Yogyakarta and Surakarta. They had grown tired of the dull drudge of garrison duty in a strange and sweaty land.

With Deen and Singh were three co-conspirators – Radhay Singh, Fakir Singh and Dia Ram – and some two dozen supporters were peering through the damp doorways to watch their little ceremony. They muttered and mumbled their mantras while the incense coiled wildly around them in smoky worm-casts, and then Matta Deen spoke. Without a Brahmin to attend to the religious needs of the Light Infantry Battalion, he had taken on the role of priest, overseeing the ceremonies in the little temples they had put together amongst the armouries and powder stores of the forts in Yogyakarta and Surakarta. He was a soldier *and* a holy man, and now he had something of divine inspiration to say. The other men kneeling beside him listened keenly. Tonight, said Matta Deen, was the moment for mutiny. On this evening of 24 October 1815, between the hours of 6 and 7.30 p.m., the British officers of the Yogyakarta Garrison were to be killed; those sepoys who stayed loyal would be locked up, and an Indian-Javanese uprising would sweep the Europeans from the island. The only thing that could possibly save the Englishmen now was the mango season …

* * *

Since the fall of Yogyakarta security in Central Java had been left largely in the hands of the sepoys. The Light Infantry Volunteers had to cover both Surakarta and Yogyakarta, with men rattling up and down the road past Prambanan as was required. The well-attested terror that the Javanese felt for the Indians gave the British officers confidence in their abilities – and certainly left them completely unconcerned about possible conspiracies. And in any case, there and all across Java there simply weren't enough European soldiers – neither officers nor rank and file – to do the job. Since 1812 when the military presence was scaled down the sepoy regiments had accounted for the bulk of the British forces in Java, and those white soldiers who remained had succumbed to sickness on a staggering scale: the 78th Regiment, the Highlanders who had tangled with the Probolinggo rebels in 1813, had arrived in Java in 1811 with 1027 men. By the time they left five years later there were only around 400 survivors, though very few of the casualties had come on the battlefield.

The sepoys were not just left with most of the responsibilities; with their senior officers mostly in the sickbay or the graveyard they were also left to their own devices, and over the course of four years there had been subtle changes. As discipline slackened sepoys had started to go AWOL. Some vanished into the green countryside around Kedu and set themselves up as dairymen; others sold their uniforms in the bazaar and married into local families in Yogyakarta. Even those who remained at their posts got used to doing as they pleased. And though some of the more respectable Javanese aristocrats maintained their horror of uncouth men with strange accents and flying moustaches, elsewhere the sepoys began to make some high level contacts with the locals, some *very* high level contacts indeed: the uprising which almost came to pass in October 1815 had the backing of none other than the slippery Susuhunan.

Quite how or why the mutinous sepoys first got in touch with the Susuhunan is unclear, but things in Surakarta were not entirely peaceful in 1815. Tensions between the Susuhunan and his irritant miniature counterpart Mangkunegara were worse than ever, and even his principal wife and his younger brother – an extremely troublesome man called Mangkoeboemi[23] who was kept in a state of loose house

---

23 This Mangkoeboemi shared a name with a rebel prince of an earlier generation – Mangkubumi, the first Sultan of Yogyakarta. In the interests of differentiation we'll know him here under the old-fashioned Dutch spelling system, in which an Indonesian 'U' gets an O and an E.

arrest within the Kraton for fear of the chaos he would cause outside – had begun plotting to place a pliant puppet of their own choosing in the post of Crown Prince, ousting the official incumbent. And there was all sorts of uncertainty about the future, for everyone in Surakarta knew that the British period was coming to a close. The Dutchmen still attached to the residency had taken to swaggering around with orange ribbons tied to their buttonholes, and the Susuhunan was getting nervous. He had, he felt, got the measure of the British. Though they had undermined his independence they had given him money, and they had forgiven him some very significant sins. If the Dutch came back, how would he handle them? Would they cut his stipends, annex more of his territory? Perhaps it was time to start stirring things up once more.

Meanwhile there was increasing unrest amongst the sepoys too. The Light Infantry Volunteer Battalion had received no leave since 1811, and neither had many of their countrymen in other divisions in other parts of Java. They had also found it impossible to remit their salaries to families in India, thanks to the currency crisis and general ineptitude of the British administration. They had also, like the Susuhunan, heard that the British would soon be leaving, but in a classic clumsy oversight, none of the British officers had ever bothered to explain political developments in Batavia, Calcutta or Europe to their men. They were left to cook up conjecture along with their chapattis, and by the dry months of 1815 a disturbing rumour was doing the rounds: the kings of England and Holland, the story said, had married their children and Java was to become part of the dowry, with the entire Light Infantry Volunteer Battalion tossed into the deal. A few of their number might have gone native, but all that the vast majority of the sepoys wanted to do was to go home. If there had ever been a moment to take the law into their own hands, then this was surely it.

* * *

The men who found themselves at the head of the conspiracy were an odd pair. Matta Deen spoke Malay; Dhaugkul Singh did not. Deen was the man of religion who dealt with the ceremonies; Dhaugkul played on his background as a high-born Rajput of the *Kshatriya* warrior caste. They should, perhaps, have been rivals in rebellion, vying jealously for the crown of the Righteous Prince. But in the end they seemed mainly to egg each other on like schoolboys, while simultaneously striving to pass responsibility and command to the other man. They seem, above all, to have been dreamers, and they talked at one time of making Dhaugkul the governor of all Java with an airy palace in the mountains above Surakarta.

Their early communications with the Susuhunan, during the months that followed the Tambora eruption, seem to have focused primarily on matters of religion, for it seems that the middle-aged Susuhunan, who in his youth was said to have had an entourage 'swarming with priests' of the Muslim variety, had begun to take an interest in Indian Hinduism. He asked Dhaugkul and Deen all sorts of cultural questions, and took to turning up incognito to watch the sepoys at prayer at a little water temple they had set up outside their barracks. The Susuhunan was, and always had been, a Muslim first and foremost. But he was a Muslim of the old Javanese variety – where Sanskrit ranked as highly as Arabic as a sacred language, and where Ramayana myths were better known than Old Testament prophets. At one of his meetings with the sepoys in the Kraton it was said that an old Javanese image of a Hindu god had been introduced (whether the king gave it to the sepoys, or the other way around depends on who told the tale), and that Dhaugkul Singh, holding the statue in outstretched hands, had said to the Susuhunan, 'If you are a descendent of a worshipper of Rama, you are my master'.

But before long the talk had taken a more sinister turn. With fear and discontent at the prospect of being abandoned by the departing British mounting in the ranks of the Light Infantry Volunteers, Matta Deen and Dhaugkul Singh had begun to mature their plans. They had gone so far as to send insurrectionist messages to kinsmen in

Batavia, and had drawn the other key conspirators – Radhay Singh, Dia Ram and Fakir Singh – more closely into their plot, the details of which remained indistinct. Now, the Susuhunan offered them his backing. His own motivations were the old ones that had driven all his clumsy conspiracies, and he named various conditions of his own: he wanted Purbaya, the young prince that the Queen and the royal brother Mangkoeboemi were trying to have appointed as heir, placed on the throne of Yogyakarta once the rebels had toppled the boy-Sultan. The Susuhunan was not entirely happy at the idea of slaughtering the entire European population of Java, however, and was perhaps a little nervous of a vision of an unhinged army of Indians under the command of no one and on the rampage in Java. But by now the hell-raising brother Mangkoeboemi – later described by the Surakarta prime minister as 'a mad man always abusing the Europeans' – had been drawn into the scheme, and was keeping cash and encouragement flowing to the sepoys. At some point in August a reply arrived to Matta Deen's note to Batavia, stating that 'You are the Light Battalion, if you mutiny or do anything we will follow you'. And then, in September, Matta Deen and the other conspirators were transferred to Yogyakarta.

* * *

The British officers and civilian administrators in Central Java had had absolutely no idea that any of this had been going on, and when, on the evening of 20 October 1815, a loyal sepoy told Christopher Macdonald, the sergeant-major at the fort in Yogyakarta, that 'something was going on in the Battalion that was not right and seemed to indicate a mutinous spirit', he refused to believe him. He 'did not suppose the men would dare to do such a thing after being treated so well and every indulgence shown them'.

But the story was true, and that night, as on all the other nights in recent weeks, men gathered on the ramparts, settled on the steps leading to the corner bastions of the fort, kicked off their shoes and incited insurrection. Four days after Macdonald heard that disquieting rumour, came the meeting in the Water Palace and the final, decisive decision to launch the massacre that very night between the hours of six and 7.30.

In the event, however, nothing happened. Though a mob of would-be murderers did gather on the ramparts, that curious tendency of Deen and Dhaugkul to try to foist the definitive authority onto the other man meant that no one would take the ultimate responsibility of ordering the start of the action. The appointed ninety minutes passed, and then, by means of deflecting criticism perhaps, someone suggested that they take advantage of the fact that the most deliciously decadent of all fruits was now in season in Java, and going very cheap. If they weren't going to kill the Englishmen, then why not throw a mango party? The suggestion seems to have prompted the first decisive action of the evening, and before long the ringleaders and the hangers-on were all sitting cross-legged in Matta Deen's quarters in the fort, with sticky fingers and mounds of mango rinds at their feet.

The mutiny was not cancelled, the sepoys claimed, just postponed, and they fell to juicy fantasies about the future of Indian-ruled Java. When Dhaugkul Singh was raised to Governor of Java, it was decided, they would celebrate with a sky-shattering 101-gun salute. At some point another aspiring mutineer who had listened to Matta Deen's fiery talk on the ramparts over the previous weeks, and who had been quite ready to act at the first sound of gunfire at 6 p.m., burst angrily in and accused the ringleaders of cowardice. Matta Deen told him to shut up and offered him a mango. Nobody was a coward; they just needed more time.

It is at the mango party on the night of 24 October that something suddenly becomes apparent, something which had eluded the Susuhunan earlier in the year and which apparently escaped the notice of the understandably alarmed British when finally they found out what had been going on: Matta Deen and Dhaugkul Singh were all mouth and no trousers. These were not the men to lead a revolution, and unless some new rabble-rouser had unexpectedly emerged from the ranks it seems unlikely that any Englishmen were ever really in danger of being beheaded in Yogyakarta in late 1815. But it also shows just how close to a real uprising sepoy troops – not just in Java, but throughout the East India Company's domains – could come without their commanders knowing anything about it. How many other times over the decades did the balance in garrisons in Malaya, Madras, Bombay or Bengal teeter on the brink between mutiny and mangos for a few hot hours until the want of a real leader tipped things in favour of the fruit?

If there had ever been a real moment to act, it had almost certainly passed now, but over the coming days the hot words continued. Matta Deen stomped around, calling the British '*banchodes*' ('sister-fuckers') and telling everyone that he was going to command their slaughter sometime very soon – but not right now. The whole thing was rapidly descending into farce – with the most ridiculous aspect being that the conspirators were still at large in the fort and still coming out with their filthy language and fantastical plans while their senior officers remained oblivious. As late as 29 October, an acquaintance who was shopping in the Yogyakarta bazaar bumped into Matta Deen who told him openly that all the Europeans in the city were to be killed that night.

But by now the loyal sepoy had returned to Sergeant-Major Macdonald's quarters with another warning: there was *definitely* something going on, and at last the British took notice. The commanding officer, Lieutenant Steel, ordered a full parade, lined all the sepoys up on the dusty space at the heart of the fort and announced in stern tones that the stories that the British were planning on handing over the battalion to the returning Dutch were lies, that anyone found talking of treachery would be blasted to pieces from the barrel of a cannon – the standard mutineers' execution in British India – and that a significant cash reward would be dished out to anyone who came forward with information. It did the trick. There were no more late night meetings on the ramparts and no more mango parties. Matta Deen tried to run away to Surakarta to ask the Susuhunan for help, but he – and all the other key conspirators – were soon under arrest and sent off separately to outlying forts while an investigation got under way.

* * *

With hindsight it seems as though the British approached the abortive mutiny of October 1815 from completely the wrong angle. They were genuinely very frightened by the fact that their Indian soldiers had been plotting against them. But the court of enquiry that sat in Yogyakarta in the second week of November turned up little more than comic ineptitude and cowardice on the part of the plotters. But it did reveal something *much* more significant than wild talk over ripe mangoes – that the Susuhunan had been involved in the conspiracy. By the earlier standards of the Interregnum the Surakarta Kraton should have immediately crumbled under a rain of chastising cannonballs. It did not.

Otho Travers had returned to Java from England by this stage, and scribbling the December entry in his diary he noted that 'Early this month we had accounts of a most extraordinary and alarming [rebellion] which broke out in one of the Sepoy battalions to the eastward'. It amounted, he spluttered, to 'the most shocking and disgraceful proceedings ever yet known attaching to the name of a Sepoy', and would cause 'much alarm and very great speculation abroad'. It certainly would have done – and it might even have offered the kind of lessons that could have averted a much bigger uprising in India forty-two years later. But Raffles seems to have decided that a cover-up was the best way to proceed. The hapless Matta Deen and Dhaugkul Singh, and the main co-conspirators, were shot and another twenty sepoys were shipped off in chains for hard labour in India, but news of the affair was not made public. During August – while the sepoys had been consorting most closely with the Susuhunan – Raffles had written that 'universal tranquillity prevails, and confidence is everywhere established'. Publicly to reveal that Britain's *own troops*, in cahoots with one of the two most important signatory kings in the colony, had been planning to murder the entire European population would have made Raffles look ridiculous.

It would be impossible to ignore the Javanese involvement in the plot altogether, but a decision seems to have been taken to blame everything on the mad, bad Mangkoeboemi. On 8 December Raffles wrote to Lord Moira in India 'with extreme regret' to tell him of the failed uprising. It did not, of course, reflect well on his lieutenant-governorship to have presided over a near mutiny, but he did all he could to downplay the possibility that the Susuhunan had been a major mover in the matter. There was 'no reason to believe that the Susuhunan had any idea of hostility or opposition to the British Government', he wrote. By the New Year, Raffles and his Council colleagues in Batavia had decided 'to receive the excuses of the Susuhunan'. It would be, they felt, 'expedient and advisable not to take further notice of the detailed informations that may come out regarding the Emperor's [Susuhunan's] personal knowledge of and share in the intrigue'. A more detailed enquiry into these very matters was due to get underway in Semarang, but before it even started, Raffles had handed the Susuhunan a pardon. He had done it again: the ruler of Surakarta, inept, debauched and unrealistic though he may have been, had wriggled, jiggled, and slipped off the hook once more. Of all her problematic protégées, the Queen of the Southern Ocean seemed to show this one by far the most indulgence.

Not everyone was impressed by Raffles' decision. The mild Miles Nightingall had been called back to India by this stage, and his second in command, Colonel Burslem, an upright and aristocratic soldier with an impeccable military pedigree, had been left in charge. Raffles had started squabbling with him immediately. Burslem and others felt – with considerable justification – that the Susuhunan really had gone too far this time and really ought to be punished. The obviously outraged English judge presiding over the later enquiry into the Javanese aspect of the conspiracy in Semarang demanded of the Surakarta Prime Minister, who had given full and frank answers throughout, 'After all this are you not concerned that the emperor is deeply implicated and that this has been a bad business?' to which the canny courtier replied, 'I ask forgiveness if I don't reply, the Governor has granted pardon, and everybody is gratified ...'

In fact, a rumour that the British *were* about to attack Surakarta had prompted a good deal of flapping in the Kraton in December and the Susuhunan had gone as far as gathering weapons from hidden caches in readiness for war. But in the end Mangkoeboemi was made a sacrificial scapegoat and shipped off to exile in Ambon. Colonel Burslem stomped off muttering about Raffles' poor judgement. The ineffectual resident at Surakarta protested that if you didn't ask then the Javanese would never tell you anything when he was pointedly pressed as to why the entire court there seemed to have been aware of the conspiracy while he had known nothing about it; and John Crawfurd, the most capable British civilian in Java, was sent back to Yogyakarta to make sure that nothing else embarrassing happened in the final months of British rule.

Meanwhile, persistent rumours of other rebels, proclaiming themselves Righteous Princes and raising armies of angry men on the western fringes of Yogyakarta territory and in the wild backwoods of East Java, were quietly ignored. Raffles, it seems, was already thinking about future mythmaking, and there was no room for seething undercurrents of unrest in the tranquil legend of British-ruled Java. He probably also rather relished the idea of leaving a few booby traps for the returning Dutch. He did, however, pick up one piece of trivia from the secretive enquiries into the Susuhunan's involvement in the abortive mutiny – the fact that the royal had taken to watching the worship of the Hindu sepoys. When he wrote *The History of Java* the following year Raffles declared, on the basis of this one little snippet of information, that had the uprising come to pass 'it would probably have been followed by the almost immediate and general re-conversion of the Javans themselves to the Hindu faith'. This was, of course, an idea as ill-informed and improbable as anything Matta Deen and Dhaugkul Singh ever came up with over their half-eaten mangos.

* * *

On the second day of 1816 Raffles set out on a final circuit of Java. He was a sick and miserable man. Fever was harassing him like an irate constituent and the yellowish tint of jaundice had coloured the edges of his wonky eyes. His last year as Lieutenant-Governor had been a strange mix of depression, anger, denial, and rogue operations. He seemed to alternate between raging against the dying of the light and thrusting his head deep into the sand. Throughout 1815 he talked of a desire to resign his post after completing a full five-year term in October 1816, and he laid out complex plans for the future British administration under his unnamed successor. But everyone already knew that the British would be gone from Java before the end of 1816; the Dutch inhabitants of Batavia were beginning to get a little shifty with impatience, and the *Java Government Gazette* was carrying frequent classified advertisements for the unwanted slaves of hurriedly departing Englishmen.[24]

Elsewhere Raffles had gone completely rogue and laid the

---

24 The last edition of the *Java Government Gazette* went out to its dwindling body of subscribers, after the official handover to the Dutch, on 10 August 1816. It was replaced shortly afterwards by the Dutch language *Bataviasche Courant*. Quite what the unemployed editor, Amos H. Hubbard did when his newspaper folded is unclear, though a sad little 'situation wanted' adverted on Page One of the final edition offers a clue: 'A YOUNG MAN, who understands the Dutch Language, would have no objections to engage himself in any of the Merchant Houses – for particulars enquire at the Printing Office'. Evidently he found himself a posting – and a lucrative one too, for the following year he chartered a ship, stocked it with cargo, and sailed home to America. It was the best option in the circumstances – he would have had a long time to wait for another editorial post on an English-language newspaper in Java: the *Indonesian Observer* didn't roll off the presses until 1955.

groundwork for the fomentation of future ferment in the Javanese courts. On his orders, in June 1815 the same Captain Baker who had surveyed the temples at Prambanan was equipped with plane tables and compasses and sent off to the wilder regions on the edge of the domain of the Queen of the Southern Ocean. He was to produce a highly secretive survey 'on a very large scale' of the Indian Ocean coast of the Yogyakarta and Surakarta territories. Raffles gave him specific instructions to search for any hidden harbours or river mouths on this wild shoreline and stated that 'The particular points to which I wish your attention to be directed are such as occur in the provinces of the Native Princes, and the practicality of effecting a communication and establishment among them in the event of a force being landed on the southern coast of the Island.' He was, it seems, dreaming of leading some future British reinvasion of Java, or at the very least of sneaking ships in from Sumatra to incite uprisings against the Dutch in the native courts. Baker did indeed find a surprisingly fine harbour – almost the only one on the whole south coast – at Cilacap on the fault-line between Yogyakarta lands and the start of Sundanese country. But when he was sent to Calcutta to deliver his findings the Supreme Government there were disinterested in the results and deeply disapproving of the sentiments. As far as they were concerned this kind of thing was *exactly* why Thomas Stamford Raffles was such a liability.

And now Raffles had to pay a visit to the Susuhunan to accept his well-honed apologies for that unseemly business with the sepoys. He also wanted to take his leave of other, less important princes. Dispatches detailing the handover to Holland had finally arrived the previous month, and they seem finally to have caused Raffles some small flicker of guilt on behalf of the native rulers of Java. Over the course of the previous four years he had hacked away the last vestiges of their independence. The big beasts of Central Java might still be able to cause trouble, but the others – the Panembahan of Sumenep in Madura, the man who had translated so many old manuscripts at Raffles' behest, and the Sultans of Banten and Cirebon – had been turned into nothing more than state pensioners. He was beginning to wonder 'how far the British Government might not be subjected to reproach, were they unconditionally to hand these princes over, thus reduced, to the mercy of their former rulers'.

Sick and sorry, slouching in the back of a carriage with Travers looking on in tender concern, Raffles rattled one final time along the road through the hills between Semarang and Surakarta. The rain came cascading out of the afternoon sky, and the track was a mushy mess of mud. The local villagers had been ordered from their fields to push the Lieutenant-Governor's vehicle whenever it got stuck in a rut. They stood shivering patiently at the roadside as he came lumbering along with a sodden accompaniment of dragoons trotting behind on mud-splattered ponies. Thunder crackled over Gunung Merapi, and the groves of palm trees swayed like knots of grief-stricken mourners.

There were royal salutes, red wine and fulsome understanding in Surakarta, and then a jolting journey down the road to Yogyakarta where the courtiers complained quietly of the difficulties of having Raffles meet the Boy Sultan. The feverish Lieutenant-Governor couldn't speak Javanese; Hamengkubuwono IV knew no Malay. They could do little more than sit side by side in embarrassed silence in the guest pavilion in the trees beside the Surakarta Road, with the shuffling princes looking on with lowered heads at the vision of a drooping thirty-four-year-old Englishman and the fidgeting eleven-year-old child he had seen fit to place on the grandest throne in Java.

There were furious rainstorms over the coming days, and the rivers around the Kraton overflowed their banks and washed away the roads. Raffles had to sit through another tiger fight. This time the buffalo won, and to hammer the point home four more tigers were then skewered to death by a platoon of Javanese spearmen. Next there were performances from some delectable dancing girls in the audience hall of Pakualam's palace, and then the guests had to watch the sorry spectacle of a billy goat vanquishing a wild hog and a common mongrel in the courtyard outside.

And then, with the last animal entertainments over and the

last leaves taken, Raffles and his party rattled off north through the drenched countryside, back towards the Pasisir. The mountains swam away into leaden cloud, and paths through the rice fields faded into grey cataracts of rain. On 18 January at Pekalongan, a shabby little port of batik workshops and mosques, they were met by a messenger carrying a letter from Lord Moira in India. Raffles read it in the residency there, exhausted and aching, and surrounded by a world of broken roads, grey mud and puddles.

For the moment, the letter stated, the threat of prosecution had retreated. There had been no final verdict, but it was unlikely that Raffles would ever be impeached over Gillespie's accusations. However, Lord Moira made it clear that this was not some kind of outright exoneration, and in other circumstances there would have been much sterner questions asked, especially about the shady subject of the Cianjur land sales. 'I must confess that from the first I have never been quite satisfied of the propriety of letting this Enquiry end in the explanations which have been forwarded by the Lieutenant-Governor', he wrote. But Java was about to be handed back to the Dutch happily, and to have an investigation into the character and capabilities of the outgoing Lieutenant-Governor underway at the time of the transition would have been 'a considerable embarrassment'. Raffles was getting off very lightly indeed.

This, however, was no consolation whatsoever, for attached to the letter was a minute from the Governor-General in Council in Calcutta, ratifying a resolution from the Board of Directors in Leadenhall Street:

Of the various measures of the Lieutenant-Governor of Java which have been commented upon in the Dispatch now before us we shall merely observe that we cannot but lament that the just and accurate view of political and commercial economy that have served to detect the numerous errors that have been committed by the Lieutenant-Governor were not directed to the prevention of acts which have rendered the occupation of Java a source of financial embarrassment to the British Government. With reference to these considerations, whatever may be the result of the investigations of the charges preferred against Mr Raffles, we are of the opinion that his continuance on the Government of Java would be highly inexpedient.

The Dutch would be back within a few short months, but it had been decided that some reliable civil servant from the India administration 'to whom the charge of the Colony can with confidence be entrusted' would be shipped in as a caretaker in the meantime. The man currently at the helm had done more than enough damage already. There was no polite way to say it, no softening euphemism with which to dull the cutting edge: Thomas Stamford Raffles had been sacked.

* * *

At the beginning of March 1816 a ship of a kind that had not been seen in Indonesian waters for half a decade anchored off Batavia. It was a frigate flying a Dutch tricolour from the topmast. Someone wandering the dockside must have spotted it first, called to a friend to come and look, and then sent word whistling up the road to Weltevreeden and beyond. The usual lethargy of European Batavia gave way to excited twittering in the old Dutch merchant houses, and by the time a tender had been lowered from the ship a welcoming party had gathered at the mouth of the Ciliwung River. As the little boat came closer the excited Hollanders strained to make out who it was carrying. In the bright light he was little more than a silhouette, and it was only as the rowers raised their oars and skulled for the dockside that they saw his clothes, his medals, and his finery. It was a Dutch officer in full uniform.

In the words of the man himself, Colonel Huibert Gerard Nahuijs, the one-time Dutch resident at Surakarta and sometime British prisoner-of-war, it was 'as if an electric shock had run through the assembled crowd and turned them all instantly mad.' The dock erupted into patriotic fervour with fevered cheers of 'Long live the King of Holland'. Nahuijs was half-carried from his little craft in a maelstrom of happy noise.

He had come ahead of the returning fleet to find out just how much of a mess the house-sitters had left. At first glance it did indeed seem that the rumours of British mismanagement were true, but the sheer delight that his arrival had prompted amongst the old burghers of Batavia boded well. 'The feelings my arrival created in Java were various', wrote Nahuijs; 'as amongst my worthy countrymen they were those of unbounded delight, so amongst the civil and military servants of the English Government it created universal consternation and dejection.'

Nahuijs had been on shore just three days when another ship arrived, this one flying the Union Jack. John Fendall, a time-served fifty-three-year-old civil servant and a *very* safe pair of hands had arrived to take up his post as the second – and last – British Lieutenant-Governor of Java. Up the road in Buitenzorg a snivelling Travers brought Raffles the news. The outgoing chief had been in bed for weeks. On the announcement of his dismissal his health had gone to pieces altogether. He had managed to scribble out a few letters of protest, had had some fights with Colonel Burslem in the Council Chamber, and had then collapsed. Some people said he was dying. Still, he had to keep up appearances, and they scraped him into a carriage and carried him down to Batavia to meet his replacement – a man of 'a mild, placid temper' thought Travers. Fendall treated the sick man kindly, and ordered that during his final days in Java he should continue to receive the courtesies he had been afforded as Lieutenant-Governor: as the carriage carried Raffles back to his sickbed, no one dared to overtake it.

Over the coming fortnight he hauled himself upright and arranged for the sale of his books and belongings, pressed a jumble of policy recommendations on the newcomer, and penned a final howl of protest to the Directors in Leadenhall Street. After blithely predicting year after year from 1811 onwards that Java was on the brink of turning a profit he now wanted to point out that he had taken over the island 'at a moment of peculiar financial difficulty'. Nothing, he stressed, had been his fault, and next year – if only there had *been* a next year – British Java would finally have made money.

And then, at dawn on 25 March 1816, a thin and feeble Thomas Stamford Raffles was ferried offshore from Batavia, four years, thirty-one weeks and six days after John Leyden had leapt whooping from the landing craft eight miles up the coast at Cilincing. Travers – who would be tagging along, of course – had organised a comfortable cabin for the invalid on a ship called the *Ganges*, namesake of the boat that had first carried a young clerk and his new wife out to India a decade earlier.

Several years earlier the late Lord Minto had promised the post of resident at Bengkulu, Britain's feverish white elephant on the skeleton coast of west Sumatra, to Raffles if Java slipped from his grasp. The offer was still tentatively open – Lord Moira had written that if Raffles was eventually acquitted of 'those charges in which his moral character is implicated, still there is no reason why he should not be employed in a situation of minor responsibility and of more strictly defined duties, of which description the Residency of Bencoolen may be considered'. However, there seems to have been a distinct official reluctance to let him take the post while there were still *some* questions about Gillespie's charges and the land rent chaos that needed addressing. And in any case Raffles was so sick that a return to English mists and temperate airs in the interim was likely to save his life.

The luggage loaded onto the *Ganges* amounted to some twenty tons of looted Javanese manuscripts, Hindu statuary, *gamelan* sets and other treasures and trinkets. The supercargo included Raffles' doctor Thomas Sevestre, a shadowy Englishman called Graham who had managed to accrue a private fortune of £60,000 in Batavia during the cash-strapped British Interregnum, and who clearly realised that the good times were now over, a pair of Malay clerks, a young Javanese man from a good family, and a child slave from Papua.

Back on shore John Fendall was beginning to take stock of a mountain of administrative arrears and a very empty treasury, while a worried Colonel Nahuijs was touring unprepared barracks. In the graveyard at Tanah Abang Olivia was lying beside John Leyden, and far away beyond the mountains in Yogyakarta they were making plans for the royal wedding of a boy a week short of his twelfth birthday. Outside the Kraton, John Crawfurd was making the best of his last months as resident and the surviving sepoys of the Light Infantry Volunteer Battalion were still waiting to go home. Six hundred miles to the east the villagers of ash-covered Sumbawa were starving; in the fields around Surabaya thin farmers were thinking of another visit to the moneylender, and three days' sailing due north in Banjarmasin vagrants and working girls dragged away from Java were still submitting to the unhinged whims of a crazed Englishman in a half-built palace.

Up over the mudflats and fishponds of the Pasisir, beyond the brown river mouths and the flat rice fields, up through the palm stands and mango groves, over the rising terraces and the coffee gardens and into the first banks of deep forest, with a temple freshly stripped of creepers in a clearing here and there; on up through the steeper slopes where there were meditation caves and the hidden camps of long-haired *jagos*, and places that no Englishman had ever visited, up and up until the forest thinned to scored brown slopes, and then across the great grey cups of the smoking craters of the island's spine and down the other side to the stormy southern shoreline, a breeze was rising. It travelled back across the green breadth of Java in the midday heat of 25 March 1816, picking up a scent of blossoms and decay and cloves and coffee, and in the evening, with clouds over the mountains, cattle egrets beating homewards through the warm air, and bloody stains streaking the sky across Sumatra, it breathed gently into the sagging sails of the *Ganges*, chasing slow waves up through the heavy canvas until they filled. The timbers of the hull flexed and creaked and shifted, and the ship moved slowly away to the west.

The Righteous Prince

On a clear July morning in 1826, a decade after the British had sailed away from Java, Thomas Stamford Raffles rose before dawn and hobbled quietly out of the bedroom of his modest manor house at High Wood near Hendon in Middlesex. Outside the first soft light was seeping over the gentle contours of the English countryside. The weather had been hot in recent weeks; the trees were in full leaf and the labourers would soon be cutting the long yellow grass for hay. But Raffles was a sick man now, crippled by crushing headaches and haunted by a sense of failure and injustice; he paid no attention to the early birdsong. He was forty-five, but he carried himself like an old man. He shuffled unsteadily for the stairs.

In the ten years since the *Ganges* had sailed slowly away from Batavia Raffles had never returned to Java. Indeed, though he had spent the rest of his career in Southeast Asia, he seems rarely even to have thought about the place where he had tried so hard and failed so badly. But, seven thousand miles to the southeast, the aftershocks of the British Interregnum were still rattling the *kratons* and *kampungs* of the Land of Promise.

* * *

The island that the Dutch authorities took back in 1816 was not the same place they had departed in 1811. In five years the British had done many strange things, and at first glance it had seemed like most of them were bad. The administration was a mess; pointless paperwork stood in piles in back offices, while the more essential reports had never been filed at all. The account books made for toe-curling reading, and most of the budgetary projections seemed to be based on fantasy. Barracks had been left to decay while all manner of seemingly inconsequential laws had been laid. Road traffic for example had never amounted to more than a trickle of carriages and carts, even in Batavia, and drivers had been free to steer their ponies and bullocks whichever way they pleased around the potholes. Now, however, though the roads were in urgent need of repair, everyone was obliged to keep strictly to the British-style left. It seemed a little silly in the circumstances.

The biggest mess of all was the new revenue system. As the Dutch accountants scratched their heads over the files they found in Batavia and Buitenzorg in late 1816 they discovered that Raffles' land rent system had detached itself from all reality. There were figures – astronomical figures – set for the supposed income in cash to be gathered from farmers in many districts, but the actual tally of rents collected amounted to a fraction of the projections. In some cases nothing had been collected at all. There had already been reports of a mess of money-lending and hunger in some of the eastern districts of the island, and it was essential that something was done quickly. The new governor-general, Van der Capellen, sent a man named De Bruijn to tour the island and to try to make sense of what had been going on.

De Bruijn did indeed find chaos. The British, he decided, had simply conjured the rent figures out of thin air, and had then failed to collect even a quarter of them. But as he travelled he came to an unexpected conclusion: Raffles may have failed miserably, but as far as De Bruijn was concerned he had probably had the right idea. Under the old VOC regime Java's fabulous fertility had somehow always failed to deliver a decent deposit into the Dutch accounts. But Raffles had come up with a new concept: if a fixed amount – be it in money or in kind – was demanded of the Javanese peasants, regardless of how much they actually managed to harvest, then the colonial income was assured, and the colonial subjects would have no choice but to work hard for their masters. For the system to work properly the rents would need to be radically reassessed and set at levels that people might have a chance of actually paying. But, wrote De Bruijn, it was 'beyond all doubt that the land rent, modified and improved on a well-considered and regulated plan, is the only true and sufficient way to pour out the rich produce of these remote regions into the lap of the Motherland ...'

Elsewhere the Dutch found that opium use had increased exponentially, and though they reinstated the old government monopoly they kept prices at a populist level. Before long opium sales were generating 12 per cent of the colonial income in Java.

And then there were the native courts. The British seemed to have done a very great deal to advance the colonial cause. Little fiefdoms that had had at least a modicum of independence five years earlier, whose rulers had at least to be soft-soaped, had been turned into outright vassals. The sultans of Cirebon and Banten were now nothing but pretty caged birds, hanging from the eaves of the colonial veranda and singing whatever song the governor-general asked of them. Their lands been hived off and now belonged to Holland. Even the great powerhouses of Central Java were not what they once were. The Susuhunan of Surakarta had been suitably chastised; his realm had been trimmed and pared back, and Europeans had been given a yet greater say in what he did and where he went. His irritant off-shoot, Mangkunegara, was a still tamer lackey. In Yogyakarta meanwhile, where the court had always burned so brightly, and where the Dutch had always failed to gain the upper hand, there was now a pliable adolescent on the throne and a good few lingering bruises from the wanton destruction of 1812.

It seemed at a glance as though the British had handed over after their brief and surreal interregnum the very thing that 200 years of VOC rule had never achieved: a Java in which the European power really was 'for the first time paramount'. This was not quite the whole story, however. The Chinese toll keepers and bazaar managers who the British had left in place had choked off small-scale commerce with their crippling levies, even as the rents rocketed. Opium was causing its own problems; there were *jago* bands moving in the wilder woods and robbers on the roads. And in Yogyakarta meanwhile, the Kraton was still traumatised and unstable. There had been no response to all the humiliation that the court had suffered, but pride and protocol seemed to demand one, and indeed royal Java would blaze briefly and brilliantly one last time before the light went out completely. The name of the final flourishing flare was Diponegoro, the feisty son of the Raffles-appointed third sultan who had fled through the Kraton on 20 June 1812 with his father and his uncle Arya Panular as the British shells rained down and the sepoys surged over the walls. In 1825 he went into rebellion.

* * *

Diponegoro had never been cut from the same sumptuous batik cloth as the other princes. As the son of a concubine rather than a queen he was never a likely candidate for the Yogyakarta throne, and he had spent his early childhood outside the Kraton, in the house of his grandmother out in the glowing green countryside at Tegelreja on the road to the Southern Ocean. The old queen had steeped the little batik-clad boy tales of the old court, in the glory days of the first sultan, Mangkubumi. Back then, she had said as the child sat wide-eyed at her feet, there had been so much light, so much lustre, that no one behaved crudely or coarsely, and the courtiers had run rings around the uncouth red-faced clowns of the VOC.

When he returned to the court as a young man Diponegoro saw much that was not fitting. At the age of twenty-six he had watched the destruction of the Kraton in horror; he had seen cannonballs falling through *pendopo* roofs and wild-eyed Indians harassing the ladies and hacking up the marble floors. He had watched a king manhandled by overgrown foreigners and had seen his cousins and uncles kissing the knees of a nervy young man who could do nothing but babble in bad Malay when he came calling on the court. He had watched a swaggering John Crawfurd – a non-Muslim and a non-Javanese; an infidel on both sides of the coin – orchestrating the wedding of the boy king in the Royal Mosque in 1816, and much else besides that was uncouth and undignified. It was more than he could take.

Diponegoro claimed that he was the *Ratu Adil*, the Righteous Prince, and that the Queen of the Southern Ocean was on his side. He hated to hear anyone speaking Malay – 'the language of chickens' he called it – and during his rebellion captured Dutchmen were forced to dress in batik sarongs and made to learn polite Javanese at the tip of a sword. Fifteen of the Yogyakarta Kraton's twenty-nine princes and forty-one of the eighty-eight senior courtiers joined his uprising; many of those who stayed loyal to the Dutch and the reigning sultan ended up dead – Arya Panular amongst them.

For five years in the 1820s Diponegoro rampaged around Java. He offered the perfect mix for a rebel prince – anti-Chinese, anti-Dutch, proudly Javanese, Islamic, mystic, and righteous – and for a while it really did look as though the buffalo might defeat the tiger once more; the Dutch lost control of the Javanese countryside, and their outlying fortresses fell to the rebels.

In the end, however, the Europeans offered guerrilla tactics to guerrillas. Diponegoro's rebel army collapsed and he was captured and shipped off into exile in Makassar where he saw out his days locked in a cramped white room. The Dutch had lost 8000 European soldiers and a similar number of native troops. Some 200,000 Javanese had died, in the fighting and in the famines that followed.

* * *

The Diponegoro War was both a reflexive reaction to the indignities of the British Interregnum and its aftermath, and a last gasp of the old independent Java that had gone before. Everything that the Land of Promise had to offer – Buddhist, Hindu, Muslim and mystical – had flowed into the person of the Righteous Prince, but in the end it had not been enough. Too much damage had already been done.

In the wake of their final shabby victory, and despite the fact that it had been the Kraton itself that had been the first object of Diponegoro's ire, the Dutch decided to cow the Yogyakarta court altogether. They annexed the last of the outlying royal lands, and then they decided to do the same thing to Surakarta too. The old Susuhunan – he who wriggled unscathed through the British Interregnum – had died in 1823. Unlike his father the new incumbent had managed to keep his hands remarkably clean, and had really done nothing worthy of Dutch complaint during Diponegoro's rebellion. When he received notice that his remaining territories too were to be taken from him he was understandably outraged. He gathered his closest advisors and did the most obvious thing – he set out for the beach at Parangtritis to confer with the Queen of the Southern Ocean. But the Dutch hauled him back before he reached the shore and shipped him off to exile in Ambon.

It was the last gasp. From now on the princes and aristocrats of old Java would have no choice but to become puppets, agents and tools of the Dutch regime. If they were willing to forget the old days of lustre and glory they could keep to their thrones or take a job as a regent; they could pose for sepia photographs on the arms of their paternal Dutch residents, and they could patronise the arts. But they could not be like the great kings of old. Meanwhile, there was a great deal of expenditure on troops and fortresses to recoup – it was time for Java to start making money.

Ultimately the method that the Dutch chose for managing the agricultural economy of the island they now ruled without rival was not Raffles' land rent system; they went back to a regime of monopoly and prescribed cash crops. But a key concept remained: the people of Java were to work as hard as they could and to make as much money as possible for their European masters. It had taken a decade-and-a-half to finish the job, but the zeitgeist of the British Interregnum had finally been made good. The scene was set for the colonial century in Indonesia.

Real liberalism and genuine compassion for the people of Asia were retrospective legends to be written in a later age; in the 19th century there were other achievements worth celebrating. Back in 1816, as he prepared to leave Java, Otho Travers had reflected admiringly on everything that Raffles and his cronies had done in the years since they came ashore at Cilincing and conquered Batavia. 'Should Java ever become free of the Dutch nation,' he wrote, 'it must be attributed to the want of conduct in the Colonial Government. The path is now open to them and if only they follow the road cut open for them by the British Government, they may ensure themselves the easy administration of one of the finest Islands in the world'.

* * *

Such sentiments had been little comfort to Raffles when *he* left Java. In 1816 the *Ganges* had carried him back to England a broken man, and his homecoming was hardly met with a hero's welcome. Though the captain of the ship had fired the requisite salute for a colonial governor as he disembarked in Falmouth on 11 July, the Cornish boatmen overcharged him for their ferrying services, and he, Travers, and the rest of their sick, sun-scorched party were left to lodge in a dockside inn while the customs officials scratched their heads over twenty tonnes of looted Javanese antiquities.

But back in the temperate airs of London and Cheltenham his constitution had managed some kind of partial recovery. Circumstance had allowed him to avoid actual impeachment over his behaviour in the Land of Promise, and in 1817 he had published his book, *The History of Java*, to great acclaim (the only person to give it a harsh notice was the only person actually qualified to review it – John Crawfurd. Writing in the *Edinburgh Review*, he sneered at the *History's* litany of chronological howlers and pointedly remarked on its 'propensity to magnify the importance of the early story of the Javanese'. Raffles would repay the compliment with an equally hostile notice for Crawfurd's own book when it appeared three years later). Though pen-pushers in the East India Company's headquarters would still curl their lip at the mention of his name, the book helped Raffles to earn the attention of the bright lights of society, and to earn a title too. He and his remaining acolytes had been hoping for rather more – a baronetcy perhaps – for a mere knighthood was all but guaranteed to even the most mediocre of returned Indian Residents. But in any case, from now on he would always be Sir Stamford Raffles.

He had also found himself a new wife – a respectable thirty-year-old spinster called Sophia Hull. Otho Travers, whose standards were always exacting when it came to his master's connections, declared the new Mrs Raffles 'amiable, affectionate, sensible, personable, tho' not very handsome, with a good figure and extremely well brought up'. She also presumably had fewer skeletons in her closet and fewer empty brandy bottles under her bed than her predecessor. And with a new title, a new book, and a new wife, Raffles had returned to Southeast Asia to take up that 'situation of minor responsibility' – the residency of Bengkulu.

Bengkulu, a little knuckle of land a quarter of the way up the wrong side of Sumatra, was the ultimate hardship posting, and not a place to which the East India Company sent its most valued employees. The British had moved in in 1685 hoping to make money from pepper and passing ships. Instead the place had turned out to be an unremitting disaster in a very literal sense. The mortality rate amongst Company servants was atrocious; Bengkulu had never made a profit, and by the turn of the 19th century it was worth a guaranteed £100,000 annual deficit on the East India Company's books.

The ramshackle settlement there was a lonely spot. The vast emptiness of the ocean opened before it, and the coast stretched away to the north in a fading line of pale sand backed by a dark bank of casuarinas. Inland rose a wall of blue mountains. Even when the sea breeze was running the heat was close and cloying, and hordes of zebra-striped dengue mosquitoes coalesced under the trees. At the centre of the settlement stood the skewed walls of Fort Marlborough, like slices of mildewed wedding cake, squatting atop a low grassy hillock. Set haphazardly around the ramparts were a few grubby white buildings, their windows gaping, their porticoes slumping, their roof tiles slipped. Within days of arriving Raffles was writing that 'This is without exception the most wretched place I ever beheld'.

And yet, despite all the evidence, Raffles had somehow managed to convince himself that he had been sent to Bengkulu, not as a nuisance put out to grass, 'but in fact [as] Political Agent for the Malay States', and that it was 'the wish of the authorities in England that I should as far as possible check the Dutch influence from extending beyond its due bounds'. Nothing that had happened in Java had served to leave him chastised.

Over the coming years he caused still more trouble with the neighbours across the Bukit Barisan in Palembang, where repercussions of his incautious letter-writing at the start of the decade were still being felt. Elsewhere he continued his scholarship, collected tales of cannibalism with which to titillate society ladies back in England, and organised various energetic reforms in Bengkulu itself. From time to time he still embarked on the kind of flight of orientalist fancy that John Leyden had originally inspired. Sumatra lacked the epic history of Java, but Raffles had still managed to conjure up a great fallen civilisation from the historical ether, and to invent a glorious fantasy role for himself as lord of the entire island:

I would assume supremacy without interfering with the just independence of other states. I would be the protector of the native states. I would, in fact, re-establish the ancient authority of Menangkabu [Minangkabau, the people of the central Sumatran mountains], and be the great Mogul of the Island.

Raffles had also become a father. Sophia had bravely shipped out with him from England, and had given birth to their first child – a girl called Charlotte – before they had even reached Sumatra. Three siblings followed in swift succession – two little boys called Leopold and Marsden, and a baby girl called Ella. And then, of course, there was his other child, a muddy little island in the Riau Archipelago.

For decades the idea of a British base at the southern mouth of the Straits of Melaka had been batted about in parlours and council chambers all over the East, and at the end of 1818 Raffles received the strictly limited sanction of Calcutta to pursue a project in those parts: a British outpost should be founded somewhere near the southern tip of the Malay Peninsula if – and *only* if – it would contravene no existing treaty that the Dutch might have with the local rulers. The former British resident of Melaka, William Farquhar, a man who knew the waters and the ways of the southern Straits better than any other foreigner, had already been scouting out such a spot. Raffles rapidly muscled in on his project, and in the first month of 1819, paying no heed whatsoever to any pre-existing Dutch paperwork, they founded their foothold. Its name was Singapore.

The founding of Singapore is today proclaimed as Raffles' greatest achievement (despite the fact that he only ever spent a total of nine months in the place, and ought, by rights, to share the glory with William Farquhar who was there for three years as the island's first British resident). His final years in Southeast Asia, then, should have been the Indian summer of a great visionary resting on well-earned laurels. They were not. Singapore itself had been little more than a last shot, and doubt still hung like monsoon clouds over its continued existence (the Dutch *did* have a pre-existing treaty with the local rulers, it turned out, and for several years a low level diplomatic crisis continued between Britain and Holland over what their Man in Southeast Asia had done). All of Raffles' greater hopes and dreams, meanwhile, had been frustrated. He had established no greater British realm in Indonesia, founded no Empire of the East, and made himself no great mogul. Java had been lost; Bangka had gone back to the Dutch, and even Alexander Hare's Borneo fiefdom had not endured: Banjarmasin had become a Dutch signatory, and the half-built palace in the jungle had rotted away to nothing. The climate was again slipping its feverish fingers into Raffles' constitution, and he was already beginning to suffer from 'the dreadful headaches I am doomed to suffer in this country'. There were days when he could not write, could not speak, could do nothing but lie in a darkened room.

The final years of his career were marked by tragedy. Bengkulu was no place to raise a family, and as a new decade opened the children started to die. Leopold, pale and sweating in a corner cot in a dark room, slipped away on 4 July 1821. Any mitigating illusion of domestic tranquillity amongst the jungles of Sumatra went with the little boy. 'My heart has been nigh broken, and my spirit is gone', wrote Raffles; 'I have lost almost all that I prided myself upon in this world'. Sophia was utterly broken by the loss. She locked herself in her room and shunned the surviving children. News of other deaths amongst friends and family trickled in over the coming weeks, and the headaches got worse.

'I sometimes think it very doubtful that I shall ever reach England again', Raffles noted at the time; 'at other times I rally a little, but on the whole I begin to be more indifferent to the result than I used to be.'

Six months after his brother, Marsden died too. And ten days later bouncing, bubbling, first-born Charlotte succumbed to dysentery. It was the kind of trauma that the local people of the *kampungs* of Java and Sumatra knew only too well. They blamed bad spirits and black magic and went to the *dukuns* – the witchdoctors – for cures and preservatives. Then they staunched grief as best they could with strict funeral regimes and interlocking family bonds across the web of cousins and aunties. But for Raffles and Sophia it was the end of everything. In a state of near panic they had the last surviving child, little Ella, shipped home to England, and a ruined Raffles finally sent in his resignation.

It was 18 months before he was actually able to leave his post. Though he was crippled by 'terrible, nervous, wretched sensations' he still managed to engineer an undignified conflict with the man he had left in charge of Singapore, William Farquhar. Much as he had once turned against incompliant secretaries in Java, Raffles now turned against the resident. Farquhar, he decided, had disobeyed his orders about the management of the new colony, and what was more, he had a certain 'Malay connexion' which might 'afford an opening for such an undue combination of peculiar interests as not only to impede the progress or order and regularity but may lay the foundation of future inconvenience which it may hereafter be difficult to overcome.'

Farquhar was an old-school Company man of the 18th-century type: Englishmen who, on realising that they might well never see home again, made commitments and compromises and settled themselves into the local scene in Asia. They were pragmatists and realists, and though they were often heat-rotted and corrupt, they went half-way native when it came to family, lifestyle and even religion. Farquhar's 'Malay connexion' came in the form of a native wife and close personal relationships with many of the island chieftains. In his previous posting the locals had called him the 'Raja Melaka', and many of the earliest settlers in British Singapore were the traders and families who had voluntarily followed him there. But there would be no room for men like Farquhar in the coming decades of the Raj, when 'connections' with the natives were mostly a matter of contracts with princes, and where 'sympathy' was an academic matter of economic theory. There was no room for him in Raffles' Singapore either. He had him kicked out.

Raffles could not by this stage run Singapore himself, however. The 'attacks in the head' were almost constant now, and more than once he convinced himself that he was about to die. Travers – who had joined him during the first years in Bengkulu – had gone home, having accrued far more than enough to live on through his long years in Raffles' train. One-time faithful Java secretary Charles Assey had died in India the year before, and so had many, many others from the ranks of the Raffles party. There was only one person left to turn to: the one man who Raffles had somehow never been able to shun, but had been equally unable to dominate, the man whose competence and knowledge he simply *had* to credit and who had been rattling around East Asia on diplomatic missions since the end of the British Interregnum in Java. As Raffles made his own preparations for a final return to England, Singapore was to be left in the capable, unromantic hands of the man who had said very unkind things about *The History of Java*. John Crawfurd was to be its next resident.

* * *

Raffles returned to England for good in the summer of 1824, numbed and empty and ill. Before they left Bengkulu Sophia had given birth to another child, a sickly little girl called Flora, but she died before 1823 was out. And then there had been the disaster of departure. Raffles had initially chartered a ship called the *Fame* to carry him home and loaded it with all his papers and much of his money, but an accident with a candle had seen it go up in flames just two days after it weighed anchor. Raffles, Sophia and all of the crewmen escaped in a longboat and paddled back to Bengkulu, but everything that had been on board was lost – the mountains of maps and manuscripts and material on Sumatra and Singapore that would surely have made for a sequel to *The History of Java*. The seas off Sumatra were still within the realm of the vengeful Queen of the Southern Ocean, it seemed.

Raffles eventually made it home in another ship with an achingly empty hold. He was forty-three, not particularly young by the standards of the day, and not young at all by the standards of returned East India Company servants. He had lost his entire academic trove and much of his money, and the Company had never really cleared him of the queasy questions about his behaviour in Java. But between the headaches he carved out some small kind of English existence. If many old Asia hands shunned him, there were still plenty of bright society things who enjoyed his company, and when he was well enough there was always an invitation to dinner. He forgot all about the women he had sacrificed to Alexander Hare in Banjarmasin, and discussed the evils of slavery with William

Wilberforce. And he teamed up with the Cornish scientist Humphry Davy to found London Zoo.

There were very few compatriots from the Java adventure still alive, but Otho Travers was in rude health, and he dropped in to see his old patron whenever he was passing, accompanying the invalid on gentle country walks, and reminiscing about the glory days. In his last years Raffles shuttled between Cheltenham and London, and finally to that modest manor house in the countryside near Hendon in Middlesex. It was called High Wood and it had its own acres. Raffles settled there and played at being a gentleman farmer in between pestering the East India Company for a pension and a final judgement on his career. He deserved at least £500 a year, he felt.

On 12 April 1826 the Company Directors did finally deliver a very modest exoneration. Their reflections on Raffles' two decades in Southeast Asia were suffused with the damning perfume of faint praise, but with the exception of the 'questionable proceeding' of the Cianjur land sales, they conceded that he had not actually committed any identifiable offences, and declared that though the effects of his actions were often of dubious value, his motivations were always pure, and 'his exertions for the interests of literature and science are highly honourable to him'. He would not be getting his £500 pension, however. Attached to the copy of the recognition of service was a bill: the East India Company had decided that Raffles owed them £22,000 (well over £1 million in modern terms).

It was an accumulation of glitches and loopholes. Raffles had filed invoices for his salary as resident at Bengkulu from the moment he left Java in 1816. It was two years before he actually took up the post, but the accounts department had paid out anyway. At the end of his time in Java, meanwhile, Raffles and other senior administrators had taken part of their salaries in the useless paper money in an attempt to stabilise it – with the promise that any deficit in market value would be made up in real cash when they left their posts. Again the Company accountants had paid out on Raffles' initial claim on the difference. Now, however, the Directors had decided that they wanted both the two years' salary and the paper currency reimbursement back, along with sundry other unsanctioned commissions which their man had taken at Bengkulu and Singapore.

The whole thing was a hard and seemingly deliberate blow. It made the mild approval of his career seem like a joke. Such financial irregularities were by no means unusual. The margins of error for confusing salaries paid alternately in rupees, dollars and pounds sterling over the course of tropical decades could easily amount to small fortunes, but a well-behaved yes-man hobbling home from India to eke out his dying days in Cheltenham could usually expect to enjoy the benefit of the doubt – and a decent pension too. But Raffles had racked up a litany of offenses small and large over his convoluted and contrary career. The bill was the Company's way of letting him know that whatever decent gentlemanly standards had obliged them to record about his abilities, nothing he had ever done had really had their approval.

* * *

What had marked Raffles out from the very start was his utter self-belief, his utter, unwavering conviction that he – and only he – knew best. The Dutch were demonic; the Javanese courts had to be crushed; an Indian-style land system had to be implemented in decidedly un-Indian Java. Slavery was to be stopped – unless doing so was inconvenient; Bangka ought to be British; and anyone who raised a voice of protest or even an alternative idea should be shipped out post-haste. And bestriding all of this, the glittering mantles of Majapahit and Minangkabau resting atop his aching head, should be Sir Stamford Raffles. From the moment he turned up in Calcutta in 1810 to claim the Java expedition for his own, to the dreary dog days in Bengkulu a decade later, he never faltered, never wavered.

This inflexible conviction, be it wrong-headed or visionary, had cost hundreds of lives and had done strange things to Javanese society. At times – such as when he arrived in Bengkulu somehow convinced that the British authorities wanted him to embark on an anti-Dutch crusade – this absolute absence of doubt made Raffles seem quite mad; at others – such as during the Palembang letter-writing and the Banjarmasin Enormity – it made him utterly amoral. But in the end, with the deaths of his children and the indignity of the financial censure from his old employers, it merely made him a tragic figure, the wise clown of the *wayang kulit* whose wisdom was somehow flawed, who could speak up against the gods, but who found that the gods had no interest in listening.

The East India Company's bill was precisely the kind of attack that had always raised Raffles to heights of energetic and affronted self-righteousness. It was just like the dark days back in Java when the first notice of Gillespie's charges arrived. He did his best to shrug off the headaches – they were truly crippling and frighteningly frequent by now – and began to pen raging replies. He could not, in any case, pay the bill.

In the end, however, he did not get beyond the first engagement of this last great battle. On that fine summer morning – July 5 1826 – before the servants were awake, he slipped out of bed and edged out onto the landing without waking his wife. Perhaps it was a dream of green mountains and monsoon rains, or of a tiger locked in mortal combat with a buffalo that had started him from an uneasy sleep. But most probably it was simply that the weight of the ever-present headache had passed beyond the point of bearing – for Thomas Stamford Raffles, it seems most likely at a distance of 200 years, had a brain tumour.

He edged painfully down the short spiral of stairs towards the ground floor, and then sat down heavily on the bottom step. He was still sitting there when Sophia found him several hours later. He was already dead.

Epilogue

The Queen of the Southern Ocean

On a damp December day I rode out of Yogyakarta on my motorbike, heading for the Southern Ocean. To the north the thunderheads were already filling over the mountain spine of Java, and the sky hung low above the city in pearly slabs. I cut through the flowing traffic between concrete shop-fronts, shabby food stalls and sagging jackfruit trees, skirted the old walls of the Kraton, dodged pedicabs and pedestrians and bore away to the south through the rice fields. I was making a pilgrimage.

For three months I had sat at a desk in a room in a boarding house in the north of the city with the light coming in green through the window on my left and the ceiling fan chopping the air above my head in slow circles. There were books piled against the wall at the back of the desk – old books with stiff covers and foxed pages picked up from second-hand dealers in England, and limp academic tomes ordered from specialist shops in Singapore. Their pages were marked with scraps of paper and sticky labels and their margins were full of notes. On either side of my laptop computer there were piled print-outs of scholarly articles from obscure journals and dog-eared PDF page images of 19th-century volumes, and beneath an empty coffee cup and a clutch of gnawed and chewed pencils was a little pile of blue notebooks full of scribbled references to manuscripts far away in the archives of the British Library.

The wet season had started early this year, and it had rained every day while I wrote, the water coming in cascading cataracts, cutting the midday light to a gloomy gloaming and shorting the electrics to leave me tapping frantically in darkness against a draining battery. My mornings were a litany of coffee and indexes, but in the dripping afternoons I would venture out with aching eyes to wander in the old quarters. Yogyakarta in the 21st century had sprawled far beyond the Kraton walls and the little European Quarter. A shambles of red-tiled roofs and tangled power lines spread north and south across what had once been farmland. Trucks and buses roared back and forth along the Surakarta road, and from first light jets bowled in from the west, bearing for the airport on the edge of town.

But buried within all that, the lines of the court city that Arya Panular, John Crawfurd and Thomas Stamford Raffles had known were still there. The grubby walls of the old Dutch fort still stood behind the trees at the bottom end of Jalan Malioboro, and the barrack rooms where redcoat soldiers had rested before their final thrust for the Inner Kraton in June 1812 now housed crude dioramas depicting set-pieces from the legend of the Indonesian independence struggle. Girls in grey jeans posed for photographs on the corner bastions where the sepoys had once gathered to plot mutiny and mango parties. On the other side of the road, across a slab of well-watered lawn, the white hulk of the residency still stood. The place where the princes had kissed Raffles' knees was the official state guesthouse now, and every other day a gaggle of students protesting with paint-splattered banners against some obscure iniquity or other gathered on the pavement outside.

Further south, beyond the white gateway that marked the edge of the royal city, the northern Alun-Alun was still an open space before the frontispiece of the Kraton. But it was no longer a stretch of pristine grass plied by magnificent Javanese troopers; it was a balding field of litter and puddles where boys without shoes played football in the rain and student couples came to drink coffee and slap at mosquitoes after dark. The sacred twin banyans still stood, but they had been trimmed back to low circles of dense green foliage and thin men sold plastic toys beside the path that ran between them. To the right, hemmed in by the houses, the pyramid roof of the Royal Mosque still rose – the place where Gillespie was shot in the arm – and at the lower end of the Alun-Alun the *Siti Inggil*, the High Place, still marked the entrance to the Inner Kraton. Behind it the white-walled courtyards were still scattered with black sand from the southern beaches, and were still haunted by aging, barefoot courtiers with polished *krises* jutting from the top of their batik sarongs. The palace had an air of dignified shabbiness, like the old barns of a farm that no longer keeps livestock.

The whole city was like that – sad and a little careworn. It was still a royal capital, the last survivor of an earlier age, a constitutional anomaly in the Republic of Indonesia, ruled by a sultan. And it was still the lodestar of Java, the place where they spoke the best Javanese, where the graffiti was art and the art was everywhere. The heart of Yogyakarta, within the line of the old walls, was a place of pot plants and birdcages, where pedicabs were left pulled up on the pavements beneath the mango trees and where bulky ladies rambled along cracked pavements from the market. Yogyakarta was a place resting, slumping, subsiding on its laurels.

Sometimes I wandered in the Taman Sari, the Water Palace where the fleeing princes had tried to seek refuge from the falling shells and where the Indian conspirators had sworn their oaths. The great lake that once filled its walls had been drained and turned into a batik-workers' *kampung* where feisty fighting cocks preened under upturned wicker baskets and children rode battered bicycles in shaky circles. The salmon-pink walls had cracked and faded, and the cloistered pools where princesses had frolicked had turned lime-green with algae. Other days I wandered along what was left of the city walls. The gateways that the sepoys had stormed were still there, and the bastions still stood, squat and whitewashed at busy road junctions. But the city had swollen around them; they defended nothing but an invisible line now, and courting couples looking for quiet corners huddled in the parapets.

Sometimes, when the rain held off and the writing was

finished early I rode out of the city to stroll between the temples at Prambanan. The mountains of mossy masonry that Colin Mackenzie had clambered over had been restored and stripped of their creepers now. There were flowerbeds between them, a car park for tour buses and a nightly dance performance under floodlights in the gardens. To find places that still offered a glimpse of the shadow-haunted chaos of tumbled blocks that Mackenzie had marvelled over I had to follow narrow hill roads to smaller temples, marked only by a faded signboard from the Archaeological Department, and unmentioned in tourist guidebooks.

In the evenings, when the rain had stopped, I often rode down through the darkened, dripping city to the southern Alun-Alun, the smaller royal square within the walls where they used to hold the tiger fights. It had fared a little better than its northern counterpart over the years. It was still ringed by a white wall with the quiet, tree-studded quarters stretching around it, and the twin banyans here were still great globes of dark foliage. Even when there was no wind the branches shifted softly, as though there were unseen things moving amongst them. Blindfolded teenagers, giggling and shuffling, tried to pass between them in a straight line as a test of fortune. At night the surrounding pavements were lined with little stalls where you could sit cross-legged on a worn bamboo mat, slurping from a bowl of sweet, gingery *ronde*, and listening to the bursts of Indonesian and low Javanese from the other customers. Bats flickered in the street-lit space between the trees; lightning sparked and guttered far away to the south, and people talked of the recent volcanic eruption – the worst for decades – that had destroyed thousands of homes and killed dozens of people on the slopes of Gunung Merapi, just fifteen miles north of the room where I wrote. People had seen leopards sneaking down from the burnt-out forests below the peak in search of food, and the old man appointed by the Sultan as the mystic guardian of the mountain had died at prayer when a wave of scorching smoke drove through his home. Ash had fallen on the city and snuck in through the mosquito netting on the windows to coat the keys of my computer, but it had all seemed strangely unreal as I buried myself in the explosions of an earlier century.

But now the work was done, and there was a journey that I had realised it would be unwise to avoid making, a debt of gratitude that ought to be paid. I cut along the edge of the old walls between mechanics' workshops and batik showrooms, passed the southeast bastion where the sepoys had tossed the bodies of dead defenders into the ditch, shifted gear and rode away into the rice fields. Behind me, over the mountains to the north, it was already raining.

* * *

There is no popular recollection of the British Interregnum in 21st century Java. People are vaguely aware that a monument to an Englishwoman called Olivia stands in the botanical gardens of Bogor, the town that was once called Buitenzorg, but no one wonders why the howling Indonesian traffic sticks – in theory, at least – to the left side of the road rather than to the continental European right. Day-tripping high school girls in pink headscarves, taking photos of each other with their mobile phones on the steps of Borobudur, might remember reading somewhere that the man who gave his name to the most famous hotel in Singapore also uncovered this monumental tourism object, still squatting in the green hills of Kedu. But they know nothing else of what Raffles did in Java.

Even in Yogyakarta, where you might at least expect a bitter memory of looting and humiliation to linger, the only popular link to the British days is a story about a street name that happens not even to be true. Ask any of the stallholders selling cheap tee-shirts, machine-made batiks, and crude *wayang kulit* puppets along the pavements of Jalan Malioboro, the once-grand thoroughfare of the city, and they'll likely tell you it was named by the British – quite possibly after a brand of American cigarettes – at some vague and indeterminate time in the distant past. But there is no record anywhere in the contemporary British sources of a rebranding of the royal Yogyakarta approach road, and in the second decade of the 19th century the Duke of Marlborough would have made a particularly obscure inspiration for a colonial street name. Malioboro, it seems most likely, is really a corruption of *malybhara* – a Sanskrit term meaning 'adorned with garlands' in reference to the flower-bearing flunkies who greeted the Sultan on his grand progresses along the street.

It is perhaps understandable if there is little room for the British period in the received modern history of the Republic of Indonesia. It is a carefully crafted construct, after all, in which the Dutch are given a role every bit as dastardly as that which Raffles wrote for them in his energetic propagandising. Squeezing in sundry other foreigners – from Portuguese pioneers to American botanists – would only blur the shadows against the screen. The Interregnum lasted only five years anyway, and the fact that the overture for the colonial century in Indonesia was played by Englishmen and Indians, with Thomas Stamford Raffles wielding the conductor's baton, is one of those historical anomalies too strange to trouble with. But it is where the period *has* been remembered that there is cause for consternation. At times while I was reading and writing I had been utterly flabbergasted. It was not Raffles himself who troubled me, but those who crafted his legend in the later decades.

The man that Lady Sophia found slumped at the bottom of the stairs that summer morning in 1826 was no hero. He was given a modest funeral in the parish church at Hendon, and a few polite obituaries in the press, but though the bereft Otho Travers was proclaiming his deceased master's 'first rate genius and Talents' from the very start, there were precious few who agreed with him. There were no stately statues carved and no epic epitaphs chiselled; there was no outpouring of national grief at the loss of a visionary, and there were plenty of old Asia hands who still sneered at the very mention of Raffles' name.

Singapore *might* – with hard work from competent administrators and industrious settlers – have a bright future as a bustling free port, but it was not yet in full bloom, and in any case, Raffles had not even nurtured the buds on his own (Farquhar was on the scene in England by the time Raffles died, and he would hang around for years afterwards, furiously protesting that he deserved credit for founding the city). Raffles might have managed a few positive changes on the steamy Sumatran shore, but within twelve months of him leaving his post at Bengkulu the place had been handed over to the Dutch in a permanent trade-off for Melaka (which they had previously regained at the same time as Java). The trouble Raffles had caused in Palembang, meanwhile, was more noteworthy than indulgent reforms in a dying backwater. And then, of course, there was the grand set-piece of Raffles' career – the administration of Java – and *that*, most sober observers in the 1820s were convinced, had been a monumental failure. He might have been a talented writer and an enthusiastic orientalist, but those were very minor deposits in the account book of reputation. But by the end of the century Raffles *had* become a hero; there *were* statues and epitaphs, and incredibly, while those of his contemporaries have toppled sideways into the long grass, his own images in copper and marble remain standing today.

On my way back out to Java after my summer in the archives I had come face to face with Raffles as he was reincarnated after death during a stopover in Singapore. His statue stands on a white plinth near the river in front of the creamy columns of the Victoria Theatre. Sweating in the soft heat I sat down on the edge of a flowerbed and looked up at him. It was a quiet corner of a busy city, and Raffles stood there, double life-size and magnificent. There was no slouch now; no squint or limp-fringed nervousness. He posed with best foot forward and shoulders squared. His arms were sternly folded, but the fingers of his left hand splayed open in the fan of a thinker. This is Raffles the hero, Raffles the pioneer, and around him stood all that Singapore has become. Air-conditioned buses swung past and Indians in hard hats and eyeshades were laying fibre-optic cables nearby. Chinese girls on lunch-break from the offices across the river came by, looking for a place to eat their sandwiches amongst the well-tended flowerbeds, and a few bumbling academics wandered across from the pale pastel walls of the Asian Civilisations Museum. The great grassy square of the Padang and the grand British-built City Hall stood to the right, and to the left the towering skyscrapers of the business district rocketed into a cloying purplish sky. There was building work everywhere. The statue, with an inscription proclaiming Raffles' 'Foresight and Genius', seemed to suggest he had done this all himself. It was erected in 1919.

After her husband's death Lady Sophia Raffles could easily have faded away into bitter obscurity. A few of the old aristocratic connections might have remembered her and pitied her from time to time, and Otho Travers would always have remained a loyal friend, but the party invitations would have dried up, and before long even her name would have raised scarcely a flicker of recognition. But Sophia had sacrificed her children and whatever dreams she might have harboured of great wealth to her husband's career. There had been iniquity at the end with that monstrous bill from the East India Company Directors, and although as a bereaved wife she had managed to convince them to show a little compassion, to cut the claim and to accept the meagre remnants of her inheritance as a sufficient return, she was still indignant at the infamy of it all. Raffles might not have died a hero, but his widow would do everything she could to turn him into one. She started work on a biography.

Sophia's *Memoir of the Life and Services of Sir Thomas Stamford Raffles* was published in 1830. She had gathered all of her late husband's letters, and all of the replies he had received – and then she had edited them ruthlessly, expurgating the unfavourable and excising the embarrassing. Only what made Raffles look good – like a hero in fact – was selected for publication. Sophia annihilated her unfortunate predecessor Olivia, whittling her down to a single, inaccurate footnote, and inserted herself into the story as a dignified character called 'the Editor', who appeared in the linking passages between the excerpts. For the long years – the Java administration foremost amongst them – before she had arrived on the scene herself she called on dear Travers to help fill in the blanks, which, as one of the few surviving veterans of the Interregnum, he did with all the retrospective adoration he could muster. A less impartial, more partisan pair of biographers could hardly be imagined and the finished work was a monument of celebratory beatification.

It ought to have been greeted with cruel cynicism, but somehow Sophia got lucky: the *Life* chimed with the times. There were still almost three decades to run before the Indian Mutiny would bring an end to the long rule of the East India Company and turn a trading concern into a true crown empire, but things were already swinging that way. Men who crushed Asiatic princes, vanquished European foes and put the natives to work had the floor, and though Raffles might have been ahead of his time in the 1800s, by the middle of the century his ghost found itself amongst kindred spirits. And to help matters along, John Crawfurd's canny administration had done its job: he had had the dot of land at the bottom of the Malay Peninsula ceded in entirety to the British Crown, and Singapore *was* prospering. Peering up ponderously from the pages of Sophia's *Life* as the Victorian era beckoned in the background, the upright agents of the burgeoning British Empire began to feel that perhaps Raffles really *had* had the right ideas after all.

All the biographers who came after the Editor (the first, Charles Demetrius Boulger, published his tome in 1897 in the heady glory days of the Raj) simply followed suit. At times, flicking through their pages for a cross-reference, I had been left shaking my head in slack-jawed disbelief. They were chronically uncritical. Every one of them – from the 1890s to the 1990s – had taken Sophia's word at face value, regarded her book as a definitive archive, and believed everything that Raffles himself had said too. They seemed to have *started* with the assumption that he was a liberal, a visionary and a hero, and then kicked any suggestions to the contrary – Palembang, Yogyakarta, Banjarmasin and many others – away into the rice fields. Raffles' own version of the British Interregnum was what they ran with, and *The History of Java* seemed to have constituted their only background reading. Sultans and Susuhunans had been scheming Asiatic despots, bent on annihilating the European inhabitants of the island; war had been inevitable. Slavery *had* been checked; the Dutch had been ignorant and evil without exception, and the land reforms had been a success – or if not a success then hampered only by a lack of time and funds. Robison had been wrong, and Gillespie a cad; Blagrave, Farquhar, Crawfurd and everyone else who ever dared to protest the views of the visionary had been wrong-headed fools. No guns and bullets had been sent to Sultan Badruddin in Palembang with an instruction to 'throw out and finish utterly' the Dutch civilians living there, and no kidnapped women had been shipped across the Java Sea to Banjarmasin. No hint of dubious ideology could be detected in the scholarship, nothing had been looted, and Raffles had personally translated *Kawi* epics from the original and delighted the speakers of courtly Javanese with his uniquely eloquent market Malay.

But though I enjoyed the sense of iconoclastic outrage, I had slowly come to recognise the real problem that had hobbled the earlier tellers of the tale of the strange five years when the British ruled the Land of Promise. If you first came to Java in the company of Raffles, if you clambered aboard the *Modeste* alongside him in Melaka knowing nothing of your destination but that it was green, exotic and strange, and if you took your very first step on fertile Javanese soil at Cilincing on 4 August 1811, then you would always be likely to see things his way. The biographers – all of them – had indeed first come to Java only in the company of Raffles.

But if you happened to be in the island already, if you had already wandered its back roads and climbed its volcanoes, if you had dipped your hands into the cold water flowing from sacred springs deep in the forest and had seen the temples standing amongst the rice fields, if you had already sat cross-legged in the haze of clove smoke at *wayang kulit* performances and brushed your fingers over the stones of the tombs of the *Wali Songo*, if you had visited *kampungs* and *kratons* and felt the strange shiver that comes in places where they say there are ghosts, if you had walked down countless streets named for

Diponegoro and had heard the stories of Sultan Agung and Senopati, if you already knew what Daendels had done, what a Susuhunan was, and who had built Borobudur – if, in fact, you watched the British warships approaching from Melaka in 1811 from a vantage point somewhere on the slopes of the volcanoes above the Pasisir, then the whole episode looked radically different. It was nothing more than a matter of perspective.

* * *

By the time I reached Imogiri the sky was the colour of wet buffalo hide and the hills hung above a creeping floodtide of lavender haze. It was very still, and the villages in the palm trees at the foot of this royal hill were full of cockcrows and cooking smoke. This was the burial place of kings, the sanctuary to which Uncle Abubakar had fled from the rout of the Kraton, and where they had interred the third Sultan at the end of 1814. And it is still the sacred cemetery for the Sultans and Susuhunans of the 21st century.

This afternoon the inner tombs of Sultan Agung and all his descendants were closed and there were few pilgrims. I picked my way slowly up the steep cascade of steps towards the top of the hill in short-of-breath silence. It was one of those days in Java when the heat hides itself well, softens its edges and blunts its burning fire to the point where you can walk a mile in a comforting illusion of cool before you realise that your shirt is sodden and that sweat is dripping from the tip of your nose. The hillside was thick with rampant greenery; sturdy banana plants sprouted from the leaf mould and banyans trailed their tendrils from the canopy. The sound of the afternoon prayer call floated in from a village mosque somewhere in the forest. Everywhere amongst the vegetation there were the tombs of courtiers and aristocrats. Little pathways branched off the main flight of white stairs to platforms marked by a pair of gravestones, angled towards Mecca but cleaving close to the resting places of kings descended from the gods.

After the Diponegoro War the royal houses of what was once Mataram had rolled on through the 19th century and beyond. With their outlying lands annexed by foreigners they had drawn back ever deeper into the recesses of formality and *kraton* life. The old fire that had burnt in the breasts of Sultan Agung, Mangkubumi and Diponegoro cooled to an icy refinement, and high Javanese art flourished. Princes penned ever more flowery *babads*, and mysticism spiralled to new heights between garden parties with Dutchmen and photo opportunities with visiting white women. The progressions continued, old sultans giving way to new sultans and old susuhunans to new susuhunans without intrigue or poison. The secondary houses – of Mangkunegara in Surakarta and Pakualam in Yogyakarta – continued their own hereditary relay too.

All these royals remained calm and quiet during the early decades of the 20th century when the buffalo began to look as though it might defeat the tiger once more, but when it came to the grand finale the uneasy balance finally tipped in favour of Yogyakarta. The reigning Susuhunan kept aloof from the anti-Dutch Indonesian nationalists, and lost his status in the new republic they founded as a consequence. The Ninth Sultan, however, gave himself over with gusto to the anti-colonial cause, and the little county-sized slice of Central Java that had remained within the sway of the Kraton until the end was made into an indulgence of royal prerogative. By a special dispensation Yogyakarta, the battered stump of old Mataram, remains the last real monarchy in the Republic of Indonesia. The sultan of the day is still the governor by default, and his deputy is the reigning Pakualam, the head of the secondary royal house created by the British.

The sultan who engineered royal Yogyakarta's endurance in independent Indonesia was interred in magnificent style at Imogiri in 1989. Today his son, Hamengkubuwono X, is king and governor. On the day of his coronation, they say, a soft, melati-scented breeze from the south moved through the Kraton.

At the top of the steps a few slim, upright men in full formal royal attire, with gold-brown sarongs and head cloths, bright buttons and polished *krises,* were minding the bolted double gateways that led to the inner sanctum of the compound. Both the *kratons* – the enduring Yogyakarta and the neutered Surakarta – keep a permanent detachment of courtiers on duty here. The sky was hanging lower and darker by the minute now, but I turned left for a circuit of the cemetery walls. Beyond the main locked gateway the place was deserted, and a green, half-rotten smell leached out of the undergrowth. A stony path looped behind the compound. The *joglo* roofs that sheltered the flower-strewn graves rose into the damp air, and a view opened out across tiers of thickset, forested hills, fading from green to blue to grey in the haze. A distant sound of traffic and children's voices rose from somewhere down in the green countryside. Swamped in the trees at the foot of the hill I could see the red roofs, the small stainless steel dome, and the turquoise walls of a *pesantren,* an orthodox Islamic seminary, a place of green paint and white skullcaps. But closer at hand, on a level rock beside the path, was a heap of rotting petals and a forest of burnt-out incense sticks where someone had spent the night in meditation, drawing on the sacred energy from the tombs behind the walls.

Raffles had sneeringly dismissed all this as 'the accumulated delusions of two religious systems', but it was what gave Java its depth and its meaning, and it still has a hold on the imagination of the island in the 21st century, long after his reforms have been forgotten. As for my own pilgrimage to mark the end of the months of writing, there was another place more dangerously loaded than Imogiri, with an energy more potent than that of dead kings. The day was darkening; I hurried back down the steps through the trees, wheeled my motorbike onto the road, and continued southwards through the shining sheets of the rice fields.

* * *

The dying day had taken on an air of anger by the time I reached the edge of the ocean at Parangtritis. I could smell the coming rain, and a gritty wind was driving down the coast from the west. The beach, a place for Sunday strolls and horse rides on quieter days, was a long strip of grubby grey sand. Furious brown waves were charging onto the shore, and the high cliffs to the east loomed threateningly. Day-trippers from Yogyakarta were thin on the ground today and the souvenir hawkers were packing up their strings of shells and hurrying home before the storm broke.

Squinting at the wind-whipped sand I rode slowly along the bumpy track at the head of the beach, and pulled over at a scruffy little food stall as the first hard droplets hurtled out of the sky. It was a place built of bamboo and tarpaulin, stocked with dusty Coca-Cola bottles and green coconuts on a rack made of driftwood. It had a single chipped Formica table. I ordered a glass of thick black Java coffee with sugar poured in in heaps, and as I sat sipping the stallholder came to sit beside me and to look out at the lashing rain and the angry ocean beyond. His name was Arianto. He had an oldest daughter at college in Surakarta, and a last-born child who had not yet started school. We passed through the usual first round of Indonesian small talk with a stranger – the where and the how and the why – and then fell into a moment of dripping silence. Thunder was throbbing over the hills inland now and great smears of rain were marching along the shore. A little two-wheeled pony trap – a *dokar* – trundled by with the driver huddled over the reins. It had occurred to me only a few weeks earlier that the name for these old-fashioned vehicles was another little leftover from British days: *dokar* – dog cart. The waves were tumbling ever more angrily onto the sand, and night was riding in early on the back of the storm clouds.

'From England, eh?' Arianto repeated my answer to an earlier question and sucked his teeth sadly. Water was pooling in the loose folds of the tarpaulin above our heads and dribbling down the bamboo supports. 'They're all doing well, the ones that used to belong to England – Singapore, Malaysia, Hong Kong.' He shook his head; 'Not like Indonesia ...'

I knew the lines with which to respond well enough now, and I repeated them wearily. He frowned at me for a moment, unconvinced, and then happily changed the subject.

'Do you have mysticism in England?'

'Some,' I said – thinking of new age hippies and summer solstices, and then changing my mind – 'but not really, not like in Java.'

He nodded as if this was quite normal, and then told me that the first day of the Javanese month of *Suro* was coming soon, when the Kraton people would come down to Parangtritis to place elaborate offerings into the waves. The offerings were for someone very important.

'Do you know about the Queen of the Southern Ocean?' he asked, eyeing me closely.

'I do,' I said, but for some reason I didn't add 'that's why I came to Parangtritis today …'

She had been such a powerful presence in Java for so long, and she was rumoured capable of such malevolence, that it would have seemed amiss not to make some small obeisance to her when the book was finished. Raffles, Gillespie, Crawfurd – none of them had taken the unseen side of Java seriously; I would not make the same mistake, and this stretch of grubby, wave-lashed sand was *her* shore.

By the time I had finished my coffee the angriest of the squalls had passed, and the rain had eased to a grey drizzle. But the afternoon would not recover and within a sodden hour night would fall. I left my bike beside Arianto's stall and wandered across the wet beach, stepping over wind-blown litter to the edge of the stormy sea. I had made sure that I was wearing no green, but I still trod carefully as the foam surged across my feet. The water, stained by the run-off from the flooding rivers, was the colour of tea, and almost as warm. There were patches of pale, pearly light between the columns of rain out on the horizon. I walked along the sand to the west for a while, the drizzle seeping through my shirt and misting my eyes, then cut inland to Parangkusumo, the spot where Senopati, founder of Mataram, had waded ashore after his three-day sojourn beneath the waves. This was still the place to go if you wanted to ask something of the

Queen of the Southern Ocean.

It was almost dark now; everything was sodden and mist was smoking across the green hills to the north in white tendrils. The great hulk of black stone where the shining star had descended above Senopati's head still stood beside a patch of damp grass picked over by a pair of skinny cows. Next to it a low white wall ringed a compound of dripping trees and shabby pavilions. There was a mildewed Muslim prayer room off to one side, but the core of the compound was a walled stretch of wet earth, punctured by a pair of small black rocks rising from the substrata.

It was Thursday evening, a good time in the Javanese week to come to places like this, and later, after evening prayers, there would be more visitors despite the rain. But for now there were just a few old men sheltering under the pavilions, and a gaggle of cackling old women in floral bandanas waiting to sell petals and incense to pilgrims by the gate.

'Ah-ha! Mister!' they leered at me, sucking at their corn-leaf cigarettes. One of them hauled herself up from her seat to fill a woven rattan basket with frangipani, melati and jasmine. She dropped a chunk of incense on top. 'To make you lucky,' she said with a snaggle-toothed grin, then added, 'don't ask "how much?" mind you, mister; don't be like that,' and pocketing the too-large banknote I had helplessly handed her she cackled and pushed me on my way across the puddles.

The whole world seemed to be drowning in the wet twilight and I could still hear the waves roaring onto the shore a hundred yards away. At the gate of the inner compound I kicked off my sandals and stood, ankle-deep in the rainwater. A young couple in city clothes were making an offering ahead of me, but there was no one else waiting and when they had gone the shrine guardian waved me forward to a wooden pallet fronted by a smouldering brazier. He was a tall, slim man, dressed in a batik sarong and a blue high-collared Javanese jacket. He knelt before the brazier and bade me do the same.

'Your name?' he hissed. I told him; he took the incense from the top of my pile of petals and dropped it onto the glowing embers. It hissed and crackled and a sweet scent of sandalwood cut through the wet gloaming. He raised his palms in prayer and mumbled an old Javanese mantra, my own name buried somewhere within it, and when he was done he nudged me towards the pair of stones, surrounded now by some two inches of water and covered with the heaped petals left by those who had come before me. I tiptoed across and squatted down. The rock was black and smooth beneath its blanket of soggy flowers, and burnt-out incense sticks, some still smouldering damply, were thrust into the crevices.

I spread my own offering liberally, and then placed my hands on the cold, wet stone and closed my eyes, thinking of nothing in particular, but hoping that this was enough. Everything smelt of water and mud and salt and flowers. The rain was dribbling down the back of my neck. After a long moment with the noise of the far-off waves and the falling water washing around me I stood up and padded back across the puddles. I thanked the guardian softly, slipping the ten-thousand rupiah note across in the limp, two-palmed handshake, and wandered away between the drooping palm trees. Night had fallen over Java.

Notes and Sources

The vast majority of the primary source material for this book is to be found in the archives of the India Office, now housed in the British Library's Asia, Pacific and Africa Collection. This is where most of the reams of paperwork churned out over the centuries by the British East India Company have ended up. The single most significant source on the British Interregnum within this enormous archive is the Raffles-Minto Manuscript Collection. This collection amounts to around fifty somewhat disorganised files spanning the entire period of the Interregnum, its run-up and aftermath. Some of the individual files are vast, and they contain much more than just the private correspondence between Raffles and Lord Minto. Unexpected interlopers pop up at every turn as you plod your way through them under the stern gaze of the portraits of long dead maharajas that line the Reading Room walls – here an angry letter from William Robison protesting his mistreatment, there a translation of an impertinent demand for a toy sailing boat from the Balinese Raja of Buleleng; here a map of a temple sketched by Colin Mackenzie, there a letter scrawled by Olivia Raffles in some Buitenzorg drawing room (could that be a faint whiff of brandy rising from the page?).

Besides this collection, many of the official reports and letters sent from Java appear in the Bengal Secret and Political Consultations. Enormous quantities of correspondence turned up in the East India Company headquarters in Calcutta each week, and that from Java is buried deep amidst obscure accounts from all corners. The notes for each chapter follow below, as does a select bibliography listing the most important of the many published books and scholarly articles I referred to during the research.

Chapter One – The Land of Promise

The official account of the British arrival at Cilincing in August 1814, with details of the order of landing and the problems caused by wind and tide, can be found in Major William Thorn's Memoir of the Conquest of Java. John Leyden's fancy-dress shenanigans on the beach are described in a rather disapproving tone by Captain Thomas Taylor, Lord Minto's military secretary, in a letter quoted in C.E. Wurtzburg's Raffles of the Eastern Isles.

All manner of books cover the history of early European involvement in Indonesia. M.C. Ricklefs' A History of Modern Indonesia is one of the best known, while specifically on the early Anglo-Dutch rivalry over the spice trade Giles Milton's highly readable Nathaniel's Nutmeg is excellent.

Chapter Two – The First Sigh of the East

Most of the details of Raffles' early life and career prior to the preparations for the Java campaign are drawn from the myriad past biographies of the man. The most significant are Lady Sophia Raffles' Memoir of the Life and Public Services of Sir Thomas Stamford Raffles, Demetrius Charles Boulger's Life of Sir Stamford Raffles, Emily Hahn's Raffles of Singapore, and C.E. Wurtzburg's Raffles of the Eastern Isles. Of these Wurtzburg provides by far the most detail, and draws from the widest range of materials – but it is by no means a book to be read for pleasure. Emily Hahn's book – while much less scholarly in tone – is exceptionally well written, makes a good job on local and historical contexts, and draws on some unusual sources. It is probably the single best traditionalist Raffles biography for general readers. These books are important supplementary sources to the archive materials for all subsequent chapters – though Nadia Wright's essay Sir Stamford Raffles – a Manufactured Hero? is essential corrective reading for anyone working from these books, or even just perusing them for pleasure.

Specifically on the topic of Olivia Raffles, Wurtzburg provides some information, but it is John Bastin's The Wives of Sir Stamford Raffles that gives the more scandalous details. John Leyden's wonderful story – and much of his rather less wonderful verse – can be found in The Poetical Remains of the Late Dr John Leyden by Reverend James Morton.

Details of conditions in Batavia in the years before the British invasion can be found harvested from various European accounts in Sketches Civil and Military of the Island of Java, a book hurriedly cobbled together in London in 1811 by the somewhat disreputable publisher John Joseph Stockdale.

Various intriguing glimpses of Raffles and others in Melaka can be found in the Hikayat Abdullah of 'Munshi' Abdullah bin Abdul Kadir. Abdullah's book is frequently criticised for its chronological inaccuracies and contradictions, and in a post-colonial context the man himself might earn a certain amount or ire for his presumably self-serving dedication to the British. But he does offer all manner of insights into daily life, character traits and physical appearance of the kind that are usually missing in contemporary European sources.

Vast amounts of correspondence and planning materials from the months prior to the departure of the British fleet from Melaka can be found in the Raffles-Minto Manuscript Collection, now held in the British Library. Files f148/1 to f148/6 contain the bulk of this material, while there is more in the Bengal Secret and Political Consultations for1810 and 1811. There is some particularly amusing correspondence in f148/6 between Raffles and the Balinese Raja of Buleleng, in which the king makes multiple impertinent demands for such luxuries as a camera obscura and a miniature sailing ship, a very specific six fathoms in length. In anticipation of these gifts he sent Raffles an eight-year-old slave by way of recompense.

Chapter Three – Glorious Victory

The main source for the details of the campaign around Batavia in August 1811 is Captain (later Major) William Thorn's Memoir of the Conquest of Java. For the mindboggling life story of Rollo Gillespie there is A Memoir of Major-General R.R. Gillespie, also by William Thorn, and The Bravest Soldier by Eric Wakeham.

The original charts and plans made during the campaign are in file f148/10 of the Raffles-Minto Manuscript Collection. The correspondence dating from the campaign – including Janssens' ink-splattered French missives – is in file f148/11, with a few more letters in f148/15.

Chapter Four – A Thousand Little Questions

The background story of the royal courts of Central Java is covered in most major histories of Indonesia. M.C. Ricklefs' Jogjakarta under Sultan Mangkubumi 1749-1792 is particularly detailed, drawing on both Dutch and Javanese sources, and explaining the contexts of the partition of Mataram.

The key source for the early part of this chapter is the account of Captain William Robison of his first visit to the Javanese courts in September 1811. This can be found in file f148/17 in the Raffles-Minto Manuscript Collection. Robison was also responsible for collating a mass of reports from the various Dutch residents still at their posts around Java. These, and the correspondence he collected from the Susuhunan and Sultan, are in f148/18.

A very large number of official and private letters and reports from Raffles, Lord Minto and others dating from the early months of the Interregnum can be found in files f148/12 and 15, as well as in the contemporaneous Bengal Secret and Political Consultations. The descriptions of the methods of torture used by the Dutch are from Stockdale's Sketches Civil and Military of the Island of Java.

A source used first in this chapter, and which remains important for subsequent chapters, is The Journal of Thomas Otho Travers 1813-1820, in the published version edited by John Bastin.

Besides Raffles' own accounts in file f148/30 of the Raffles-Minto Manuscript Collection, a very useful second perspective on his journey to the Javanese Courts in late 1811 – giving, amongst other things, a unique indication that military action against the courts may have already been being prepared at this stage, and mentioning the complaints of the villagers who were forced to carry Raffles' luggage unpaid – comes from the journal of Colonel Colin Mackenzie, which can be found in file f148/47.

Chapter Five – Hearts of Darkness

The vital correspondence between Raffles and the Palembang Sultanate is in file f148/6 in the Raffles-Minto Manuscript Collection. Raffles' own letters sent to Minto once the massacre had been discovered and the expedition planned are in f148/30. The affair is examined in an article by John Bastin, 'Palembang in 1811 and 1812' in edition 110 of the journal Bijdragen tot de Taal, Land- en Volkenkunde, and is also given a brief critical examination by Syed Hussein Alatas in Thomas Stamford Raffles: Schemer or Reformer? Both writers dwell excessively on the largely irrelevant issue of the translation of the phrase 'buang habiskan sekali-kali' while seemingly missing the much more important context of the plan to annex Bangka (revealed in the above listed archive files, and in f148/3 and f148/15). Bastin does, however, provide a helpful appendix with some of the original Malay-language correspondence transliterated into roman script from the Jawi.

Detailed accounts of the advance on Palembang, vividly conveying the 'Heart of Darkness' atmosphere of the journey, can be found in William Thorn's Memoir of the Conquest of Java, and A Memoir of Major-General R.R. Gillespie. Gillespie's letters and reports on the expedition are in file f148/21 of the Raffles-Minto Manuscript Collection. A special edition of the Java Government Gazette, published on 30 May 1812, gives a public account of the campaign – and a good deal of heavy-handed editorialising on the theme of 'Asiatic treachery' to boot.

On the idea of 'amok' see Hobson-Jobson, the great dictionary-encyclopaedia of the British Empire in Asia, and for more on European perceptions of 'the Malay Race' see the excellent The Myth of the Lazy Native by Syed Hussein Alatas.

A key source for the second part of this chapter and for subsequent chapters is the official weekly newspaper, the Java Government Gazette. The entire 1812-1816 print run of the paper is held on microfilm in the British Library's Asia and Pacific Collection. Olivia Raffles' letter to Lord Minto is in file f148/30 of the Raffles-Minto Manuscript Collection, as are various key letters in which Raffles discusses his plans to attack Yogyakarta. More letters from shortly before the assault are in f148/31, while Thorn's Memoir of the Conquest of Java details the military preparations for the assault.

Chapter Six – A New Field of Glory

The vital source for this chapter – and for sections about Yogyakarta in subsequent chapters – is the Babad Bedhah ing Ngayogyakarta of Arya Panular. The original manuscript of this colourful, digressive account of the British assault on the Kraton and the years that followed is in the British Library, but it has helpfully been transliterated into roman script with a canto-by-canto English synopsis by Peter Carey in The British in Java 1811-1816: A Javanese Account, which also contains an absolute treasure trove of very detailed endnotes.

Arya Panular's British counterpart as principal chronicler of the attack on the court is, once again, William Thorn. There are detailed descriptions of the military manoeuvres in the Memoir of the Conquest of Java. The 4 July edition of the Java Government Gazette covers the assault, and gives details of the last stand of the Javanese in the Royal Mosque.

Raffles' private letters and public proclamations on the Yogyakarta campaign are in files f148/23, 24 and 31 of the Raffles-Minto Manuscript Collection. The treaty forced on the court is in f148/24 in both English and Javanese.

Chapter Seven – Making History

The key sources for the first part of this chapter are the journal, reports and letters of Colonel Colin Mackenzie. These are all written in a rather lovely – if somewhat ornate – hand, and are to be found in file f148/47 of the Raffles-Minto Manuscript Collection. For background and biographical details on this 19th-century answer to Indiana Jones, see John Bastin's article 'Colonel Colin Mackenzie and Javanese antiquities' in Bijdragen tot de Taal, Land- en Volkenkunde 109 and Jennifer Howes' Illustrating India: The Early Colonial Investigations of Colin Mackenzie.

For a look at early 19th-century orientalism in action, as discussed in the middle part of the chapter, see Raffles' own The History of Java, and John Crawfurd's History of the Indian Archipelago, and for an assessment of those approaches see Gareth Knapman's Race, Empire and Liberalism: Interpreting John Crawfurd's History of the Indian Archipelago, and Syed Muhd Khairudin Aljunied's Raffles and Religion.

Dr Thomas Horsfield's reports from the field are in file f148/46 of the Raffles-Minto Manuscript Collection.

Details of life in British Java in the early years of the Interregnum can be found in the Java Government Gazette. For the changes wrought by the British on the older Indo-Dutch culture of Batavia see V.T. van de Wall's The Influence of Olivia Mariamne Raffles on European Society in Java. Lord Minto's thoughts and instructions to Raffles on the issue of slavery are to be found in file f148/15 of the Raffles-Minto Manuscript Collection. The translated Dutch slave laws and Raffles' ponderings thereon are in f148/8, while details of his household staffing are in Emily Hahn's Raffles of Singapore. There is more relevant detail in Wurtzburg's Raffles of the Eastern Isles. Raffles' extensive musings on opium – in which he gnaws on the unanswerable conundrum of how to increase demand for the drug without having a negative impact on society – are in file f148/7.

Letters and reports detailing the beginnings of the major disagreements between Raffles and Gillespie are in files f148/32, 33 and 34, while another view on the deteriorating relationship comes from the Journal of Otho Travers.

Chapter Eight – The Buffalo and the Tiger

On the unrest in Probolinggo see Sri Margana's Java's Last Frontier: The Struggle for Hegemony of Blambangan c.1763-1813, and William Thorn's Memoir of the Conquest of Java. See also Claudine Lombard-Salmon's article 'The Han Family of East Java. Entrepreneurship and Politics' in Archipel Volume 41 for the family history of the Chinese landlords. For background on the regiment of the soldiers who got caught up in the events see The Historical Records of the 78th Highlanders by James MacVeigh, which also gives some important insights into general conditions for the British troops serving in Java, particularly on the mortality from tropical diseases. Raffles' own reactions to the Probolinggo affair, and John Crawfurd's remarkably even-handed official investigations, are in file f148/25 of the Raffles-Minto Manuscript Collection. For the role of jago in Java see Jean Gelman Taylor's Indonesia: People and Histories, and for more on jago, albeit in a later period of Indonesian history, see Java in a Time of Revolution by Benedict Anderson.

The issue of the Cianjur land sales is dealt with in all the major Raffles biographies, though disentangling the hard facts from the apologetics is a tough task. Papers detailing Raffles' efforts to annex the remaining territory of the Sultan of Banten are also in file f148/25 (an interesting point is that the accounts of Raffles' meetings with the Banten Sultan are by his official Malay translator, M. Juoid, indicating that his own Malay may not have been strong enough to handle formal negotiations).

Raffles' attempts to overhaul the system of obtaining revenue from Javanese peasants are dealt with in considerable detail by John Bastin in The Native Policies of Sir Stamford Raffles in Java and Sumatra, and in an article entitled 'The working of the early land rent system in West Java' in Bijdragen tot de Taal, Land- en Volkenkunde 116. Colin Mackenzie's preparatory notes from the field are in file f148/47. More reports from Mackenzie and John Crawfurd are in f148/44, and Crawfurd's public criticisms of the attempts are in his History of the Indian Archipelago.

On the scandal caused by William Robison in Palembang, see the Journal of Otho Travers. Raffles' private responses to the formal accusations levelled in Calcutta by Gillespie, Blagrave and Robison are in f148/38 of the Raffles-Minto Manuscript Collection, while the official letters about the impeachment attempt and Raffles' public responses are in separate files also held in the British Library – mss.eur.w2417 and mss.eur.w2423. The blow-by-blow account of the tiger and buffalo fight during Raffles' visit to Yogyakarta is in the Java Government Gazette.

On the sad saga of William Robison's later tussles with authority in India over what he regarded as corruption and bad governance, see the early campaigning journal The Oriental Herald and Colonial Review, Volumes 1 and 2.

Chapter Nine – Mutiny and Mangos

On matters beyond Java during the Interregnum, see various editions of the Java Government Gazette. For letters and reports about British dealings in Borneo over piracy see file f148/26 in the Raffles-Minto Manuscript Collection.

The first readily accessible account of Raffles' relationship with Alexander Hare over the 'Banjarmasin Enormity' appeared in Syed Hussein Alatas' Thomas Stamford Raffles: Schemer or Reformer? The affair is also covered in a Dutch-language paper, 'De Bandjermasinsche Afschuwelijkheid', published in 1860 in Bijdragen tot de Taal, Land en Volkenkunde van Nederlandsch Indie 3, which contains some original correspondence pertaining to the episode. This suggests that what is already known about the affair may be but the tip of the iceberg. A thorough scholarly investigation would be a very worthwhile undertaking.

Private and public correspondence from Raffles and others during the late stages of the British Interregnum can be found in f148/36, 37 and 38 in the Raffles-Minto Manuscript Collection. Details of Rollo Gillespie's last great battle against the Ghurkhas are found in William Thorn's A Memoir of Major-General R.R. Gillespie, and Eric Wakeham's The Bravest Soldier. The death of Sultan Hamengkubuwono III is described in Arya Panular's Babad, and Caroline Currie's account of Olivia Raffles' funeral can be found in John Bastin's The Wives of Sir Stamford Raffles.

Contemporary accounts of the portents and aftermath of the Tambora eruption can be found in Sophia Raffles' Memoir of the Life and Public Services of Sir Thomas Stamford Raffles and in Raffles' own The History of Java. A thorough modern overview of the cataclysmic event is found in an article by Bernice de Jong Boers, 'Mount Tambora in 1815: a volcanic eruption in Indonesia and its aftermath' in Volume 60 of the journal Indonesia.

The abortive sepoy uprising in 1815 is examined by Peter Carey in the article 'The Sepoy conspiracy of 1815 in Java' in Bijdragen tot de Taal, Land- en Volkenkunde 133. Carey pays particular attention to the role of the Surakarta court in the affair, but there is much more detail – including an account of the mango party, and the transcripts of the subsequent trials – in the official papers dealing with the aftermath of the episode. These are found in the Bengal Secret and Political Consultations Volumes 278-283 for 1816. Raffles' apparent provisions for a possible future reinvasion of a Dutch-ruled Java are revealed in the reports of Captain Baker, which are also in Volume 283 of the 1816 Bengal Secret and Political Consultations.

Chapter Ten – The Righteous Prince, and Epilogue – The Queen of the Southern Ocean

On developments in post-Interregnum Java see major histories, including M.C. Ricklef's A History of Modern Indonesia. On issues specific to land reforms see John Bastin's The Native Policies of Sir Stamford Raffles in Java and Sumatra, and J.S. Furnivall's Netherlands India: A Study of Plural Economy. For a discussion of the etymology of Yogyakarta's famed Malioboro Street, see Peter Carey's article 'Jalan Maliabara: The Etymology and Historical Origins of a much Misunderstood Yogyakarta Street Name' in Archipel Volume 27

For the Raffles' life after his departure from Java, see the various past biographies, in particular those of Wurtzburg and Hahn, while for a very sharp assessment of the construction of the popular discourse on 'Raffles as hero' see Nadia Wright's essay, Sir Stamford Raffles – a Manufactured Hero?

For the rest you'll need to make a visit to Central Java in person, which I heartily recommend. Motorbike rental is available from any number of hole-in-the-wall travel agencies in the Sosrowijayaan area of Yogyakarta, just across the road from the train station ...

Select Bibliography

Abdullah bin Abdul Kadir, *Hikayat Abdullah* (trans.), Kuala Lumpur 1955

Alatas, Syed Hussein, *Thomas Stamford Raffles: Schemer or Reformer?* Sydney 1971

Alatas, Syed Hussein, *The Myth of the Lazy Native*, New York 1977

Aljunied, Syed Muhd Khairudin, *Raffles and Religion*, Petaling Jaya 2004

Allen, Charles, *Tales from the South China Sea*, London 1983

Anwar, Rosihan, *Sejarah Kecil "Petite Histoire" Indonesia*, Jakarta 2004

Barley, Nigel, *In the Footsteps of Stamford Raffles*, Singapore 2009

Bastin, John, 'Palembang in 1811 and 1812', in: *Bijdragen tot de Taal-, Land- en Volkenkunde 110*, Leiden 1954

Bastin, John, 'Colonel Colin Mackenzie and Javanese antiquities', in: *Bijdragen tot de Taal-, Land- en Volkenkunde 109*, Leiden 1953

Bastin, John (ed), *The Journal of Thomas Otho Travers 1813-1820*, Singapore 1957

Bastin, John, *The Native Policies of Sir Stamford Raffles in Java and Sumatra*, Oxford 1957

Bastin, John, 'The working of the early land rent system in West Java', in: *Bijdragen tot de Taal-, Land- en Volkenkunde 116*, Leiden 1960

Bastin, John, *Sir Thomas Stamford Raffles*, Liverpool 1969

Bastin, John, *The Wives of Sir Stamford Raffles*, Singapore 2002

Boers, Bernice de Jong, 'Mount Tambora in 1815: a volcanic eruption in Indonesia and its aftermath', in: *Indonesia 60*, New York 1995

Boulger, Demetrius Charles, *Life of Sir Stamford Raffles*, London 1897

Brown, Colin, *A Short History of Indonesia*, Crows Nest 2003

Carey, Peter, 'The Sepoy conspiracy of 1815 in Java', in: *Bijdragen tot de Taal-, Land- en Volkenkunde 133*, Leiden 1977

Carey, Peter. 'Jalan Maliabara: The Etymology and Historical Origins of a much Misunderstood Yogyakarta Street Name', in: *Archipel Volume 27,* Paris 1984

Carey, Peter (ed), *The British in Java 1811-1816: A Javanese Account*, Oxford 1992

Collis, Maurice, *Raffles*, London 1968

Coupland, R, *Raffles of Singapore*, London 1946

Crawfurd, John, *History of the Indian Archipelago Volumes I-III,* Edinburgh 1820

Furnivall, J.S., *Netherlands India: A Study of Plural Economy*, Cambridge 1967

Geertz, Clifford, *The Religion of Java*, Chicago 1960

Gomperts, Amrit, and Carey, Peter, 'Campanalogical Conundrums: a History of Three Javanese Bells', in: *Archipel Volume 48*, Paris 1994

Hahn, Emily, *Raffles of Singapore*, New York 1946

Horsfield, Thomas, 'An Essay on the Oopas, or Poison-Tree of Java', in: *The Asiatic Journal* Volume 1, London 1816

Howes, Jennifer, *Illustrating India: The Early Colonial Investigations of Colin Mackenzie*, Delhi 2010

Keay, John, *Indonesia: From Sabang to Merauke*, London 1995

Knapman, Gareth, *Race, Empire and Liberalism: Interpreting John Crawfurd's History of the Indian Archipelago*, Melbourne 2008

Koentjaraningrat, *Javanese Culture*, Singapore 1985

Lombard-Salmon Claudine. 'The Han Family of East Java. Entrepreneurship and Politics (18th-19th Centuries)', in: *Archipel Volume 41*, Paris 1991

Margana, Sri, *Java's Last Frontier: The Struggle for Hegemony of*

Blambangan c.1763-1813, Leiden 2007

MacVeigh, James, *The Historical Records of the 78th Highlanders*, Dumfries 1887

Milton, Giles, Nathaniel's Nutmeg, 1999 London

Morton, Rev. James, *The Poetical Remains of the Late Dr John Leyden*, London 1819

Raffles, Sophia (ed), *Memoir of the Life and Public Services of Sir Thomas Stamford Raffles*, London 1830

Raffles, Thomas Stamford, *The History of Java Volumes I and II*, London 1817

Ricklefs, MC, *Jogjakarta under Sultan Mangkubumi 1749-1792*, London 1974

Ricklefs, MC, *A History of Modern Indonesia*, London 2001

Ricklefs, MC, *Polarising Javanese Society*, Singapore 2007

Stockdale, John Joseph (ed), *Sketches Civil and Military of the Island of Java*, London 1811

Tayler, Jean Gelman, *Indonesia: People and Histories*, New Haven 2003

Thorn, Major William, *Memoir of the Conquest of Java*, London 1815

Thorn, Major William, *A Memoir of Major-General R.R. Gillespie*, London 1816

Wakeham, Eric, *The Bravest Soldier: Sir Rollo Gillespie*, London 1937

Wall, V.T. van de, *The Influence of Olivia Mariamne Raffles on European Society in Java*, Batavia 1924

Wright, Nadia, *Sir Stamford Raffles – a Manufactured Hero?*, Melbourne 2008

Wurtzburg, CE, *Raffles of the Eastern Isles*, London, 1954

The Oriental Herald and Colonial Review Volumes 1 and 2, London 1824

Bijdragen tot de Taal, Land en Volkenkunde van Nederlandsch Indie 3, Leiden 1860

Index